COMMUNICATION AND CYBERSPACE

COMMUNICATION AND CYBERSPACE

Editor

Débora Terrazas

scitus academics

Communication and Cyberspace

Edited by **Débora Terrazas**

This Book is Printed on Acid-Free Paper. ♾

ISBN: 9781681178462

Library of Congress Control Number: 2017948873

SCITUS Academics LLC,

616, Corporate Way, Suite 2, 4766,

Valley Cottage, NY 10989

www.scitusacademics.com

Printed in United States of America.

Preface

Technology is everywhere; it has changed every aspect of our lives, the way we buy our books, listen to our favorite music, book our holidays, even the way we stay in touch with family and friends; it rules everything and most importantly how and why we communicate. Technology has revolutionized our daily routines but if there is one thing that has really evolved beyond recognition that would be the way we work. Over the past years, electronic communication and new technologies have been progressively reshaping traditional communication practices. The Internet has become an arena for many voices and languages and has created new communication channels for people from different parts of the globe. Social media is changing at a fast pace and it´s creating new trends in the marketplace. Such a shift in access to information and opportunities for cross-cultural interactions have brought a new set of research questions, challenges, and dilemmas that professional communicators need to discover so as to ensure a productive intercultural dialog among different people. These facts confirm how overwhelmingly important social media has become not only for us but also for businesses. Research into intercultural online communication should also maintain opportunities for the distribution of products and services, intellectual and cultural exchanges, humanitarian efforts, and successful collaboration in the internet era.

'Communication and Cyberspace' brings together discussion and research on cybernetworks and cyberspaces, studies of new senses of cybernautics and explorations of cybercommunication and cyberculture. It covers on the issues of intercultural communication and cyberspace, contains a set of recent theoretical approaches and research studies that present an excellent overview of some of the ways electronic technologies affect cultures and the ways cultures affect electronic discourses.

Table of Contents

CHAPTER 1

Cyberspace Security Using Adversarial Learning and Conformal Prediction

Harry Wechsler

Department of Computer Science, George Mason University, Fairfax, VA, USA

ABSTRACT

This paper advances new directions for cyber security using adversarial learning and conformal prediction in order to enhance network and computing services defenses against adaptive, malicious, persistent, and tactical offensive threats. Conformal prediction is the principled and unified adaptive and learning framework used to design, develop, and deploy a multi-faceted self-man- aging defensive shield to detect, disrupt, and deny intrusive attacks, hostile and malicious behavior, and subterfuge. Conformal prediction leverages apparent relationships between immunity and intrusion detection using non-conformity measures characteristic of affinity, a typicality, and surprise, to recognize patterns and messages as friend or foe and to respond to them accordingly. The solutions proffered throughout are built around active learning, meta-reasoning, randomness, distributed semantics and stratification, and most important and above all around adaptive Oracles. The motivation for using conformal prediction and its immediate off-spring, those of semi-supervised learning and transduction, comes from them first and foremost supporting discriminative and non-parametric methods characteristic of principled demarcation using cohorts and sensitivity analysis to hedge on the prediction outcomes including negative selection, on one side, and providing credibility and confidence indices that assist meta-reasoning and information fusion.

Keywords: Active Learning, Adversarial Learning, Anomaly Detection, Change Detection, Conformal Prediction, Cyber Security, Data Mining, Denial and Deception, Human Factors, Insider Threats, Intrusion Detection, Meta-Reasoning, Moving Target Defense, Performance Evaluation, Randomness, Semi-Supervised Learning, Sequence Analysis, Statistical Learning, Transduction

1. INTRODUCTION

Cyber security affects the fabric and infrastructure of modern society. It encompasses the interplay between science, technology, and engineering practices to protect networks, computers, programs, and data from attacks, damage, insider threat, or unauthorized access (e.g., intrusion) for criminal and nefarious purposes. Cyber security is first and foremost about all-encompassing recognition. It is about intrusion detection and is adversarial in nature. It is crucial for both biological (e.g., immune system) and machine Oracle systems to recognize patterns as friend or foe and to respond to them appropriately. Failure to recognize pathogens or subterfuge such as Trojan horses, characteristic of malware, can be fatal. Recognition is continuous and multi-layered. It includes detection (e.g., intrusion detection system), categorization, and continuous re-authentication. This paper considers the use of adversarial learning as the methodology of choice to enhance cyber security defenses against adaptive, malicious, persistent, and tactical offensive threats. To meet such goals the paper proposes conformal prediction as the principled and unified learning framework to design, develop, and deploy a multi-faceted protection and self-managing defensive shield that supports adversarial learning.

Intrusion detection bears many analogies to biological immunity including the challenges raised by the lack of abnormal patterns (e.g., imposters or pathogens) for modeling and training that would most likely afflict the network and its components, and cause therefore significant harm. Additional challenges come from countering the possibility for denial of service (DoS) and reduced quality of service (QoS) while maintaining high sensitivity (e.g., high detection or true positive rates) for detection purposes and high specificity to avoid high false (positive) alarm rates. Training and learning, which are responsible for model selection and prediction is the core for intrusion detection and depends much on the quality, quantity, and type of data available in order to demarcate normal from abnormal traffic.

It is also highly desirable that the decisions made on intrusion carry reliability indices suitable for further processing and protection. Both noisy and faulty data due to poor observations and recordings, annotation mistakes, and deliberate attempts for obfuscation and spoofing, affect training and the safeguards in place for protection purposes.

One can approach intrusion detection using either supervised or unsupervised learning or some mixture of both. Supervised learning, which involves binary or multi-class classification with classes making reference to normal traffic, on one side, and attacking traffic, on the other side, can be therefore addressed using discriminative methods (e.g., decision trees trained over normal and known abnormal data). There is always, however, innovation and novelty about both legitimate and illegitimate traffic so supervised learning cannot be expected to handle zero-shot (unseen) attacks and/or deviations from normal behavior. To address both novelty and lack of enough and representative data for intrusions, one is advised to substitute unsupervised learning for supervised learning vis-à-vis anomaly or outlier detection using amongst others one-class classification (e.g., K-nearest neighbors (KNN) and one-class SVM). Both anomaly detection and the provision of reliability indices for the decisions made are addressed using conformal prediction, in general, and transduction, in particular, as discussed throughout this paper. Here the analogue to outlier detection comes from assessing the extent to which observations are more extreme or strange than normal data. The higher the strangeness or atypicality for a new observation, the more likely it is that the observation of concern can be traced to illegitimate traffic. There is always the possibility that the quality for training data is lacking due to intrusions (e.g., noise) labeled as normal data, and notwithstanding if the noise is deliberate (e.g., insider threat) or not. This is characteristic of adversarial learning and is addressed next.

Annotation for training can be lacking on purpose (e.g., deliberate) or not. Poor annotation affects not only cyber security (e.g., spam, phishing, fake internet accounts, and fraud detection) but basic science as well, as it is the case with coronal mass ejection (CME) events that are fed to design detection and tracking methods for solar physics [1] . It is often difficult to obtain annotated data for pattern recognition tasks; however, public email service providers have the ability to solicit annotation support from their users. A select set of users (e.g., Amazon Mechanical Turk (AMT)), can be asked to occasionally provide a class label for a randomly selected incoming email message. This, of course, allows an adversary (including insider threats) to taint the data used to train the spam detection method. An adversary might mislabel a spam message as not spam in order to allow similar spam messages to be delivered in the future, or alternatively it might mislabel a non-spam message as spam. The same adversary can also overwhelm intrusion detection system (IDS) with highly unbalanced and/or corrupt training data to further compromise the integrity of the spam detection method. While it may be possible to restrict invitations for annotations to well-established accounts, an adversary may create fake accounts with the intent to influence the training of the spam detection method. Even under the best of circumstances annotators may still make unintentional errors.

Adversarial learning (AL) involves effective allocation of finite resources including but not limited to human and/or machine annotation. The nominal (e.g., computational) and representation (e.g., descriptive) aspect is handled by active learning (ACL) and includes both importance sampling and feature extraction and selection using feature relevance and reputation. To undermine defenses, the adversary places emphasis on denial and deception (D&D) to evade detection and to deceive defenses. The motivation behind active learning comes from the need for promptness and selectivity in separating (e.g., filtering informative contents) from obfuscation using limited resources. This involves what is best to annotate (e.g., queries of interest) and when, the annotation process itself (e.g., the Oracle), and countering what are perceived to be potential vulnerabilities (e.g., to compromise the Oracle) affecting the learning processes involved in intrusion detection systems (IDS) training and/or the reputation of the features involved in social network analysis (SNA).

Miller et al. [2] have recently surveyed the field of ACL to promote Security-oriented Active Learning Testbed (SALT) architecture in order to experiment and evaluate diverse strategies surrounding active learning to counter adversarial contexts and deliberate manipulation. SALT evaluation has been so far relatively limited to the continuous 2D feature space where the aim is usually that of learning a binary classifier while evaluating different active learning strategies to prioritize requests (e.g., queries) for annotation. The results reported indicate that for "the system which is not under attack, the maximum uncertainty strategy performs significantly better than random choice. When the system is under attack [the case of interest here], randomization of training samples becomes the best strategy, while the maximum uncertainty choice suffers severe degradations" [2] . Principled randomization using conformal prediction inspired transduction (see Sect. 3 and 4) and randomness (see Sect. 11) are better ways to engage in importance sampling for active learning purposes. Vulnerabilities, both known and unknown are many and each of them affects cyber security differently including functional creep bearing on privacy and interoperability bearing on use across different platforms [3] . Exploratory vulnerabilities, which focus on modifying test samples once a model has been trained, and causative vulnerabilities, which aim to modify both training and test data can be handled using inductive conformal prediction (ICP) driven by conformal prediction and incremental transduction, when unlabeled and training data are complementary to each other in the execution of annotation. The i.i.d. assumption held by SALT and others is relaxed later on using online compression models (see Sect. 10).

Conformal prediction supports a multitude of functional blocks that address the major challenges faced by adversarial learning including denial and deception, pattern representation and classification, and vulnerabilities, deliberate or not, affecting learning, training, and annotation. The solutions proffered are built around meta-reasoning, active learning, and most important and above all adaptive Oracles seeking to be effective and efficient regarding the prediction outcomes. Effective to be resilient to malicious attacks aimed at subverting promptness and selectivity in separating the wheat (e.g., informative patterns) from the chaff (e.g., obfuscation), and efficient to minimize the costs incurred. Additional motivation for using conformal prediction and its immediate offspring, those of semi-supervised learning and transduction, comes from the simple but important realization that such intertwined learning methods are consonant with the deployment of discriminative methods using likelihood ratios; demarcation using cohorts, local estimation, and non-conformity measures; randomness for hypothesis testing and incremental inference using sensitivity analysis; reliability indices, such as credibility and confidence using relative strangeness or a-typicality, to augment the current practice of bare prediction outcomes; high-dimensional change detection using martingale; open set recognition (including the reject option) and negative selection using transductive p-values and skew; and consensus reasoning to upend questionable label annotations, deliberate or not, using aggregation and importance sampling.

Additional motivation for using conformal prediction comes from biometrics and forensics. Many analogies hold between adversarial learning and biometric mass screening and identity management with both vulnerable to impersonation, with ground truth annotation lacking for the non-self, and with uncontrolled settings and change (e.g., covariate shift) the norm rather than the exception. Impersonation and spoofing in biometrics are directly related to obfuscation seeking to confuse training during cyber security engagements.

The structure and outline for the paper address motivation and justification throughout, theoretical foundations, and overall methodology and development tools. The discussion covers both existing methods and promising venues for future R&D. The particular outline for the paper goes as follows. Background for the whole cyber security enterprise continues in Sect. 2 the discussion started in this introductory section. The theoretical foundations on machine learning are discussed in Sect. 3, while conformal prediction, the novel learning core advanced in this paper, is introduced in Sect. 4. Particular methods and development tools including active learning and change detection, semantics and stratification, and the symbiosis of immunity and intrusion detection, which draw and support conformal prediction, are presented in Sections 5 - 7, respectively. The design and development of an all-encompassing software environment methodology where one can explore and exploit in a coordinated fashion different functional modules that complement each other and address conflicting asymmetries is discussed in Sect. 8 using meta-reasoning and meta-recognition. The remaining sections are dedicated to additional topics that support and provide value-added to a self-management and protective shield vis-à-vis malware attacks, in general, and intrusion detection, in particular. The particulars topics of interest for innovation and their potential impact on cyber security include insider threats and moving target defense, online compression models, randomness, distributed semantic models and vector space representation that substitute context and prediction to traditional bag of words and counting, and human factors (see Sections 9 - 14). Quo Vadis and prescriptive conclusions discuss promising venues for future R & D and bring closure to the paper in Sections 15 and 16, respectively.

2. BACKGROUND

We review briefly here on current and relevant background and literature regarding adversarial learning [4] . The review takes place at the interface between machine learning, robust statistics, cyber security, and computing. We recall that adversarial learning can be deliberate or not in nature, that information can be missing, corrupt, or superfluous, and that it is most important to assess and respond properly to the very possibility that the Oracle involved with decision-making, including detection and classification, can be compromised. Spam filter (e.g., Spam Bates) can be rendered useless even if the adversary's access is limited to only 1% of the training messages with relatively little system state information and relatively limited control over training data [5] . Focused attacks assisted by insider threat with extra domain specific knowledge can do even more harm. This suggests that the defense should exercise great caution in its use of training data. Towards that end, labeling errors characteristic of lacking proper annotation can be detected and redressed in many ways including constrained regularization driven optimization and label flipping [6] with label flipping best done in a principled way characteristic of importance sampling [7] . The use of soft rather than hard labeled data is more resistant to (adversarial) label noise [3] with soft labels integral to conformal prediction, the learning framework proposed here, and to incremental transduction, in particular [8] .

Questions relevant to adversarial learning inquire about how to integrate and process new information, possibly mistaken, which does not fit within the existing mold. Those are also hard questions for medical diagnosis and their resolution will be of great help to clinical practice (e.g., NYU Langone Medical Center announced significant changes in its procedures after the death by septic shock of a 12-year-old boy who was sent home from the center with fever and a rapid heart rate under the erroneous presumption of a run-of-the-mill ailments in children, such as stomach bug). The use of active learning (see Sect. 5) and semantics and stratification (see Sect. 6) would have helped to prevent such fateful misdiagnosis. The mutual relationships between rudimentary biological immunity subliminal to artificial immune system (AIS) and intrusion detection (e.g., IDS) would have further helped with avoiding the above misdiagnosis (see Sect. 7).

The way society conducts its business depends more and more on broadening the cyber space while maintaining proper security and privacy norms of behavior for the very purpose of ensuring the trustworthiness of the cyberspace. Among many concerns deceit and its prevention make the top list. There is offense and there is defense with both attempting to guess and learn from each other. This is the core for adversarial learning. There are many dimensions along which adversarial learning is played out, among them active learning that is tasked to choose what to learn and how to build robust Oracles, moving target defense to counter advanced persistent threats (APT), and moving target defense (MTD) to increase the time it takes to mount and execute an attack while decreasing the time it takes to deploy defensive moves. Much of the adversarial aspect is driven by greed and monetary rewards so the economics of the cyberspace play a major role. Adversarial learning therefore benefits and impacts on the way social and behavioral economics (SBE) are conducted and safeguarded in the cyberspace.

The challenges, which are typically of adversarial nature, are many and they are succinctly tabulated here in context along possible solutions we describe throughout. Adversarial is meant as any attempt to either deceive or defend against deception. Detecting adversarial advertisements in the wild [9] expands on the adversarial aspect. It involves intertwined minority-class and multi-class issues with scale affecting both. The majority of ads are from good-faith advertisers and those of adversarial (e.g., malicious) nature are few and spread between counterfeit goods and inaccurate claims. Local estimation using open set recognition driven by non-conformity measures and ranking putative classification assignments address both such (minority and multi-class) aspects (see Sect. 3 for TCM-DR) with large scale addressed using cascade implementations that trade false positive and false negative rates and can be efficiently run using Map Reduce. One could also consider 1) adversarial behavior aiming to affect personalized recommender systems; and 2) adversarial attempts to tamper the use of mobile devices (e.g., location wise) while seeking for spatial-temporal trajectories when using the sequence of messages as the basic unit of information. This is relevant for both SBE and social network analysis (SNA). Another aspect of interest for adversarial learning is to what extent human experts should be involved and when, something active learning is best qualified to engage in for purposeful annotation with adaptive Oracles (e.g., machine) and/or human expertise competing for the job (see Sect. 13).

Adversarial learning that is conducive to cyber security can be conducted using reactive and/or proactive modes of operation [10] . In the reactive mode, the offensive side devises and engages in the attack while the defense is limited to analyzing the attack and developing countermeasures. The proactive case learns from the past and seeks to anticipate and forecast. The defense gets more involved as it models the adversary, simulates attacks, evaluates attacks' impact, and develops countermeasures to prepare for that time when it is under attack and has to raise and deploy adequate defenses. It is a game like environment with learning and adaptation substituting for formal game theory to contend with practical issues of implementation and use of computational resources. The taxonomy for adversarial learning takes place along three axes: influence (exploratory/reconnais- sance or causative), specificity (targeted or indiscriminate), and security violation (integrity, availability, or privacy) [11] . The particulars of adversarial learning including task and mode of operation are therefore primed by meta-planning to distinguish between different attacking behaviors, and where are they encountered and for what purpose (e.g., advertising and marketing, sentiment analysis). The persistent arms race between defense and offense brings up continuous tradeoffs between reverse engineering where the attackers want to divine the Oracle used by defense and/or compromise it, and randomization schemes that are used by defense to confuse the attackers. It has been reported that the defender's optimal policy tends to be either to randomize uniformly (ignoring baseline classification accuracy), which is the case for targeted attacks, or not to randomize at all, which is typically optimal when attacks are indiscriminate [12] . This suggests the need for meta-recognition (see Sect. 8) to choose among the arsenal of methods available while considering random matrix theory (see Sect. 11) and random projections for message representation [13] .

We have explored both adversarial and active learning along several dimensions and found promising solutions for a number of challenges that involve representational aspects and/or detection methods. Regarding representation we have reported recently a number of innovations: 1) clustering (e.g., stratification) and active learning that yield a 90% reduction in the need for annotation, which is expensive to start with [14] ; 2) social network analysis (SNA) reputation features that yield an increase of 70% in detection rate compared to content filters that ignore server reputation [15] ; 3) spectral clustering of URL n-grams and transductive semi-supervised learning that yield a 100% increase in detection rate (e.g., doubling the detection rate while maintaining the same false positive rate) of adversarial message modification compared to filters that rely on contents only for classification [16] ; 4) reputation and similarity features that yield a 13.5% increase in cost savings when challenged by changes in data distribution [17] ; and 5) random boost that yields 75% reduction in computational costs compared to random forest, where both random projections and boosting help with feature randomization to counter adversarial attacks [13] .

3. MACHINE LEARNING

The learning themes addressed by adversarial learning are those of model selection and prediction and they are dealt with using statistical learning theory (SLT) [18] [19] . SLT involves non-parametric learning and inference from finite samples (rather than asymptotic in nature). It is conceptually modeled using system imitation (e.g., mimicry) rather than accurate identification for both generalization and prediction purposes (e.g., SVM). SLT, which trades margin (for better generalization) against complexity (e.g., MDL), estimates local functional dependencies (e.g., Oracles) and putative classifications using relatively small rather than big collections of data. This helps with the deployment of robust IDS that cannot be easily compromised by adversarial learning using sporadic but dense subversion. There are three learning frameworks that draw from SLT and used here. First comes semi-supervised learning (SSL) [20] , with its basic assumptions: the smoothness assumption, characteristic of supervised learning, where similar samples (e.g., messages) share similar labels; the cluster assumption, where samples in the same cluster are likely to be of the same class and their subsequent stratification and prototyping helps with both performance and scale; and the low density separation assumption that seeks for decision boundaries in low-density regions. Transduction, similar in spirit to SSL, comes next. It leverages the complementary use of training and test data, the latter providing insights on its own data distribution. Transduction employs the strangeness or alternatively the typicality of messages to mediate between randomness deficiency (and regularity), Kolmogorov complexity, and minimum description length (MDL). Conformal prediction (CP) hedges and punts on labels to determine putative sets of predictions including their inclusion, order, and ranking in terms of likelihoods. Similar to the immune system, CP engages in open set recognition to distinguish the “self” (e.g., proper training data) from the “non-self” (e.g., adversarial training data) and thus to detect and reject unfamiliar patterns. The proposed learning frameworks go beyond bare predictions and provide reliability indexes (e.g., credibility and consistency) for the classification choices made on missing labels. This facilitates information fusion, meta-reasoning (e.g., control and gating), and meta-recognition, which leads to learning consistency and stability for Oracles and helps with reliable and robust classification including operational resilience to recover from misdiagnoses once changes in the data distribution are observed and tracked.

Randomness deficiency and Kolmogorov complexity are intricately related. The larger the randomness deficiency is the more regular and more probable some string (e.g., message or attack) is. Transduction chooses from all the possible labeling for unlabeled data the one that yields the largest randomness deficiency, i.e., the most probable one. Towards that end, one employs randomness and complexity using similarity and corresponding rankings driven by strangeness and p-values. The strangeness, which stands for non-conformity measures (NCM), measures the lack of typicality with respect to its true or putative (assumed) identity label and the labels for all the other patterns known. The strangeness α is the (likelihood) ratio of the sum of the K nearest neighbor (KNN) distances d from the same class y divided by the sum of the KNN distances from all the other classes $(\neg y)$. The smaller the strangeness, the larger its typicality and the more probable its (putative) label y is, where the use of KNN corresponds to lazy learning. Alternative definitions for the strangeness more suitable for anomaly detection (e.g., unsupervised learning) framework (rather than the supervised learning framework) on intrusion detection involve only the numerator and dispense with the denominator from the earlier definition. This makes the strangeness for samples far away from normal traffic (e.g., illegitimate traffic) larger than the strangeness of samples that belong to normal traffic. The strangeness further facilitates both feature selection (similar to Markov blankets) and variable selection (dimensionality reduction) to decrease the time the defense spends on detection. One finds empirically that the strangeness, classification margin, sample and hypothesis margin, near miss, posteriors, and odds are all related via a monotonically non-decreasing function with a small strangeness corresponding to a large margin. This is similar in spirit to cohort (e.g., context-aware estimation and learning) models using likelihood ratios, universal background model (UBM), and logistic regression [21] . One further notes that the KNN error approaches the Bayes error (with factor 1) if $k = O(\log n)$, that the strangeness α is related to the optimal decision boundary $(\alpha = 1)$ and the posterior $P(c_j|x_j)$; and that the KNN strangeness would smooth boundaries and generalize better than KNN, particularly for overlapping distributions.

The likelihood-like definitions for strangeness are intimately related to discriminative methods. The p-values described next compare ("rank") the strangeness values to determine and rank the credibility and confidence in the putative classifications made. The p-values aggregate information on relative strangeness and inform on the degree of typicality. The p-values bear resemblance to their counterparts from statistics but are not the same [22] [23] . They are derived using the relative rankings of putative classifications against each one of the classes known. The standard p-value construction, where m is the cardinality of the training set T, constitutes a valid randomness (deficiency) test approximation for some putative label y assigned to a new pattern z and is associated with $p_y(z) = \#\left(i : \alpha_i \geq \alpha_{new}^{y}\right) / (m+1)$. The p-values are used to assess the extent to which data supports or discredits the null hypothesis $H0$ (for some specific label). The largest p-value defines the credibility of the classification chosen (e.g., all other alternative classifications are stranger and thus more a-typical). The confidence measure is the difference between the top two p-values. It indicates how close to each other the first two classifications are and it thus measures for ambiguity and uncertainty. The larger the confidence the smaller the ambiguity is.

Demarcation, using the transduction confidence machine (TCM) [24] , follows from the above discussion. TCM chooses for classification that label that is most consistent with the current and well-localized training set (e.g., the self) and yields therefore the highest p-value (e.g., most typical and thus least strange label) for credibility of the class (e.g., label) assignment made. The associated confidence measure records the difference between the top two p-values and indicates the degree of ambiguity in the class assignment made. Credibility and confidence are the particular reliability indices that TCM provides for further processing, e.g., meta-reasoning, meta-recognition, and information fusion (see Sect. 8). Note that once one iterates through putative label assignments for the probe of interest, the KNN for training instances can change and their corresponding strangeness and thus p-values may change too. The intuition behind TCM is to model the test sample in a fashion most similar to the training set while minimally changing the original (predictive) model learned. Note that TCM- KNN includes different versions indexed by the number of n nearest neighbors K involved, with the class of demarcation machines referred to as TCM-KNN.

TCM-KNN is most suitable for closed set recognition. It does not, however, address the detection aspect needed for open set recognition, in general, and IDS, in particular. One needs to quantify how strange something needs to be before it can be thought of as non-self and thus be rejected as novel and unfamiliar (see Sect. 7). Towards that end, one expands the basic TCM into TCM-DR (with DR standing for detection and recognition), with detection and rejection suitable for open set recognition and outlier (e.g., intrusion) detection, in general, and impersonation (of legitimate training instances) detection, in particular. The question left for TCM-DR to answer is when to exercise the reject option non-self detection purposes. The challenge here is that one can model only the "normal" class and this leads to one-class classification problems. The approach pursued by TCM-DR leverages the distinction between individual strangeness and ("context aware") p-values, when some novel (e.g., slightly but not much different) pattern characteristic of the "self" is not necessarily a-typical overall compared to alternative interpretations for which the non-self (e.g., alternative putative labels) yields much smaller p-values. One-way to determine the threshold needed for rejection is to re-label each self-pattern as non-self, derive the corresponding p-values distribution under such a false assumption, and then empirically determine a suitable threshold that demarcates self from non-self. Similar to SSL, changing label assignments (characteristic of impersonation) provides the bias needed to determine the rejection threshold required to demarcate the self from non-self. This is characteristic of revision using "ghost" or "virtual" examples subsumed by the symmetrization lemma [25] when one replaces the true risk by an estimate computed on an independent (e.g., auxiliary) set of data, e.g., unlabeled or test data. Towards that end, one re-labels the training samples, one at a time, with all the putative labels except the one originally assigned to it. The PSR (peak-to-side) ratio, $PSR = (p_{\max} - p_{\min}) / p_{stdev}$, records the resulting p-value distribution and determines, using cross validation, the [a priori] threshold used for self-authentication. The PSR values found are low because their relative strangeness is high (and p-value low) and the threshold used is empirically chosen as several standard deviations away from the PSR mean [26] . The PSR distribution derived in such a manner supports negative identification (e.g., negative selection). Edits and revisions, similar to learning from hints and/or side information, are basic mechanisms available throughout for recovery and self-healing from attacks.

4. CONFORMAL PREDICTION

Conformal prediction (CP) mediates the incremental use of discriminative methods (e.g., likelihood ratios) using varying non-conformity measures (NCM) for strangeness. The purpose for NCM is to support hedging and punting when making predictions and to provide reliability indices such as accuracy (e.g., credibility) and certainty (e.g., confidence). Such indices, radically different from indices such as support and confidence (see Sect. 5) derived during data mining search for associations (e.g., A Priori), are well-calibrated (see below) and are generated assuming only that the data are generated independently by the same (but unknown) (i.i.d.), probability distribution, a standard assumption in machine learning that can be, however, relaxed (see Sect. 10). Transduction, in general, and both the Transduction Confidence Machine (TCM) and the Transduction Confidence Machine for Detection and Recognition (TCM-DR), in particular, which are examples of CP offspring, yield credibility and confidence as reliability indices using different NCM variants for strangeness, p-values, and skew (see Sect. 5). Furthermore, the credibility index is well calibrated (or conservatively valid) to ensure that the frequency of prediction errors does not exceed t (between 0 and 1) at each confidence level $1-t$ (in the long run). Smaller values of t correspond to greater reliability. The confidence measure, which expresses the extent of ambiguity, becomes efficient as the TCM and TCM-DR prediction (nested) sets (regions) Γ shrink (in terms of number of possible outcomes) with the prediction regions as small as possible, e.g., the inductive conformal (e.g., transductive) predictor (ICP) maps a (labeled) data sequence (training set) T and a new data sample x as $\Gamma^t(T,x)=\{y\in Y : p_y > t\}$ with $\Gamma^{t_1}\subseteq\Gamma^{t_2}$ for $0\le t_1\le t_2\le 1$. Empty predictions correspond to impersonation and spoofing that are therefore rejected. Transduction, similar to CP, is incremental in nature. It leverages the complementarity between training and test data for the purpose of robust and stable predictions (e.g., test data participate in its own disposition and classification). One can use for computational efficiency the following ICP method [27] similar to incremental transduction [8] . Divide the training set T into proper training set $T1$ and calibration set $T2$. Construct prediction rule F for classification using $T1$. Compute NCM (e.g., strangeness) score α for samples (x_i, y_i) in $T2$ using difference $\Delta(y,y')$ with $\alpha_i=\Delta(y_i,F(x_i))$. For each sample x_j and every possible label $y\in Y$, compute $\alpha_j=\Delta(y,F(x_j))$ and the corresponding p-value against calibration set $T2$ using for cardinality $|T1|-|T2|$. The prediction set is $\Gamma^t(T,x)=\{y\in Y : p_y > t\}$ and one can show that ICP is valid.

5. ACTIVE LEARNING AND CHANGE DETECTION

Adversarial learning leverages data and information contents to detect and counter attacks in order to ultimately build robust defenses. Rather than being passive in randomly selecting data instances for learning Oracles, one engages instead in purposeful collection and processing [28] . While collecting large amounts of data lacking annotation for training is straightforward and quite feasible, their annotation requires that significant effort needs to be chosen for inquiry on their annotation are selected dynamically for the purpose of learning and generalization. This follows the resolution and annotation of previous queries made using abstract but intertwined notions of margin, separability, and importance sampling. The choice on queries is made with the implicit expectation for lesser ambiguity and corresponding error reduction. Selection takes place using online or pool-based methods realized as serial or batch, the latter to avoid frequent retraining. Active learning is the functional block that addresses the requirements and objectives listed above. It is incremental and progressive in nature, with data instances once primed for selection subject to online and/or batch annotation expected to augment the training set for further principled selection, annotation, and periodic but timely IDS retraining. Fundamental to active learning is the uncertainty about what is best to query for possible annotation leading to better generalization, with the pseudo-metrics and costs sorting out and ranking the candidates for annotation.

Active learning is about making optimal choices to improve accuracy (including tradeoffs between false positives and false negatives), trading latencies between defense and offense, and generating cost savings on the resources used. Active learning, however, is not only about data instance selection. It is also about data reduction for better use of computational resources and deployment of more powerful intrusion detection methods. Active selection addresses both anomaly-based intrusion detection, which is most suitable to unknown attacks, and signature-based intrusion detection, which is most suitable for detection of known attacks. Anomaly detection, similar to immunity (see Sect. 7) is usually afflicted by high rates of false positives due to lack of knowledge about the non-self (e.g., unknown types of attacks) relative to possible deviations from legitimate behavior (e.g., the self) that are characteristic of signature-based intrusion detection. One can observe that anomaly detection or alternatively intrusion detection can benefit from the use of TCM-KNN [29] [30] to achieve higher true positive rates and lower false positive rates. In addition, data reduction in terms of less instance samples for training using active learning and lower dimensionality for those samples using feature selection becomes feasible at reduced computational costs. Note that one can redefine to advantage strangeness using only the KNN distances to normal instances. This is similar and consonant with the concept of one-class classification when anomalies are not known ahead of time.

Conformal prediction driven by algorithmic randomness, hypothesis testing, and transductive inference, provides rigorous theoretical guarantees on the error frequencies of the predictions made on unseen data samples. Transductive active learning is much cheaper in a stream-based setting (especially with the use of incremental classifiers such as ICP) where data instances are observed sequentially. It is therefore intuitive to use p-values for active learning in the stream-based (online) setting (e.g., query by transduction (QBT) [31] . The samples are queried based on the difference between the top two p-values computed using the likes of TCM-KNN. Using existing relations between transduction, Bayesian statistical testing, Kullback-Leibler divergence, and Shannon information, QBT was found related to the Query-by-Committee (QBC) paradigm for active learning. The specifics for QBT are straightforward. Let p_i be the p-values obtained for a particular instance x_{n+1} using all the possible class labels $i=1,\cdots,M$ and let p_j and p_k be the two highest p-values when sorted in descending order. The absolute difference between p_j and p_k provides a degree of information contents for the unlabeled instance, with a smaller value of the difference denoting a larger ambiguity regarding the proposed label. To quantify the uncertainty of the information contents possessed by each instance or sample, one defines its ambiguity as $I(x_{n+1})=|p_j-p_k|$. As $I(x_{n+1})$ approaches 0, the uncertainty in classifying the unlabeled instance increases. Thus, the addition of this unlabeled sample with its actual label (obtained using a human or machine Oracle and with incremental machine transduction the Oracle of choice here) to the training set provides substantial information regarding the structure of the data model. Such an unlabeled instance represents a promising data sample from an active learning perspective.

One can expand on QBT to advance a generalized version based on eigen-decomposition of matrices, where the p-values corresponding to all the putative class labels of a given sample point are integrated to decide whether or not to query any particular data sample [32] . As an example, lightweight TCM-KNN [33] subjects the input space (e.g., web transactions) with attributes such as one-way delay, request/response delay, packet loss, overall transaction duration, and delay variation (jitter) (similar to Covert Time Channels (CTC) [34]) (see Sect. 9) toward instance selection. The result for lightweight TCM-KNN is that 5600 rather than the original 98,000 training points yield similar (TP, FP) indices but at a much-reduced computational cost, e.g., original TCM-KNN (100%, 1.28%) vs. light TCM-KNN (98.38%, 1.87%). Savings of 98.65% building time for the training set and 66.45% detection time for TCM-KNN are further reported using active learning and feature selection, respectively [35] .

Yet another dimension for active leaning is that of data reduction "to avoid the curse of dimensionality and alleviate the annotation workload" [30] . First and foremost and characteristic of data reduction is feature selection. There are many methods for feature selection including (Pearson) chi-square and/or Fisher discriminant tests, to determine whether there is a significant difference between the expected ("feature") and observed ("class") frequencies in one or more categories, entropy and mutual information, and/or (filter and/or wrapper) methods using genetic algorithms (GA), characteristic of evolution and including generational GA (GGA), steady-state GA (SGA), heterogeneous recombination and cataclysmic mutation adaptive search algorithm (CHC), and population-based incremental learning (PBIL) [33] .

As information contents and ambiguity are further primed by changes in the data distribution, another dimension for active learning is to first seek for and detect such changes and then to leverage them. This takes place in particular for the purpose of online change (and drift) detection for multidimensional data sequences based on testing exchangeability using martingale [23] [31] . We recall first that some patterns found strange are not counted as a-typical or novel when compared to alternative non-self samples. We also recall that both the strangeness and p-values provide the information needed for open set recognition. This holds for both anomaly (e.g., outlier) and novelty detection using the relative order of p-values for ranking. Change detection seeks to identify those time instances when the underlying distribution for time-varying data streams (e.g., attacks) undergoes a significant change, which shows as a break down in exchangeability. Given unlabeled training set $T = \{x_1, \cdots, x_n\}$, the strangeness of a sample x_i with respect to a cluster model induced by T is $s(T,x) = \|x_i - c\|$ with c standing for cluster centers. Using the strangeness, a family of martingales, indexed by ε drawn from $[0,1]$ and referred to as the randomized power martingale, is defined as $M_n^{(\varepsilon)} = \prod\left(\varepsilon p_i^{\varepsilon-1}\right)$ with the p-values p_i approximately distributed uniformly over $[0,1]$. One notes that the skewness, a measure of the degree of asymmetry of a pdf distribution, deviates from close to zero (for uniformly distributed p-values) when the underlying model changes, due to adversarial learning, in general, and impersonation, in particular. The skewness is small and stable when there is no change. The skewed p-value distribution plays an important role in the martingale test for change detection as small p-values inflate martingale values. As a result, the martingale $M_n^{(\varepsilon)}$ increases, and evidence starts to accrue against the null hypothesis $H0$ of exchangeability in a data sequence. The increase in martingale value is used to test for change detection. The martingale, non-parametric, incremental, single-pass and working on both labeled and unlabeled data instances, does not require a sliding window on the data stream or the need to monitor the explicit performance of the classification or clustering model as data samples are streaming. The martingale is most suitable for high-dimensional data streams, compared to the Sequential Probability Ratio Test (SPRT) and Cumulative Sum (CUSUM) [36] that are suitable for time-series confined to 1D. The martingale method has a theoretical false positive error bound given a specific threshold, and the delay time between the true change point and the detected change point can be approximated.

6. SEMANTICS AND STRATIFICATION

The motivation here is to confront attack diversity and scale using semantics and stratification using clustering (e.g., Chinese Restaurant Process and spectral clustering), topic discovery using probabilistic latent semantic analysis (PLSA) and latent Dirichl et al. location (LDA)) [37] , and aggregation and consensus reasoning using RANSAC and Random-Hough Transform) [7] . Defense can be further enhanced using feature reputation [17] .

We start by reviewing here our own ongoing efforts on semantics and stratification. Towards that end we have developed phish GILLNET, a multi-layer methodology characteristic of meta-reasoning, for phishing detection [38] . The first layer (phishGILLNET1) employs PLSA to build a topic model that captures diversity using semantics for stratification. The topic model handles synonymy and polysemy (words with multiple meanings) and other linguistic variations found in phishing to counter adversarial attacks that involve deception. Deliberate misspellings are handled using Levenshtein editing and Google APIs for correction. The term document (TD) frequency matrix is fed to PLSA to find phishing and non-phishing topics using tempered expectation maximization. The performance of phish GILLNET1 is evaluated using PLSA fold-in technique with classification driven by Fisher similarity. The second layer, phishGILLNET2 employs AdaBoost [39] to build a robust ensemble classifier using the topics found earlier for stump classifiers. The third layer, phish GILLNET3, expands on phish GILLNET2 while learning a classifier from labeled and unlabeled examples using co-training [40] . Experiments conducted using one of the largest public corpora of email data containing 400,000 emails show phish GILLNET3 outperforms state of the art phishing detection methods to achieve an F1-score of 100%. Moreover, phish GILLNET3 requires only a small percentage (10%) of data to be annotated thus saving significant time for defense and avoiding errors incurred in annotation.

We expanded on phish GILLNET for the dual purposes of phishing detection and impersonated entity discovery using conditional random fields (CRF) and LDA, the first leveraging and the latter adding a Dirichlet prior for per-document topic distribution that serves as a proper generative model for new messages [37] . Impersonated entity discovery helps with black hat characterization and locks on potential attackers, which pretend to be from a legitimate organization and direct users to fake websites, which resemble legitimate sites aiming to collect users' personal information. Towards that end, phishing web side detection (PWD) involves LDA, intelligent web crawler, image to text conversion, and is device and language neutral. Our approach engages name entity recognition (NER) and discovers the impersonated entity from messages that are classified as phishing at a rate of 88.1% [41] .

The Chinese Restaurant Process (CRP) is a recent application of non-parametric clustering that does not fix in advance the number of clusters. This is relevant to situations when attacks are varying and characteristic of multi-class environments, as it is the case when detecting adversarial advertisements in the wild [9] . Similar to the infinite Gaussian mixture model (IGMM) but different from K-means, CRP does not need to manually set in advance the number of clusters to be found. The arriving "customers" (e.g., messages or attacks) can choose to sit alone at the first free/unoccupied table or join other "customers" at any of the already occupied tables.

The corresponding probabilities for the nth arriving customer are $a/(n-1+a)$ and $n_k/(n-1+a)$, respectively, where a determines how likely it is that a customer would choose to sit by herself at the first unoccupied table and n_k is the number of customers already seated at one of the k tables with k ranging from 1 to the number K of tables currently seating customers. The CRP distribution of table assignments for any arriving customer, proportional to either a or n_k, thus favors crowded tables.

The goal for most customers is to get seated with similar or familiar customers with the possibility to "open" new tables for customers who don't have much to share with those already seated. This is the motivation behind the recently introduced distance-dependent CRP (dd-CRP) [42] where table assignments are dependent on direct familiarity or through customers' connections. The distribution of table assignments for customer c_i is now a (for an unoccupied table) and $f(d_{ij})$ to join customer j at her table with similarity distance d_{ij} between customers i and j, and with f standing for the (exponential or logistic) decay function, e.g., $f(d)=\exp(-d/a)$ or $f(d)=\exp(-d+a)/(1+\exp(-d+a))$ [43] . One can expand on dd-CRP using NCM that leverage Levenshtein editing to choose among alternative readings of the attacks (e.g., hallucinate and revise). Another possibility is to have dd-CRP operate in a lower dimensionality manifold generated using spectral clustering.

Table assignments would use NCM and TCM-DR, including the reject option characteristic of open set recognition, for impersonation detection (e.g., new customers unfamiliar with those already seated) and have them seated at a new table. Imposters, characteristic of unfamiliar customers (e.g., obfuscation attacks to confuse training), can be reassigned to earlier tables (e.g., known attacks) as more evidence streams in and links are established with customers (e.g., attacks) already seated at tables.

One goes beyond active learning to leverage the relative importance of data instances and build better defenses using importance sampling, characteristic of RANSAC and Random-Hough Transform (RHT) for consensus reasoning methods.

The motivation is to pursue evidence accumulation and accrue cues for aggregation and ultimate detection of intrusions. The whole is more than the sum of its parts. RANSAC, characteristic of robust estimation methods, starts with a small but randomly chosen data set of instances and estimates some parametric model that fits data best. It then iteratively enlarges the set with consistent data when possible and re-estimates the model and its error. Starting from different subsets, The Randomized Hough Transform-Support Vector Machine (RHT-SVM) [7] leverages multiple versions of the decision boundary to identify messages that have been mislabeled deliberately, as result of persistent attacks, or not deliberately but due to poor Oracle annotation. The RHT-SVM uses the product of the actual classification label and the average signed distance of an observation from the decision boundary to determine if a training message has been mislabeled. The labels for messages, which on the average appear on the wrong side of the boundary, are flipped and a final SVM model is trained using the modified data.

We note that RHT expands on agnostic active (A2) learning [44] [45] that maintains both a current version space and a region of uncertainty. Two data sets, TREC 2007 and CEAS 2008 were used for comparing the performance of RHT-SVM to the performance of Reject On Negative Impact (RONI) [5] as well as the performance of an SVM trained on the tainted training data. To preserve the time ordered nature of the data stream, for each of the data sets the first 10% of the messages are used for training and the remaining 90% of the messages are used for evaluation. Separate adversarial experiments are conducted for flipping spam labels and non-spam labels. For 10 iterations, labels are flipped for a randomly selected subset of 5% of the training data and the final RHT-SVM is evaluated on the test set. RHT-SVM shows an average 9.3% increase in the F1- (harmonic mean of precision and recall) score compared to RONI (99.0% versus 90.6%).

The flip sensitivity for RHT-SVM is 95.9% and the flip specificity is 99.0%. It also takes over 90% less time to complete the RHT-SVM experiments compared to the RONI experiments (20 minutes per experiment instead of 360 minutes).

7. IMMUNITY AND DETECTION

The observation that biological immune system (BIS) and information detection systems (IDS) aims are functionally similar is not new. This observation has led to the design of artificial immune systems (AIS) that interface between BIS and IDS using concepts borrowed from evolutionary computation (EC) and genetic algorithms (GA). AIS analogies for IDS are appealing for two reasons in terms of reach and scope. First, BIS provides a high level of protection from invading pathogens but can still fail as one knows very well. Second, computer security techniques "are not able to cope with the dynamic and increasingly complex nature of computer systems and their security" [46] . The immunity characteristics of AIS are not a literal translation of BIS, which is still shrouded in mystery, but rather a conceptual and functional transliteration of BIS. Note that AIS help also with misbehavior detection (e.g., routing misbehavior) in mobile ad-hoc networks [47] , recommender systems, and detecting security attacks in software-defined networks (SDN).

Conformal prediction and open set recognition (e.g., TCM-DR) provide a suitable framework to emulate the immunity paradigm. Basically, AIS have to demarcate adversarial attacks that have never been seen before (e.g., non-self) from current self (e.g., normal patterns of behavior and expression). This is accomplished using self-generated antibodies and evaluating them for fitness and avidity to match (e.g., negative selection) continuously morphing antigens (non-self) (e.g., network access patterns) characteristic of pathogens that use clonal selection. Both affinity and avidity are readily available using transduction. Affinity, between detector and specific antigen, is similar to strangeness; avidity, which reflects on the interactions between one detector and all the antigens, is similar to p-values including credibility and confidence for fitness. Together, affinity and avidity support attribute weighting and priorities needed to establish the degree of matching and to facilitate clonal selection including positive selection (PS), when new and advantageous genetic variants sweep a population [48] . A good intrusion detector should have a high non-self avidity and low self-avidity. Additional AIS functionalities that cope with dynamics include apoptosis (e.g., programmed cells death), and the provision of danger SOS signals that indicate damage to self-cells during positive selection. Negative selection and recognition takes place using open set recognition, with innovations on re-identification that seek among others for similar antigens that can be traced to the same source of attack. This leverages consensus reasoning (e.g., RANSAC) and helps with both adversarial learning and clonal selection. The motivation behind re-identification comes from the fact that the multitude of antigens share common characteristics and can be traced to some common source(s) using amongst others longest common sequence (LCS) (e.g., positive selection) for similarity using dynamic programming and/or RANSAC/Random Hough Transform for realization [7] . Positive selection further helps with better designs for adversarial attacks as they anticipate weak points in defense susceptible to be overwhelmed by persistent attacks.

It is important to know not only what works and to what extent it works, but also to know what does not work and why. This affects AIS (e.g., detection and re-identification). Anecdotal evidence suggests that 90 percent of mass screening errors is due to only 10 percent of the biometric (face) patterns and that even 1% obfuscation and spoofing are enough for cyber security attacks to win. The contribution made by varying attacks patterns on the overall system error is not even. Pattern Specific Error Inhomogeneity (PSEI) analysis [49] shows that the error rates vary across the population being screened according to its diversity. This has led to the jocular characterization of the target population as being composed of "sheep" and "goats." In this characterization, the sheep, for whom classification systems perform reasonably well, dominate the population, whereas the goats, though in a minority, tend to determine the performance of the system through their disproportionate contribution of false reject errors. Impersonation has additional barnyard appellations, which follow from the observed inhomogeneity in performance observed across the population. Specifically, there are some malicious attacks, which have unusually good success at impersonating many different targets. These are called "wolves." There are also some targets that are easy to imitate and thus seem unusually susceptible to many different impersonations. These are called "lambs." PSEI can be addressed using meta-reasoning and transduction [26] to recognize attack patterns that are difficult to defend against, and thus to gate and process them accordingly (see Sect. 8). PSEI spans the analogue of a biometric/forensic menagerie [50] . It expands on the type of attacks and also addresses covariate shift (e.g., changes in the data distributions characteristic of the arm race encountered during evolution) on one side, and change and drift detection, on the other side. PSEI and fraud detection can further leverage reputation and implicit NCM toward deploying one-class SVM [17] in order to mediate between different types of attacks and their constructive resolution.

One can observe and investigate (rather than be constructive and proffer solutions) different automated evasion techniques in the "wild" that "enable malware writers to generate highly variable polymorphic versions of malware that all exploit the same software vulnerability" [51] . Two quantitative measures, similar to evolution and immunity, were proposed for the evaluation of the strength of polymorphic engines: the variation (e.g., diversity) strength and the propagation (e.g., survival) strength. Using these measures, "the authors [51] analyze variability of real shell code samples and claim that the degree of variability attainable by polymorphic engines raises a strong doubt that attacks can ever be modeled by the simple generative approach (i.e., attack signatures) used in many common intrusion detection and antivirus tools" [52] . This could be handled, however, using anomaly detection methods, on one side, and techniques similar to those deployed using PSEI, randomness, and distributed semantic models using vector space representations (see Sect. 12), on the other side. Such observations suggest that negative and clonal selection is ultimately better off using cohort (e.g., context aware) learning and open set recognition rather than the intricacies of polymorphic engines and signature-based intrusion detection.

For completeness we mention that [53] have reported that they built and deployed a coherent, scalable, and extensible real time system, the Facebook Immune System (FIS), to protect users and the social graph (SG) they span. The use of "Immune" refers to overall defense against attackers (e.g., intruders similar to pathogens) without any specific adherence to AIS except a reference to generic mutation. The FIS has two advantages over the attacker: user feedback and global knowledge, something that is not usually pervasive and therefore available to neither AIS nor much of IDS. User feedback for FIS is both explicit and implicit. Explicit feedback includes mark as spam or reporting. Implicit feedback includes deleting a post or rejecting a friend request. Both implicit and explicit feedback is valuable and central to FIS defense. In addition to user feedback, the system has knowledge of aggregate patterns and what is normal and unusual, again something that is not usually available to standard and continuous IDS operation.

Some of the findings and solutions reported by FIS are consonant with the statistics and methods reported throughout this paper about the mode and effectiveness of current attacks. A 2% false-positive rate today on an attack affecting 1000 users is better than a 1% false-positive rate tomorrow on the same attack affecting 100,000 users. As time progresses, attacks mutate and training data becomes less relevant. Similar to learning good is often better than perfect when the complexity involved is lower because it yields better generalization. Optimizing the classification methods or reducing their feature space further improves the classification latency. FIS performs real time checks and classifications on every read and write action. As of March 2011, this was 25B checks per day, reaching 650 K per second at peak.

The effort to design, develop, and deploy FIS has been major, with many Facebook (FB) engineers involved in addition to the authors of the reference paper. FIS findings, which are specific to social media, are helpful overall with both meta-reasoning and meta-recognition (Sect. 8), on one side, and with the immunity aspect discussed in this section, on the other side. Attackers target the social graph in two ways: either by compromising existing graph nodes or by injecting new but fake nodes and relationships.

The defense is tasked to protect the graph from attackers who aim to hide patterns and subvert detection. "To be effective, the defense must respond fast and target the features that are most expensive for the attacker to change, being careful to avoid over-fitting on the superficial features that are easy for the attacker to change. The defender seeks to shorten Attack and Detection phases while lengthening the Defense and Mutate stages. The attacker seeks the opposite: to shorten Defense (by obscuring responses and subverting attack canaries) and Mutate while lengthening Attack and Detect" [53] . This illustrates why detection and response latencies are so important for effective defense with any AIS designed to shorten the phases controlled by attackers and to lengthen the phases under defense control. FIS ultimately deploys an integrated IDS that is scalable and responsive to attacks coming from multiple and heterogeneous channels. This affects "the metric interplay between fitness and immunity as response and detection latencies become more important than precision and recall". Damage accumulates quickly [53] . The above interplay and further analogies between AIS and IDS support evolution and co-evolution for both defense and offense whose role are interchangeable, and ultimately affect the effectiveness of the self-protection shield to buttress the defense. Topics of further interest for investigation in the context of adversarial learning include the digital analog of immune disease and immunosuppression using sensitivity analysis driven by cohorts and NCM related concepts.

We note here for completeness that data mining methods have also been used for intrusion detection [54] . Data mining, however, lacks the local estimation and training aspects characteristics of conformal prediction, in general, and transduction, in particular, which provide for locality that reveals specific context, location, and time stamps. One early example for data mining use is audit data analysis and mining (ADAM) system [55] to discover attacks in a TCP dump audit trail using KDD 1999 for test bed and seeking DOS and PROBE attacks. ADAM leverages A Priori association mining to derive (antecedent to consequent) rules of legitimate behavior (e.g., profiles free of attacks) in terms of "normal" frequent item sets. The data mining output augments the rules found with support and confidence indices, which are characteristic of the whole transaction data set T. This is different from the reliability indices for putative class assignments found using TCM-KNN, which correspond to different types of localized attacks. The rules $X \rightarrow Y$ found using association mining have support s in the (big data) transaction set T if s% of transactions contains $X \cup Y$, and confidence c if c% of transactions that contains X also contains Y.

8. META-REASONING AND META-RECOGNITION

There are two complementary dimensions discussed in this paper. One dimension is about advancing and developing a unified learning framework built around conformal prediction for adversarial learning purposes. The other dimension is about designing and developing a software environment where one can explore and exploit in a coordinated fashion different functional modules that complement each other and address conflicting asymmetries. The proposed integrated environment should expand on the likes of SALT [2] and optimally engage and gate modules that challenge both offense and defense while at the same time enhances and evaluates both. Such an enterprise is supported by meta-reasoning and meta-recognition, whose workings are intertwined. Meta-rea- soning plans the best layout and disposition of functional modules, and meta-recognition navigates the maze of data and detection options in order to sort out and rank alternative hypotheses and feasible solutions according to reliability indices and sensitivity analysis. Best defense is multi-prong as contents are multi-varied in reach and scope. This is where re-identification comes in. It is broader than both stand-alone static and/or dynamic recognition and it is incremental in nature. The patterns (e.g., messages) characteristic of adversarial attacks are sporadic rather than continuous in terms of location and time stamps, and can be at times only partial in appearance and disposition. Re-identification [56] is about threading, on one side, and countering disparate and sporadic events, on the other side. This takes place as prior information is lacking and with nothing yet available to track when defenses start looking around for possible attacks.

Isaiah Berlin recalls in his landmark work The Hedgehog and the Fox that "There is a line among the fragments of the Greek poet Archilochus which says: 'the fox knows many things, but the hedgehog knows one big thing. For there exists a great chasm between those, on one side, who relate everything to a single central vision, one system less or more coherent or articulate, in terms of which they understand, think and feel—a single, universal, organizing principle in terms of which alone all that they are and say has significance—and, on the other side, those who pursue many ends, often unrelated and even contradictory, connected, if at all, only in some de facto way, for some psychological or physiological cause, related by no moral or aesthetic principle; these last lead lives, perform acts, and entertain ideas that are centrifugal rather than centripetal, their thought is scattered or diffused, moving on many levels, seizing upon the essence of a vast variety of experiences and objects for what they are in themselves, without consciously or unconsciously, seeking to fit them into, or exclude them from, any one unchanging, all-embracing, sometimes self-contradictory and incomplete, at times fanatical, unitary inner vision. The first kind of intellectual and artistic personality belongs to the hedgehogs, the second to the foxes [57] . The clash between "monist and pluralist", with the latter aware of the permanence of ambiguity and uncertainty, parallels the competition between generative (hedgehog) and discriminative (fox) methods. For modern audience the fox is "divergent" as it displays many not necessarily complementary traits. What is unique are only the philosophical underpinnings for using conformal prediction to learn, on one side, and hedging and punting for demarcation purposes, on the other side, while all along training and querying for annotation and testing are complementary to each other.

Best defense needs to be multi-prong with adversarial learning expected to leverage both contents and context. Contents are multi-varied in reach and scope. Their description starts from raw messages and/or events and moves up the information ladder to include pragmatics and semantics, expected vulnerabilities, and linkages that seek to tie everything together. This is where re-identification comes in. It is about threading and explaining disparate and sporadic events lacking prior information and without anything yet to track when defenses get started to look around for possible attacks. Some functional modules have been motivated and described in the preceding sections. Additional functionalities are introduces in subsequent sections including moving target defense, on-line compression, randomness, and distributed semantic models and vector space representation.

The motivation for meta-reasoning including meta-planning and gating networks draws from anticipation and control, on one side, and context and goals, on the other side. It has been apparent to all that there is no single method for all pattern recognition problems but rather a bag of tools and a bag of problems. Pragmatic and constructive context-aware information fusion supports reliable adversarial learning for intrusion detection and re-identification using principled conformal prediction, in general, and incremental transduction and consensus reasoning for aggregation and stratification, in particular. Inference leverages localization and specialization to combine and deploy expertise. This bears analogies to ensemble of methods, mixtures of experts, and voting machines. Re-identification, which is integral to meta-recognition, accrues evidence for recognition of sporadic (site and time wise) and partial but potentially adversarial events, and supports incremental learning about the adversary. Re-identification helps to interface and mediate between AIS and IDS deployment for the dual purposes of negative and positive selection, on one side, and clonal selection, on the other side.

Meta-reasoning mediates among functional modules while making strategic choices among methods, strategies, and tactics. Adversarial architectures, in general, and IDS architectures, in particular, should be modular and integrated, on one side, and discriminative and incremental in nature, on the other side. The ultimate goal for cyber security is that of deploying a protective defense shield that at its core implements the analogue of autonomic computing [58] and W5+. Autonomic computing, referred to as self-management, provides basic functionalities, e.g., self-configuration (for planning and organization), self-optimization (for efficacy), self-protec- tion (for security purposes), and self-healing (to repair malfunctions and display resilience). W5+ answers questions related to WHAT data to consider, When to get/capture the data and from WHERE, and HOW to best process the data. The WHO question, about adversarial identity (e.g., source and reputation), is about identity management. Directed evidence accumulation seeks also to explain intent or mal-intent using the WHY question. This question is tasked with linking observations and hypotheses (models) (abducted using analogy reasoning or inferred using Bayesian (belief) networks). The Bayesian networks (for inference and validation purposes) can assist with optimal and incremental/progressive smart data collection, e.g., multi-view integration. In a fashion similar to signal processing and transmission, the incremental aspect signifies continuous access and/or use of crucial evidence, which at some point is enough to solve the IDS "puzzle" and/or make re-identification apparent. Exploration and exploitation, training and detection, active learning, adaptation and co-evolution, can be threaded according to the confidence placed in prediction outcomes and the calibration of the confidence obtained when using ICP, TCM, and TCM-DR. As an example, Integrated Adaptive Cyber Defense (IACD) where autonomic computing is coupled to human-centric automation (see Sect. 14), promises "to create a healthy cyber ecosystem by automating many risk decisions and optimizing human oversight of security processes too complex or important for machines alone to solve" [59] .

Meta-recognition [60] , complementary to meta-reasoning, is a post-recognition and score normalization analysis that considers the underlying nature of the prediction sets and their score distribution, and evaluates the extent to which a recognition algorithm succeeds or fails. It can adjust the recognition outcomes if necessary, and it feeds control information to signal to meta-reasoning that a specific response action, e.g., operator intervention or further acquisition of data, is needed. Three basic but different techniques can address the interplay between non-match and matching distributions for putative intrusions: score normalization using cohort analysis and non-conformity measures, statistical extreme value theory (EVT) (without requiring training data), and machine learning. Score normalization essentially leverage varying cohorts, which are not available during real-world operation [61] and the corresponding prediction sets that ICP and its variants yield. The key insight for EVT is that "if the best score is a match, then it should be an outlier with respect to the non-match (tail distribution) model" [60] . P-values and skew discussed earlier are the extreme value solutions that are advanced here using conformal prediction, in general, and transduction, in particular. While machine learning using SVM is reported to perform undertook on cyber security. The motivation for such findings is aligned with the sensible observation already made that a multitude of methods and algorithm instantiations including randomness is needed to face a diversity of attacks. As an example, anomaly detection renders itself to meta-recognition using the choice or (stage-wise cascade or weighted) combination of one-class SVM to account for access to the normal class only, TCM-DR introduced earlier that avails itself of the reject option of open set recognition for anomaly detection of the novel and unfamiliar, the sequential Hausdorff NN conformal anomaly detector (SHNN-CAD) [62] for online learning and sequential anomaly detection, and the discords algorithm characteristic of SAX for time- series [63] .

Incremental transduction similar to ICP augments the training set T with sample (q, y(q)) for query q that has been annotated as $y(q)$. One endows the new instance with some reliability index to measure the difference between the T distributions before ($T1$) and after instance augmentation ($T2$) using Kullback-Leibler (KL) divergence (e.g., sensitivity analysis), i.e., $r(q,y(q))=1-KL(T1,T2)$. The strangeness (e.g., NCM) for the instance is $\alpha(q)=1-r(q,y(q))$. The reliability index r can be revised using information on class (label), e.g., priors and the sensitivity and specificity of the classification method C used by ICP. Confidence intervals for both prediction and sequential importance sampling are established accordingly. Assume now a regression model where the strangeness for putative label y is defined as $\alpha(y)=p(x)|y-f(x)|/\exp(g(x))$ with regression function f built upon training set T, error of regression function $|y-f(x)|$, estimate of accuracy for re-gression $g(x)$ built using Support Vector Regression (SVR) from data set $G=\{(x_i,\ln(|y-f(x_i)|)),i=1,\cdots,N\}$, and with $p(x)$ characteristic of the input data density. Assuming confidence level t and predictive region $\Gamma^t(T,x)=\{y\in Y:p_y>t\}$ or equivalently the set $\{y:\alpha(y)<\alpha a\}$, which is a valid $(1-a/(N+1))\times 100\%$ confidence region with $t=\#\{\alpha_i:\alpha_i\geq\alpha_a\}/(N+1)$, the predictive region is then $|y-f(x_{new})|<\alpha_a*\exp(g(x_{new})/p(x_{new}))$. The obtained predictive region will then be smaller for points at which SVR prediction is good and large for points where the prediction is bad, with more confidence in the regions of high input density [64] . Similar sensitivity analysis leverages the observed changes in class posteriors due to guided perturbations and informed edits.

The decision about how to proceed in a step-wise fashion depends on both the current prediction sets (see above) and on management and/or policy considerations. For example, an action in one region (e.g., prediction set) might be more undesirable than in another region. Another example would be applying a more aggressive spam classifier to pages depending on admin preferences. Towards such ends, meta-reasoning includes mechanisms to evaluate classifier performance and leverage in an incremental fashion the prediction sets that are advanced by ICP-like methods (e.g., transduction). Subsequent gating is realized using a multi-layer architecture that includes 1) PSEI (see Sect. 7); 2)

Psychology and (behavioral) economics using biases (see Sect. 14); 3) AIS and IDS (see Sect. 7); 4) incremental ICP and sensitivity analysis (see above); 5) stratification using topics (see Sect. 6); and 6) targeted strategies and tactics. Other anti-abuse and adversarial learning problems are likely to benefit from focusing on fast detection and response, sharing data across information channels, and integrated feedback loops.

Adversarial learning is challenging because attackers can detect defenses and mutate their exploits relatively quickly. Towards that end, an important functionality is that of sequential anomaly detection and mining of trajectories, which is relevant amongst other to moving targets defense (MTD) that modify network environments in response to adversarial activity and persistent threats following reconnaissance undertaken by adversary (e.g., data collection on targets of interest). "Existing methods are not designed for sequential analysis of incomplete trajectories or online learning based on an incrementally updated training set [as ICP and incremental transduction do] and involve ad-hoc thresholds, and may suffer from over fitting and poorly calibrated alarm rates"; the sequential Hausdorff NN conformal anomaly detector (SHNN-CAD) is a sequential "parameter-light anomaly detection that offers a well-founded approach to the calibration of the anomaly threshold" [62] and is consonant with re-identification that threads to fill in for missing or corrupt information.

Traffic can also be approached using time series encoded using discrete representations including symbolic aggregate approximation (SAX) like methods that replace standard representations of time series (e.g., DWT, DFT) in order to find discords and most unusual time series subsequences [63] . Complementary to SAX is the search for indexing and mining very large collections of time series (e.g., iSAX2.0) [65] to demarcate self from non-self (e.g., alien DNA). Search and storage can be accommodated to advantage using locality sensitive hashing (LSH) [66] .

9. MOVING TARGET DEFENSE

Another desirable functionality for adversarial learning is to leverage the cognitive footprints including their timing left [34] by both legitimate and adversarial users, while at the same time covertly deploying decoys (e.g., hotspots) that do not interfere with the normal operation of the network and/or mobile devices. One now seeks to ensure that the current user is still one of the legitimate ones who were initially authenticated in order to prevent intrusions characteristic of advanced persistent threats (APT). This is similar in concept to moving target defenses (MTD), in general, and to continuous and covert re-authentication (CCA), in particular, it searches among others for "active indicators and corresponding automatic detection tools to ferret out individual with privileged access who are engaged in malicious behaviors such as espionage, sabotage, or violence" and the development of inference enterprise models (IEMs) designed to forecast an enterprise accuracy in detection potential threats [67] .

Expert ("voting") methods (e.g., random forests) support the deployment of active indicators for user engagements using command streams [68] or scrolling behaviors [69] . As both MTD and CCA have to cope with change and novelty detection, solutions built around zero-shot learning [70] using one-class SVM, are yet another possibility [71] [72] , while the control strategy is to explore and exploit. Similar to decoys, MTD challenges any potential adversary to divine and fathom friend from foe, on one side, and exploit the outcomes the decoys trigger in order to make future engagements (e.g., exploration) better focused and effective. MTD is adaptive by nature. It is complementary to gating in supporting meta-reasoning and meta-recognition, can leverage the conformal prediction sets competing to become effective (e.g., shrink), while at the same time striving for better intrusion detection.

The exploitation dimension seeks for enhanced re-authentication using the analog of recommender system like strategies, e.g., user profiles (e.g., contents filtering) and crowd out sourcing (e.g., collaborative filtering). Similar strategies also support system agility. This "[to engage] in any reasoned modification to a system or environment in response to a functional, performance, or security need" using MTD [73] . System agility is expected to be responsive to W5+ like questions (see Sect. 8), in particular to those of when, what, and how to employ autonomic computing to improve the security of an environment, as well to consider how to measure and weigh the effectiveness of different approaches to agility. Challenges of interest to moving target defenses include concealing the strategy from the adversary (e.g., randomness and subliminal covert challenges), sustaining security across layers, and managing costs including utility and usability (see Sect. 14).

Covert Time Channels (CTC), both active and passive in nature, manipulate the timing of existing traffic (e.g., ordering of network events) for exfiltration purposes. Towards that end, obfuscation takes place when one rather than transmitting at a high rate of speed in order to achieve large bandwidth would deliberately extend the duration of the CTC transmission process. IDS are tasked currently to handle CTC by analyzing deviations from legitimate network traffic statistics. Such approaches, however, are not applicable to highly dynamic and noisy environments because they rely on historical traffic and tedious model training. One could instead use traffic- mining [62] and/or transduction (with/without i.i.d. assumptions) (see Sect. 10) and its variants. An NCM-CTC combination can model slow CTC and use wavelet-based detection (WBD) [34] that does not require historical traffic data and still yields a high detection rate and a low false positive rate. WBD measures the distance between outbound traffic generated by two virtual machines (VM), one the potentially infected VM and the other a benign VM. The detection metric employs observable variables derived from the discrete wavelet-based multi-resolution transform (DWMT) to measure the variability of the timing difference at all decomposition scale. Yet another possibility is to expand on NCM-CTC using random matrix spectral theory (see Sect. 11).

10. ON-LINE COMPRESSION MODELS

We expand here the scope of conformal prediction using online compression models (OCM) that start from scratch (e.g., zero-shot learning) and without assuming that the samples are i.i.d. and exchangeable. This supports the adversarial and incremental aspect of the arm race waged between defense and offense. Conformal inductive predictors (CIP) including their validity and efficiency or alternatively their credibility and confidence regarding their prediction outcomes become relevant here. The OCM are lossy in nature and one "can argue that the only information lost is noise, since the summary is required to be a 'sufficient' statistics" [27] . OCM-like summaries include the Gauss and Markov models, which are stronger models than exchangeability. The summary statistics for the Gaussian model are, as one would expect, the mean and variance (or alternatively the first two moments) of the data sequence T seen so far. The non-conformity measure (NCM) for some data sequence $T(x_1, \cdots, x_{n+1})$ is $|x_{n+1} - mean(x_1 \cdots x_n)|$ and the prediction regions Γ^{ε} are built around the t-distribution with $n-1$ degrees of freedom using the t-test with the bonus feature of errors being independent of each other in the online setting [27] .

11. RANDOMNESS

Another dimension that needs to get embedded in the self-protective shield is that of random matrix theory (RMT). This test the degree and distribution of randomness observed using novel non-conformity measures (NCM) that support demarcation for data lacking proper annotation. A random matrix (RM) is a matrix of given type and size whose entries consist of random numbers from some specified distribution. Random matrix theory, similar to statistical mechanics, can describe the dynamics of socio-economic systems and is a basic tool for financial markets that consist of many components (e.g., stocks) and complex interactions between stock prices (e.g., macroscopic variables $g_i(t)$).

The cross-correlation matrix C (e.g., between stock prices) is time-dependent and varies, with meaningful correlations described by large any random matrices. One can then compare the eigenvalues of C against a "null hypothesis"-a random correlation matrix R constructed from mutually uncorrelated time series [74] [75] and derive NCM of interest. The eigenvectors of C corresponding to the eigenvalues outside their RMT bound display systematic deviations from RMT predictions, with the deviating eigenvectors showing distinct groups (e.g., explaining factors).

Such randomness tests support conformal prediction, in general, and adversarial learning, in particular, in their search for demarcation and grouping. Similarity (e.g., agreement and regularity) characteristic of randomness and deviations characteristic of contents can therefore inform on advanced persistent threats (APT) and/or purposeful (spear) attacks. RMT is particularly useful when there is no informative historical data (e.g., traffic) available (e.g., zero-day attacks) and one still seeks to connect the dots for seemingly disparate and sporadic events and patterns. RMT provides also additional insights in problems related to detection (e.g., number of sources embedded in noise) [76] . Yet another use of randomness is to hash and salt, with the latter about random data that augments the hash. There are also links to be leveraged between RMT and Covert Time Channels (CTC).

In particular, one would use RMT and/or transduction to detect CTC, which for obfuscation purposes rather than transmitting at a high rate of speed in order to achieve large bandwidth would deliberately extend the duration of the CTC transmission process for information leak purposes. The expanded RMT-NCM-ICP framework can further leverage the benefits accrued from using random matrix spectral theory and conformal prediction (e.g., NCM-ICP).

12. DISTRIBUTED SEMANTIC MODELS AND VECTOR SPACE REPRESENTATIONS

Chinese restaurant process (CRP), clustering, and stratification models can use any of TD/IDF, bag of words (BOW), or latent Dirichl et al. location (LDA) for message representation. An alternative spectrum of representations, which has been recently proposed, makes reference to distributional semantic models (DSM) including semantic vector space representations (VSR) that span the universe of classic context-counting (e.g., co-occur- rence) and context-predicting (e.g., embedding or neural language models) semantic vectors, with the latter claimed to "obtaining a thorough and resounding victory against their count-based [only] counterparts" [77] . VSR using continuous bag-of-words (CBOW) (e.g., predict a word given the context) and continuous skip-gram (CSG) (e.g., predict context given a word) models [78] . Both CBOW and CSG, characteristic of context-pre- dicting VSR models, have recently become available (e.g., word2vec) from Google using Python. There is also the possibility to combine global matrix factorization (e.g., latent semantic analysis (LSA)) and local context window (e.g., skip-gram) methods (e.g., Global Vector (GloVe) [79]) to enjoy both worlds (e.g., BOW and CBOW). VSR, one among several directions for developing new NCM in support of adversarial learning, facilitates message detection and stratification, on one side, and can overcome message obfuscation using quasi vector operations, on the other side. The justification and motivation come from one moving away from simple scalar or angle distances between word vectors toward measuring instead for varying word analogies and relational similarities using vector arithmetic in the embedded space. The NCM can further encode the difference between predictions and observations, use likelihoods (similar to GloVe) and strangeness to filter out noise, and leverage the complementarity between CBOW and skip-grams. DSM and VSR are similar in their use of analogies for learning with the use of auxiliary side information including higher-order similarities and chorus of prototypes.

13. EXPERIMENTAL METHODS AND PERFORMANCE EVALUATION

Experimental design and performance evaluation include nested and multiple k-fold cross-validation ((train, tune/validate), test)) for model selection and generalization for ultimate prediction on sequestered data.

This includes parameter setting, pruning (e.g., feature selection and dimensionality reduction) for complexity control, and stopping criteria (e.g., using extreme values and/or lowest perplexity). Note that first and foremost one is most interested in model selection and prediction using the expected prediction risk for any method M contemplated. The prediction risk for method M is found as that $\text{prediction risk}(M) = \text{empirical risk}(M) * f(d/n)$, with "$d$" the number of degrees of freedom (e.g., parameters) for the prediction method M trained on "n" instances/samples/examples/and "f" a monotonically increasing penalty function. As the number of degrees of freedom increases and the data sample size decreases the prediction risk on sequestered or new test data increases. One therefore seeks to decrease the number of parameters for any given training data set. Additional dimensions of interest include the use of randomized control trials (RCT) to avoid correlation to become causation and substitute foresight to hindsight (e.g., back stacking), and sampling and resampling strategies including balanced training populations using over and under sampling and/or mixed strategies (e.g., 0.632 bootstrap). In addition to the reliability indices for confidence on the decisions associated with conformal prediction (e.g., risk for misdetection), one also employs standard performance metrics including overall accuracy, ROC and AUC, and sensitivity (e.g., recall), precision, specificity, and F1-score. Similarity, which is intrinsic to both metrics and non-conformity measures, includes cosine, Jaccard, Hamming, Hausdorff (e.g., maximum distance from a point in set A to the closest point in set B, quite useful for anomaly detection), and weighted distances. Scale is addressed using vector space representations, (distributed) semantics and topics, and stratification and importance sampling (see Sects. 6 and 12), the latter expanding on active learning using consensus reasoning and guided perturbations that are characteristic of sensitivity analysis (e.g., mutations using flipping annotation and/or revising contents to assess the extent to which the Oracles become affected). Last but not least we recall that what to evaluate is as important as how to evaluate.

Yet another factor affecting overall cyber security and malware detection, which is traced to epidemiology, is the intrinsic relationship between prevalence (e.g., proportion of a population to show a condition of interest) and fallacy (e.g., invalid reasoning) [80] . The corresponding base-rate fallacy and its implications for the difficulty of intrusion detection [81] are examined next. The (Sensitivity, Specificity) and (Recall, Precision) pairs, which are set according to the entries of the confusion matrix (e.g., TP for true positives and FN for false negatives) and serve as useful figures of merit (FOM) to characterize overall intrusion detection performance, An intrusion detection engine with constant sensitivity of 99.9% and specificity of 99.9% would appear to provide excellent performance when just 1% or 10,000 out of 1,000,000 of messages are adversarial attacks. Since the engine is 99.9% sensitive, it will detect 9990 attacks and miss 10 attacks. To continue this analysis, recall that out of one million messages, 990,000 are adversarial attacks. If the specificity is also 99.9%, one can see that 989,010 legitimate messages (e.g., true negatives (TN)) have to be allowed to pass through, while 990 legitimate messages, or approximately 0.1% of the original population, are labeled as false positives (FP) and need to be denied access. What is still needed to complete a meaningful analysis is the prevalence of adversarial attacks in the general population, which is referred to as the prior odds. Assume now that the prevalence for adversarial attacks is 0.1% rather than 1%, i.e., there are 1000 rather than 10,000 adversarial attacks. At 99.9% sensitivity, the intrusion detection engine will pick up 999 of them, leaving only one adversarial attack to slip through. Of the 999,000 genuine messages, the detection engine lets through 998,001 of them, and falsely labels 999 of them as attacks. The evaluation yields now the same number of false positive as true positive, and the PPV (+ predictive value) for attacks is now only 50%. Each other message labeled as an attack is a mistake! When the prevalence is 1%, the decision on detection is worth much more because the PPV changes drastically and goes up to 90%, i.e., only one tenth rather than half of genuine messages are quarantined. PPV is further affected by sensitivity and specificity changes that are related to the differences in the populations trained on and then screened for detection purposes.

14. HUMAN FACTORS

Human factors are about tactics, in general, and insights, ingenuity and intuition in particular. Such characteristics are hard to replicate by machines but are most important for human learning, critical thinking, and problem solving [19] , with automation expected to amplify human skill and therefore enhance cyber security infrastructure. Human factors should ease, facilitate and induce human "serendipity" in exploring and exploiting alternative scenarios leading to better and original security solutions. The ultimate challenge is to move away from "technology-centered automation toward human-centered automation where the human operator is kept in the decision loop, which is a continuous process of action, feedback and judgment making" [82] . Furthermore, the same author [82] argues that the best decision-support systems provide professionals with "alternative interpretations, hypotheses, or choices." This entails adaptive automation, which employs "cutting-edge sensors and interpretive algorithms to monitor people's physical and mental states, then uses that information to shift tasks and responsibilities between human and computer. When the system senses that an operator is struggling with a difficult procedure, it allocates more tasks to the computer to free the operator of distractions.

But when it senses that the operator's interest is waning, it ratchets up the person's workload to capture their attention and build their skills." Conformal prediction supports such adaptive automation using sensitivity analysis driven by reliability indices, randomness, and self-adaptation surrounding active learning.

Another dimension of interest for future research is that usability and security go hand in hand [83] . Most recently (in February 2015), and following recent attacks on Target and Sony, medical insurance giant Anthem was hit by a massive data breach affecting personal information for about 80,000,000 of its customers and employees in one of the largest attacks in corporate history with tens of millions of records stolen. The security breach exposed names, birthdays, and social security numbers among others. It appears that Anthem didn't encrypt the data, "the result of what a person familiar with the matter described as a difficult balancing act between protecting the information and making it useful" [84] . This balancing act reflects on what the National Academy of Engineering (NAE) has recently noted "if security systems are burdensome, people may avoid using them, preferring convenience and functionality to security." Usability and security involves first and foremost human factors and purposeful adaptation to ensure that "usable privacy and security researchers adhere to human activity-centered design to improve system security" and that "usable security research frequently benefits from studying user behavior in the presence of an adversary including deliberate deception" [83] . The self-protective shield, promoted in this paper and characteristic of autonomic computing, would go a long way to lessen the burden of security and increase the usability of the defenses deployed, and ultimately reach "the best security interface that would generally be no security interface." To achieve usability gains, researchers must go beyond adopting human-centered design principles and embrace user decision-making, moving from "command by direction, to command by plan, and ultimately to command by intention" [83] . Additional factors that bear on usability or alternatively utility come from differential privacy (see Sect. 15).

Adversarial learning is complex in nature with many strategies (e.g., overall plans) and tactics (e.g., maneuvers that achieve specific missions) in play. This aspect, related to cognitive biases arising from limits on optimization and/or characteristic of psychology and (behavioral) economics (e.g., systematic deviations from rationality) rather than formal game theory, concerns adversaries (e.g., user) habits and profiles. Examples of biases include anchoring (e.g., focusing on one trait) and attention bias (e.g., focus on preponderance of information), which are triggered by unbalanced populations, base rate fallacy (e.g., ignore base rate information), characteristic of intrusion detection (e.g., seeking for a needle in a haystack), confirmation bias (e.g., tendency to search for information that confirms prior beliefs), hyperbolic discounting (e.g., display stronger preference for payoffs sooner rather than later). First interpretations tend to be decisive including stubbornness in abandoning prior but still cherished beliefs.

Most recently Stahl and Feigenson [85] have shown that babies are better scientists than adults often are. The adults are usually afflicted by confirmation bias and ignore current information most likely to enhance their behavior and better their performance. Human factors and cyber security reach and scope, however, are tightly intertwined and should mimic the babies in their hunger for the unexpected.

Similar to Popper the babies seek for those facts that falsify their current theories and understanding about how the world surrounding them works. The unexpected after all enhances both adaptation and exploration geared for choosing what to learn about and what to ignore. Towards such ends the authors show that 11-month-old infants used violations of prior expectations as special opportunities for further exploration and hypothesis testing for learning purposes. "Much as scientists faced with unexpected patterns of data are propelled to think harder, run further experiments, or change their methods of inquiry, untutored preverbal minds are sensitive to conflict between the predicted and the observed, and use this conflict as a scaffold for new learning" [85] . Active learning using the NCM introduced earlier can seek and lock on the unexpected.

Defense and immunity from such cognitive biases further comes from using randomness and/or implementing strategic aims reminiscent of Sun Tzu's Art of War that advises on competition and conflict. In particular, the conformal prediction framework must be able to anticipate and repair, and to quote from Sun Tzu "deep knowledge is to be aware of disturbance before disturbance, to be aware of danger before danger, to be aware of destruction before destruction, to be aware of calamity before calamity"; and that "by deep knowledge of principle, one can change disturbance into order, change danger into safety, change destruction into survival, change calamity into fortune" [86] . Such lofty aims can be achieved by deploying a self-defensive and protective shield using sensitivity and stability analysis for exploration and exploitation (e.g., control, gating, and navigation), which predates events, determines weaknesses and anticipates vulnerabilities, and self-heals as much as it can before harm is caused.

This is similar to what vaccination does in administering antigenic material (e.g., non-self) to stimulate the IDS immune system to develop adaptive immunity to adversarial attacks (e.g., pathogens). The challenge is to heal, repair, and transform the battlefield before calamity strikes.

15. QUO VADIS

Adversarial learning using conformal prediction is a major direction on the road leading to better cyber security but not the end of the road. Worth to note that learning requires both better classification and detection for IDS purposes and better human-centered problem solving skills. Adversarial learning goes beyond cyber security and can serve intelligence analysis on intruders and their threats. This will entail linking between the dots in analogy to solving gumshoe stories that make authentication and detection hard. A majority of detective stories follow the "whodunit" format. The events of the crime and the subsequent events of the investigation are presented such that the reader is provided with enough clues from which the identity of the perpetrator of the crime and her intent may be deduced. The solution is usually not revealed until the final pages of the book. This is similar to expanding re-identification into multiple event re-identification (MERI) to account and detect sporadic and partial events, thread the clues found and trace them to multiple and different causative events and entities while accounting for intrinsic sources of vulnerabilities. An additional outcome that should be sought by adversarial learning is to preclude functional creep and to enable functional interoperability for similar methods across different infrastructure and platforms.

The lessons learned from the 1998 DARPA off-line intrusion detection evaluation still hold today as they did back then. One major challenge, which still waits for feasible but satisfactory solutions, is that further research should focus on developing techniques to find new attacks instead of extending rule-based approaches [54] (see Sect. 7 for ADAM). The conformal prediction framework, open set recognition using TCM-DR for KNN, and the synergy between natural immunity and intrusion detection, are the solutions advanced here to cope with new attacks. Such zero-day attacks can be detected even if training data for them is lacking using zero-shot learning [87] and self-taught learning [88] . Such an approach draws from cross-modal transfer learning, which leverages large corpora of known attacks and unsupervised learning, side information using domain knowledge and shared distributed semantics (see Sect. 12), and adaptive and smart mutations (see Sect. 7) geared for both better immunity and continuous and targeted testing.

The ultimate challenge is to have cyber security avail itself of a self-protective shield that can engage in precision intrusion detection. Similar to challenges and goals recently set for optimal delivery of precision medical care what cyber security is expected and has to do is to be context-aware and cure the particular service or user engagements from specific intrusions while taking into account the specific infrastructure and platform where the intrusion momentarily takes place rather than handling the open-ended generic "disease" of intrusion detection. It is here and now, it is local, and it is consonant with conformal prediction and the advice proffered by Vapnik [85] that everything is local in nature and one should not solve a problem more general than needed to be. An interesting line of future research concerning lack of information for attacks and their attribution would consider differential privacy, anonymity, and meta-data, with a constant "tension between minimizing privacy loss and maximizing utility" [89] . Loss of privacy concerns amongst others identity theft using spear phishing.

One can pursue important leads for future research by expanding the earlier discussion on immunity and intrusion detection (see Sect. 7) using social network analysis and herd immunity. Towards that end and using the obvious relationships between vaccination and overall network protection using the likes of antivirus protection and firewall policies, one can follow and benefit from the current discussion on how anti-vaccine views hurt herd immunity. In particular, when large segments of a population are immunized against measles, it reduces the risk of exposure in the community, including families who refuse vaccines. The concept is called herd immunity. But when too many healthy people forgo vaccinations, the whole herd becomes more vulnerable, not just those who skipped the shots. "Without vaccines measles, other infectious diseases can proliferate, and people who were previously protected may become imperiled" [90] . Future studies on quantitative and qualitative aspects of cyber security should therefore leverage links between social networks and epidemics using the importance of contact patterns for outcomes including but not limited to the "informatics of complex interacting systems scaling the microbiome to the entire globe" [91] [92] .

Epidemics and their spread depend first and foremost of the vaccination rate that confers protection to the herd (e.g., about 93% for measles). Further relevant to this discussion is to recall that immunity is never 100%, that "even people who have gotten the vaccine need the protection provided by the herd to minimize their odds of contracting the disease" (e.g., being afflicted by cyber-attacks), and that the economics of malware attacks require the equivalent of epidemics to justify investment and ensure that significant profits are made. Proliferation is such that "highly infectious diseases like measles ricochet through a community, leaping from person to person until the chain of transmission is interrupted" [90] . Furthermore, "it's not that no one will be infected, but the chain of infections will burn out before it spreads to a large population" and "social mixing fundamentally changes the epidemiological landscape and, consequently, that static network approximations of dynamic networks can be inadequate" [93] . Vaccines "help by breaking the chain of transmission and lowering a disease reproduction rate" [92] . To avoid spread and pandemics the reproduction rate has to stay below 1 and this determines the fraction of the population that needs to be inoculated.

Additional challenges that need to be addressed include better carving of space and time and not necessarily all reductionist in nature. Some things don't bear dissection [94] [95] . Proper layers of representation and execution including mutual dependencies and recurrent feedback are important. The ecosystems of interest for cyber security are intricately complicated with the possibility of indeterminacy always present despite the very ability to improve the odds. Resolution of perennial philosophical questions on forecast ability between description, explanation and prediction, nature vs. nurture, and "holistic conundrums," on one side, and correlation and causality, on the other side, come immediately to mind. Is the future predestined or emergent? It is really the case that to understand the whole all what one needs is to understand its parts or to conflate simpler with smaller when lacking proper layers of description and aggregation? Possible solutions include consensus (e.g., aggregation) and context-aware reasoning that makes problem solving circumscribed and consonant with basic statistical learning theory tenets as expressed in conformal prediction, in general, and transduction, in particular. Additional goals would include investigating integration issues ranging from fusing multiple information channels (e.g., appearance, behavior, location, and profiles) using conformal prediction, best ways and means to combine conformal prediction with deep learning using vector space representations, models that incorporate in a competitive fashion particular strategies and tactics and avoid human biases, and addressing W5+ in an integrated fashion. One notes in particular that "it is now widely recognized that traditional approaches to cyber defense [including boundary controllers, firewalls, and virus scanners] have been inadequate. Nevertheless, sophisticated adversaries using zero-day exploits are still able to get in and, in many cases, establish a persistent presence, so we need to study and engage the adversary on the defender's turf in order to influence any future moves. The key component in this new paradigm is cyber denial and deception (D & D) [96] . Denial prevents the adversary from capturing information, while deception provides misleading information. Together D & D lessen the amount of reliable information available to an adversary to pursue its malfeasance purposes, whatever they might be. The net result of D & D is increased uncertainty that requires more (precious time) deliberation to move on with attacks, which are less focused and allow the defense to have better and more opportunity to counter the perceived threats. The tradeoffs, which are dynamic in nature and affect D & D effectiveness, are about what to reveal and what to conceal, on one side, and facts or fiction for make believe information, on the other side. The threat-based active defense using D & D can leverage the multi-faceted virtual protective shield described throughout with adversarial learning and conformal prediction engaging both immunity and immunosuppression, on one side, and human factors, on the other side.

16. CONCLUSIONS

This paper promotes cyber security using adversarial learning and non-parametric conformal prediction. It advances reliable, robust, and resilient intrusion detection or alternatively consistency in performance and the ability to withstand and recover from adversarial, hostile, and malicious attacks and subterfuge to improve system resilience across networks and computing platforms. This is achieved using strong fundamentals driven by intertwined learning themes that combine statistical learning, semi-supervised learning, and transduction, in general, prediction validity and calibration and reliability indices on outcomes, non-conformity measures and open set recognition, change detection, and active learning. The methodology proposes links and leverages natural immunity and intrusion detection. Venues for future research including economics, epidemics and pandemics, denial and deception, interoperability, and zero-day attacks are motivated and addressed as well. The envisioned software environment would challenge both offense and defense while at the same time enhance defenses for continuous and better cyber security performance.

There is awareness at all times of the permanence of ambiguity, risk, and uncertainty. The infrastructure proposed displays many complementary traits built using conformal prediction to learn, on one side, and to hedge and punt for demarcation purposes, on the other side. The traits include training, querying, and re-training for annotation, detection, disruption, and protection, which are complementary to each other with helping defenses. This comes courtesy of conformal prediction (using non-conformity measures that quantify the resemblance of a data point or event to a particular class) that draws from validation, calibration, and efficiency (e.g., the frequency of prediction errors does not exceed some a priori chosen confidence level in the long run and the prediction outcomes sets are as small as possible), incremental transduction and sensitivity analysis that guarantee the confidence values derived match actual errors, anomaly detection using active learning for self from non-self demarcation, and self-adaptation using randomness.

The objectives here, to enhance and protect cyber security, are multi-pronged. The habitat for both defense and offense is that of an ecosystem where mutual adversarial learning takes place. The functional goals, similar to those espoused by autonomic computing, aim to deploy a self-management protective shield, which coordinates and parcels recurrent activities geared to detect, disrupt, and deny intrusive attacks and subterfuge. Diversity, scale, and utility, which come from using annotation, co-evolution, randomness, and semantics and stratification, raise attack costs to enable and facilitate better defenses. This gains expression in terms of layout and purposeful disposition of functional modules using meta-reasoning and meta-recognition that leverage aggregation, context, traffic, and trajectories, to carve space and time better and to undermine hostile and malicious behavior. In particular, purposeful coordination involves control and gating to navigate the maze of data and detection options, and to sort out and rank alternative hypotheses according to reliability indices, risk, and sensitivity analysis, which are intrinsic to active learning. Significance comes from advancing a science of cyber security built around exploration and exploitation that has learning, anticipation and imputation, control, self-adaptation and self-healing, and prevention work in tandem towards detecting the alien and malicious DNA and making it less harmful as much as possible.

The impact for cyber security is wide open and versatile. Beyond the obvious need to maintain quality of service, safeguard proprietary information and privacy, there is also much to gain from straightforward economic well-being. This comes from the simple observation that cyber-crime can be pervasive and relatively facile to undertake, that lack of violence makes cyber-crime less susceptible to further investigation and leads to underreporting due in part to lack of full awareness, on one side, apprehension not to have reputation compromised, on the other side, the economic harm can be huge when cyber security is not properly safeguarded. Additional applications bear on social and behavioral economics and social network analysis include cyber economics and mobility. Cyber security is multi-faceted as it is expected to protect financial, power, and water grids, and smart identity management [97] interests. It provides in particular immunity to exfiltration and identity theft, protection of intellectual property and e-commerce, and coming and emergent applications geared for mobile wearable devices and personal health surveillance, machine-to-machine (M2M) communication including smart transportation, and Internet of Things (IoT). Cyber security also contributes to big data as it promotes effective and efficient access and leverage of rich lodes of data that might lack proper annotation and safeguard them against disruptive and malicious attacks.

A recent cyber security outlook for the future reports on six potential cyber game changers and priorities for future research [98] . The game changers include new computing paradigms and new territories for network complexity for cyber environment changes, big data analytics and resilient self-adaptation for technology trends, and mixed-trust systems and active defenses for cyber technology breakthroughs. This paper involves many of the changers contemplated. This includes adversarial learning using conformal prediction and immunity for new computing paradigms, meta-reasoning and meta-recognition to support the emergence of a self-protective management shield for resilient self-adaptation, and human factors for mixed-trust systems and usability. Additional directions and factors for promising and rewarding future R & D are discussed throughout and in particular in the preceding Sect. 15 on Quo Vadis.

Last but not least any advances in cyber security are predicated on some astute remarks expressed recently about the computer security industry itself. Among them Amit Yoran from RSA makes users aware that "first, much commercial software is riddled with flows, making it tricky for any technology to make it secure after the fact" and "second, security companies are competitive, and pitch their own solutions as a cure-all. Executives are loath to suggest that customers would be more secure if they used other technologies as well [99] ". This calls for the deployment of secure and sustainable cyber ecosystems, in general, and similar to autonomic computing seeking for "computer architectures that are engineered from the foundation to promote hardware-enhanced security-for example, creating combined hardware-software architecture to support self-protecting data, secure enclaves for executing trusted software components, and new hypervisor models for more security in cloud environments. A more fundamental goal is to engineer secure hardware than can itself limit security breaches, such as the cache side-channel attacks that today's cache architectures allow" [100] .

REFERENCES

1. Olmedo, O., Zhang, J., Wechsler, H., Poland, A. and Borne, K. (2008) Automatic Detection and Tracking of Coronal Mass Ejections (CMEs) in Coronagraph Time Series. Solar Physics, 248, 485-499.
2. Miller, B., Kantchelian, A., Afroz, S., Bachwani, R., Dauber, E., Huang, L., Tschantz, M.C., Joseph, A.D. and Tygar J.D. (2014) Adversarial Active Learning. Proceeding of the 2014 Workshop on Artificial Intelligent and Security Workshop AI, Scottsdale, 3-7 November 2014, 3-14.
3. Thiel, C. (2008) Classification on Soft Labels Is Robust Against Label Noise. Proceeding of the 12th International Conference on Knowledge-Based Intelligent Information and Engineering Systems, Zagreb, 3-5 September 2008, 65-73.
4. Tygar, J.D. (2011) Adversarial Machine Learning. IEEE Internet Computing, 15, 4-6.
5. Nelson, B., Barreno, M., Chi, F.J., Joseph, A.D., Rubinstein, B.I.P., Saini, U., Sutton, C., Tygar, J.D. and Xia, K. (2008) Exploiting Machine Learning to Subvert Your Spam Filter. Proceeding of 1st Usenix Workshop on Large Scale Exploits and Emergent Threats, San Francisco, 15 April 2008, 1-9.
6. Bootkrajang, J. and Kaban, A. (2012) Label-Noise Robust Logistic Regression and Its Applications. Proceedings of the 2012 European Conference on Machine Learning and Knowledge Discovery in Database, Bristol, 24-28 September 2012, 143-158.
7. DeBarr, D., Sun, H. and Wechsler, H. (2013) Adversarial Spam Detection Using the Randomized Hough Transform-Support Vector Machine. Proceedings of the IEEE International Conference on Machine Learning and Applications (ICMLA), Miami, 4-7 December 2013, 299-304.

8. Basit, N. and Wechsler, H. (2011) Function Prediction for in Silico Protein Mutagenesis Using Transduction and Active Learning, Proceedings of the IEEE International Conference on Bioinformatics and Biomedicine, Atlanta, 12-15 November 2011, 939-940.
9. Sculley, D., Otey, M.E., Pohl, M., Spitznagel, B., Hainsworth, J. and Zhou, Y. (2011) Detecting Adversarial Advertisements in the Wild. Proceeding of the 17th ACM SKIGKDD International Conference on Knowledge Discovery and Data Mining, San Diego, 21-24 August 2011, 274-282.
10. Biggio, B., Fumera, G. and Roli, F. (2014) Security Evaluation of Pattern Classifiers under Attack. IEEE Transaction on Knowledge and Data Engineering, 26, 984-996.
11. Huang, L., Joseph, A.D., Nelson, B., Rubinstein, B. and Tygar, J.D. (2011) Adversarial Machine Learning. Proceedings of the 4th Workshop on Artificial Intelligence and Security and Artificial Intelligence, Chicago, 17-21 October 2011, 43-57.
12. Vorobeychik, Y. and Li, B. (2014) Optimal Randomized Classification in Adversarial Settings. International Conference on Autonomous Agents and Multi-Agents Systems (AAMAS), Paris, 5-9 May 2014, 485-492.
13. DeBarr, D. and Wechsler, H. (2012) Spam Detection using Random Boost. Pattern Recognition Letters, 33, 1237- 1244.
14. DeBarr, D. and Wechsler, H. (2009) Spam Detection Using Clustering, Random Forests, and Active Learning. Proceedings of the 6th Conference on E-Mail and Anti-Spam (CEAS), Mountain View, 16-17 July 2009, 16-17.
15. DeBarr, D. and Wechsler, H. (2010) Using Social Network Analysis for Spam Detection. Proceedings of the 3rd Conference on Social Computing, Behavioral Modeling and Prediction (SBP), Bethesda, 30-31 March 2010, 62-69.
16. DeBarr, D., Ramanathan, V. and Wechsler, H. (2013) Phishing Detection Using Traffic Behavior, Spectral Clustering, and Random Forests. Proceedings of the IEEE International Conference on Intelligence and Security Informatics (ISI), Seattle, 4-7 June 2013, 67-72.
17. DeBarr, D. and Wechsler, H. (2013) Fraud Detection Using Reputation Features, SVMs, and Random Forests. Proceedings of the 9th International Conference on Data Mining, Las Vegas, 22-25 July 2013, 238-244.
18. Cherkassky, V. and Mulier, F. (2007) Learning from Data. 2nd Edition, Wiley, Hoboken.
19. Vapnik, V. (1998) Statistical Learning Theory. Springer, Berlin.
20. Chapelle, O., Scholkopf, B. and Zien, A. (Eds.) (2006) Semi-Supervised Learning. MIT Press, Cambridge.
21. Wechsler, H. and Li, F. (2014) Biometrics and Face Recognition. In: Balasubramanian, V., Ho, S.S. and Vovk, V., Eds., Conformal Predictions for Reliable Machine Learning: Theory, Adaptations, and Applications, Elsevier, Amsterdam, 189-215.
22. Ho, S.S., and Wechsler, H. (2010) A Martingale Framework for Detecting Changes in The Data Generating Model in Data Streams. IEEE Transaction on Pattern Analysis and Machine Intelligence, 32, 2113-2127.
23. Ho, S.S., and Wechsler, H. (2014) On Line Change Detection Using Exchangeability. In: Balasubramanian, V., Ho, S.S. and Vovk, V., Eds., Conformal Predictions for Reliable Machine Learning: Theory, Adaptations, and Applications, Elsevier, Amsterdam, 99-114.
24. Proedrou, K., Nouretdinov, I., Vovk, V. and Gammerman, A. (2002) Transductive Confidence Machine for Pattern Recognition. Proceeding of the 13th European Conference on Machine Learning, Royal Holloway, 19-23 August 2002, 81-390.
25. Vapnik,V. (2000) The Nature of Statistical Learning Theory. 2nd Edition, Springer, New York.
26. Li, F. and Wechsler, H. (2005) Open Set Face Recognition Using Transduction. IEEE Transaction on Pattern Analysis and Machine Intelligence, 27, 1686-1698.
27. Vovk, V., Gammerman, A. and Shafer, G. (2005) Algorithmic Learning in a Random World. Springer, Berlin.
28. Wechsler, H. and Ho, S.S. (2011) Evidence-Based Management of Data Collection and Decision-Making Using Algorithmic Randomness and Active Learning. Journal of Intelligent Information Management, 3, 142-159.

29. Li, Y., Fang, B., Guo, L. and Chen, Y. (2007) Network Anomaly Detection based on TCM-KNN Algorithm. Proceeding of the 2nd ACM Symposium on Information, Computer and Communications Security, Singapore, 20-22 March 2007, 13-19.
30. Li, Y. and Guo, L. (2007) An Efficient Network Anomaly Detection Scheme Based on TCM-KNN Algorithm and Data Reduction Mechanism. Proceeding of the IEEE Workshop on Information Assurance, West Point, 20-22 June 2007, 221-227.
31. Ho, S.S. and Wechsler, H. (2008) Query by Transduction. IEEE Transaction on Pattern Analysis and Machine Intelligence, 30, 1557-1571.
32. Balasubramanian, V., Chakraborty, S., Ho, S.S., Wechsler, H. and Panchanathan, S. (2014) Active Learning. In: Balasubramanian, V., Ho, S.S. and Vovk, V., Eds., Conformal Predictions for Reliable Machine Learning: Theory, Adaptations, and Applications, Elsevier, Amsterdam, 49-70.
33. Li, Y., Guo, L., Fang, B.X., Tian, Z.H. and Zhang, Y.Z. (2008) Detecting DoS Attacks Against Web Server via Lightweight TCM-KNN Algorithm. Proceeding of the ACM SIGCOMM 2008 Conference on Data Communication, Seattle, 17-22 August 2008, 497-498.
34. Liu, A., Chen, j.X. and Wechsler, H. (2013) Real-Time Covert Timing Channels Detection in a Networked Virtual Environment. Proceeding of the 9th Annual International Federation for Information Processing, Orlando, 28-30 January 2013, 273-288.
35. Li, Y. and Guo, L. (2007) An Active Learning based TCM-KNN Algorithm for Supervised Network Intrusion Detection. Computers and Security, 26, 459-467.
36. Basseville, M. and Nikiforov, I.V. (1993) Detection of Abrupt Changes: Theory and Application, 104. Prentice Hall, Englewood Cliffs.
37. Ramanathan, V. and Wechsler, H. (2013) Phishing Detection and Impersonated Entity Discovery Using Conditional Random Field and Latent Dirichlet Allocation. Computer and Security, 34, 123-139.
38. Ramanathan, V. and Wechsler, H. (2012) PhishGILLNET—Phishing Detection Methodology Using Probabilistic Latent Semantic Analysis, AdaBoost, and Co-Training. EURASIP Journal of Information Security, 2012, 1.
39. Freund, Y. and Shapire, R.E. (1996) Experiments with a New Boosting Algorithm. Proceeding of 13th International Conference on Machine Learning (ICML), Bari, 3-6 July 1996, 148-156.
40. Blum, A. and Mitchell, T. (1998) Combining Labeled and Unlabeled Data with Co-Training. Proceedings of the Workshop on Computational Learning Theory, Morgan Kaufmann, 24-26 July 1998, 92-100.
41. Ramanathan, V. and Wechsler, H. (2012) Phishing Website Detection using Latent Dirichlet Allocation and AdaBoost. Proceedings of the IEEE International Conference on Intelligence and Security Informatics, Washington, 11-14 June 2012, 102-107.
42. Blei, D.M. and Frazier, P. (2010) Distance Dependent Chinese Restaurant Process. Proceedings of the 27th International Conference on Machine Learning (ICML), Haifa, 21-24 June 2010, 87-94.
43. Sun, H., Chen, J.X. and Wechsler, H. (2014) A New Segmentation Method for Broadcast Sports Video. Proceedings of the 8th International Conference on Frontier of Computer Science and Technology (FCST), Chengdu, 19-21 December 2014, 1789-1793.
44. Balcan, M.F., Beygelzimer, A. and Langford, J. (2009) Agnostic Active Learning. Journal of Computer and System Sciences, 75, 78-89.
45. Balcan, M.F., Beygelzimer, A. and Langford, J. (2006) Agnostic Active Learning. Proceedings of the International Conference on Machine Learning (ICML), Pittsburgh, 25-29 June 2006, 65-72.
46. Kim, J., Bentley, P., Aiklelin, U., Greesmith, J., Tedesco, G. and Twycross, J. (2007) Immune System Approaches to Intrusion Detection—A Review. Natural Computing, 6, 413-466.
47. Boudec, J.Y. and Sarafijanovic, S. (2004) An Artificial Immune System Approach to Misbehavior Detection on Mobile Ad-Hoc Networks, Proceeding of Biologically Inspired Approaches to Advanced Information Technology, Lausanne, 29-30 January 2004, 96-111.

48. Tang, W., Yang, X.M., Xie, X., Peng, L.M., Youn, C.H. and Cao, Y. (2010) Avidity-Model based Clonal Selection Algorithm for Network Intrusion Detection. Proceedings of the 18th International Workshop on Quality of Service (IWQoS), Beijing, 16-18 June 2010, 1-5.
49. Doddington, G.R., Liggett, W., Martin, A., Przybocki, M. and Reynolds, D. (1998) Sheep, Goats, Lambs and Wolves: A Statistical Analysis of Speaker Performance. Proceedings of 5th International Conference Spoken Language Pro- cessing, Sydney, 30 November-4 December 1998, 1351-1354.
50. Yager, N. and Dunstone, T. (2010) The Biometric Menagerie. IEEE Transaction on Pattern Analysis and Machine Intelligence, 32, 220-230.
51. Song, Y., Locasto, M.E., Stavrou, A., Keromytis, A.D. and Stolfo, S.J. (2010) On the Infeasibility of Modeling Polymorphic Shell Code. Machine Learning Journal, 81, 179-205.
52. Laskov, P. and Lippmann, R. (2010) Machine Learning in Adversarial Environments. Machine Learning Journal, 81, 115-119.
53. Stein, T., Chen, E. and Mangla, K. (2011) Facebook Immune System. Proceeding of the 4th Workshop on Social Network Systems (SNS), Salzburg, 10-13 April 2011, 1-8.
54. Lippmann, R. et al. (2000) Evaluating Intrusion Detection Systems: The 1998 DARPA Off-Line Intrusion Detection Evaluation. Proceedings of the DARPA Information Survivability Conference and Exposition (DISCEX), Los Alamitos, 25-27 January 2000, 12-26.
55. Barbara, D., Couto, J., Jajodia, S., Poypack, L. and Wu, N. (2001) ADAM: Detection Intrusions by Data Mining. Proceedings of the IEEE Workshop on Information Assurance and Security, West Point, 5-6 June 2001, 11-16.
56. Nappi, M. and Wechsler, H. (2012) Robust Re-Identification Using Randomness and Statistical Learning: Quo Vadis. Pattern Recognition Letters, 33, 1820-1827.
57. Berlin, I. (1953) The Hedgehog and the Fox. Weidenfeld & Nicolson, London.
58. Ganek, A. and Corbi, T. (2003) The Dawning of The Autonomic Computing Era. IBM Systems Journal, 42, 5-18.
59. Fonash, P. and Schneck, P. (2015) Cybersecurity: From Months to Milliseconds. Computer, 48, 42-49.
60. Scheirer, W.J., Rocha, A., Parris, J. and Boult, T.E. (2012) Learning for Meta-Recognition. IEEE Transactions on Information Forensics and Security, 7, 1214-1224.
61. Wechsler, H. (2007) Reliable Face Recognition Methods. Springer, New York.
62. Laxhammar, R. and Falkman, G. (2014) On-Line Learning and Sequential Anomaly Detection in Trajectories. IEEE Transaction on Pattern Analysis and Machine Intelligence, 36, 1158-1173.
63. Keogh, E., Lin, J. and Fu, A. (2005) HOT SAX: Efficiently Finding the Most Unusual Time Series Subsequence. Proceeding of the 5th IEEE International Conference on Data Mining (ICDM), Houston, 27-30 November 2005, 226-233.
64. Nischenko, I. and Jordaan, E.M. (2006) Confidence of SVM Predictions Using a Strangeness Measure. Proceedings of the International Joint Conference on Neural Networks (IJCNN), Vancouver, 16-21 July 2006, 1239-1246.
65. Camerra, A., Palpanas, T., Shieh, J., and Keogh, E. (2010) iSAX 2.0: Indexing and Mining One Billion Time Series, Proceeding of the 10th IEEE International Conference on Data Mining (ICDM), Sydney, 13-17 December 2010, 58-67.
66. Leskovec, J., Rajaraman, A. and Ullman, J.D. (2015) Mining of Massive Data Sets. 2nd Edition, Cambridge University Press, Cambridge.
67. Rockwell, M. (2015) IARPA Eyes Insider-Threat Tech. http://fcw.com/articles/ 2015/ 03/30/iarpa-insider-tech.aspx
68. El Masri, A., Likarish, P., Wechsler, H. and Kang, B.B. (2014) Identifying Users with Application-Specific Command Streams. Proceedings of the 12th International Conference on Privacy, Security and Trust (PST 2014), Toronto, 23-24 July 2014, 232-238.
69. El Masri, A., Likarish, P., Wechsler, H. and Kang, B.B. (2015) Active Authentication Using Scrolling Behaviors. Proceedings of the 6th IEEE International Conference on Information and Communication Systems (ICICS 2015), Amman, 7-9 April 2015, 257-262.

70. Socher, R., Ganjoo, M., Sridhar, H., Bastani, O., Manning, C.D. and Ng, A.Y. (2013) Zero-Shot Learning through Cross-Modal Transfer. Proceedings of the Advances in Neural Information Processing Systems (NIPS), 26, Lake Tahoe, 5-10 December 2013, 935-943.
71. SchÖlkopf, B., Williamson, R.C., Smola, A.J., Shawe-Taylor, J. and Platt, J.C. (2000) Support Vector Machine for Novelty Detection. MIT Press, Cambridge, 582-588.
72. Tax, D.M.J. and W Duin, R.P. (2004) Support Vector Data Description. Machine Learning, 54, 45-66.
73. McDaniel, P., Jaeger, T., La Porta, T.F., et al. (2014) Security and Science of Agility. Proceedings of the 1st ACM Workshop on Moving Target Defense, Scottsdale, 3-7 November 2014, 13-19.
74. Plerou, V., Gopikrishnan, P., Rosenow, B., Amaral, L., Guhr, T. and Stanley, H.E. (2002) A Random Matrix Theory Approach to Quantifying Collective Behavior of Stock Price Fluctuations. Empirical Science of Financial Fluctuations, 88, 35-40.
75. Rosenow, B. (2005) DPG-School on Dynamics of Socio-Economic Systems. Bad Honnef, Germany.
76. Kritchman, S. and Nadler, B. (2009) Non-Parametric Detection of the Number of Signal: Hypothesis Testing and Random Matrix Theory. IEEE Transactions on Signal Processing, 57, 3930-3941.
77. Baroni, M., Dinu, G. and Kruszewski, G. (2014) Don't Count, Predict! A Systematic Comparison of Context-Counting vs. Context-Predicting Semantic Vectors. Proceeding of the 25nd Annual Meeting of the Association for Computational Linguistics, Baltimore, 23-25 June 2014, 238-247.
78. Mikolov, T., Chen, K., Conrado, G. and Dean, J. (2013) Efficient Estimation of Word Representations in Vector Space. Proceedings of the Workshop at ICLR, Scottsdale, 2-4 May 2013, 1-12.
79. Pennington, J., Socher, R. and Manning, C.D. (2014) GloVe: Global Vectors for Word Representation. Conference on Empirical Methods in Natural Language Processing (EMNLP 2014), Doha, 26-28 October 2014, 1532-1543.
80. Kraemer, H.C. (1992) Evaluating Medical Tests: Objectives and Quantitative Guidelines. Sage Public-ation, Thousand Oaks.
81. Axelsson, S. (1999) The Base-Rate Fallacy and Its Implications for The Difficulty of Intrusion Detection. Proceedings of the 6th ACM Conference on Computer and Communications Security, Sing-apore, 1-4 November 1999, 1-7.
82. Carr, N. (2014) http://online.wsj.com/articles/automation-makes-us-dumb-1416589342
83. Cranor, L.F. and Buchler, N. (2015) Better Together: Usability and Security Go Hand in Hand. IEEE Security and Privacy, 12, 89-93.
84. Yadron, D. and Beck, M. (2015) Investigators Eye China in Anthem Hack. http://www.wsj.com/articles/investigators-eye-china-in-anthem-hack-1423167560?mod=WSJ_hp_LEFTWhatsNewsCollection
85. Stahl, A.E. and Feigenson, L. (2015) Observing the Unexpected Enhances Infants' Learning and Exploration. Science, 348, 91-94.
86. Sun, T. (1988) The Art of War. Thomas, C. (Translator), Shambhala Publications, Boston & London.
87. Rohrbach, M., Stark, M. and Schiele, B. (2011) Evaluating Knowledge Transfer and Zero-Shot Learning in A Large Scale Setting. Proceedings of the Computer Vision and Pattern Recognition (CVPR), Colorado Springs, 20-25 June 2011, 1641-1648.
88. Raina, R., Battle, A., Lee, H., Packer, B. and Ng, A.Y. (2007) Self-Taught Learning: Transfer Learning from Unlabeled Data. Proceedings of the 24th International Conference on Machine Learning, Corvalis, 20-24 June 2007, 759-766.
89. Dwork, C. (2009) The Differential Privacy Frontier. Proceedings of the 6th Theory of Cryptography Conference (TCC), San Francisco, 15-17 March 2009, 496-502.
90. McGinty, J.C. (2015) How Anti-vaccine Views Hurt Herd Immunity. Wall Street Journal.http://en.wikipedia.org/wiki/Self-information
91. Eubanks, S. (2003) Social Networks and Epidemics. http://silver.ima.umn. edu/ talks/workshops/11-3-6.2003/eubank/eubank.html

92. Eubank, S., Kumar, V.S., Marathe, M., Srinivasan, A. and Wang, N. (2006) Structure of Social Contact Networks and Their Impact on Epidemics. AMS-DIMACS Special Volume on Epidemiology, 70, 181-213.
93. Volz, E. and Meyers, L.A. (2009) Epidemic Thresholds in Dynamic Contact Networks. Journal of The Royal Society Interface, 6, 233-241.
94. Lewontin, R. (2000) The Triple Helix. Harvard University Press, Cambridge.
95. Rothman, S. (2002) Lessons from the Living Cell: The Limits of Reductionism. McGraw-Hill, New York.
96. Heckman, K.E., Stech, F.J., Schmocker, B.S. and Thomas, R.K. (2015) Denial and Deception in Cyber Defense. Computer, 48, 36-44.
97. Wechsler, H. (2012) Biometrics, Forensics, Security, and Privacy using Smart Identity Management and Interoperability: Validation and Vulnerabilities of Various Techniques. Review of Policy Research, 29, 63-89.
98. Kott, A., Swami, A. and McDaniel, P. (2014) Security Outlook: Six Cyber Game Changers for the Next 15 Years. Computer, 47, 104-106.
99. Yoran, A. (2015) Computer-Security Industry Critiques Itself Following High-Profile Breaches. http://www.wsj.com/articles/computer-security-industry-critiques-itself-following-high-profilebreach-es-1429573277
100. Lee, R.B. (2015) Rethinking Computers for Cyber Security. Computer, 48, 16-25.

CHAPTER 2

Information and Inference

Paul Walton

Capgemini UK, Forge End, Woking, Surrey GU21 6DB, UK

ABSTRACT

Inference is expressed using information and is therefore subject to the limitations of information. The conventions that determine the reliability of inference have developed in information ecosystems under the influence of a range of selection pressures. These conventions embed limitations in information measures like quality, pace and friction caused by selection trade-offs. Some selection pressures improve the reliability of inference; others diminish it by reinforcing the limitations of the conventions. This paper shows how to apply these ideas to inference in order to analyse the limitations; the analysis is applied to various theories of inference including examples from the philosophies of science and mathematics as well as machine learning. The analysis highlights the limitations of these theories and how different, seemingly competing, ideas about inference can relate to each other.

Keywords: information; philosophy of science; inference; induction; information quality; information friction; machine learning

1. INTRODUCTION

Inference pervades society. Examples include legal trials, science, computer modelling and those inferences that routinely form the basis of individual or organisational decisions. Increasingly, new forms of inference, based on business analytics and machine learning are becoming embedded in digital services [1]. However, inference uses information and is therefore subject to the difficulties inherent in information. This paper examines inference in this context building on the techniques developed in [2,3,4], summarised in Section 2 and showing how they apply to inference.

Section 3 explores the relationship between information and inference and, in particular, the impact of information ecosystems (just "ecosystem" where the context is clear) that have developed under the influence of a range of selection processes. In each ecosystem, conventions have developed that define the ways in which information is abstracted, processed and exchanged by the various actors in the ecosystem, which we call Interacting Entities (IEs). In different ecosystems, people, animals, organisations, parts of organisations, living cells [5,6] and computer systems are all IEs. The conventions incorporate the trade-offs made to information measures like pace and friction and, in particular, the impact on information quality [1,3]. Inside the envelope of environmental circumstances in which selection pressures apply, IEs need to be able to rely on inference to achieve favourable enough outcomes; this is how the term "reliable" is used in this paper. However, the conventions that drive these inferences may not provide sufficiently reliable inferences for other purposes or under different selection pressures [7].

These trade-offs and the constraints of individual circumstances (shortages of time or resources, for example) affect information in two ways. Individual interactions may not achieve the quality standards of the ecosystem embedded in ecosystem conventions. Secondly, ecosystem conventions may impose limitations on the effectiveness of inference. Inference uses a number of different mechanisms like induction, deduction and probability and the constraints that apply to information may be different in each case. Section 4 examines the reliability of inference.

In addition to selection trade-offs, there are pragmatic issues with inference—chaotic effects [8] and the impossibility of completely accurate measurement mean that it may not be possible to discriminate different environment states reliably. At a deeper level, reliable models of complicated systems do not exist (think of economics); and even for the simplest system models may not exist (think of the three-body problem). In [7], the authors express this in the following way:

"What makes relevant inferences possible [...] is the existence in the world of dependable regularities. Some, like the laws of physics, are quite general. Others, like the bell-food regularity in Pavlov's lab, are quite transient and local. [...] No regularities, no inference. No inference, no action."

The corollary of this is that, generally, an approach to inference is reliable only to the extent that selection pressures have challenged it thoroughly. Moreover, it is reliable enough only within the envelope in which the selection pressures have applied.

In Section 5, we use the ideas of Section 3 and Section 4 to analyse some examples in the philosophy of science, mathematics and machine learning. By considering how the types of inference are subject to selection processes and how closely they match the generic inference pattern we can identify their limitations. We can also show how different, seemingly competing, ideas about inference in the philosophy of science relate to each other.

2. THE MODEL FOR INFORMATION

This section sets out the approach to information contained in [1,2,3,4]. In this approach, information corresponds to a set of physical properties that conform to conventions that evolve in information ecosystems. Consider the elements of this statement in turn.

Information processing entities interact with their environment and so we call them Interacting Entities (IEs). Through interaction, IEs gain access to resources like money, food, drink or votes for themselves or related IEs, and develop new capabilities including channels to other IEs and sources of information (see Figure 1).

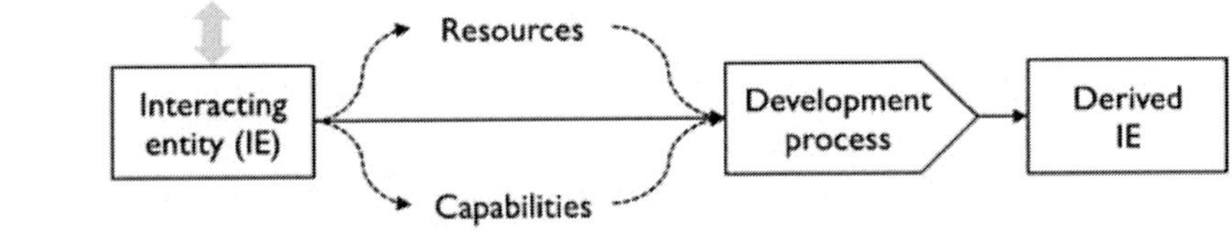

Figure 1. Selection processes.

These ideas apply very broadly. In [5,6], the authors discuss information in relation to living cells and say that "living existence is informational" and that "the signaling system provides the cell with a generic ability to 'grab' or 'abduct' information from the environment". With this starting point they discuss meaning, value and adaptability in the context of information.

Through a range of processes and feedback mechanisms, derived IEs (e.g., children, new product versions, changed organisations) are created from IEs. The health of the IE—its ability to continue to interact and achieve favourable outcomes—and the nature of any derived IE depend on the resources and channels the IE has access to and the outcomes it achieves. The nature of interactions and the outcomes available create selection pressures that affect the characteristics of derived IEs. Examples of selection processes include the market, natural selection, elections, personal choice and sexual selection but for any IE different combinations of selection process may apply.

As selection pressures change, there is an incentive to combine the conventions of different ecosystems where this will achieve more favourable outcomes. In [5,6], the authors discuss knowledge recombination and its relationship with "separate, specialized disciplines", relating to information ecosystems, and the "disciplinary reliance on accepted paradigms", relating to ecosystem conventions. They relate the dynamics of science to the evolutionary nature of technological change, quoting [9]:

"Technologies therefore share common ancestries and combine, morph, and combine again to create further technologies. Technology evolves much as a coral reef builds itself from activities of small organisms—it creates itself from itself."

The ability of an IE to achieve favourable outcomes from an environment state requires information processing—information enables connections to be made between the environment state, potential outcomes and the actions to help achieve them. So, we can talk of descriptive, predictive and prescriptive information, respectively.

Selection processes lead to the formation of information ecosystems. Note that the use of the term "ecosystem" here is consistent with [1,2,3,4] and is based on an evolutionary perspective like that of ecology in the natural world but differs from that used in [10]. Examples include English speakers, computer systems that exchange specific types of banking information, Mathematicians and many others. Each ecosystem has its own conventions for exchanging and processing information. Within different ecosystems, modelling tools such as languages, Mathematics and computer protocols have evolved to structure information within the ecosystem. The conventions shape how potentially arbitrary physical properties are interpreted. The existence of ecosystem conventions confirms that information is relative (see, for example, [11]—"the information in a message is a function of the recipient as well as the message" or [12]—"information is not an absolute but depends on the context in which it is being used"). An IE outside the ecosystem may not be able to interpret the information—

think of a classical languages scholar trying to understand quantum mechanics.

Call a slice a contiguous subset of space–time. A slice can correspond to an entity at a point in time (or more properly within a very short interval of time), a fixed piece of space over a fixed period of time or, much more generally, an event that moves through space and time. This definition allows great flexibility in discussing information. For example, slices are sufficiently general to support a common discussion of nouns and verbs, the past and the future.

Information corresponding to ecosystem conventions we call content with respect to the ecosystem. Content is structured in terms of chunks and assertions. A chunk specifies a constraint on sets of slices (e.g., "John", "lives in Rome", "four-colouring"). An assertion hypothesises a relationship between constraints (e.g., "John lives in Rome") that may or may not correspond to the actual relationship. Pieces of information are connected in an associative model (for example, Quine's "field of force whose boundary conditions are experience" [13], the World Wide Web, or Kahneman's "associative memory" [14] for people) with the nature of the connections determined by ecosystem conventions and constraints.

In [10], the author defines epistemological information for a human subject in terms of its ontological information: "the state in which the thing is and the way by which the state varies from others". In this paper, "state" corresponds to properties of slices where, in any ecosystem, a property is measured using an ecosystem process. Also, an ecosystem may include non-human actors. Assertions are the mechanism for relating the properties of different slices and how they vary from each other. The relationship with other definitions of information is discussed in [2] but, as discussed above, the approach in this paper and [2] is based on the idea that information is relative and that it is the ecosystem conventions that determine how content is processed and linked to actions and outcomes.

The effect of selection pressures over time is to improve the ability of IEs and ecosystems to process information in a number of different ways. The quality of information may improve, in the sense that it is better able to support the achievement of favourable outcomes; it may be produced with lower friction [15] or it may be produced faster [5]. These three measures, pace, friction and quality, are limited by ecosystem conventions.

Selection pressures ensure that information is generally reliable enough for the purposes of the ecosystem and within the envelope in which the selection pressures apply. However, quality issues and ecosystem limitations mean that outside the envelope we should not expect ecosystem conventions to be reliable. This is particularly important in an era of rapid change, such as the current digital revolution, in which ecosystem conventions cannot keep pace with the change.

3. INFORMATION AND INFERENCE

IEs make inferences to guide their actions and improve their chances of favourable outcomes. Inferences are based on information received as well as that stored in IE or ecosystem memory. Depending on ecosystem conventions, inference can use a variety of mechanisms including, for example, association, correlation, induction, deduction, machine learning, probability and the scientific method. This section analyses the relationship between information and inference using the model described in Section 2.

3.1. Selection and Inference

The relationship between information and selection processes is examined in [1,2]. The ability of an IE to achieve favourable outcomes depends on how well it can respond to interactions with the environment. The question that IEs address, often implicitly, is: what is the action to take, if any, that has the best chance of a favourable outcome? Better quality information and relevant connections between different pieces and types of information improve the chances of favourable outcomes. So, it is clear that there is a selection advantage in understanding what can be inferred from descriptive information.

However, inference is subject to huge combinatorial problems and rigorous inference incurs very high friction (think, for example, of the cost of science). So we would expect that selection pressures would drive trade-offs between the measures and, indeed, this is what happens. For example, in [7], the authors make the case that many specialised inference mechanisms have evolved in people; they say: "inference, and cognition more generally, are achieved by a coalition of relatively autonomous modules that have evolved [...] to solve problems and exploit opportunities."

In a similar way, organisations implement computer systems that automate many different routine activities in different ways but richer, more complex information processing requires people. In the field of machine learning, there are many different approaches [16] and one of the key tasks is to understand where to hand off decisions to a human being [17].

Table 1. Challenge.

Ecosystem	Inference	Challenge
English criminal law (prosecution)	The defendant is guilty	The defence (plus, potentially, the appeals process)
Science	A prediction made by a hypothesis is true	Experiments to refute or confirm the prediction
Mathematics	A theorem is proved	Peer review
Computer systems	The system will perform as required	Tests that the system meets its requirements

Selection processes select for conventions that embed these trade-offs in ecosystem processing and communication including, as described in [7,14], into the fundamental design of the IE.

3.2. Reliability

For an IE, an inference is reliable if it helps achieve a favourable-enough outcome—the IE can rely on the inference under the ecosystem selection pressures.

So, how do ecosystems improve the reliability of inference? An element that many ecosystems have in common is that of challenge. Table 1 shows some examples.

The objective of each challenge is to identify weaknesses in the inference either in terms of its output (e.g., refutation in scientific experiments), the input assertions it is based on (e.g., the evidence in a trial) or the steps of the inference (e.g., peer review of Mathematics).

The generic mechanism is similar in each case. A related ecosystem has selection processes in which favourable outcomes correspond to successful challenges. The degree to which the challenge is rigorous depends on the selection pressures that apply to it and, in some cases, the degree to which a different IE from the one making the inference conducts it.

However, selection pressures can also diminish quality. "Conflict of interest" is a term used widely to capture the difficulties of such selection pressures. In [18], the author gives examples of the impact on science.

3.3. Inference Patterns

Different types of inference have a structure in common. In each, there is a set of input assertions and from different combinations of assertions further assertions can be inferred. As Quine says in [13] the set of input assertions to consider may be much larger than those under immediate consideration and include IE or ecosystem memory. In making any inference, there may be intermediate steps, so an overall inference will have the form of an acyclic, connected, directed graph, as shown in Figure 2 (although in many cases inference may have just a single step).

There will also be a measure of quality associated with the derived assertions. When an IE makes an inference the result may add, delete, confirm or change those assertions and quality measures in the IE's memory (and potentially in the ecosystem memory) not directly associated with the inputs.

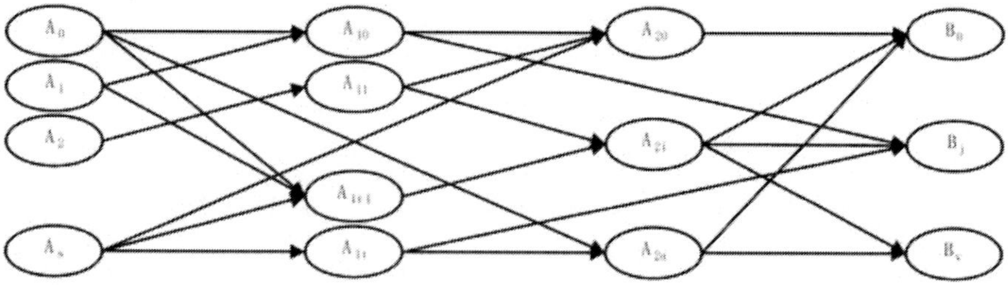

Figure 2. Inference instance.

What does each connection (based on a single inference) look like? Inference patterns and inference instances can be modelled using linnets [2,3]—a generalisation of graphs in which connectors (generalising edges) can connect other connectors as well as vertices. Figure 3 shows the general case.

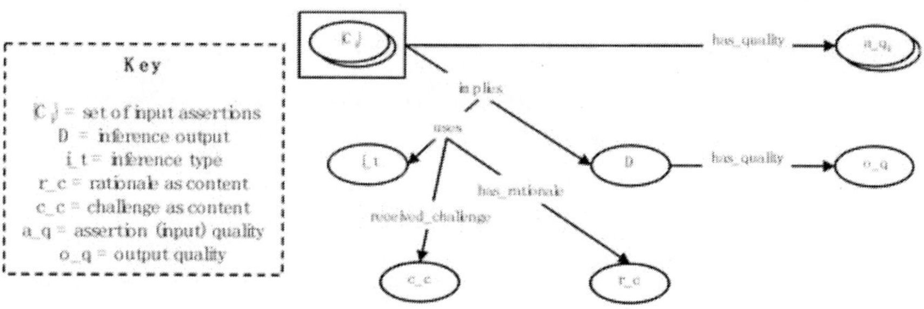

Figure 3. Single inference patterns.

As shown in Figure 3, apart from the initial assertions {A_i} any assertion (D) is derived from other assertions (for clarity, the figure shows one output—there may be more than one). Each input assertion has a measure of quality (that may or may not be captured). The inference uses some type of inference that determines how this step in the inference is accomplished.

The overall rationale may be expressed as content and may be challenged independently of the inference process itself or embedded as part of the inference process. The following sections expand on these ideas.

3.4. Content and Event Inference

In [13], Quine discussed the prevailing "fundamental cleavage" between analytic and synthetic truth and, in the context of science discussed the "field of force whose boundary conditions are experience". In [4], the "cleavage" is discussed in term of ecosystem conventions and their limitations. Some limitations are associated with the distinction between content interpretation and event interpretation that depends on the ecosystem-specific difference between content slices and event slices. Content slices are those that are interpreted as content within the ecosystem—all others are event slices. So, content slices include speech, animal calls, computer messages corresponding to particular protocols, documents and many others (each within its own ecosystem). IEs interpret information by connecting it with sets of other slices and so the question of which slices are considered in the search is highly pertinent. As it is expressed in [4]:

"does the search include content only [...] or also events [...]? Call the former 'content interpretation' and the latter 'event interpretation'. In both cases, the interpretation connects the [information] with sets of slices, but in the first case, the slices will be content slices only. For example:

- *a Logician or Mathematician may treat the content of [information] as a set of symbols with rules (content interpretation);*
- *a computer query may just search for the string "John Smith" (content interpretation);*
- *a person may also consider memories of John Smith as a person (event interpretation);*
- *more generally, people may relate content to events that they remember (for example, relating people to holidays, parties, or other social events)—this is a major focus of modern social media (event interpretation)."*

We can apply the same approach to inference. Inferences using inference models that apply to content only we can call content inference. Event inference includes the rest.

3.5. Types of Inference

This section considers different types of inference and how they relate to the inference pattern shown in Figure 2 and Figure 3. In each case, the inference can be expressed in terms of properties of slices where a property is measured by an ecosystem process. In terms of the discussion so far there are the following types:

- Content inference;
- Causation—in this case, the inference is based on one or more causation processes;
- Similarity—in this case, the inference is based on the similarity between sets of slices and the assumption that the similarity will extend.
- Before we look at these, some terminology:
- P $(\sigma, t) = V$ means that the set of properties P of slice σ at time t has value V (P and V are tuples);
- P $(\sigma) = V$ means that P $(\sigma, t) = V$ is true for all t under consideration;
- P $(\Sigma) = V$ means that P $(\sigma) = V$ for all $\sigma \in \Sigma$.

V can be any content allowed by the ecosystem (so it can be a single value, a range or a more complex function, depending on the ecosystem).

Each of these statements may be considered either to be defining a chunk or an assertion. For example, P $(\Sigma) = V$ defines a chunk where Σ is the set of all slices that meet this constraint. However, if Σ is defined elsewhere then it is an assertion.

Consider the following syllogism (E/C means that event or content interpretation are possible):

- (E/C) Socrates is a man.
- (E/C) All men are mortal.
- Therefore, Socrates is mortal.

As discussed below, the difference between event and content interpretation is important. If we use event interpretation, this captures simple set containment based on the slices defined by the sets {Socrates}, {men} and {mortal entities}. In this case there is a direct relationship between the assertions and the sets.

In the more general case we have in which (C) indicates that this is content interpretation:

(C) $P \rightarrow Q$.
(C) $Q \rightarrow R$.
Therefore, $P \rightarrow R$.

This syllogism is an example of a general case that applies to modelling tools like Logic and Mathematics as well as any reasoning that only considers rules about symbols and content rather than the event slices they refer to. We can describe the general case using properties of slices. Suppose that:

- C_i and D_j are assertions in an ecosystem for various i, j;
- Δ_i is the set of slices representing C_i in the ecosystem;
- Φ_j is the set of slices representing D_j in the ecosystem;
- R is ecosystem content that represents application of ecosystem rules to demonstrate that $\{C_i\}$ implies $\{D_j\}$;
- Ψ is the set of slices that represent the content R in the ecosystem;
- T is the ecosystem representation of truth;
- $E(\Omega) = T$ represents the application of an ecosystem process to measure the ecosystem truthfulness of Ω and the process returns T.

With these definitions we can express the general case as:

(E/C) $E(\Delta_i) = T$ for all i.
(C) $E(\Psi) = T$.
Therefore, $E(\Phi_j) = T$ for all j.

This case includes deduction in both formal and less formal senses, depending on the ecosystem in which it is applied.

Consider causation and the following example from [19]: A = "The rain caused the wheat to grow". There are many assumed assertions here. In particular, it is assumed that there is a slice σ in which wheat is growing over a period of time; also that t' is a time period that is sufficient to demonstrate growth. So, A means the following: "It rains on σ at time t implies that the wheat will have grown by time t + t'" (in the absence of other factors).

In any example of causation there is an implied slice (like σ), a starting time period, t, an elapsed time period, t', and a physical process that operates from t to t + t'. As in the example above, none of these may be immediately apparent in the content and the slice of interest at time t + t' may be different from σ (call it σ') and we may be interested in a different set of properties of it. So, any example of causation takes the following form:

(E) P (σ, t) = V. (e.g., the height of the wheat)
(E) There is a slice τ containing σ from time t that instantiates an ecosystem process pattern. (e.g., it rains)
Therefore, $\exists\ \sigma' \subseteq \tau$ and time t′ for which Q (σ', t + t′) = U. (e.g., the wheat has grown).

The property values are established through ecosystem measurement processes and values are provided in ecosystem content. The property values $\{(p_i, v_i)\}$ match the input assertions of the inference (but also see Section 4 for a discussion of the reliability of the match).

Inference associated with causation works forward (as in this case), but also backwards:

$$\text{(E) } P(\Sigma_1 \cup \Sigma_2) = V.$$
$$\text{(E) } Q(\Sigma_1) = U.$$
$$\text{Therefore, } Q(\Sigma_2\ \Sigma_1) = U.$$

In this way, inference based on causation can be indirect—it can work forwards and backwards, through slices σ, σ′, ..., σ′…′, and corresponding times to draw conclusions seemingly remote from the starting point.

In all of these cases, there is an underlying ecosystem pattern (perhaps based on science at one extreme or folklore at the other) that forms the basis for establishing inference. For example, causation is the basis for computer simulations for subjects as diverse as economics and climate change.

The degree to which causation-based inference makes sense in people-based ecosystems depends, in part, on the degree to which the type of causation accords with human psychology (like the example A above). Kahneman [14] points out the "innate biases" of System 1; these biases, and limitations in human senses, form the basis, for example, of magic tricks. In [20], the authors show how the tricks involved in magic are linked to neuroscience. A more extreme example is quantum mechanics and Einstein's quote [21]:

"Quantum mechanics is certainly imposing. But an inner voice tells me that it is not yet the real thing. The theory says a lot, but does not really bring us any closer to the secret of the "old one." I, at any rate, am convinced that He does not throw dice."

Correspondingly, causation that accords with human psychology is more likely to be adopted in human ecosystem conventions than causation, which does not. Or, expressed differently, human psychology can apply selection pressures.

Now for similarity. In this case, inference is based on the similarity between sets of slices with the assumption that the similarity will extend, assuming the "dependable regularities" discussed in [7]. We can express a pattern for similarity-based inference as follows (for sets of slices Σ_1, Σ_2):

(E) $P(\Sigma_1 \cup \Sigma_2) = V$.
(E) $Q(\Sigma_1) = U$.
(E) For all σ for which Q has been measured, if $Q(\sigma) \neq U$, then $P(\sigma) \neq V$. (i.e., there are no known counter-examples)
Therefore, $Q(\Sigma_2\ \Sigma_1) = U$.

We can compare this pattern with the taxonomy of inductive inference created by Carnap [22]. Table 2 relates them in terms of various specialisations of the "similarity" pattern.

Table 2. Carnap's taxonomy of inductive inference.

Variety of Inductive Inference	Specialisation of the "Similarity" Inference Pattern
Direct inference	$\Sigma_1 \subset \Sigma_2$, Q measures the frequency of $P = V$. $Q(\Sigma_2) = U$. Therefore, $Q(\Sigma_1) = U$.
Predictive inference	$\Sigma_1 \cap \Sigma_2 = \varnothing$. $P(\Sigma_1) = P(\Sigma_2) = V$. $Q(\Sigma_1) = U$. Therefore, $Q(\Sigma_2) = U$.
Singular predictive inference	As for predictive inference but, in addition, $\lvert \Sigma_2 \rvert = 1$.
Inference by analogy	$\lvert \Sigma_1 \rvert = \lvert \Sigma_2 \rvert = 1$. $\Sigma_1 \neq \Sigma_2$. The rest follows as per the general similarity case.
Inverse inference	$\Sigma_1 \subset \Sigma_2$. $Q(\Sigma_1) = U$. Therefore, $Q(\Sigma_2) = U$.
Universal inference	As for inverse inference but with the stronger version of similarity.

Each of the examples above is based on properties of slices including the existence of slices with particular properties. The input assertions correspond to relationships between properties of slices and so do output assertions. So, each form of inference has the following form:

$P_i(\Sigma_i) = V_i$, for sets of slices Σ_i.
Therefore $Q_j(\Phi_j) = U_j$, for sets of slices Φ_j.

The reliability of inference with respect to the physical world is based on the level of confidence that the model applies correctly to the given inputs (and that the known regularity described in [7] can be extended). This is the traditional problem of induction [23]. The uncertainties apply at two levels: those that result from the particular inference instance not meeting the ecosystem conventions and those that result from the ecosystem conventions themselves. In the former case there is a reference point; the ecosystem determines what quality means in terms of inference is like and we can use an approach to analyse the quality like the approach for descriptive information described in [2,4]. In the latter case we can use an equivalent of viewpoint analysis, as described in [4], to highlight the limitations of the ecosystem conventions.

4. INFERENCE RELIABILITY

In this section we use the ideas developed in Section 3 to analyse the reliability of inference using a similar approach to that followed in [4]. First, we need to understand more about the processes that IEs and ecosystems undertake to draw inferences, since these processes are the source of the limitations. Subsequent sections consider the quality of inference as measured against ecosystem standards and then the limitations of the ecosystem conventions themselves.

4.1. Inference Strategy

Ecosystem conventions define norms for making inferences. However, to make an inference an IE has to (implicitly or explicitly) decide how to instantiate the pattern in Figure 2 and Figure 3. For example, as the authors put it in [7], "humans are like other animals: instead of one general inferential ability, they use a wide variety of specialized mechanisms".

This shows the importance of inference strategy—the approach taken to inference. Inference strategy addresses the factors shown in Figure 4 based on the corresponding figure in [3]. Inference strategy is constrained at two levels: the ecosystem conventions (some of which are embedded in the basic capabilities of the IE) and the circumstances in which the IE finds itself (including, for example, time or resource constraints).

The context factor is driven by the set of inputs ($\{A_i\}$ in Figure 3) that are taken into account—how much should be included from memory as well as the specific assertions under consideration? At one extreme, only the assertions in question would be included; at the other, all of ecosystem memory as well.

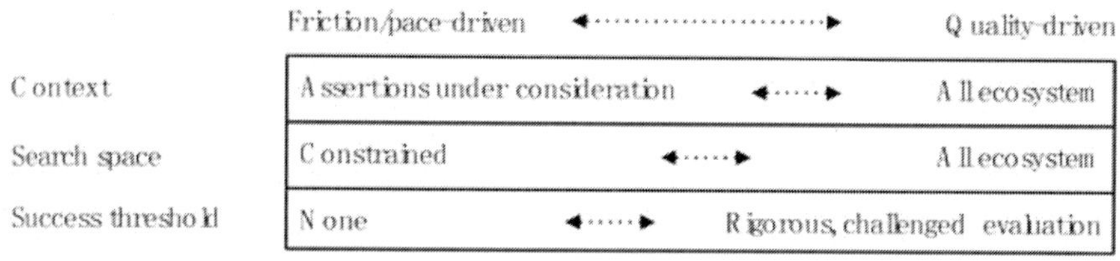

Figure 4. Inference strategy factors.

The search space factor determines the rigour with which the inference pattern is sought—how much IE and ecosystem memory is searched to find the inference pattern(s). The success threshold option considers how the search for a model completes: is there a rigorous evaluation incorporating multiple options?

4.2. Inference Quality

The quality of descriptive information is discussed in [2,3]. With respect to inference, the measures relate to the components shown in Figure 2 and Figure 3: the input assertions; the structure of the inference instance; the quality of the challenge; interim and output assertions. The input assertions can be distinguished from the inference in the same way as unconditional and conditional probability.

Consider the reference point provided by the ecosystem. This will be an ecosystem inference instance that conforms to an ecosystem inference pattern. An example of such a pattern is the UK government 5-case model for making business cases [24]—business cases make an inference that with a particular starting point specified actions undertaken by an organisation will produce specified outcomes. Other examples are the rules that apply to mathematical or logical deductions. The ecosystem inference pattern (and there may be more than one for an ecosystem) expresses the convention in the ecosystem for making inferences of the level of quality expected.

The structure of both the ecosystem inference instance and the inference instance in question can be expressed as linnets, extensions of graphs described in Section 3.3. This allows a comparison of:

1) the completeness of the assertion vertices (i.e., including input assertions, interim assertions and output assertions) and the absence of extraneous vertices (Figure 2);

2) the completeness of the connections and absence of extraneous connections (Figure 2);

3) the inference model used for each connection (Figure 3).

Items 1 and 2 correspond to calculations about sub-linnets and so represent a partial order under set inclusion. Item 3 may represent just a comparison or there may be a richer relationship between inference models in the ecosystem. Again, in general, this a partial order.

Input assertions are covered by the quality measures discussed in [2,3]. The various quality measures discussed are summarised in a single measure called trustworthiness. Trustworthiness combines the quality of the chunks forming an assertion and the plausibility of the assertion itself—the degree to which the actual relationship between the chunks is the same as that hypothesised by the assertion.

Does the same apply to interim and output assertions? The idea of plausibility transfers directly to inference so consider the quality of chunks. Interim and output assertions are created by the inference and so we are interested in the following question: to what extent does the inference instance match the ecosystem inference instance? The content of the two instances could be expressed very differently, so a direct analysis of the content may not be helpful. Instead, using ideas from [2,3], we can measure the differences between the interpretations of the content and, to do this in a standard way, we can use the ecosystem interpretation. Figure 5 shows the comparison.

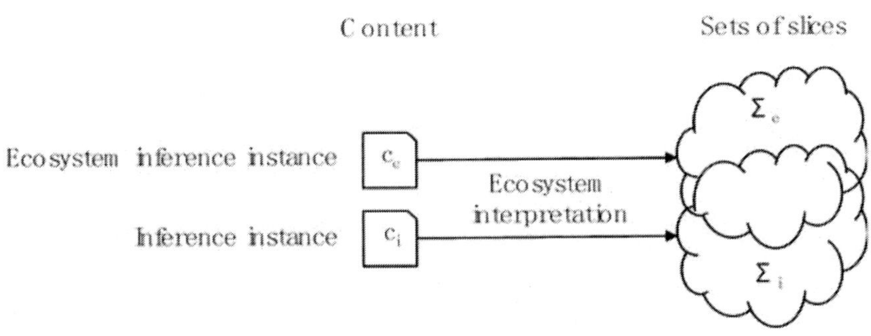

Figure 5. The quality of interim and output assertions.

Consider accuracy first. The accuracy of descriptive content addresses the relationship between ecosystem and IE interpretations of the same content. Here, we are concerned with the ecosystem interpretation of different pieces of content. However, the calculation, in both cases, is based on set inclusion (of sets of slices) and we can apply it to Σ_e and Σ_i (see Figure 5). In this sense, we can measure the accuracy of the inference instance.

The precision of descriptive content applies to interpretations of the same content at different times or in different assertions (or parts of the same assertion). We can use the same concept.

The other measures described in [2,3] apply either to the content itself or to the nature of the IE's interpretation so they do not apply to the question we are addressing here.

So, accuracy and precision can be used to measure the quality of chunks in interim and output assertions. As before, we cannot guarantee that these form a total order. So we cannot (in general) assign numbers to the overall quality of an inference; nor can we guarantee to assess the relative quality of different inferences. The best we can say is that we can assess the relative quality of some pairs of inferences.

To consider the quality of the challenge we can look at the characterisation of inference discussed in Section 3.5. Each form of inference has the following form:

1. $P_i (\Sigma_i) = V_i$, for sets of slices Σ_i.
2. Therefore $Q_j (\Phi_j) = U_j$, for sets of slices Φ_j.

The challenge takes the following form: do there exist the following sets of slices for which the input assertions are trustworthy but not the output assertions:

1. $\{\sigma_i : \sigma_i \in \Sigma_i\}$
2. $\{\phi_j : \phi_j \in \Phi_j\}$
3. $P_i (\sigma_i) = V_i$
4. $Q_j (\phi_j) \neq U_j$.

The purpose of the challenge is to identify what the software industry calls test cases [25]—a set of inputs and outputs designed to cover the range of possibilities thoroughly enough to provide confidence in the context of the ecosystem. The quality of the challenge determines how effectively the ecosystem model has been applied.

When there is high friction we should expect selection processes to find a trade-off. In practice, it is too difficult for IEs to assess quality so they often use proxies and the provenance of an inference (linked to authority, brand, reputation, conformance to a data model or other characteristics) provides a shortcut. In [26], the authors express this idea elegantly with respect to documents:

"For information has trouble, as we all do, testifying on its own behalf... Piling up information from the same source doesn't increase reliability. In general, people look beyond information to triangulate reliability."

4.3. Inference Limitations

Ecosystem conventions apply to each element in Figure 2 and Figure 3 and the conventions are derived from trade-offs between quality, friction and pace and so we should expect there to be limitations in the conventions. In this section, we examine the following limitations:

- Ecosystem inertia: this applies when an ecosystem inference pattern has not kept up to date with the changes in selection pressures;
- Selection conflict: this applies when there are selection pressures that diminish the quality of inference (and ecosystem inertia may be a source of selection conflict);
- Inference tangling: this applies when different ecosystem conventions apply to different parts of the inference instance; an inference that is assumed to have been derived using a set of ecosystem conventions has not been;
- Output collapse: this applies when only one inference output is produced rather than a range;
- Inference strategy: this applies when the inference strategy is limited in its scope as described in Section 4.1.

These are discussed in turn below.

Ecosystem inertia is described in [4] and, with respect to digital change, in [1]. Ecosystem conventions take time to develop and may not keep up with the rate of change in the environment. In this case, the conventions that apply may not suit the changed environment and reduce the IE's chances of favourable outcomes. Kuhn's discussion of paradigm shifts in science [27] is an example.

In organisations, "change resistance" is a well-known concept. For example [28]:

"One of the most baffling and recalcitrant of the problems which business executives face is employee resistance to change."

Or, in the social arena, some people find it difficult to keep up with changing digital technology, causing a "digital divide" [29] as they lose access to digital services.

One of the drivers for ecosystem inertia in human disciplines is the proliferation of knowledge. In [5,6], the authors discuss this and suggest that "all major research areas have to be surrounded by a 'cloud' of disciplines in order to convey the necessary [...] knowledge". With respect to information science itself, the authors suggest a move from "self-centred inward looking", driven by ecosystem conventions, towards "outward seeking".

Selection conflict occurs when there are selection pressures that reduce the quality of inference. Goldacre [18] provides examples in science. The term "conflict of interest" applies more widely and covers many such selection conflicts including, for example, applications in the law and politics. The extent to which an ecosystem has mechanisms to detect the presence and influence of selection conflict has a corresponding impact on reliability.

Inference tangling occurs when different ecosystem conventions apply to different parts of the inference. An example of inference tangling is mentioned in Section 3.5—there are examples of content inference (like the "Socrates" example mentioned) for which content or event inference is possible. Formal systems apply to symbols but whenever sentences are written in English (or another language) then event interpretations are also possible, potentially leading to difficulties (especially in the light of Kahneman's "innate biases" [14]). Elements of an inference can be based on the informality and, often, poor information quality of language.

Inference tangling also occurs when content inference is associated with event interpretation—when a rigorous formal argument is applied, without a correspondingly rigorous event interpretation, to events in the physical world. Examples of this, with respect to well-known paradoxes, are discussed in [4].

Inference is about making connections between descriptive information and outcomes and in the most general case includes a range of different outputs (like, for example, a probability distribution). Although a particular inference may link to different outcomes with different levels of quality, in many cases the IE needs to act, so it needs to focus on one outcome. As a result, many ecosystem conventions collapse the range of outputs down to a single one resulting in output collapse.

The inference strategy captures the parameters of an inference instance. There are always constraints on the scope of the inference strategy (the combinatorial difficulties are formidable) and these constraints limit the quality of the inference. Any inference instance draws on the associative memory of the IE and ecosystem (for example, Quine's "field of force whose boundary conditions are experience" [13], the World-wide Web, Kahneman's "associative memory" [14]) to support the individual elements of the inference (see Figure 2). So, the impact of the limitations and quality may vary between parts of the inference and may also vary as the circumstances of the IE change. Outside the envelope of reliability, inference may be very sensitive to initial conditions and these may not be measured accurately enough to overcome the sensitivity. In addition, selection pressures are not static, as currently demonstrated by developments in digital technology [1]

Information suffers from extreme combinatorial issues that ecosystem conventions overcome at a cost. So, why should we expect reliability? Kahneman [14] indicates why: "System 1 is radically insensitive to both the quality and quantity of information that gives rise to impressions and intuitions". Selection pressures have given us a level of confidence but that confidence can be misplaced.

Constraints on reliability are embedded in ecosystem conventions and may be further exacerbated by the individual circumstances of an IE (e.g., shortages of resources or time or the application of an inappropriate pattern to the inference).

Deductive logic gives a semblance of reliability but, again, at a cost. Apparent reliability is linked to content inference but only if it is divorced from physical events. Any attempt to apply content inference to physical events suffers from the limitations of event interpretation—the huge enterprise that is modern science testifies to the difficulty of this.

5. EXAMPLES OF INFERENCE

The approach presented in Section 3 and Section 4 can be applied to different examples of inference. It can be used to analyse both individual examples of inference and general theories of inference and the extent to which they incorporate considerations of quality, ecosystem limitations and the need to consider all relevant selection processes. In this section, we consider some aspects of the philosophy of science, the philosophy of mathematics and machine learning.

5.1. Science

Different approaches to the philosophy of science examine different parts of the inference mechanism discussed in Section 3 and different subsets of the selection pressures that apply. Based on the approach in this paper we can ask the following questions:

- to what extent do theories consider the full selection environment and the limitations of ecosystem conventions?
- to what extent do theories consider the components of information quality discussed in Section 4.2?
- what does the selection-oriented view of information say about the structures of knowledge that persist over time?
- how can we interpret "truth" or "approximate truth" in relation to the theories?

The answers provide a mechanism to understand the scope of theories—what they take into account and what they leave out—and therefore understand their limitations. It also helps to demonstrate how the theories relate to each other. Let us consider selection pressures first.

Popper [30] focuses on the importance of refuting assertions through experiment, which forms part of the challenge shown in Figure 3. In his theory, experiments provide the selection processes and the number and type of experiments define the scope of the challenge. The focus on refutation highlights one of the selection pressures in science, but Popper does not consider other selection pressures and the ecosystem more widely (see [18] for examples in which additional selection pressures can subvert the challenge).

In [13], Quine touches on selection pressures and ecosystem inertia. As he puts it:

"[...] it turns upon our vaguely pragmatic inclination to adjust one strand of the fabric of science rather than another in accommodating some particular recalcitrant experience. Conservatism figures in such choices, and so does the quest for simplicity."

The conservatism and quest for simplicity he discusses are selection pressures. Conservatism is an element of ecosystem inertia.

There are strong selection pressures in science to apply resources to refutation. However, Kuhn's discussion of paradigm shifts in science [27] adds a wider range of selection pressures. As well as experimentation, Kuhn adds in wider societal pressures and it is the ecosystem inertia associated with these that leads to the nature of the paradigm shifts he describes. As Max Planck [31] (quoted in [27]) describes it:

"A new scientific truth does not triumph by convincing its opponents...but rather because its opponents eventually die, and a new generation grows up that is familiar with it."

This is a more rounded view of the selection pressures than Popper provides but, again, it is limited. As Goldacre demonstrates in [18], there can be a further set of selection pressures associated with the nature of the funding, publication and review processes that lead to selection conflict and consequent reduction in quality. These three types of selection pressure, identified by Popper, Kuhn and Goldacre, show the nature of the selection conflict in science. However, they also demonstrate the complex relationships between different selection pressures of different types.

Now consider quality. Through the idea of degrees of corroboration, Popper touches on the trustworthiness of input assertions. However, he does not address the concept of quality measures in more detail, and nor does Kuhn. Quality measures are useful in determining the reliability of inference but also in determining the impact of what Quine calls "contrary experiences". This is the problem of holistic underdetermination. In [32] this problem is expressed in the following way:

"Holist underdetermination [...] arises whenever our inability to test hypotheses in isolation leaves us underdetermined in our response to a failed prediction or some other piece of disconfirming evidence. That is, because hypotheses have empirical implications or consequences only when conjoined with other hypotheses and/or background beliefs about the world, a failed prediction or falsified empirical consequence typically leaves open to us the possibility of blaming and abandoning one of these background beliefs and/or 'auxiliary' hypotheses rather than the hypothesis we set out to test in the first place."

Quine based his discussion of underdetermination on a connection-oriented view like that Kahneman [14]. Because of the interconnectedness, Quine argues that all input assertions may be challenged:

"The totality of our so-called knowledge or beliefs [...] impinges on experience only along the edges. [...] the total field is so underdetermined by its boundary conditions, experience, that there is much latitude of choice as to what statements to reevaluate in the light of any single contrary experience."

Rudner [33] makes the following argument:

"[S]ince no hypothesis is ever completely verified, in accepting a hypothesis the scientist must make the decision that the evidence is sufficiently strong or that the probability is sufficiently high to warrant the acceptance of the hypothesis."

The approach to inference in this paper is helpful in analysing this issue. Rudner's use of the term "sufficiently" relates directly to quality (either of information or inference). We can therefore reframe the question of holistic underdetermination in terms of the relative quality of input and interim assertions and the inference itself (see Section 4.2and [3]). Low quality will then become a guide to those assertions or elements of the inference to challenge more rigorously.

Other limitations may also play a role. Quality is often assessed by proxy within an ecosystem (see Section 4.3) and these proxy assessments may contribute to ecosystem inertia and the difficulty of Kuhn's paradigm shifts. Relative assessments, as Rudner suggests, are the best we can expect, since quality measures do not generally support a total order.

We can also consider the relationship with structures of information and knowledge. When linked with an analysis of selection pressures, the connection-oriented approach to information has implications for the likelihood of structures to persist over time. The model for information presented in this paper embeds different types of structure in complicated sets of connections that we can model using linnets [2,3]. Selection pressures trade off friction against quality, so highly connected structures that are difficult to change (i.e., where the change incurs very high friction) are likely to persist—this is an aspect of ecosystem inertia. So, we should expect some structures to be preserved under selection pressures. Whether we can anticipate in advance which structures will be preserved is another question.

Structural realism, as discussed by Worrall in [34], provides an example. Worrall says:

"The rule in the history of physics seems to be that whenever a theory replaces a predecessor, which has however itself enjoyed genuine predictive success, the 'correspondence principle' applies. This requires the mathematical equations of the old theory to re-emerge as limiting cases of [...] the new. [...] The principle operates, not just as after-the-event requirement on a new theory [...] but often also as a heuristic tool in the actual development of the new theory."

That an existing structure will operate as a heuristic tool, which we can describe as a pattern with respect to connection-oriented information, is what we would expect from ecosystem conventions. We can also expect that successful theories will be very highly connected (to information about experiments as well as to other theories) and that there will be very high friction associated with dismantling these connections.

This idea is developed in [5,6] in which the authors discuss scientomics, which they describe as "a genuine informational approach to science" with an evolutionary approach to the development of knowledge in which knowledge recombination between disciplines plays a major role. In this sense, scientomics is explicitly about connecting different ecosystems, which naturally incurs high friction, the possibility of inference tangling and, implicitly, about overcoming the limitations of ecosystem conventions. As discussed in [5], "scientomics posits an inner structure of major recombination events along science history".

Naturally, theories of the philosophy of science are concerned with truth. However, Worrall discusses one of the underlying difficulties when he addresses approximate truth, which is similar to the concept of truthlikeness discussed in [35]. He asks the question: "what exactly is involved in approximate truth?" but does not provide a detailed analysis. A rigorous analysis requires a more detailed understanding of this concept and its relationship with the quality of information and inference. This analysis is provided in [3] in which truth, truthlikeness and other concepts are analysed as measures of information. As discussed in [3], truth is not a rich enough measure of information to capture the comparisons suggested by Quine and Rudner. The idea of trustworthiness, which brings together different measures of quality and plausibility (see Section 4.2), provides a more useful tool to analyse "approximate truth" and its relationship with quality. In this way, using the inference pattern in Figure 2 and Figure 3 integrates the notion of "approximate truth", via quality and truthlikeness, into the structure of any inference.

In summary, a limited view of selection pressures handicaps any theory. Without an understanding of the selection pressures a full understanding of the ecosystem conventions in play is not possible. In turn, this means both that the impact of the conventions on quality and the nature of the limitations will not be clear. Similarly, theories that rely on over-simplistic measures of information do not have the richness to handle concepts like quality, "degrees of corroboration" and "approximate truth".

Each of the theories discussed focuses on a subset of the overall inference pattern. This highlights their limitations but also their position in the inference pattern highlights the relationships between them.

5.2. Mathematics

We can also apply the ideas above to mathematics. Mathematics straddles the worlds of content inference and event inference; the nature of inference is very different in these two cases.

Popper [36] discussed a related point when he suggested that a statement can be logically true but also falsifiable as a statement about the world. His example was "2 apples + 2 apples = 4 apples". The first interpretation ("logically true") relies on content interpretation and inference using mathematics. By contrast, the second interpretation relies on event interpretation and inference. The first uses mathematics as the modelling tool and the second uses both language and mathematics. For his example, it is easy to see that the interpretations coincide fairly readily. However if we consider the example "2 piles + 2 piles = 4 piles" (included in [4]) then it is more difficult. The second form of interpretation depends on what "+" means since it is also possible that "2 piles + 2 piles = 1 pile" (or other numbers).

Content ecosystems for mathematics deal with mathematics as a formal system. In this case, inference consists of proofs of conjectures or the demonstration of counter-examples. These can be long-term and ecosystem-wide as in the case of Fermat's Last Theorem before it was proved by Wiles [37] or within a single IE for a short time (perhaps for individual elements of a proof as discussed by Villani in [38]). This is consistent with Curry's formalist view [39].

Some ecosystems deal with applications of mathematics, for example in applied mathematics or science. In this case the inference to be challenged is an event inference of the form: there is a trustworthy relationship between a hypothesis expressed in mathematics and a set of slices. This form of inference is very different from content inference and the relationship between the two is complicated by the use of language in mathematics. Human language is used in mathematics to make it understandable. Wittgenstein referred to this idea in [40,41]:

"[I]t is essential to mathematics that its signs are also employed in mufti"

"[i]t is the use outside mathematics, and so the meaning ['Bedeutung'] of the signs, that makes the sign-game into mathematics"

This means that there is considerable scope for inference tangling (see Section 4.3) and so we cannot necessarily be sure of the exact nature of the inference process.

5.3. Machine Learning

As the name implies, selection is built into concepts of machine learning. There are several different approaches to machine learning that Domingos [16] summarises as "symbologists, connectionists, evolutionaries, Bayesians, and analogizers". As he says:

"Symbolists view learning as the inverse of deduction and take ideas from philosophy, psychology, and logic. Connectionists reverse engineer the brain and are inspired by neuroscience and physics. Evolutionaries

simulate evolution on the computer and draw on genetics and evolutionary biology. Bayesians believe learning is a form of probabilistic inference and have their roots in statistics. Analogizers learn by extrapolating from similarity judgments and are influenced by psychology and mathematical optimization."

The tribes form ecosystems: "each tribe has a set of core beliefs, and a particular problem that it cares most about". Each has its own conventions.

Machine learning uses data. As Domingos says: "[machine] learners turn data into algorithms". They assume what he calls the unwritten rule of machine learning: "whatever is true of everything we've seen is true of everything in the universe" and they "induce the most widely applicable rules [...] and reduce their scope only when the data forces [them] to". This point of view pushes the "dependable regularities" discussed in [7] to their limits and emphasises the importance of challenge.

Machine learning quality has been analysed in depth. Machine learning finds patterns in data and the patterns depend both on the data and the type of pattern. It is prone to overfitting—"hallucinating patterns that aren't really there" [16]. At the extreme, machine learning will find patterns that fit the learning data but no others, so effective machine learning relies extensively on testing with data that has not been used for learning.

This demonstrates the main selection pressure they experience—what they infer is defined by the data used to define and test them. However, some types of machine learning, for example using neural networks, make the rationale for an inference opaque which exposes a different type of selection pressure. As Bostrom concludes [17]:

"It will become increasingly important to develop AI algorithms that are not just powerful and scalable, but also transparent to inspection—to name one of many socially important properties."

"It is also important that AI algorithms taking over social functions be predictable to those they govern."

These points demonstrate that, although machine learning is explicitly exposed to some selection pressures (by training and testing on selected inputs), these selection pressures only include a narrow assessment of function and quality. Wider issues, such as those presented by Bostrom are not necessarily yet part of the learning. As he says:

"...it will require an AGI [Artificial General Intelligence] that thinks like a human engineer concerned about ethics, not just a simple product of ethical engineering."

There is an analogy with Popper [30] and Kuhn [27]. Machine learning is currently addressing a narrow set of selection pressures (by analogy with Popper's description of refutation). Only when the machine learning ecosystem can also incorporate societal selection pressures (by analogy with Kuhn) will the wider questions raised by Bostrom be addressed.

6. CONCLUSIONS

The model for information presented here provides a set of tools with which to analyse information. These tools (about selection, ecosystem conventions and measures of information) highlight the limitations of inference.

Under the influence of selection processes, ecosystem conventions develop that establish the norms for inference. These conventions will provide inference that is reliable enough (but possibly not more) within the envelope of environment states determined by the selection pressures. The corollary of this is that, generally, an approach to inference is reliable only to the extent that all relevant selection pressures have challenged it thoroughly. And it is reliable only within the envelope in which selection pressures have applied.

If we use the pattern for inference in Figure 2 and Figure 3, we can analyse different forms of inference in different ecosystems. This highlights the degree to which ideas in the philosophy of science, mathematics and machine learning, for example, match up to the generic pattern and, therefore, where their limitations may be found. It also shows how different, seemingly competing, ideas about inference in the philosophy of science relate to each other within the general model.

ACKNOWLEDGMENTS

The author would like to thank the referees for their constructive comments.

CONFLICTS OF INTEREST

The author declares no conflict of interest.

REFERENCES AND NOTES

1. Walton, P. Digital information and value. Information 2015, 6, 733–749.
2. Walton, P. A Model for Information. Information 2014, 5, 479–507.
3. Walton, P. Measures of information. Information 2015, 6, 23–48.
4. Walton, P. Information and Meaning. Information 2016, 7, 41.
5. Moral, R.; González, M.; Navarro, J.; Marijuán, P.C. From Genomics to Scientomics: Expanding the Bioinformation Paradigm. Information 2011, 2, 651–671.
6. Marijuán, P.C.; Moral, R.; Navarro, J. Scientomics: An emergent perspective in knowledge organization. Knowl. Organ. 2012, 39, 153–164.
7. Mercier, H.; Sperber, D. The Enigma of Reason; Harvard University Press: Cambridge, MA, USA, 2017.
8. Lorenz, E.N. Deterministic Nonperiodic Flow. J. Atmos. Sci. 1963, 20, 130–141.
9. Arthur, B.W. The Nature of Technology: What It Is and How It Evolves; The Free Press and Penguin Books: New York, NY, USA, 2009.
10. Zhong, Y. Unity-Based Diversity: System Approach to Defining Information. Information 2011, 2, 406–416.
11. Burgin, M. Theory of Information: Fundamentality, Diversity and Unification; World Scientific Publishing: Singapore, 2010.
12. Logan, R. What Is Information?: Why Is It Relativistic and What Is Its Relationship to Materiality, Meaning and Organization. Information 2012, 3, 68–91.
13. Quine, W.V.O. "Two Dogmas of Empiricism", Reprinted in from a Logical Point of View, 2nd ed.; Harvard University Press: Cambridge, MA, USA, 1951; pp. 20–46.
14. Kahneman, D. Thinking, Fast and Slow; Macmillan: London, UK, 2011.
15. Gates, B.; Myhrvold, N.; Rinearson, P. The Road Ahead; Viking Penguin: New York, NY, USA, 1995.
16. Domingos, P. The Master Algorithm: How the Quest for the Ultimate Learning Machine Will Remake Our World; Penguin: London, UK, 2015.
17. Bostrom, N. The Ethics of Artificial Intelligence (PDF); Cambridge University Press: Cambridge, MA, USA, 2011.
18. Goldacre, B. Bad Science; Harper Perennial: London, UK, 2009.
19. Simon, H.A.; Rescher, N. Cause and Counterfactual. Philos. Sci. 1966, 33, 323–340.
20. Macknik, S.L.; Martinez-Conde, S. Sleights of Mind; Picador: Surrey, UK, 2011.
21. Einstein, A. Letter to Max Born (4 December 1926); The Born-Einstein Letters (Translated by Irene Born); Walker and Company: New York, NY, USA, 1971.
22. Carnap, R. Logical Foundations of Probability, 2nd ed.; University of Chicago Press: Chicago, IL, USA, 1962.
23. Vickers, J. The Problem of Induction, Zalta, E.N., Ed.; Spring 2016 Edition; The Stanford Encyclopedia of Philosophy: Stanford, CA, USA; Available online: https://plato.stanford.edu/archives/spr2016/entries/induction-problem/(accessed on 25 May 2017).
24. The Green Book: Appraisal and Evaluation in Central Government. Available online: https://www.gov.uk/government/publications/the-green-book-appraisal-and-evaluation-in-central-governent (accessed on 25 May 2017).
25. Sommerville, I. Software Engineering; Addison-Wesley: Harlow, UK, 2010.
26. Brown, J.S.; Duguid, P. The Social Life of Information; Harvard Business Press: Boston, MA, USA, 2000.
27. Kuhn, T.S. The Structure of Scientific Revolutions, Enlarged 2nd ed.; University of Chicago Press: Chicago, IL, USA, 1970.
28. Lawrence, P.R. How to Deal with Resistance to Change. Harv. Bus. Rev. 1954, 32, 49–57.
29. Norris, P. Digital Divide: Civic Engagement, Information Poverty and the Internet Worldwide; Cambridge University Press: New York, NY, USA, 2001.
30. Popper, K.R. The Logic of Scientific Discovery; Hutchinson: London, UK, 1959.
31. Planck, M. Scientific Autobiography and Other Papers; Gaynor, F., Translator; Williams & Northgate: London, UK, 1950.

32. Stanford, K. Underdetermination of Scientific Theory; Zalta, E.N., Ed.; The Stanford Encyclopedia of Philosophy: Stanford, CA, USA, Spring 2016 Edition Available online: https://plato.stanford.edu/archives/spr2016/entries/scientific-underdetermination/ (accessed on 25 May 2017).
33. Rudner, R. The Scientist qua Scientist Makes Value Judgments. Philos. Sci. 1953, 20, 1–6.
34. Worrall, J. Structural Realism: The Best of Both Worlds? Dialectica 1989, 43, 99–124.
35. Floridi, L. The Philosophy of Information; Oxford University Press: Oxford, UK, 2011.
36. Ryle, G.; Lewy, C.; Popper, K.R. Symposium: Why are the calculuses of logic and arithmetic applicable to reality? In Proceedings of the Logic and Reality, Symposia Read at the Joint Session of the Aristotelian Society and the Mind Association, Manchester, UK, 5–7 July 1946; pp. 20–60.
37. Wiles, A. Modular elliptic curves and Fermat's Last Theorem. Ann. Math. 1995, 142, 443–551.
38. Villani, C. The Birth of a Theorem: A Mathematical Adventure; The Bodley Head: London, UK, 2015.
39. Curry, H. Outlines of a Formalist Philosophy of Mathematics; North-Holland: Amsterdam, The Netherlands, 1958.
40. Wittgenstein, L. Remarks on the Foundations of Mathematics, Revised Edition; Anscombe, G.E.M., Translator; von Wright, G.H., Rhees, R., Anscombe, G.E.M., Eds.; Basil Blackwell: Oxford, UK, 1978.
41. Wittgenstein, L. Wittgenstein's Lectures on the Foundations of Mathematics; Diamond, C., Ed.; Cornell University Press: Ithaca, NY, USA, 1976.

CHAPTER 3

Security Awareness of the Digital Natives

Vasileios Gkioulos [1,*,†], Gaute Wangen [1,†], Sokratis K. Katsikas [1,2,†], George Kavallieratos [2,†] and Panayiotis Kotzanikolaou [3,†]

[1]*Department of Information Security and Communication Technology, Norwegian University of Science & Technology, 2802 Gjøvik, Norway,*

[2]*Department of Digital Systems, University of Piraeus, 18532 Piraeus, Greece*

[3]*Department of Informatics, University of Piraeus, 18532 Piraeus, Greece*

ABSTRACT

Young generations make extensive use of mobile devices, such as smartphones, tablets and laptops, while a plethora of security risks associated with such devices are induced by vulnerabilities related to user behavior. Furthermore, the number of security breaches on or via portable devices increases exponentially. Thus, deploying suitable risk treatments requires the investigation of how the digital natives (young people, born and bred in the digital era) use their mobile devices and their level of security awareness, in order to identify common usage patterns with negative security impact. In this article, we present the results of a survey performed across a multinational sample of digital natives with distinct backgrounds and levels of competence in terms of security, to identify divergences in user behavior due to regional, educational and other factors. Our results highlight significant influences on the behavior of digital natives, arising from user confidence, educational background, and parameters related to usability and accessibility. The outcomes of this study justify the need for further analysis of the topic, in order to identify the influence of fine-grained semantics, but also the consolidation of wide and robust user-models.

Keywords: security; mobile devices; digital natives; security awareness; user behavior; education

1. INTRODUCTION

Mobile devices (i.e., cellphones, laptops, tablets) have become an indispensable part of our everyday life, since they fulfill the increasing users' desire for Internet connectivity and access to information, social and private networks at any time and place. Owing to the proliferation of "smart" devices and the escalating dependency on them with respect to the execution of everyday tasks, they have evolved from a communication medium to a multifunctional equipment. The reduced cost, in combination with the increasing computational and storage capacity of mobile devices, allow them to accommodate critical functionalities with significant security and safety related impact such as e-banking, control systems and Internet of things architectures. Such devices do not simply store information related to their owners, but also receive data on people and infrastructure related in some way to them. As a result, they can retrieve, store and modify extensive quantities of diverse and potentially sensitive information.

Furthermore, the users are accustomed to the notion of continuous connectivity, even across networks with potentially unknown configurations. Such transmissions are likely to be vulnerable to unauthorized access and, consequently, they constitute a security risk. In many cases, these risks materialize as direct criminal attacks, such as privacy intrusions or unauthorized disruptions of communication. Moreover, they can expose the users to more complex types of malicious activity, such as identity theft, blackmailing, active data collection, or defamation. In light of the increasing risks due to the aforementioned use of mobile devices, it is important that users are aware of the risks they are exposed to and, more importantly, that they are informed about how to protect themselves.

Therefore, the aim of this study is to investigate the user behavior of digital natives from distinct educational backgrounds and levels of security competence. We seek to identify how user confidence, security awareness and background affect their decisions, in aspects related to the use of their mobile devices that can inflict significant security related impact. More specifically, this study investigates how the background and technical competence influences the digital natives' security awareness within five focus areas: (i) Use of Mobile devices; (ii) Connectivity and Network Access; (iii) Management of Credentials; (iv) Knowledge and Fear of Risks; and (v) Self-evaluation of security awareness. With this study, we aim to understand how young people use their mobile devices, how well they know them, and what their concerns are, in order to help improve the secure and safe use of these devices. Our results outline the generic properties of the whole sample and the categorical differences across the groups (see Section 3) within the focus areas.

The results of this study are useful both for designing educational and awareness campaigns, but also for purposes of user behavior modeling. With this article, we aim to highlight areas in which current security related knowledge dissemination is sufficient, areas where there is a clear difference in behavior across the digital natives, and areas where they lack knowledge as a whole or they choose usability over security. The remaining of the paper is structured as follows: Section 2 discusses related work, while Section 3 presents the methodology used for this study. Subsequently, in Section 4, we present the results of the executed surveys, identifying categorical differences across the groups and discussing their origins. Finally, Section 5 summarizes the results extracted from our analysis, while we conclude with presenting the limitations of our study and potential paths for future work.

2. RELATED WORK

Since 2014, mobile devices have been becoming the leading digital platform, displacing the desktop PC [1]. Prensky [2] writes that the digital natives have radically changed their way of thinking by being exposed to technology almost since birth, while other scholars [3] have contested such claims. However, there is no denying that the digital natives have a different view of technology than older generations.

The scope of this article is the digital natives and their security awareness, related in particular to mobile devices. A considerable number of studies concerning user behavior, with regards to selecting and installing applications on smartphones, have found that users do not consider security and privacy issues during app selection, as they tend to ignore privacy policies and EULAs (End-user license agreement) [4]. Furthermore, Android users were found not to pay attention, understand, and act on permission information during installation [5,6]. Mylonas et al. [7] have explored the security awareness metrics of smartphone users who download applications from official application repositories. The authors of that study applied these to measure how the security background affects the smartphone security awareness of their sample, concluding that security background has a slight impact on awareness. The key differences between the current study and Mylonas et al. is that the latter applied self-rating as the independent variable for determining skill level, did not explicitly target the digital natives and investigated different areas of smartphone security awareness.

Furthermore, Mylonas et al. [8] explore the security awareness of smartphone users who download applications from official application repositories. The findings from said study show that users are complacent in their smartphone security behavior and display high levels of trust towards smartphone application repositories. In addition, they rarely consider privacy and security when installing new applications, and do not install adequate protection mechanisms [9]. Additional research into users and protection mechanisms partially contradicts the idea that smartphone users are not security aware, and finds several correlations between security awareness and smartphone OS, language, and gender [10]. However, the said study [10] does not specifically target the digital natives, despite them being the majority of users. More related to the topic are the studies conducted by Markel and Bernik [11] and Markel and Zgaga [12]. These papers report the findings of a survey carried out in 2011 among 281 students of Slovenian faculties, investigating threat perception on mobile devices [11] and in cyberspace [12]. The findings show that the sample student population had a low awareness of security threats and security measures, and the authors suggest that education and awareness levels must be increased in Slovenia to counter this development.

A common argument towards the reviewed studies is that, although they address a similar topic, they are geographically limited [11,12,13] or they investigate behaviors in relation to subsets of technologies [5,6,9] and problems [4,7,8,9] that are not specifically related to the digital natives. Ariu et al. [14] have worked on filling this gap by studying the level of awareness and perception of IT security amongst university students, paying particular attention to the world of mobile devices. Their report analyses the answers given by 1012 students from over 15 Italian universities to a multiple-choice questionnaire. The analysis shows that students' perception of their knowledge is generally wrong and that they are unaware of the risks arising from their behavior. This paper builds on the Ariu et al. results and supplements with two additional datasets, thus expanding the knowledge base. The second data set targeted generic computer science students, while the third dataset targeted information and cyber security students specifically.

3. METHODOLOGY

This article builds on a previous study [14] on the topic of security awareness of the digital natives, and was conducted to investigate the differences in risk perception across three distinct groups categorized by their technical background. This section has the following structure: the first sub-section addresses the choice of data collection method and instrument, followed by the sample description, and a brief overview of the statistical methods used for data analysis.

3.1. Data Collection and Instruments

The survey aimed to explore the security awareness of the digital natives addressed to students of the digital age, i.e., persons who were born in the years of the technological boom in Information Technology and Communications (ICT), between 1987–1997. Universities are ideal since they comprise a diverse population. Thus, the sample of this study comes from students born within range. We found the online questionnaire to be the best option for data gathering as it reaches a broad audience and provides a strong level of anonymity; therefore, the presented datasets were collected using Google Forms.

The original survey was developed by Ariu et al. and initially ran in multiple Italian universities [14]. The survey had 60 questions that investigated security awareness aspects within the five areas outlined in the introduction. As for the level of measurement, the questionnaire had categorical, ordinal, and continuous type questions. Category type questions are used here mainly for demographics, while the main bulk of the questionnaire was designed using several mandatory scale and ranking questions.

3.2. Sample and Analysis

This study utilises three distinct samples:

- The data set collected by Ariu et.al., which was targeted at the Italian digital natives, is included in this study and corresponds to our general security competence group (GSCG). The sample consists of 1012 respondents from various university departments (Including law, engineering, computer science, humanitarian, marketing, and multiple other faculties not directed to IT education), which are mapped for the purposes of this study to the general population of digital natives.

- Secondly, we collected data for the medium security competence group (MSCG) by targeting digital natives from Greece with education exclusively in computer science. This group is expected to a have wider knowledge over the use of mobile technologies and increased awareness over security related aspects due to their educational background. The sample consists of 303 responders in total at the undergraduate (234), postgraduate (54), and doctoral (15) levels.
- Finally, the target population for the high security competence group (HSCG) was undergraduate, postgraduate and doctoral students of information security from Norway. These were expected to have a higher security awareness regarding the four main areas than the medium and generic groups, due to their specialized education. For this group, we had 35 respondents in total, of which 21 are undergraduate students, 10 postgraduate, and four doctoral students.

The difference in quantity of respondents for each survey reflects the scarcity of each group in the general population; for example, there are more respondents in GSCG than MSCG, and more in MSCG than HSCG, with the latter group was large enough for the central limit theorem to apply [15]. For the descriptive data analysis, we primarily consider differences in the frequency distributions, while we used the security competence groups as categorical data for bi-variate analysis. The questionnaire primarily asked categorical and ordinal multiple-choice questions, while, as a measure of central tendency for ordinal questions, we considered the median, variance, and range.

4. ANALYSIS OF RESULTS AND DISCUSSION

The individuals participating in the survey, across all competence groups, were requested to self-evaluate their knowledge on aspects related to information security, both before and after participating in the survey (Table 1 and Figure 1). A degradation is noticeable at the "before" and "after" responses across the groups, with the exception of HSCG group participants that selected "Insufficient". In conjunction with the results presented in the following sections, this is attributed to the increased user confidence that characterizes the everyday use, when security threats are not prioritized or not directly visible. This contributes to the unjustified perception of being secure, hence intensifying the security risk, and necessitates increased effort towards educating and making the users aware of the risks.

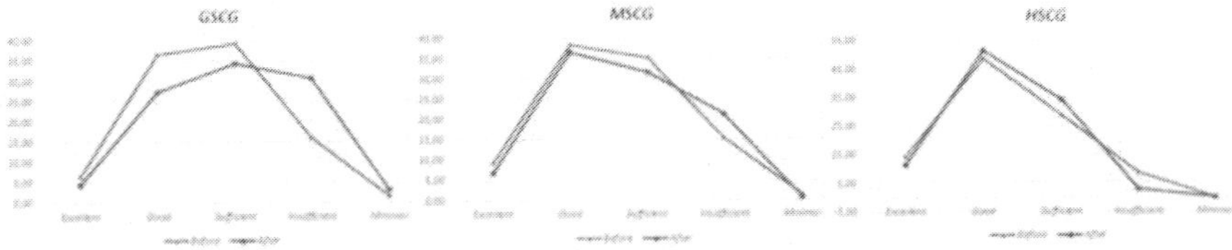

Figure 1. How do you assess your knowledge on information security?

Table 1. How do you assess your knowledge on information security?

		Excellent	Good	Sufficient	Insufficient	Minimal
Before	GSCG	6.5%	36.6%	39.3%	16.0%	1.6%
	MSCG	9.3%	38.5%	35.3%	15.4%	1.3%
	HSCG	14.3%	48.6%	28.6%	8.6%	0.0%
After	GSCG	4.4%	27.4%	34.4%	30.7%	3.1%
	MSCG	6.7%	36.5%	31.7%	21.2%	0.6%
	HSCG	11.4%	51.4%	34.3%	2.9%	0.0%

GSCG: general security competence group; MSCG: medium security competence group; HSCG: high security competence group.

4.1. Use of Mobile Devices

This section includes questions related to the use of mobile devices and applications, as well as questions related to user behavior when selling or losing a mobile device, and modifying its operating system.

We asked the digital natives what they store on their mobile devices, while a section of the question referred to personal passwords. As presented in Table 2, despite the frequent warnings, an average of 29.1% of the responders stores personal passwords in their mobile devices, regardless of their security related competence or background.

Table 2. Do you store personal passwords on your mobile device? (in plaintext).

	Yes	No
GSCG	27.7%	72.3%
MSCG	31.1%	68.9%
HSCG	28.6%	71.4%

Subsequently, we asked the digital natives if, in the case of loss/theft of their mobile device, they reported the event to the authorities. The results that are presented in Table 3 highlight the fact that the users are not widely aware of the ability to deny access to wireless networks based on the IMEI (International Mobile Equipment Identity) and other misuse countermeasures. Additionally, some of the differences in the responses between the GSCG and the MSCG/HSCG groups are likely caused due to regional variations in legislation, trust in the efficiency of the authorities, and the awareness of related countermeasures.

Table 3. Have you reported the loss/theft of your device to the authorities?

	Yes	No
GSCG	68.5%	31.5%
MSCG	33.5%	66.5%
HSCG	28.6%	71.4%

The next question focused on software updates on cellphones/tablets and laptops. The results for each category of mobile devices are presented in Table 4 and Figure 2 and Figure 3. It is noticeable that 14.5% of the GSCG group state that they do not update anything in their laptops, while across all groups, updating only the applications ranks higher than updating only the operating system. Furthermore, comparing the results of the two categories, we observe that the GSCG and MSCG groups better maintain the software of their cellphones/tablets in comparison to their laptops.

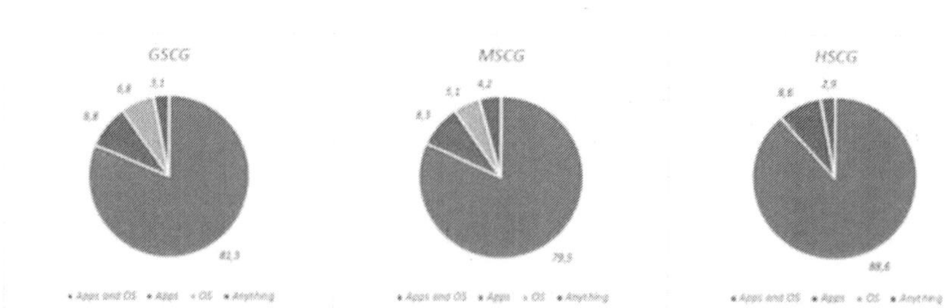

Figure 2. Do you regularly update the software on your mobile device? (cellphone/tablet).

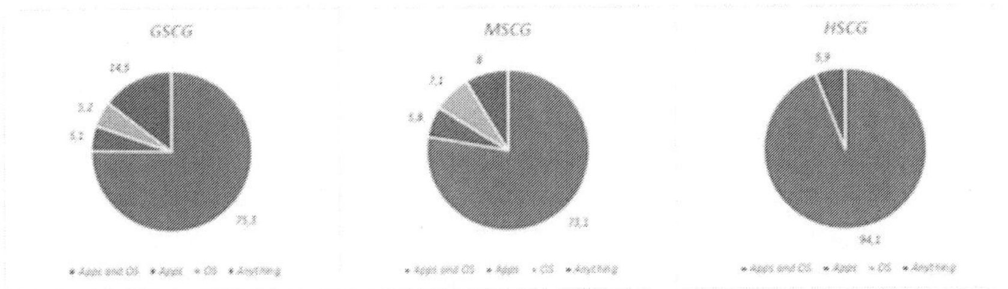

Figure 3. Do you regularly update the software on your mobile device? (laptop).

Table 4. Do you regularly update the software on your mobile device?

		Apps and OS	Apps	OS	Anything
Cellphone/tablet	*GSCG*	*81.3%*	*8.8%*	*6.8%*	*3.1%*
	MSCG	79.5%	8.3%	5.1%	4.2%
	HSCG	88.6%	8.6%	0.0%	2.9%
Laptop	*GSCG*	*75.3%*	*5.1%*	*5.2%*	*14.5%*
	MSCG	73.1%	5.8%	7.1%	8.0%
	HSCG	94.1%	5.9%	0.0%	0.0%

Regarding the use of applications, the next question focused on the sources that the digital natives use in order to download applications from, as presented in Table 5. Over 80% of the digital natives primarily use the official store, while an average of 12.3% across groups consciously uses non-official sources, regardless of the potential security threats. However, there is a positive correlation between security competence and application source.

Table 5. Where do you download applications from?

	Official Store	Other Sources
GSCG	*83.1%*	*16.9%*
MSCG	85.9%	11.5%
HSCG	91.4%	8.6%

Focusing on the behavior of the digital natives in terms of the application usage patterns, we asked how they manage their credentials when they have finished using an application. The results that are presented in Table 6 highlight that, regardless of knowledge on the potential privacy and other implications, they select usability over security, since only an average of 24.5% logs out. Furthermore, there is a notable difference between the MSCG and HSCG regarding saving the credentials, where the HSCG group more frequently chooses to save the credentials to stay logged in. Another notable finding is that a significant percentage of participants states that logging-out is "not important".

Table 6. As soon as you have finished using an application, you..?

	Save Credentials to Stay Logged in	Log out	Forget to Log out	Do Not Log out Because It Is Not Important	Do Not Log out Because I Do Not Know How
GSCG	*40.3%*	*24.1%*	*19.6%*	*10.3%*	*5.6%*
MSCG	30.8%	26.6%	16.7%	20.5%	1.9%
HSCG	48.6%	22.9%	14.3%	14.3%	0.0%

Another aspect of application usage patterns with significant security implications is the control of application access rights. Thus, we asked the digital natives how frequently they check the permissions that an application requires prior to accepting its installation. The results, in Table 7, show significant differences across the groups with a positive correlation between competence and security behavior. Analyzing these responses, in conjunction with the results of Table 6, highlights that expertise and knowledge can affect user behavior when security is not in conflict with usability.

Table 7. How frequently do you check the permissions (access rights) that the application requires before completing the installation?

	Never	Rarely	Often	Always
GSCG	*15.6%*	*38.2%*	*25.5%*	*20.7%*
MSCG	8.0%	26.3%	27.6%	34.9%
HSCG	5.7%	14.3%	40.0%	40.0%

A set of questions in this section focused on technical knowledge regarding mobile devices, in particular jailbreaking and rooting, as presented in Table 8 and Figure 4. The respondents across all groups seem to be familiar with these practices, and despite justifiably considering them potentially hazardous in terms of security, an average of 41.6% has used them in their mobile devices. The results show a difference between the groups where the competence level correlates positively with having a jailbroken or rooted mobile device, while the HSCG is slightly (8–10%) less likely to consider these practices as risky. It is evident, from the second data set presented in this table, that individuals with computer science/engineering background are less reluctant in applying such methods. This has also been traced across the GSCG group, when filtering the digital natives according to their academic background [14].

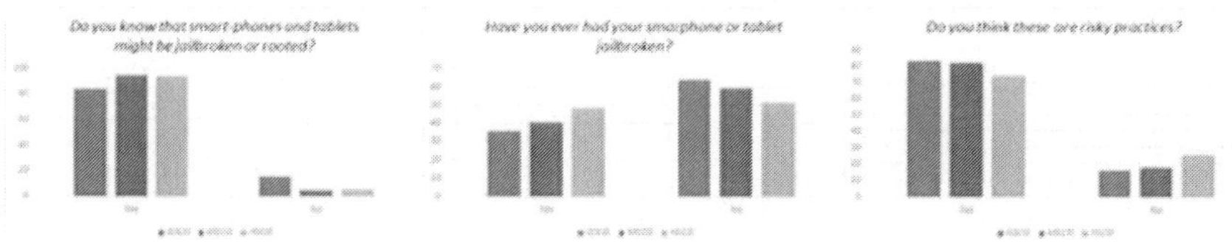

Figure 4. Visualization of Table 8 results.

Table 8. Jailbreaking and rooting mobile devices.

Do you know that smartphones and tablets might be jailbroken or rooted?		
	Yes	No
GSCG	*84.2%*	*15.8%*
MSCG	94.9%	5.1%
HSCG	94.3%	5.7%
Have you ever had your smarphone or tablet jailbroken?		
GSCG	*35.7%*	*64.3%*
MSCG	40.4%	59.6%
HSCG	48.6%	51.4%
Do you think these are risky practices?		
GSCG	*83.5%*	*16.5%*
MSCG	82.1%	17.9%
HSCG	74.3%	25.7%

Additionally to these results, the questionnaire included a number of propositions regarding the security of these techniques (jailbreaking, etc.), which the respondents had to evaluate as “True”, “False”, or

"Unknown". An example of the investigated propositions is: *"Some Jailbreaking methods delete some operating systems' protections, which can be exploited by malicious code"*. In the majority of cases, these propositions have been answered incorrectly by all groups, suggesting that the digital natives are willing to apply such methods on their mobile devices, despite being aware of the involved security risks and without the required experience/knowledge.

4.2. Connectivity and Network Access

This section was focused on analyzing the behavior of digital natives towards connectivity and network access. The results show significant variations across the groups, while one of the most notable differences relates to user behavior when they have the opportunity to connect to an unsecured wireless network, as presented in Table 9.

Table 9. If you find free Wi-Fi, what do you do with your mobile device?

		I Connect and Use the Internet without Restrictions	I Connect but Only Do Activities that Do Not Require Credential Authentication	I Do Not Connect
Cellphone/tablet	GSCG	43.6%	33.4%	23.0%
	MSCG	26.0%	44.9%	21.8%
	HSCG	22.9%	34.3%	42.9%
Laptop	GSCG	43.6%	33.4%	23.0%
	MSCG	28.0%	46.9%	25.1%
	HSCG	25.7%	45.7%	28.6%

As presented in Figure 5, there exists a significant difference between the GSCG and the other two groups when it comes to connecting to free Wi-Fi, with both mobile devices and laptops, the former having the largest divergence. The MSCG are more likely to connect their mobile devices, but restrict the use of activities that require credential authentication. Moreover, the HSCG stands out with 42.9% opting not to connect with mobile devices at all, which represents a 20% difference from the two other groups. It is also noticeable that a larger portion of the HSCG (45.7%) opts to connect their laptops, rather than their mobile devices, to unsecured Wi-Fi with restricted activities.

The results across all types of mobile devices, show that user background and knowledge of the involved risks can affect their behavior, according to the significant differences across groups in response to the "I connect and use the Internet without restrictions" question. However, the results highlight that only with small exceptions across people with a security related background do users disregard or are unaware of the involved risks. Furthermore, users tend to be less reluctant when using their laptops in comparison to other mobile devices, potentially due to a falsely increased trust level in the security of such devices.

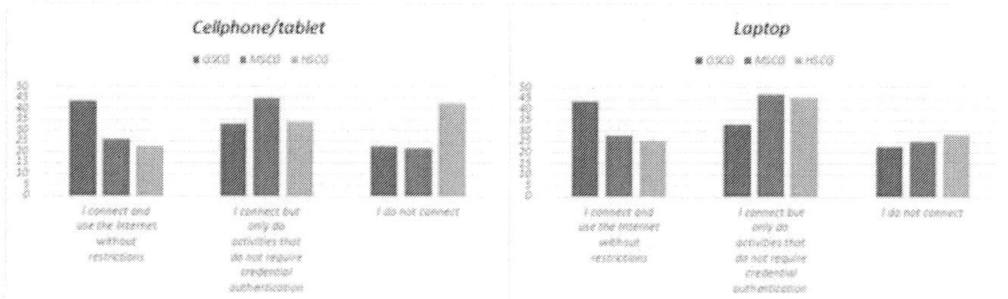

Figure 5. If you find free Wi-Fi, what do you do with your mobile device?

4.3. Management of Credentials

This section presents results in questions related to the management of credentials and the use of protection technologies. Initially, the digital natives have been asked about the solutions they use, in order to enforce access control to their mobile devices. The results revealed that 40.1% of the GSCG group, 19.9% of the MSCG group and 8.6% of the HSCG group choose to not use any access control mechanism in their mobile devices, while the pattern lock and PINs (Personal Identification Numbers) were the most popular solutions among the GSCG–MSCG groups and biometrics for the HSCG group. The results showed that the users' background can significantly affect related decisions regarding the overall use of access control mechanisms, while the exact choice of technologies can also be affected by financial or cultural agents.

Aiming to identify potential external influences on these results, we asked the digital natives to identify the reasons behind the decision to not utilize an access control mechanism. The results that are presented in Table 10 show that the usability of these mechanisms can significantly affect this decision. For the HSCG group, the use of access control was at 91.4%, with biometrics used in 54.3% of the sample, which highlights that users who are aware of the involved risks and provided with usable solutions (biometrics) will increasingly incorporate access control mechanisms.

Table 10. If you do not use a mechanism to protect access to your mobile device, why is that so?

	I Know Them but Never Thought About Using Them	I Know Them but I Am Not Interested in Using Them	I Know Them but They Make the Use of My Device Uncomfortable	I Do Not Know Them
GSCG	13.6%	27.7%	52.5%	6.3%
MSCG	3.0%	41.5%	51.0%	5.0%
HSCG	16.7%	33.3%	50.0%	0.0%

A further set of questions was dedicated to analyzing the use of passwords for authentication purposes. The results in Table 11 and Table 12 show that a mixture of best and worst practices is implemented across the groups, with significant variations among the different password types. Lasting and persistent awareness campaigns focused in the past several years on educating the public and raising awareness about best practices. However, these results show that, despite the visible positive influence, the system did not reach a stable state yet, while educating the users on security best practices requires sending a simple and clear message.

Table 11. For applications that require a password.

	I Always Use the Same Password for All the Applications	I Use Small Variations of the Same Password for Different Applications	I Always Use Different Passwords	I Do Not Use Applications that Require Passwords
GSCG	20.6%	41.3%	31.7%	6.3%
MSCG	8.7%	41.7%	39.1%	6.7%
HSCG	5.7%	51.4%	40.0%	2.9%

4.4. Knowledge and Fear of Risks

This section included questions aiming to identify how the users perceive security related risks, their level of confidence in using their mobile device and their concerns. A summary of the results is presented in Figure 6 and Figure 7, showing that the background affects the confidence of users in respect to security related risks, especially regarding laptop usage. However, a difference between the distributions corresponding to cellphones/tablets and laptops is noticeable. In correlation with the network access results presented in Section 4.2, this can be traced both to the maturity of the technologies and the roles of the distinct devices in daily use. Additionally, it is evident that, despite their increased computational capacity, access to personal data, and incorporation into critical systems, the users, to a great extent, seem to still perceive smartphones and tablets in a more liberal fashion.

Table 12. What type of password are you most likely to use?

The passwords that I use are at least 8 characters long		
	Yes	No
GSCG	*87.0%*	*13.0%*
MSCG	83.7%	11.5%
HSCG	100.0%	0.0%
I use passwords that contain personal information		
GSCG	*36.5%*	*63.5%*
MSCG	36.8%	63.2%
HSCG	17.1%	82.9%
I use passwords that contain simple strings of characters (1234, qwerty, etc.)		
GSCG	*8.7%*	*91.3%*
MSCG	29.5%	80.5%
HSCG	0.0%	100.0%
I use passwords that contain meaningful words		
GSCG	*45.0%*	*55.0%*
MSCG	27.8%	72.2%
HSCG	34.3%	65.7%
I use passwords that contain numbers and special characters		
GSCG	*74.6%*	*25.4%*
MSCG	9.1%	90.9%
HSCG	97.1%	2.9%
If the system allows it, I do not use a password		
GSCG	*6.2%*	*93.8%*
MSCG	9.4%	90.6%
HSCG	14.3%	85.7%

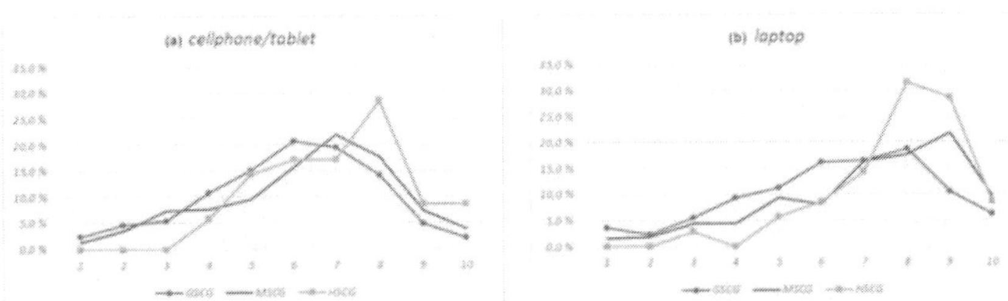

Figure 6. On a scale from 1 (none) to 10 (excellent), how do you assess your knowledge of issues and risks associated with the use of your—(**a**) cellphone/tablet, (**b**) laptop?

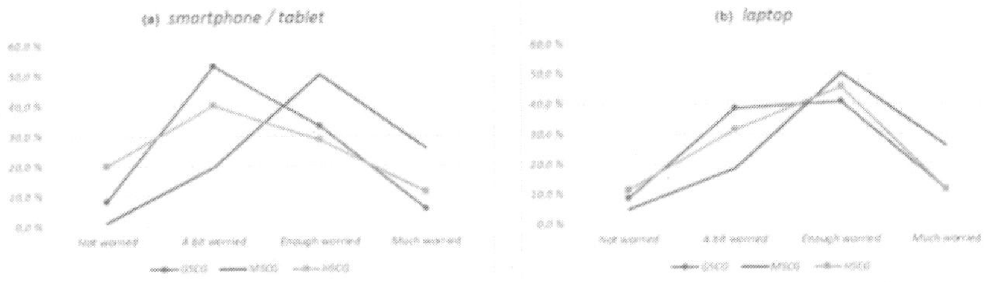

Figure 7. How concerned are you about the security of your—(**a**) cellphone/tablet, (**b**) laptop?

5. SUMMARY OF RESULTS

The most significant findings of this study can be summarized as follows:

- Users tend to have increased confidence in the daily use of their mobile devices, leading them to negligent behavior towards actions with potential security related impact. However, the digital natives seem to adopt a more constrained stance when security threats become directly visible. It would be interesting to investigate the variations in user behavior prior and after a major security incident, along with analyzing the duration and extent of this phenomenon.
- Specific areas of user behavior (such as the storage of plaintext passwords in mobile devices) are not significantly affected by their security awareness or background, with a consistent percentage of digital natives remaining willing to accept the risk. Aiming to facilitate further security improvements in such areas would require not only informing the users about the potential threats, but also channeling those who persist in the practicality of such actions into more secure alternatives (e.g., password managers).
- The digital natives still remain unaware of some countermeasures that are available at their disposal and could improve their user experience while maintaining higher security standards.
- Variations in user behavior have been identified to originate not only from their level of security awareness, but also from regional, financial and cultural agents. Thus, regional studies and campaigns aiming to raise security awareness, must be scoped and adapted accordingly.
- Users tend to prioritize access to services and the usability of their mobile devices over the enforcement of security measures, without

major differentiations based on their background. However, the results of this study have shown that users who are aware of the security risks are willing to opt for security when usable solutions become available.

- Digital natives are willing to accept risks despite of their concerns about security (e.g., jailbreaking/rooting, unofficial application sources) in order to obtain access to additional services. This decision is not significantly affected by their overall knowledge about security, while users with backgrounds in engineering, computer science or information security are less reluctant due to their increased confidence.
- The users of mobile devices seem to feel more confident and less constrained in terms of security when using their laptops in comparison to smartphones and tablets. This is attributed to the maturity of the technologies, but also the lack of recognition of the increased computational capacity and criticality of tasks allocated to smartphones and tablets.
- In some aspects, such as the selection of secure passwords, the digital natives seem to be informed of the appropriate practices. However, the results highlight that, despite the noticeable improvement, a precise framework still needs to be consolidated across the users' mindsets.

6. LIMITATIONS

This study has been conducted under the limitation that the dataset referring to the GSCG was collected in a prior investigation. Therefore, access to the raw data was not possible, something that restricted the possibility for deeper statistical analysis. Inherently, expanding the samples' geographic distribution for this study carries interlacing cultural influences. Therefore, future work in this field should also consolidate an understanding of the influences arising from such fine-grained cultural divergences.

7. CONCLUSIONS

The purpose of this study was to investigate how the digital natives use their mobile devices, their level of security awareness, and how these relate to their background and educational influences. Our goal was to identify common usage patterns with negative security impact in order to facilitate the deployment of suitable risk treatments. To this end, an initial study of students across Italian Universities has been extended, totaling 1350 participants across three countries, mirroring distinct educational backgrounds and security related competence levels. Categorical differences have been identified between the groups within all five investigated areas, allowing the extraction of findings referring to the modeling of digital natives both across and within the investigated groups.

The results of this study open multiple paths for future work. Regarding risk understanding, the digital natives tend to have increased confidence in the daily use of their mobile devices, but seem to adopt a more constrained stance when security threats become directly visible. A path for future work would be to investigate the variations in user behavior prior and after a major security incident as stated earlier. Our results may also contribute to targeted user-modeling validation studies, specifically regarding the correctness of how developers and security experts perceive the user behavior of the digital natives.

ACKNOWLEDGMENTS

We extend our thanks to Francesca Bosco for giving us access to the questionnaire used in [14]; to Elisavet-Maria Katsika for translating it from Italian to Greek; and to Marte Lunde for suggesting to extend the survey to Norwegian students.

AUTHOR CONTRIBUTIONS

These authors contributed equally to this work.

CONFLICTS OF INTEREST

The authors declare no conflicts of interest.

REFERENCES

1. Lella, A.; Lipsman, A. The US Mobile App Report. 2014. Available online: http://www.comscore.com/Insights/Presentationsand-Whitepapers/2014/The-US-Mobile-App-Report (accessed on 8 April 2015).
2. Prensky, M. Digital natives, digital immigrants part 1. On the Horizon 2001, 9, 1–6.
3. Bennett, S.; Maton, K.; Kervin, L. The 'digital natives' debate: A critical review of the evidence. Br. J. Educ. Technol.2008, 39, 775–786.
4. Chin, E.; Felt, A.P.; Sekar, V.; Wagner, D. Measuring user confidence in smartphone security and privacy. In Proceedings of the Eighth Symposium on Usable Privacy and Security, Washington, DC, USA, 11–13 July 2012.
5. Felt, A.P.; Ha, E.; Egelman, S.; Haney, A.; Chin, E.; Wagner, D. Android permissions: User attention, comprehension, and behavior. In Proceedings of the Eighth Symposium on Usable Privacy and Security, Washington, DC, USA, 11–13 July 2012.
6. Kelley, P.G.; Consolvo, S.; Cranor, L.F.; Jung, J.; Sadeh, N.; Wetherall, D. A conundrum of permissions: Installing applications on an android smartphone. In Proceedings of the International Conference on Financial Cryptography and Data Security, Kralendijk, Bonaire, 27 February–2 March 2012; Springer: Berlin/Heidelberg, Germany, 2012; pp. 68–79.
7. Mylonas, A.; Gritzalis, D.; Tsoumas, B.; Apostolopoulos, T. A qualitative metrics vector for the awareness of smartphone security users. In Proceedings of the International Conference on Trust, Privacy and Security in Digital Business, Prague, Czech Republic, 28–29 August 2013; Springer: Berlin/Heidelberg, Germany, 2013; pp. 173–184.
8. Mylonas, A.; Kastania, A.; Gritzalis, D. Delegate the smartphone user? Security awareness in smartphone platforms. Comput. Secur. 2013, 34, 47–66.
9. Ophoff, J.; Robinson, M. Exploring end-user smartphone security awareness within a South African context. In Proceedings of the 2014 Information Security for South Africa, Johannesburg, South Africa, 13–14 August 2014.
10. Parker, F.; Ophoff, J.; Van Belle, J.P.; Karia, R. Security awareness and adoption of security controls by smartphone users. In Proceedings of the 2015 Second International Conference on Information Security and Cyber Forensics (InfoSec), Cape Town, South Africa, 15–17 November 2015.
11. Markelj, B.; Bernik, I. Safe use of mobile devices arises from knowing the threats. J. Inf. Secur. Appl. 2015, 20, 84–89.
12. Markelj, B.; Zgaga, S. Comprehension of cyber threats and their consequences in Slovenia. Comput. Law Secur. Rev.2016, 32, 513–525.
13. Sheila, M.; Faizal, M.; Shahrin, S. Dimension of mobile security model: Mobile user security threats and awareness. Int. J. Mob. Learn. Organ. 2015, 9, 66–85.
14. Ariu, D.; Bosco, F.; Ferraris, V.; Perri, P.; Spolti, G.; Stirparo, P.; Vaciago, G.; Zanero, S. Security of the Digital Natives. 2014. Available online: https://ssrn.com/ abstract=2442037 (accessed on 13 October 2016).
15. Norman, G. Likert scales, levels of measurement and the "laws" of statistics. Adv. Health Sci. Educ. 2010, 15, 625–632. [PubMed]

CHAPTER 4

Investing in Cybersecurity: Insights from the Gordon-Loeb Model

Lawrence A. Gordon, Martin P. Loeb, Lei Zhou

Robert H. Smith School of Business, University of Maryland, College Park, USA

ABSTRACT

Given the importance of cybersecurity to the survival of an organization, a fundamental economics-based question that must be addressed by all organizations is: How much should be invested in cybersecurity related activities? Gordon and Loeb [1] presented a model to address this question, and that model has received a significant amount of attention in the academic and practitioner literature. The primary objective of this paper is to discuss the Gordon-Loeb Model with a focus on gaining insights for the model's use in a practical setting.

Keywords: Economics of Information Security, Cybersecurity Investment

1. INTRODUCTION

Cybersecurity is a critical concern in today's interconnected digital world.[1] In fact, the major industrialized countries throughout the world now consider having a cybersecurity strategy as a national policy priority (OECD, 2012). Private sector organizations are equally concerned about cybersecurity, especially in light of the recent wave of high visibility corporate breaches.[2]

Given the importance of cybersecurity to the survival of an organization, a fundamental economics-based question that must be addressed by all organizations is: How much should be invested in cybersecurity related activities? Since organizations have finite resources, answering the above question essentially involves a resource allocation decision. As with all resource allocation decisions, a good starting place is to assess the costs and benefits (i.e., conduct a cost-benefit analysis) associated with cybersecurity investments.[3] That is, as long as the expected incremental benefits exceed the expected incremental costs from additional cybersecurity investments, an argument can be made for increasing additional cybersecurity investments. Mathematically speaking, the optimal level of cybersecurity investment for an organization is at the point where the expected marginal investment costs equal the expected marginal benefits derived from the investment.[4] Finding this optimal level of investment in cybersecurity is, in essence, the Holy Grail that is at the heart of economic aspects of cybersecurity.

One approach for deriving an organization's optimal level of cybersecurity investment, which has received a significant amount of attention in the academic and practitioner literature, is referred to as the Gordon-Loeb Model (hereafter as the GL Model).[5,6] The primary objective of this paper is to discuss the GL Model, as well as some extensions to the model, with a focus on gaining insights for utilizing the GL Model in a practical setting. In other words, although the GL Model is based on a set of mathematical formulas, the focus of this paper is to show that the intuition underlying the model's key components, as well as the model's findings, provide a useful framework for guiding organizations in their quest for deriving the right level of cybersecurity investment.

The remainder of this paper will proceed as follows. In the next (second) section of the paper, we briefly review the GL Model. The third section of the paper focuses on the general insights that can be gleaned from the model. Based on these insights, the third section of the paper also provides a set of steps an organization could take to derive its optimal (or at least an appropriate) level of cybersecurity investment. In the fourth section of the paper, we provide a hypothetical example of how an organization can derive its cybersecurity investment level. The example also illustrates how to allocate the investment to various information sets, based on the steps provided in the third section of the paper. The fifth, and final, section of the paper provides some concluding comments, as well as limitations of the GL Model and directions for future research.

2. THE GORDON-LOEB MODEL

Following is a brief review of the GL Model. This review is based, in large part, on the original article [1] . The purpose of this review is to highlight the key components of the model, as well as the key findings from the model. The emphasis will be placed on the intuition underlying the model's key components and findings, rather than the mathematics upon which the model is based. As such, this paper builds and expands upon [7] . We refer readers interested in delving more deeply into the mathematics of the model to the original article [1] , as well as the follow-up article [8] .

The basic assumptions of the GL Model are as follows. First, information sets of organizations are vulnerable to cyber-attacks. This vulnerability, denoted as v ($0 \leq v \leq 1$), represents the probability that a breach to a specific information set will occur under current conditions.[7] Second, if an information set is breached, the value of the information set represents the potential loss (i.e., the cost of the breach) and can be expressed as a monetary value, denoted as L. Thus, vL is equal to the expected loss prior to an investment in additional cybersecurity activities.[8] The third assumption is that an investment in cybersecurity, denoted as z, will reduce v based on the productivity of the cybersecurity investment. The GL Model defines s(z,v) as the security breach probability function. More to the point, s(z,v) specifies a function that considers the productivity of different levels of cybersecurity investments and thus provides a revised measure of the probability of an information set's vulnerability after some level of investment in cybersecurity. The model also assumes that s(z,v) is twice continuous differentiable and strictly convex, such that the benefits from increasing cybersecurity investments related to a specific information set are increasing at a decreasing rate (i.e., there are positive, but diminishing, returns to additional investments in cybersecurity), as shown in Figure 1. The model also assumes that, if some level of vulnerability exists for an information set, additional investments in cybersecurity can bring the probability of a cybersecurity breach arbitrarily close to zero, but not zero.

Given the assumption discussed above, the GL Model can be summarized in a set of equations published in [1] (p. 444). These equations are provided below, where the price of a unit of investment, z, is equal to one. In these equations, the expected benefits of an investment in information security are denoted as EBIS, and are equal to the reduction in the firm's expected loss attributable to the extra security, as shown in Equation (1) below:

$$EBIS(z) = [v - S(z,v)]L \tag{1}$$

EBIS is written above as a function of z, since the investment in information security is the firm's only decision variable (v and L are given parameters for a given information set). The expected net benefits from an investment in information security are denoted ENBIS, and equal EBIS less the cost of the investment, as shown in Equation (2a) below:

$$ENBIS(z) = [v - S(z,v)]L - z \quad (2a)$$

Maximizing Equation (2a) is equivalent to minimizing the expression shown in (2b) below:

$$S(z,v)L + z \quad (2b)$$

The interior maximum at $z^* > 0$, is characterized by the first-order condition for maximizing Equation (2a), and is shown in Equation (3) below:

$$-s_z(z^*,v)L = 1 \quad (3)$$

From (3) above, it becomes clear that the optimal level of investment, z^*, in cybersecurity takes place where the expected marginal benefits from investing in cybersecurity is equal to the expected marginal cost of the investment.[9] This optimal level of cybersecurity investment is illustrated in Figure 1, at the investment level of z^*. Gordon and Loeb [1] were able to show that, for two broad classes of security breach probability functions, the optimal level would not exceed vL/e, or roughly 37% of the expected loss from a security breach, vL.[10] Following [1] (p. 451), this result is expressed as:

$$z^*(v) < (1/e)vL \quad (4)$$

Mathematicians Lelarge [10] [11] and Baryshnikov [12] generalized the results of the GL Model to a large array of security breach probability functions. When the assumptions given by Lelarge are violated, the papers of Willemson [13] and Hausken [14] provide demonstration that the 37% rule does not always hold. Gordon et al. [8] extended the GL Model to include externalities, which were not considered in the original model. The revised formulation for the social optimal cybersecurity level considering externalities, denoted as z^{SC}, is shown as the inequality (5) below (see page 8 of [8]):

$$z^{SC}(v) < (1/e)\left[1 + \left(L^{E}/L^{P}\right)\right] vL^{P} \qquad (5)$$

where L^P represents the private costs to an organization from a cybersecurity breach, L^E represents the cost of externalities to other organizations and individuals from the firm's cybersecurity breach, and L^{SC} represents the total social costs from the firm's cybersecurity breach (i.e., $L^{SC} = L^P + L^E$).[11]

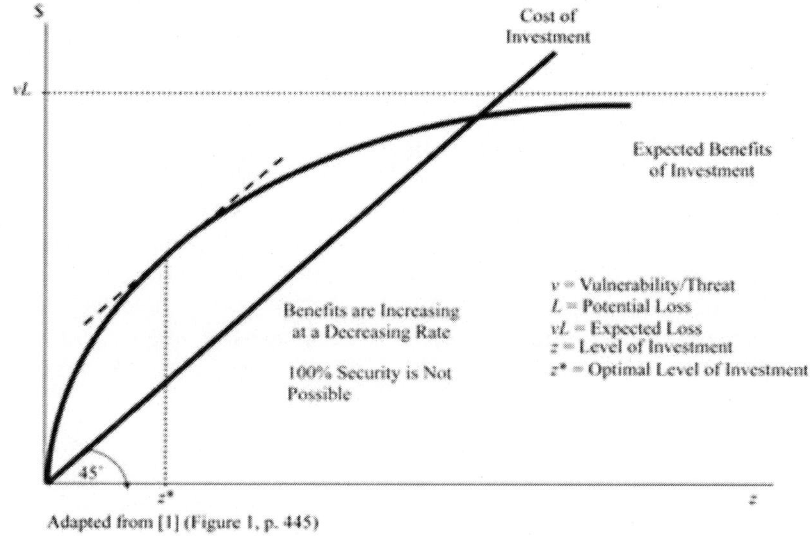

Figure 1. Benefits and costs of an investment in cyber/information security.

3. INSIGHTS FROM THE GORDON-LOEB MODEL

The GL Model provides important insights regarding the way organizations can derive the appropriate level of cybersecurity investment and the best way to allocate this investment to various information sets. These insights are most clearly seen in terms of the model's key components and findings.

There are three key components underlying the way the model derives the optimal amount to invest in cybersecurity. The first component has to do with identifying and valuing an organization's information sets. The value of each set represents the potential loss if the information set were to experience a cybersecurity breach. Since segmentation of information sets (via network segmentation) is an important part of cybersecurity, firms are likely to have several sets of information to protect.[12]

Once the organization's information sets are established and valued, the second component of the GL Model has to do with estimating the vulnerability to a cybersecurity breach for each information set. That is, the organization should estimate the probability that an information set will experience a cybersecurity breach, for each information set identified.

The third underlying component of the GL Model has to do with the way and investment in cybersecurity will reduce an information set's vulnerability to a cybersecurity breach (i.e., the productivity of a cybersecurity investment). Estimates of this investment productivity will likely vary for different information sets, depending on the specific concerns surrounding a particular information set. In addition, as noted above, it is assumed that the benefits from cybersecurity investments will increase at a decreasing rate. In fact, the finding from the GL Model that firms should generally invest an amount that is less than, or at most equal to, roughly 37% of the expected loss that could result from a cybersecurity breach to an information set is directly related to the assumption that the benefits of cybersecurity investments increase at a decreasing rate. Furthermore, it is assumed that cybersecurity investments are allocated to cybersecurity activities based on the declining marginal productivity of the investments.

Another finding from the GL Model is that the optimal level of cybersecurity investment does not always increase with the level of vulnerability.[13] For example, it may pay for a firm to spend more on protecting an information set that has a medium level of vulnerability than one with a high level of vulnerability. Again, this general finding is linked to the productivity of incremental investments in cybersecurity.

The above discussion can be summarized in terms of four steps. These steps are provided below. In the next section, an example based on these steps is provided.

Step 1: Estimate the Value, and thus the potential Loss (L), for each information set in the organization. This step recognizes the fact that the value of the information sets that you wish to protect may differ. It also recognizes the fact that segmentation of information sets is an important component of cybersecurity.

Step 2: Estimate the probability that an information set will be breached based on the information set's vulnerability. This step explicitly considers the likelihood of a successful cyber-attack on each information set within the organization.

Step 3: Create a grid of all possible combinations of steps 1 and 2 above. The grid resulting from this step should range from Low Value/Low Vulnerability to High Value/ High Vulnerability information sets. Each cell in the grid represents the expected loss (L) without any additional investment in cybersecurity. The expected loss is, in essence, the potential benefit (i.e., cost savings) from additional cybersecurity investments. The net benefit (discussed in the previous section of this paper) would be the difference between the benefit and investment cost.

Step 4: Derive the level of cybersecurity investment by allocating funds to protect the information sets, subject to the constraint that the incremental benefits from additional investments exceed (or are at least equal to) the incremental costs of the investment. Assuming the investments in cybersecurity will have different levels of productivity based on the levels of vulnerability associated with each information set, the optimal amount to invest in different information sets will vary and not necessarily increase with increases in the vulnerability of an information set. Furthermore, it is assumed that cybersecurity investments are allocated to cybersecurity activities based on the declining marginal productivity of the investments.

4. EXAMPLE FOR DERIVING THE INVESTMENT LEVEL

In this section we provide a hypothetical example of how to use the insights from the GL Model discussed in the previous section of this paper. Our approach is to focus on the four steps of the GL Model that were discussed at the end of the previous section of this paper.

The example is for the GLZ Corporation, a U.S. based manufacturing company that sells its products in several different countries as well as throughout the U.S. The company, which manufactures household appliances, has two manufacturing plants in the U.S. and one manufacturing plant in Canada.

The GLZ Company has 12,000 employees, of which 10,000 are located in the U.S. and another 1500 in Canada. The remaining 500 employees are located in a variety of other countries (i.e., other than the U.S. or Canada) and focus largely on sales related issues. The GLZ Company has patents for several of its products and has several key business partners in the U.S., Canada, China, and throughout Europe. These business partners are from various points throughout the entire supply chain, including firms that provide raw materials to the corporation and large retail stores that sell its final products.

In an effort to protect its information from cybersecurity breaches, as well to minimize the impact of any cybersecurity breaches that actually occur, the firm has been diligent in segmenting its databases (i.e., data segmentation). For example, the firm has segmented its databases according to countries, business partners, customer related information, employee information and market-based data. In addition, highly sensitive data (e.g., employee social security numbers) is separated from less sensitive data (e.g., employee names). In deriving the firm's overall level of spending, the firm has decided to follow the four steps suggested by the GL Model that were outlined in the previous section of this paper. The firms' approach to following these steps is provided below.

Step 1: For each separate database, what the company refers to as information set, the GLZ Corporation provides a rough estimate of the total monetary value in terms of the maximum potential loss (L) the firm would incur if the information set were to experience a cybersecurity breach. Stated in terms of dollars, the firm decides on five discrete categories of monetary value for purposes of grouping information sets. These five categories are $20 million, $40 million, $60 million, $80 million, and $100 million. Different information sets could have the same monetary value. These dollar values represent the potential maximum cost of a cybersecurity breach and include such things as the cost of detecting and correcting the cybersecurity breach. In addition, these dollar values include the potential costs associated with lost revenues due to the negative reputation effects of a cybersecurity breach and the potential costs associated with successful lawsuits filed against the firm as a result of the breach.

Step 2: The next step in GLZ Corporation's decision process for deriving its cybersecurity spending is to assign a vulnerability (v) score to each information set. For illustrative purposes, it is assumed that GLZ corporations assign a vulnerability score of either 0.2, 0.4, 0.6 or 0.8 to each information set. Assigning an information set a score of 0.2, 0.4, 0.6 or 0.8 means there is a 20%, 40%, 60% or 80% probability that the information set will incur a cybersecurity breach. The fact that more than one information set has the same monetary value, or in essence the same potential loss (L), does not mean that these sets will have the same probability of being breached. In fact, the probability that an information set may experience a breach is largely the result of the anticipated threats confronting the information set. In other words, the firm has decided that each level of potential loss (L) should be further segmented into the four categories of vulnerabilities (v), thereby generating 20 distinct information sets (i.e., five categories of information value, with each of these categories sub-divided into four categories of vulnerabilities).

Step 3: The next step is for the firm to develop a grid that combines steps 1 and 2 above. This grid, which is illustrated in Figure 2, contains the expected losses that the firm would incur due to a cybersecurity breach of a particular information set. The cells in yellow in Figure 2 represent the medium level of expected losses (i.e., low: $vL < 30$, medium: $69 \geq vL \geq 30$, high: $vL \geq 70$).

Step 4: The final step in the process of deciding on how much to spend on cybersecurity activities is to consider the cost-benefit aspects of investing additional funds on each information set. Executing this step requires knowledge of the potential expected loss from each information set, but it also requires knowledge of the expected productivity derived from incremental cybersecurity investments. Using $1 million as our unit of investment in cybersecurity activities, this step essentially comes down to asking the following question: How much costs will our firm save, in terms of the reduction in the expected loss, by investing another $1 million on the information set under consideration? If the firm expects to save more (less) than $1 million by making an additional $1 million investment, it pays (does not pay) to make the additional investment from a strictly economics perspective. At a cost savings of $1 million, for an additional $1 million cybersecurity investment, the firm would be indifferent to investing the additional funds.

As noted above, knowledge concerning the productivity of additional investments is crucial to carrying out the fourth step. Although there is no absolute procedure for obtaining this knowledge, we do know (or at least assume) that rational economic decision makers will generally select investment opportunities in descending order. In other words, they generally select investment opportunities that provide the largest benefits first and work their way down to opportunities with smaller benefits. This approach will essentially result in a curve that exhibits increasing benefits at a decreasing rate (as shown in Figure 1, and discussed the previous section of this paper). Exactly how the benefits curve will look is, however, a function of the specifics productivity of the investment.

For purposes of completing the fourth step in our example, we assume that investments are generally more productive where the vulnerabilities are greatest. This assumption is based on the general principle that "low hanging fruit" are easiest to pick and therefore provide a higher return for a given level of effort.

Accordingly, for our three levels of vulnerabilities (i.e., the probability that a cybersecurity breach will occur), we assume that the productivity of adding an additional $1 million dollars of investment (z) will reduce the vulnerabilities [i.e., $s(v,z)$] from Equation (3) above by $v/(1 + z)$ where v is 0.2, $v/(1 + z)^2$ where v is 0.4 or 0.6, and $v/(1 + z)^3$ where v is 0.8. Figure 3 provides a summary of the reduction inv due to incremental investments of the 1st million, 2nd million, 3rd million, and 4th million dollars for each level of v shown in that figure. Applying the results shown in Figure 3 to Figure 2, we can derive Figures 4-7. The cells in yellow in Figures 4-7 represent the information sets where it is still beneficial to make the next $1 million additional investment. Figure 8 illustrates the final amounts to invest to all of the information sets.

As shown in Figure 8, the maximum amount to invest in any information set is $4 million (the final cells in yellow). More to the point, for the cells showing that z is $1 million means that after investing $1 million, the savings from the next $1 million investment would be less than the investment cost. A similar interpretation would apply for the other cells shown in Figure 8 (i.e., where $2 million, $3 million, $4 million are invested, the savings from investing the next $1 million would be less than the investment cost).

As shown in Figure 8, the only information sets to receive a $4 million in investment in our hypothetical example would be the information sets with a $100 million value (or potential loss, L) and a vulnerability (v) score of 20% and 60%, and the information set with an $80 million value and a vulnerability score of 60%.

Value of Information Sets (in $ Million)*

Vulnerability/Threat**		Low	Medium		High	
		20	40	60	80	100
Low	20%	4	8	12	16	20
Medium	40%	8	16	24	32	40
Medium	60%	12	24	36	48	60
High	80%	16	32	48	64	80

*Value of Information = Potential Loss (L)
**Vulnerability/Threat = V

Low: $vL < 30$
Medium: $69 \geq vL \geq 30$
High: $vL \geq 70$

Figure 2. Expected loss from information security breach.

	Low Productivity		Medium Productivity		High Productivity	
z	*s*(*z*,*v*)	Reduction in breach Probability	*s*(*z*,*v*)	Reduction in breach Probability	*s*(*z*,*v*)	Reduction in breach Probability
0	*v*		*v*		*v*	
1	*0.500v*	*0.500v*	*0.250v*	*0.750v*	*0.125v*	*0.875v*
2	*0.333v*	*0.167v*	*0.111v*	*0.139v*	*0.037v*	*0.088v*
3	*0.250v*	*0.083v*	*0.063v*	*0.049v*	*0.016v*	*0.021v*
4	*0.200v*	*0.050v*	*0.040v*	*0.023v*	*0.008v*	*0.008v*
5	*0.167v*	*0.033v*	*0.028v*	*0.012v*	*0.005v*	*0.003v*
6	*0.143v*	*0.024v*	*0.020v*	*0.007v*	*0.003v*	*0.002v*

Low Productivity: $s(z,v)=v/(1+z)$ for Low Vulnerability/Threat
Medium Productivity: $s(z,v)=v/(1+z)^2$ for Medium Vulnerability/Threat
High Productivity: $s(z,v)=v/(1+z)^3$ for High Vulnerability/Threat

Figure 3. Productivity of investments in cybersecurity.

Vulnerability/Threat		Value of Information Sets (in $ Million): Low	Medium		High	
		20	40	60	80	100
Low	20%	2.00	4.00	6.00	8.00	10.00
Medium	40%	6.00	12.00	18.00	24.00	30.00
	60%	9.00	18.00	27.00	36.00	45.00
High	80%	14.00	28.00	42.00	56.00	70.00

Figure 4. Cost savings from 1st million dollar investment.

Value of Information Sets (in $ Million)

Vulnerability/Threat		Low: 20	Medium: 40	Medium: 60	High: 80	High: 100
Low	20%	0.67	1.33	2.00	2.67	3.33
Medium	40%	1.11	2.22	3.33	4.44	5.56
Medium	60%	1.67	3.33	5.00	6.67	8.33
High	80%	1.41	2.81	4.22	5.63	7.04

Figure 5. Cost savings from 2nd million dollar investment.

Value of Information Sets (in $ Million)

Vulnerability/Threat		Low: 20	Medium: 40	Medium: 60	High: 80	High: 100
Low	20%	0.33	0.67	1.00	1.33	1.67
Medium	40%	0.39	0.78	1.17	1.56	1.94
Medium	60%	0.58	1.17	1.75	2.33	2.92
High	80%	0.34	0.69	1.03	1.37	1.71

Figure 6. Cost savings from 3rd million dollar investment.

Vulnerability/Threat		Value of Information Sets (in $ Million): Low	Medium		High	
		20	40	60	80	100
Low	20%	0.20	0.40	0.60	0.80	1.00
Medium	40%	0.18	0.36	0.54	0.72	0.90
	60%	0.27	0.54	0.81	1.08	1.35
High	80%	0.12	0.24	0.37	0.49	0.61

Figure 7. Cost savings from 4th million dollar investment.

Vulnerability/Threat		Value of Information Sets (in $ Million): Low	Medium		High	
		20	40	60	80	100
Low	20%	<2M	<3M	3M	<4M	4M
Medium	40%	<3M	<3M	<4M	<4M	<4M
	60%	<3M	<4M	<4M	>4M	>4M
High	80%	<3M	<3M	<4M	<4M	<4M

Figure 8. Investment amounts.

The actual GL Model is based on continuous investment functions, whereas our hypothetical example is based on discrete investments of $1 million per unit of investment. Consequently, the investment level in our example would only serve as an estimate of the mathematical optimum. In any case, comparing, the numbers in Figure 8 with 1/e times the numbers in Figure 2, cell by cell, the example is consistent with the GL rule that the optimum investment is less than 37% of the expected loss.[14]

5. CONCLUDING COMMENTS

Today's interconnected digital world has changed the way organizations, as well as people, operate and interact. Indeed, we now live in a world that many describe as an on-demand economy (i.e., a marketplace that allows consumer demands for goods and services to be immediately met via digital communication through various sorts of electronic devices). This new kind of economy has created a business model that is characterized by large quantities of information being instantaneously transmitted through cyberspace and stored in a variety of electronic devices.[15]Although the interconnected digital world has resulted in many benefits to businesses, as well as individuals, a downside of this new way of operating and interacting with one and other has been the rapid growth of cybersecurity breaches. Unfortunately, no organization is immune to potential cybersecurity breaches. Accordingly, organizations need to make investments in cybersecurity activities so as to protect themselves against the negative effects of cybersecurity breaches. A fundamental question that must be asked, in this regard, is: How much should be invested in cybersecurity related activities?

The primary objective of this paper has been to explain how the GL Model can be used by organizations to answer the above question. More to the point, this paper has provided a conceptual explanation, accompanied by an illustrative example, of how organizations can use the Gordon-Loeb Model to derive their appropriate level of cybersecurity investment.[16]

As shown in this paper, despite its mathematical underpinnings, the GL Model provides an intuitive framework that lends itself to an easily understood set of steps for deriving an organization's cybersecurity investment level. These steps are: (1) to estimate the value, and thus the potential Loss ( ), for each information set in the organization; (2) to estimate the probability that an information set will be breached based on the information set's vulnerability; (3) to create a grid of all possible combinations of steps 1 and 2 above; and (4) to derive the level of cybersecurity investment by allocating funds to protect the information sets, subject to the constraint that the incremental benefits from additional investments exceed (or are at least equal to) the incremental costs of the investment.

Although not a panacea, the use of the intuitive framework provided by the GL Model can go a long way toward improving the decision process concerning the way organizations should go about deriving the appropriate amount to invest in cybersecurity activities. In other words, it provides a rational economic procedure for firms to use in deciding on how much to spend on cybersecurity, in light of the cybersecurity risk confronting the firm.

As with the use of all approaches to making investment decisions, there are limitations to using the above noted framework for deciding on the appropriate level of cybersecurity spending. The two most prominent of these limitations are the imprecision associated with valuing the information sets the firm is trying to protect and estimating the probability that a given information set will be breached. However, we believe that making rational, systematic, estimates of these factors is preferred to some completely ad hoc approach to considering them in the process of making cybersecurity investment decisions. Another limitation of the approach described in this paper for deriving the cybersecurity investment level is the fact that it does not explicitly consider the qualitative aspects of the decision. However, as noted in footnote 3 of this paper, we believe that using a cost-benefit approach (which is essentially what the GL Model does) is a good starting place for cybersecurity investment decisions. Qualitative concerns (e.g., the organizations overall strategy toward cybersecurity spending) should be considered before making any final decisions regarding the appropriate level of spending on cybersecurity activities. In other words, we strongly believe that economic models should be used as complement to, not as substitute for sound business judgment.

Future research could extend the analyses provided in this paper in several ways. For example, a simulation varying the number of information sets, the values for each information set, and the probabilities associated with potential breaches, could be conducted to assess the sensitivity of the resource allocation decision to these factors. In addition, the quantitative analysis provided by the GL Model could be combined with qualitative techniques for considering cybersecurity investment decisions. In this latter regard, the probabilities of potential cybersecurity breaches used in step 2 from the GL Model could be derived via an AHP (Analytical Hierarchy Process) technique, which allows for consideration of both quantitative and qualitative issues (see [18]).

REFERENCES

1. Gordon, L.A. and Loeb, M.P. (2002) The Economics of Information Security Investment. ACM Transactions on Information and System Security, 5, 438-457.
2. Gordon, L.A. and Loeb, M.P. (2006) Managing Cybersecurity Resources: A Cost-Benefit Analysis. McGraw-Hill, Inc., New York.
3. Rue, R. and Pfleeger, S.L. (2009) Making the Best Use of Cybersecurity Economic Models. IEEE Security & Privacy, 7, 52-60.
4. Cavusoglu, H., Mishra, B. and Raghunathan, S. (2004) A Model Evaluating IT Security Investments. Communications of the ACM, 47, 87-92.
5. Wang, J., Chaudhury, A. and Rao, H.R. (2008) Research Note—A Value-at-Risk Approach to Information Security Investment. Information Systems Research, 19, 106-120.
6. AFCEA (Armed Forces Communications and Electronics Association) Cyber Committee Report (2013) The Economics of Cybersecurity: A Practical Framework for Cybersecurity Investment.
7. Gordon, L.A. and Loeb, M.P. (2011) You May Be Fighting the Wrong Security Battles. The Wall Street Journal, 26September.
8. Gordon, L.A., Loeb, M.P., Lucyshyn, W. and Zhou, L. (2015) Externalities and the Magnitude of Cybersecurity Underinvestment by Private Sector Firms: A Modification of the Gordon-Loeb Model. Journal of Information Security, 6, 24-30.
9. Gordon, L.A., Loeb, M.P. and Zhou, L. (2011) The Impact of Information Security Breaches: Has There Been a Downward Shift in Costs? Journal of Computer Security, 19, 33-56
10. Lelarge, M. (2012) Coordination in Network Security Games. In: Greenberg, A.G. and Sohraby, K., Eds., INFOCOM, IEEE, 2856-2860.
11. Lelarge, M. (2012) Coordination in Network Security Games: A Monotone Comparative Statics Approach. Selected Areas in Communications, IEE Journal, 30, 2210-2219.
12. Baryshnikov, Y. (2012) IT Security Investment and Gordon-Loeb's 1/e Rule. Workshop on Economics and Information Security, Berlin. http://weis2012.econinfosec.org/papers
13. Willemson, J. (2006) On the Gordon & Loeb Model for Information Security Investment. The Fifth Workshop on Economics of Information Security (WEIS), University of Cambridge.http://www.econinfosec.org/archive/weis2006/docs/12.pdf
14. Hausken, K. (2006) Returns to Information Security Investment: The Effect of Alternative Information Security Breach Functions on Optimal Investment and Sensitivity to Vulnerability. Information Systems Frontiers, 8, 338-349.
15. Gordon, L.A., Loeb, M.P., Lucyshyn, W. and Zhou, L. (2015) The Impact of Information Sharing on Cybersecurity Underinvestment: A Real Options Perspective. Journal of Accounting and Public Policy, 34, 509-519.
16. Gordon, L.A., Loeb, M.P., Lucyshyn, W. and Zhou, L. (2015) Increasing Cybersecurity Investments in Private Sector Firms. Journal of Cybersecurity, 1, 3-17.
17. Tanaka, H., Matsuura, K. and Sudoh, O. (2005) Vulnerability and Information Security Investment: An Empirical Analysis of e-Local Government in Japan. Journal of Accounting and Public Policy, 24, 37-59.
18. odin, L., Gordon, L.A. and Loeb, M.P. (2008) Information Security and Risk Management. Communications of the ACM, 51, 64-68.

NOTES

[1]For purposes of this paper, the term cybersecurity refers to "the protection of information that is accessed and transmitted via the Internet or, more generally, through any computer network" ([2] , p. 10).

[2]For example, in the U.S., Target Corporation had a major cybersecurity breach in 2013 (see Target's 10-K Report for the fiscal year ending February 1, 2014, filed with the U.S. Securities and Exchange Commission at: https://corporate.target.com/annual-reports/pdf-viewer-2013?cover= 6725&parts= 6727). JP Morgan Chase & Co. had a major cybersecurity breach in 2014 (see JP Morgan Chase & Co.'s 8-K Report filed on October 2, 2014 with the U.S. Securities Exchange Commission at https://www.sec.gov/Archives/edgar/data/19617/000119312514362173/d799478d8k.htm).

[3]Although a cost-benefit analysis is a good starting place with all resource allocation decisions, other considerations, many of which cannot be quantified, also need to be considered when deciding on how much to spend on cybersecurity activities. More will be said about this point in the final section of this paper.

[4]The primary benefits from cybersecurity investments are the cost savings associated with cybersecurity breaches that were prevented due to investments. In some cases, however, cybersecurity investments could give an organization a competitive advantage that could generate additional benefits (e.g., increased revenues).

[5]While there is a broad literature dealing with cybersecurity investment (e.g., [3] - [5]), the Gordon-Loeb Model has been referred to as the "gold standard" for deriving the amount an organization should invest on cybersecurity activities (e.g., see the Appendix A to [6]).

[6]In the original paper, the GL Model used the term information security rather than cybersecurity. Given the role of the Internet in storing and transmitting information in today's interconnected digital economy, for purposes of this paper the two terms are considered to be interchangeable.

[7]Our notion of vas the probability that a successful breach will occur incorporates the threat that an information set will experience a cybersecurity attacked, as well as the information set's vulnerability to a cybersecurity breach. Gordon and Loeb [1] , for expositional ease, held the threat probability constant so that v was interpreted as the probability of a breach for the given threat level.

[8]Although not explicitly stated in [1] , the GL Model considers situations where some level of cybersecurity already exists within an organization and

thus the concern is to derive the optimal amount of additional investment. Also, note that measuring the actual loss from a cyber breach is not straightforward. One method used in the cybersecurity economics literature is to measure the effect of the announcement of a cyber breach on the value of firm's stock. See, for example, [9] .

[9]It should be recalled that the price of a unit of z is equal to 1. Furthermore, there are no fixed costs in the analysis, which means that that the investment curve in Figure 1 is a 45-degree linear curve.

[10]Although the GL Model discussedL andz in terms of a single breach, the analysis would be the same if L andz were considered in terms of multiple breaches within a single time period without corrections after each breach (i.e., ignoring the interdependencies among breaches during the time period).

[11]Because the socially optimal level of investment is greater than the private optimal level of investment, additional incentives are required to motivate private firms to invest more. Gordon et al. [15] [16] look at ways in which private firms may be incentivized to increase their cybersecurity investments.

[12]Each set would contain various pieces of information based on some logical grouping of the relevant information for an organization.

[13]Tanaka et al. [17] empirically verify this finding.

[14]The maximum to invest (in increments of one million) were shown in Figure 8, for all cells with the exception of the two cells (row 4, column 5) and (row 4, column 6). Although we did not carry out the example to the point where one would not wish to invest more for those information sets, one can easily carry out the example to verify that one would want to invest less 37% of the expected loss for those sets as well.

[15]The term cyberspace refers to the environment where digital communication, especially via the Internet and other computer networks, takes place.

[16]For a 3-minute-and-34 second YouTube video providing a succinct overview of the Gordon-Loeb Model, see: https://www.youtube.com/watch?v=cd8dT0FuqQ4.

CHAPTER 5

Sending Safety Video over WiMAX in Vehicle Communications

Jun Steed Huang [1], Oliver Yang [2,*] and Funmilyo Lawal [2]

[1]*Suqian College, Jiangsu University, Jiangsu 223800, China*

[2]*Computer Communication Network Research Lab, School of Electrical Engineering and Computer Science, University of Ottawa, 161 Louis Pasteur, Ottawa, ON K1N 6N5, Canada*

ABSTRACT

This paper reports on the design of an OPNET simulation platform to test the performance of sending real-time safety video over VANET (Vehicular Adhoc NETwork) using the WiMAX technology. To provide a more realistic environment for streaming real-time video, a video model was created based on the study of video traffic traces captured from a realistic vehicular camera, and different design considerations were taken into account. A practical controller over real-time streaming protocol is implemented to control data traffic congestion for future road safety development. Our driving video model was then integrated with the WiMAX OPNET model along with a mobility model based on real road maps. Using this simulation platform, different mobility cases have been studied and the performance evaluated in terms of end-to-end delay, jitter and visual experience.

Keywords: vehicular camera; WiMAX; Ad-hoc; video; modeling

1. INTRODUCTION

By virtue of its versatility and utility convenience, mobile wireless communication has now become a necessity. Over the years, different technologies have been developed to increase the data rate in wireless networks. Technologies like WiMAX (Worldwide Interoperability for Microwave Access) and 3G/4G devices can support 100 Mbps per data channel [1], and LTE (Long Term Evolution) can go as high as 200 Mbps. This has created room for different types of applications in different specialties. Users have come to desire not only the basic voice functionality of wireless devices, but also different forms of mobile multimedia communication. Video communication via a VANET (Vehicular Adhoc NETwork) is one such application.

Safety and environmental issues in managing existing road networks have become one of the greatest concerns of both the automotive industry and governmental bodies. A VANET consisting of clusters of vehicles communicating with each other and also with roadside infrastructure can provide a solution to these issues. Telematics for the telecommunications of safety information is one major tool used in this area. Progressively, sharing real-time driving video traffic among vehicles and roadside infrastructures would be the next natural step to enhance the safety feature. One motivation of this paper comes from the statistics of road traffic fatalities which shows that there were 44,192 accidental deaths in Canada from the years 2000 to 2004 [2]. California, with a population of 37 million people reports, one million vehicle accidents each year [3]. The increase in road traffic volume over the years has led to a concern among researchers to create an effective, efficient and safe automotive environment with the help of video communication. One example is the "smart car" in the state of Nevada which, as a first step towards this goal, uses video to assist hands-free driving.

Unlike other wireless environments that are mostly stationary or under slow motion, transmitting video signals in a VANET poses more challenges to resolve. Electromagnetic interferences such as those from engine electronics, from Additive White Gaussian Noise, or those due to weather conditions can affect the QoS (Quality of Service) as seen by a wireless user. Since the topology is constantly changing, a vehicle could move out of sight to cause an outage in data transmission. Obstacles along LOS (Line of Sight) communication are another major reason to cause an outage. Finally, packet loss due to data traffic congestion will definitely make things worse, and communication disruptions may become inevitable.

Understanding the characteristics of real-time video would allow the design of efficient real-time transmission/transportation protocols to address the above challenges and to allow us to carry out further study. There has been continuous and extensive work on VBR video from various specific video sources, (e.g., from video conferencing cameras, web cameras, broadcast TV or HDTV [4,5], and non real-time processing/storage of data taken from the cameras installed in a real public safety law enforcement car system [6]. However, images from a vehicular camera have higher activity around all edges than the middle portion. This is very different from a normal camera constructed for stationary scenarios, and can be addressed/utilized in the design of video communication. So far, we are not aware of any comprehensive study related to real-time driving video traffic originating in the actual vehicle camera, such as GV1500 from GenieView Inc. [7]. Furthermore, all these prior arts focus on the modeling of separate and independent video traffic before the wireless networks, and there is no work done on the video model of the traffic coming out of a wireless link, as will be needed in our later study of highway video through a VANET.

Higher layer protocols are usually required to support various video applications. TCP (Transport Control Protocol) [8] and UDP (User Datagram Protocol) [9] for real-time transportation of video have been shown to be ineffective. As is further reviewed in Section 2, TCP is best used for lossless data transfer as it ensures packet delivery by its support of packet retransmission. This poses a problem for real-time traffic, as there is no time for retransmission [10]. UDP is better for video traffic, but unfortunately still cannot guarantee real-time and loss performance. RTP (Real-Time Transport Protocol) [11] offers an alternative but has other shortcomings that need to be remedied, as is discussed later. Most of the aforementioned transport algorithms and the traffic control protocols below are built on top of TCP and have only been tested in wired networks. Quite often, packets in a wireless network are stored in a buffer waiting for proper bandwidth allocation before they can be delivered. In real-time communication, a poorer quality can be tolerated, but delay should be reduced to a minimum if not eliminated.

Since a large volume of video traffic can easily consume the limited wireless bandwidth, there is a need to throttle the video traffic for better bandwidth utilization and avoid congestion. Traffic/Congestion control can provide smooth throughput and high link utilization for real-time data. Of the two main types of traffic congestion, control in computer networking (reviewed in Section 2), implicit congestion control does not provide smooth throughput for real-time and low link utilization. Also, the control is based on packet loss-events which are not a big concern for real-time traffic as mentioned earlier. Explicit congestion control of traffic from the router node becomes impractical in a high speed when the CPU cannot catch up with the updating of events arising from changing driving speeds. Consequently, a different protocol (desirably with a low complexity) should be considered.

Finally, it is safer and more cost efficient to simulate possible solutions than actual field experimenting with highway driving. An effective VANET simulation platform/model has pertinent importance in research and industry to emulate a real world situation. One major challenge is the development of an effective platform that can bring all issues described earlier under one simulation model. A major issue is the integration of an effective mobility model that considers vehicle-to-vehicle interaction and vehicle-to-infrastructure interaction along with the full functionalities of a communication device capable of effective receiving, processing and transmitting capabilities. Although there has been work on creating a similar platform, e.g., [12,13,14], little work has been done on certain issues related to video streaming from vehicle camera such as the characterization of the data traffic (e.g., its unique packet size distribution) and the behavior under different driving conditions (e.g., highway *vs.* local).

In view of the above and others reviewed in the related work in the next section, we seek to create a robust platform for effective VANET simulation, one that can provide an environment to test, develop and deploy effective communication protocols that would enhance real-time communication of video information from vehicle camera. As forerunners, in this paper, we would like to:

1) create a real-time camera video model under VANET conditions;
2) integrate a realistic VANET mobility model to test the testbed at various speeds;
3) integrate a practical algorithm to survive network congestion;
4) demonstrate the capability of such a platform.

To achieve the above objectives, we first adopt the protocol architecture of our simulation platform as shown in Figure 1. We need to adopt appropriate protocols for the lower layers consisting of the Data Link Layer and the Physical Layer, and the upper layers for the remainder. After a comparison of several viable technologies for the lower layers such as the pros and cons as reviewed in Section 2, we have chosen WiMAX (Worldwide Interoperability for Microwave Access) for its cost-effective approach that can provide a high data rate that can satisfy the needs of our vehicle camera users (low latency and high coverage) at high speed at an affordable cost. It is scalable because its uses OFDMA (Orthogonal Frequency Division Multiple Access) to allow flexible frequency re-use. It implements full MIMO (Multiple-Input and Multiple-

Output) which is good for mobile applications by enhancing timely information delivery to save lives and improve quality of life. In view of the complexity problem in implementing an explicit congestion control mechanism in the upper layers to control streaming traffic from driving video in real-time, our present approach is not to "cure" congestion but to "survive" congestion. We propose to reduce the compression rate of the video packets once congestion is detected in the network. We use the RTCP (Real Time Control Protocol) to feed such information back to the sender.

Layer 4	Sub-layer 3	RTCP
	Sub-layer 2	RTP
	Sub-layer 1	Data Traffic Controller
Layer 3	Sub-layer 2	UDP
	Sub-layer 1	IP
Layer 2	Sub-layer 2	Data Link Port
	Sub-layer 1	Data Link Buffer
Layer 1	Sub-layer 2	Physical Port
	Sub-layer 1	Physical Transponder

Figure 1. Overall Architecture.

The next step is to find a simulation tool and a realistic vehicular mobility model for integration. Of the few available network simulation languages such as Qualnet and NS-2, we have chosen OPNET because it has different wireless models including WiMAX. It has a rich set of video streaming protocols, and it provides a good framework, which allows us to integrate our mathematical driving video model effectively so that we can explore different scenarios during network traffic congestion. After searching, we have also decided that VanetMobiSim [15,16] is the only VANET mobility model that would allow the output code generator to be modified in order to generate and output traces useable by other simulators. Consequently, we can integrate its traces into our existing OPNET model using the open-loop approach.

To support the experiments from our simulation platform, we need to use realistic driving video traffic streams. Since we do not have an additional ACE [17] license to support the feeding of life data into our OPNET simulator, we shall generate our traffic streams based on a model established from real video traffics transported over wireless networks.

Not only do we want to use this model to generate traffic traces quickly, we would also use it to alter the traffic characteristic under different scenarios later on without having to recapture traffic traces from life experiments, which can be both costly and time consuming.

The contributions of this paper lie in the following:

1) The design and implementation of a theoretical but more realistic driving video model than the traditional video model. To the best of our knowledge, there is no comprehensive study related to real-time driving video traffic originated from a vehicle camera, nor any work done on the modeling of the video traffic from the vehicular camera system through the wireless link;
2) The integration of a VANET mobility model with such a driving video model to provide a practical VANET simulation platform for the evaluation of video traffic under different scenarios;
3) The design and implementation of a practical traffic controller for driving video over RTP applications.

The rest of the paper is organized as follows. Section 2 discusses existing works related to our research, especially their deficiencies. Section 3 discusses the network operations and models used in our testbed. To illustrate the procedure of modeling the driving video traffic in VANET, Section 4 presents an example of the trace collection and stochastic analysis of the trace. We then discuss the OPNET simulation of different scenarios and evaluate their performance in Section 5.

2. RELATED WORKS

Below are works related to our research work on VANET testbeds, models for driving video, as well as the lower and upper layer protocols.

2.1. VANET Testbeds

There have been practical implementations of VANET testbeds. For example, a testbed was implemented to extract H.263 video streams through an ADSL (Asymmetric Digital Subscriber Line) gateway to an SQL server in the Internet [18]. A prototype testbed [19] using a handheld device with an Android operating system was presented for data-intensive application. While these approaches are effective, their hardware implementations are expensive and do not allow quick and easy changes to adapt to various industry scenarios and implementation of special safety applications. Video cameras make up a key component in VANET due to their ability to aid navigation safety and give road users and relevant authorities a precise and clear image of the traffic conditions when necessary. Intel Corporation has decided to lead the development of a video camera system on board of a car [20]. Others include the CogniVue system [21]. Since a special high-definition camera can pump into the network to degrade network performance and video quality, this has been a key concern in VANET design. Solving this issue will unlock the power of driving camera video applications.

In light of the outlined efforts, one of the major focuses of VANET research is the creation of an effective simulation platform that can integrate a network simulator with a realistic vehicular traffic simulation model. Unlike other network environments, VANET mobility has a peculiar and unique nature due to the randomness of human behavior. One classification groups vehicular traffic under four models [22]: Submicroscopic, Microscopic, Mesoscopic and Macroscopic. It is important to choose a realistic mobility model to correspond to each one. An open-loop integration approach and a closed-loop integration approach have been discussed for the integration of the network model with a VANET mobility model. Although there has been other work on creating a similar platform (e.g., [12,13,14]), to the best of our knowledge, there is hardly any work on the characterization (e.g., the packet size distribution) of video data streaming from the vehicle camera and the behavior under different data traffic conditions. The closest work is on UAV video [23], but this was done from an image process perspective. A broad view of the state-of-the-art mobility models adapted for VANETs was discussed [24], which also provided a detailed survey and comparison of mobility models. However, it only provides a model for data transmission and not for video transmission. Such a model needs to consider other factors (like the physical layer communication mechanism and control algorithms in the application layer for real-time video streaming) for effective VANET simulation. Note that a model or a tool may be good for one aspect/feature, but their integration is necessary to model an effective safety solution.

2.2. Modeling Driving Video Traffic

Unlike other forms of multimedia traffic (like data, voice and video), driving video traffic has a very dynamic stochastic nature. Different statistical studies [25] have already revealed that the inherent characteristics (not source nor codec specific) of Variable Bite Rate (VBR) video traffic is the LRD (Long Range Dependence) which has a significant impact on the queuing performance and characterization of video traffic [25,26]. Video traffic modeling over wireless has been studied extensively. There is work on the video traffic modeling in a wireless environment with emphasis on the streaming video over WiMAX networks [27]. The I, P and B frames have been modeled separately according to their types, and a fixed pattern is used to combine these frames together to form the GOP (Group of Picture) [27,28,29]. A video traffic model was obtained using a trace generated with a fixed frame inter-arrival time [30]. All these prior works have focused on the separate and independent video modeling before the traffic is fed into the wireless networks, and none has considered the video model after coming out of the wireless link. Such modeling is required in our highway video forwarding through a number of consecutive cars. Furthermore, we are not aware of any comprehensive study related to real-time driving video traffic originated from the actual vehicle camera, such as GV1500 made by GenieView Inc. [7]. Due to the very driving nature, such a video has an even higher statistical fluctuation that is very hard to control. More discussions can be found in further sections such as 1 and 4.3.

2.3. Lower-Layer Protocols for VANET

VANET applications can be supported through V2R (Vehicle-TO-Roadside) and V2V (Vehicle-to-Vehicle) communications. IEEE 802.11 (WiFi) [31], IEEE 802.16 (WiMAX) [32] and DSRC (Dedicated Short Range Communications) [33] technologies can be used in this model of communication.

With the DSRC standard, OBU (OnBoard Units) placed at each vehicle can send or receive data to or from roadside units (RSUs), as well as communicating directly with each other. There are thus many potential applications in urban areas (or in populated countries in Europe or Southeast Asia) such as forward collision warning, electronic parking payments, and approaching emergency vehicle warning [34]. Unfortunately, it is limited in its distance coverage and may not cover rural areas in countries like Canada and USA. Furthermore, DSRC is based on 802.11a and cannot handle high-speed mobility while maintaining an acceptable data rate. It also does not have the ability to hand over connections at high speed, which is essential for high-speed motion and cannot support high data rates. DSRC would probably be integrated with other technologies for use in the VANET if it is to be universally accepted. For example, we can use dynamic spectrum sharing for both DSRC and WiMax to improve the communication efficiency as well as the spectrum utilization to cover both the rural and urban areas [35].

WiMAX (Worldwide Interoperability for Microwave Access) [14] is a 4G equivalent technology that enables the delivery of last mile wireless broadband access. WiMAX technology [36] can eliminate the use of cables and can save costs when used in remote and rural areas. The technology is scalable and has a flexible frequency re-use scheme because it uses OFDMA (Orthogonal Frequency Division Multiple Access) technology. Unlike DSRC, WiMAX was designed to handle high data rates. It implements full MIMO (Multiple-Input and Multiple-Output) which is good for mobile and car applications by enhancing timely information delivery to save lives and improve quality of life. Many laptops in USA already support such interface even though its present price is still high. With the above observations on and comparison work with DSRC, one sees that WiMAX is the most cost effective approach by providing a data rate that can satisfy the needs of our vehicle camera users (low latency and high coverage) at high speed and at an affordable cost.

2.4. Higher-Layer Protocols for VANET

Real-time data has an arrival deadline to reach its destination, or else its information is no longer valid. TCP (Transport Control Protocol) [8] and UDP (User Datagram Protocol) [9] are protocols that have been used but were found to not be effective. TCP is best used for lossless data transfer as it ensures packet delivery via packet retransmission. This poses a problem for real-time traffic, as there is no time for retransmission [10]. UDP can be better for real-time video traffic, but unfortunately still cannot guarantee real-time nor loss performance because their flows cannot adapt their rates to congestion control mechanisms at the router [37]. They can provide the best-effort service only since they have no priority over TCP flows. Congestion will also lead to random jitter and eventually loss, as video traffic becomes prevalent in f VANET. Although in theory TCP or UDP should not be affected by the choice of physical transmission medium such as fiber optic, they often perform poorly in wireless networks [38] because their design and implementations were carefully optimized for wired networks. RTP (Real-time Transport Protocol) [11] is a protocol designed for end-to-end real-time transport of video traffic. However, it does not take many performance issues into account including channel outage, traffic congestion, the effect of overheads in uncast/multicast applications, and the end-to-end delay in a mobile environment.

In summary, the behavior of these protocols in the VANET environment are quite different as the wireless medium is prone to interference from forces of nature and manmade effects, and the situation is exacerbated when transmitter and/or receiver are moving.

Various works have been conducted on congestion control in wired environments [39], wireless environments [40,41] and VANET [42].

Congestion control protocols can also be classified into two main types [39]: window-based and rate-based. The window-based congestion control algorithms adjust the window-size according to the level of congestion detected in the network. Algorithms like RED (Random Early Detection) [43], its TCP variants (like Tahoe [44], NewReno [45]), and AIMD (Additive Increase and Multiplicative Decrease) [44] fall under this category. This type of control usually corresponds to the implicit congestion control as congestion is detected at the receiver through the observation of events such as packet loss. So many algorithms in this type of approach can cause fluctuations in the source sending rates, thus producing non-smooth throughput and low link utilization. These are evidently not effective for real-time video streaming [46] in practice.

Rate-based congestion control algorithms on the other hand, allow each source in the network to directly adjust its sending rate based on the congestion notification received, and usually from the router that knows the state of the network. TFRC (TCP Friendly Rate Control) [47] and API-RCP (Adaptive PI Rate Control Protocol) [39] falls under this category. API-RCP presents an effective way to calculate the source-sending rate based on the queue deviation, and is quite capable of producing steady queue length to meet the bandwidth requirement of a driving camera. The rate-based control usually makes use of explicit congestion control due to the nature of its operation (as a contrast to the implicit control discussed earlier). However, this type of control may not be effective when a vehicle is moving because constant updating of the router due to motion consumes more CPU resources. Eventually, the CPU cannot catch up with the events arising from high speeds.

Most of the algorithms mentioned previously are built on top of TCP and have only been tested in wired networks. In wireless networks, delay is caused mostly by wireless interference rather than network congestion. Quite often packets are stored in a buffer waiting for proper bandwidth allocation before they can be delivered. As mentioned earlier, in real-time traffic, buffering (which incurs delay) is not wanted. We can tolerate a poorer quality, but delay is unacceptable. Explicit congestion controls handle traffic more effectively by calculating the flow throughput at the router node, and then smoothing throughput and achieving high link utilization in real-time. However, they are not effective for practical purposes. This is because they are more tedious to implement; one has to take time to load the controller on every router, and constant updates are required for the router of the moving vehicles. This consumes more CPU resources, and may not catch up with the driving speed. We thus consider an automatic predictive source control to assist the explicit control. When P frames start piling up, we drop the even frames first and then the odd frames without waiting for control commands to come from the base station.

3. OPERATION AND MODELS OF THE VANET TESTBED

Figure 2 is a simple example of a VANET consisting of cars communicating their video information with each other and with the Internet (IP cloud) via the RSUs, which can be implemented as a WiMAX-enabled Base Station. The server is to forward or to archive the streaming video from the cars. Each car is acting as a WiMAX Mobile Station (MS) capable of receiving, processing and forwarding data to the destination and consequently to the backhaul network via the WiMAX Base Station.

In our VANET testbed, each vehicle has the ability to communicate with any neighboring vehicles. Depending on the nature of the messages, they will either stay within the VANET or exit the backhaul network via the RSU. For instance, tailgating, collision and braking (from preceding cars) are warning messages that can remain within the VANET network, while detailed regional weather forecast, notification of traffic jams and collision are usually exchanged between the backhaul network and the VANET. In many video applications we envision that video messages from the vehicular camera are usually required to be forwarded from the point of interest (such as traffic congestion, road block, and accidents) to a control center in the backhaul network to aid various parties (such as traffic personnel, emergency agents, insurance companies) to respond to the situations more effectively. We shall refer to these types of traffic as "safety driving video" or simply "safety video" later on.

To implement a testbed for the study safety driving video traffic among vehicles, we shall provide the operations at different layers as well as different models used in the testbed in the following two sections.

3.1. Protocol Layers and Operations

With reference to Figure 2, an RSU (BS 1 or BS 2) has the capability of handling up to N cars simultaneously. Each car/MS (Mobile Station) is associated with the closest RSU in the coverage area. Safety driving video packets are routed and given priority by recognizing their service class and scheduling type. For example, the silver service class and the rtPS (real-time Polling Service) scheduling [17] are assigned to the safety video. For each service class, there is a maximum sustainable traffic and reserved traffic rates (e.g., 384 kbps for the silver service class). Each video packet arriving from the higher layer at a MS is expected to be within a size limit. Otherwise, it will be segmented before being encapsulated into a PDU (Protocol Data Unit) with the appropriate header information, and then transmitted. For example, video packets longer than 1500 B must be segmented to fit the SDU (Service Data Unit) for the silver (safety video) service.

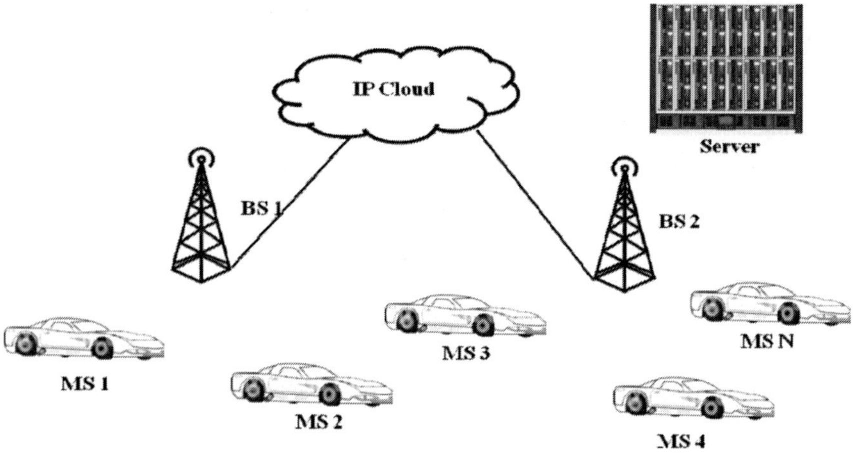

Figure 2. Vehicle camera network operation.

The driving video traffic is generated from the application layer when an MS wants to transmit. We use UDP (User Datagram Protocol) as the transport layer protocol to cater for the end-to-end delivery of packets. RTP (Real Time Protocol) is used at the application layer to combat the possible unreliability in UDP. RTP is a real-time streaming protocol designed for streaming audio and video. In conjunction, we use RTCP (Real-Time Transport Control Protocol) for controlling, signaling and quality service monitoring.

The unique nature of driving video traffic is due to its burstiness and persistence. The size of each frame generated is dependent on its previous frames and the driving speed, and the exact time a frame is generated or received also depends on previous frames and road conditions. These two correlated uncertainties contribute to the high variable bit rate characteristics of driving video communication. Coupled with the real-time and accuracy requirement of our safety applications, these factors pose a modeling challenge. Of the various video codec schemes that have been developed e.g., MPEG2/4, H.263/4, we have chosen the MPEG4 video compression for our vehicular cameras and studied its traffic model for our testbed. Our array-based MPEG encodes the input video into three types of compressed frames called the I, the Peven, and the Podd frames. I-frames are compressed using intra frame information only. Peven or Podd-frames are coded similarly but with motion compensation for even or odd lines respectively according to the previous I frame. Depending on the vehicle driving speed or congestion condition, Peven and Podd frames may be dropped alternatively, or altogether. In general, I–frames are 10 times bigger than P frames. After coding, the frames are arranged in a deterministic order, which is called GOP (Group Of Pictures). This pattern is not specified hence different coders may use different patterns for subsequent GOPs. A common feature, however, is that all video frames exhibit strong time dependent correlations among themselves. This gives rise to different queuing statistics and time-dependent rush hour congestion phenomenon. This is the subject of streaming traffic analysis and modeling later on, as well as the need for a delicate adaptive congestion controller design.

Each car has a WiMAX capability in transmitting (and receiving) at the physical and the MAC layers after receiving the safety video packets from (and delivering to) the network layer. At the MAC layer, the destination address is examined and the nearest RSU is chosen to handle the request. The packet is sent to that RSU, and further forwarded accordingly. In our investigation, the IP cloud in Figure 2 can be set to its default values and acts a router. The server is configured to accept packets generated by our simulator.

As suggested above, we shall use mobile WiMAX technology at the physical and MAC layers for our VANET. This is a revision of the fixed WiMAX IEEE 802.16e-2005 standard [48] and it provides functionalities such as Base Station handoffs, MIMO (Multiple Input Multiple output) transmit/receive diversity, and scalable FFT (Fast Fourier Transform) sizes. Table 1lists some of the more relevant features. Although WiMAX can support high data rates providing up to 128 Mbps downlink and 56 Mbps uplink using its MIMO antenna techniques, we shall use SISO antenna technique, which supports up to 1 Mbps uplink and downlink. We use the WiMAX MAC architecture to define service flows that can be mapped into gradual IP sessions to enable end-to-end IP based QoS.

Of the two-duplexing modes allowed by mobile WiMAX, we shall use the TDD (Time Division Duplexing) mode (the other is FDD (Frequency Division Duplexing) mode) as done in most deployments in order to accommodate the asymmetric VANET traffic. That is, our uplink traffic requires more bandwidth than the downlink, due to the uploading of safety (not downloading entertainment video that the other researchers are focused on) driving video traffic to the RSU. The WiMAX technology uses OFDMA frames for multiple users to receive data from the BS at the same time thereby increasing bandwidth utilization. The frames are structured into UL (Uplink) and DL (Downlink) subframe as shown in Figure 3 [49].

Table 1. IEEE 802.16e characteristics.

Sub-layers 2	Standard	IEEE 802.16e–2005
	Multiplexing	OFDMA
	FFT size	Scalable (512, 1024, 2048, *etc.*)
	Duplexing mode	TDD
Sub-layers 1	Modulation scheme	QPSK, 16-QAM, and 64-QAM
	Subcarrier spacing	10.94 kHz
	Signal bandwidths	5, 7, 8.75, and 10 MHz
	Spectrum	2.3, 2.5, and 3.5 GHz

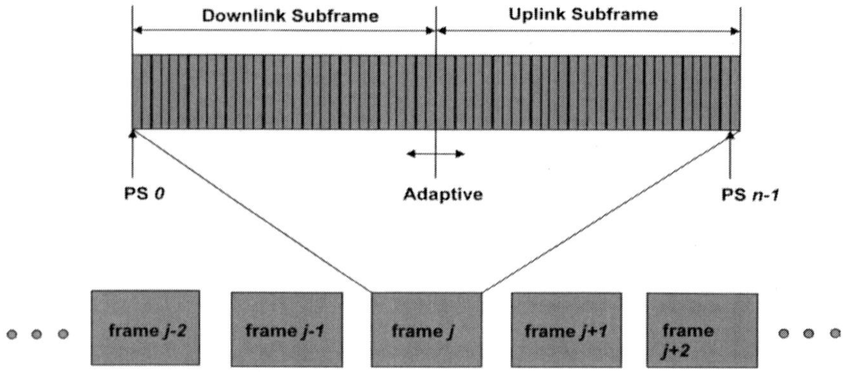

Figure 3. WiMAX frame structure.

All the MSes receive the frame control section of a DL subframe. The DL mapping field in the frame control section specifies the location and duration of DL data burst in the frame from a particular MS. Conversely; the UL mapping field specifies the location and number of time slots allotted in the frame for a particular MS to transmit its data on UL. All MSes listen to the control section in the DL frame, and receive or transmit data during the slots assigned to them by the BS [50]. As seen from Figure 3, this structure enables dynamic allocation of DL and UL resources to efficiently support asymmetric DL/UL traffic. A subchannel is allocated to each user there by reducing the channel interference in the frequency domain. OFDMA (Orthogonal Frequency Division Multiple Access) is the scheme used allowing multiple accesses to every user on our network.

3.2. Network Models

Figure 4 summarizes the various components of our Driving Video VANET OPNET model. It consists mainly of the video model and the VANET model. OPNET modeler then provides the platform for the communication model and allowed for the integration of the various components of the Driving Video VANET OPNET model and other considerations like the congestion controller. They are discussed in the following.

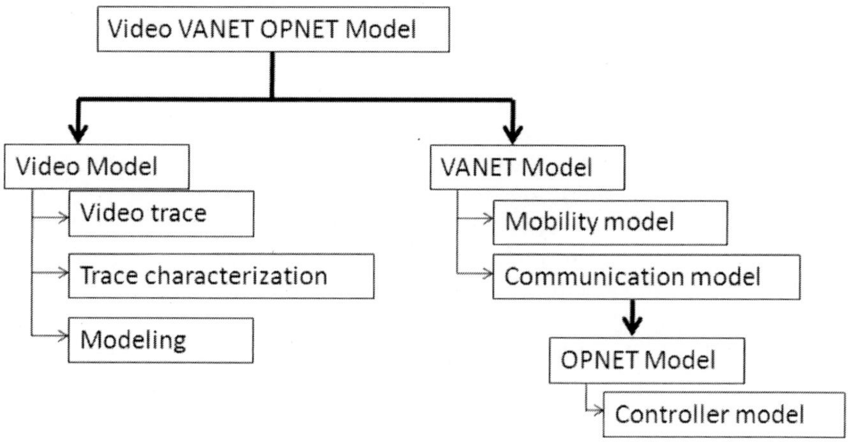

Figure 4. Driving video VANET OPNET Model structure.

3.2.1. VANET Model

The VANET model consists of the VANET mobility model for the movement of a vehicle, and a communication model for information exchange with neighboring MS and BS.

3.2.1.1. VANET Mobility Model

Of the four categories of VANET mobility models described previously, we adopted both the macroscopic and microscopic models to allow the modeling of vehicle-to-vehicle and vehicle-to-infrastructure interaction. VanetMobiSim is chosen to integrate these models in OPNET due to its flexibility to manipulate output files (by coding its output generator file to produce a format desired by our simulator). It also generates traces in a special Universal Trace Format [15] in the form of (*time node_id pos_X pos_Y velocity acceleration*) where *time* records the simulated time;

node_id identifies the specific node; pos_*X* and *pos_Y* provide the X and Y coordinates of the specific node at the given time respectively; and the *velocity*and *acceleration* show respectively the velocity at which the node moves and its acceleration at that time. With these capabilities, VanetMobiSim can model traffic lights, stop signs, human mobility dynamics and safe inter-distance management. It allows the integration of road topologies from databases such as GDF [51] or TIGER [52] to user-defined topologies as well as random topologies. VanetMobiSim provides a flexible platform in which the user can configure the shortest path during a trip based on the criteria of Dijkstra, road speed and road density. The trip can either be generated by random source-destination or according to activities [15].

3.2.1.2. RSU and Vehicle Communication Model

The RSU and the vehicles are the major communication nodes in VANET. Our RSU is a WiMAX BS. Each RSU is non-application-sensitive so that a wide range of information can be sent and received. Each vehicle has WiMAX receiving and transmitting capabilities to enable vehicle to vehicle and vehicle to infrastructure (RSU in our case) interaction. Table 2shows the basic essential characteristics of our model along with some typical settings.

Table 2. RSU parameters.

Parameter	Value	Unit
Physical Layer	IEEE 802.16e	NA
BS TX Power	5	W
Number of TX	SISO	NA
BS Antenna Gain	15	dBi
Minimum Power Density	−80	dBc
Maximum Power Density	−30	dBc
Link Bandwidth	20	MHz
Base Frequency	5.8	GHz
Physical Layer Profile	OFDM	NA

3.2.2. Driving Video Model

The driving video model is used to analyze and characterize the video trace of a live driving scene captured by a vehicle camera. The results are then used to generate models for use in our simulator for real-time driving video communication in a VANET environment. The implementation of this wireless driving video traffic model allows us to handle a wide range of burstiness in terms of packet inter-arrival and packet size arising from the unique nature of wireless video traffic during driving as mentioned above. A guideline to check the efficiency of a traffic model is, however, needed as to set a standard to be followed. Parsimony, analytic, relative accuracy, flexibility, implement ability and absolute accuracy are factors listed in [53] showing the engineering tradeoffs among different traffic models.

Using these factors on a scale of 1 to 3, 3 being the highest, Table 3 shows the settings of a few popular models including the FBM (Fractional Brownian Model) and the OPNET-emulated TCP traffic. By comparison, we adopt the Mini-Pareto model to be used later due to its overall score. In particular, we have taken a systematic approach in developing our mini-Pareto model. Driving video traffic traces were collected using the same camera used for a road test. In our testbed, we traced the frames from the receiver instead of the transmitter in order to correspond to video traveling from vehicle to vehicle, and through the RSU to the city's road monitoring center in a safety network. The traces were analyzed and stochastically represented and plugged into our simulation platform. A detailed discussion about these steps is presented in Section 4.

Table 3. Traffic model comparison.

Items	FBM	TCP Model	Mini-Pareto
Parsimony	3	1	2
Analytical	1	1	2
Flexibility	1	1	1
Implemental	2	1	3
Accuracy	2	3	2
Mobility	2	1	3

3.2.3. Traffic Controller Model

As discussed in Section 1 and Section 2.4, we only need to survive congestion to meet the QoS requirement of our real-time safety application scenario. This has given us the idea of reducing the complexity of the explicit control algorithm in order to cut down the CPU consumption when the vehicular camera is moving at higher speeds. Our careful study shows that reducing the sending bit rate is the key factor of success, and this can be achieved in two ways: dropping some frames (packets) or reducing quantization level per frame. There are different consequences and tradeoffs.

For driving video traffic, the drop pattern is very important to the quality of service as seen by user. Dropping just the even frames or just the odd frames is usually better than dropping both consecutively. The frequency of a drop can be a more critical factor than the percentage of drop. For instance, dropping 10 consecutive packets out of 100 packets is a 10% drop, which is the same as randomly dropping 1 out of 10 packets from a stream of 100 packets. However, the latter is more tolerable than the former in our system. Since there are many more P frames than I frames, we only drop P frames, first even then odd in our testbed. Thus we can use an automatic predictive source control to assist the explicit congestion control. That is, when P frames start piling up, we drop the P-frames by following a particular drop patter. For example, dropping the even frames first and then the odd frames without waiting for control commands to come from the base station. We can also set an upper limit of approximately 25% beyond which the video becomes less comfortable to watch (and may not satisfy customer expectations).

According to our industrial partners, changing the quantization level will be the next practical and cost-effective approach to reduce bit rate in terms of complexity and ease of deployment. We lower the quantization level when we use fewer coefficients from the coarse DCT (Discrete Cosine Transformation) algorithm, and thus reducing the packet size as well. Depending on the end-to-end delay, the receiver notifies the sender of the quantization level to use in encoding the subsequent video frames. This method will bring the total bit rate down to 50% of the original coding/sending rate. Beyond 50%, we need to drop the color components, thus leaving the video in its black-and-white mode.

In summary, the sending bit rate = frameRate*FrameSize which can be lowered by lowering one or both of the frame rate or frame size. There are tradeoffs between the two. Dropping packets (frames) will lower the frame rate while reducing the quantization level that will lower the resolution. The challenge in lowering the resolution is to keep the user experience/satisfaction high as long as possible, and various experiments have been conducted to find out the optimum point. Although our real GenieView camera has implemented in both methods in firmware to improve user experience, our OPNET model has chosen to drop the frames/packet only. This is reflected in Figure 5 and Figure 6 below where the called party collaborates with the calling party to determine the end-to-end delay based on how our controller uses one byte to notify the source to reduce its sending rate by dropping selected frames as discussed above. We also make use of RTP/RTCP at the application layer to provide an effective feedback mechanism.

Figure 5 depicts the video called party (receiver) procedure. Once the variables are initialized successfully, and a connection is established, data transmission can begin upon request. As soon as a frame is received, the frame count is incremented until it reaches the threshold value *p*. Once *p* is reached (e.g., $p = 5$ in our experiments), the frame count is reset to zero and the end-to-end delayassociated with the packet is checked. If the end-to-end delay is less than the threshold value *t* set by the end user on the receiving end (e.g., 100 ms), a default/designed rate of *x2* is fed back to sender via the ACK packet. Else a lower rate *x1* is returned instead. The *x1* value can be a default value such as half of *x2, or* computed according to some formula)

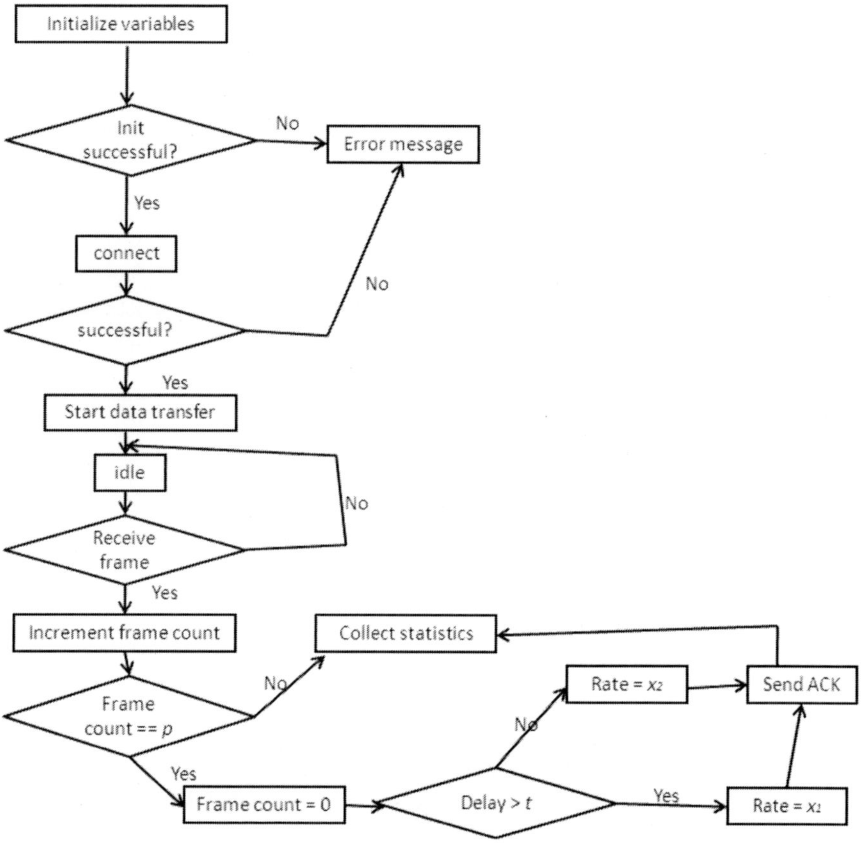

Figure 5. Video called party flow diagram with RTCP implementation.

Figure 6 shows the flow chart of the controller operation controller at the calling party manager (sender). Once the initialization process is successful, the video characteristics/properties are collected and a connection is established with the receiver. For every packet received, the algorithm checks if it is a control ACK packet. If not, the required statistics on packet type are collected and the packet is destroyed. If the packet is an ACK packet, the rate is retrieved and used to determine whether the sender should use the normal sending rate *x2* or the reduced rate of *x1*. The parameters for the call establishment are also updated according to the new value obtained.

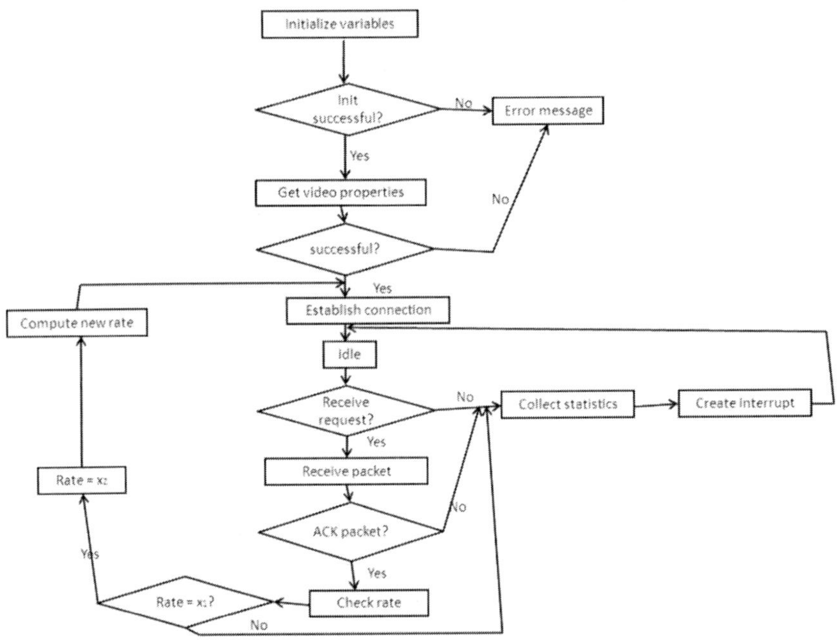

Figure 6. Video calling party flow diagram with traffic controller implementation.

4. EXPERIMENTAL SETUP

By collecting and studying video traces we want to come up with a model that can generate video traffic with characteristics as close to real life traffic as possible. This section discusses on the setup of our simulator testbed illustrates the trace collection process, its analysis and modeling.

This will set the stage for traffic generation and performance evaluation in the next section.

4.1. Trace Collection

As shown in the setup of Figure 7, we use the monitor to play a series of driving video clips at 10 min each from driving action movies. Each video was captured by a PTS (Pan Tilt Zoom) camera taken from a vehicle. The video is encrypted and highly compressed at a ratio of 250:1 at the transmitter block. Using one processor for each section of the screen, the 96-array processors in the transmitter block can achieve fast independent image processing. The transmitter sends the highly compressed encrypted video images to the control center via a wireless link using the non-licensed 900 MHz FHSS radio-band. Please note that 900 MHz is more affordable to us presently than WiMax and DSRC. Since they are all wireless links, they will all be subjected to the same noise sources, such as EM interference. We only need to obtain similar type of interference and their statistics first to verify our platform.

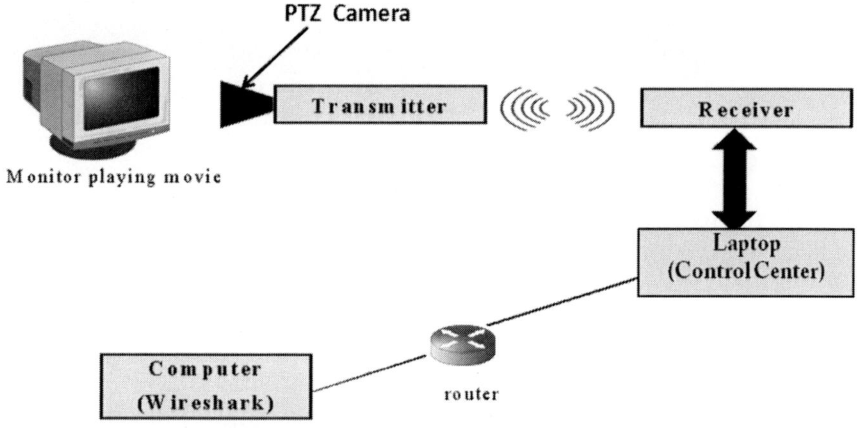

Figure 7. Setup for taking video traces.

The receiver block decodes and decompresses the received video frames and plays the image at the control center at about 20 fps. The control-center laptop and the receiver are connected using a RS232 serial port. The control center is then connected through a router to a computer hosting the packet trace-capturing tool—Wireshark™ [54]. Once the system is turned on, the computer with the Wireshark™ software is set to access the "capture" folder in the control center which would then stream the video via a router for trace capture.

A video trace (a record sequence of time and size of each arriving packet) captured by Wireshark is shown in Figure 8. Due to the loss and duplication that will change its original characteristics, this type of traffic trace is closer to those from our application in the real environments.

We want to characterize such a life driving video trace using proven stochastic processes and integrate it into a model that has as few parameters as possible but which can produce traces to match the real measurements.

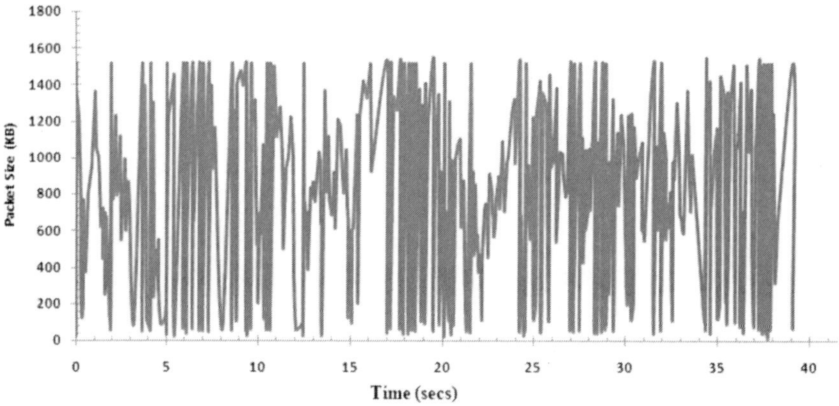

Figure 8. Live driving video trace.

In order to model video traces of different correlation/fractal characteristics arising from different activities, we collected traces playing three different video clips.

The video clips were chosen based on their activity rates. Actions like highway chasing movies (with a lot of movement on the edge of the screen/camera and hence unique variation in frame sizes), stories in a parking lot (with less and slower movement) and dramas on the street (on the average driving speed) were chosen.

We combine these clips to form a two-hour video trace (consisting of the time and size of each arriving frame), which is sufficient to characterize the fractal nature of the driving video traffic as well as the wireless channel effect.

4.2. Trace Analysis and Modeling

The next challenge is to analyze the trace and to create a driving video traffic model for traffic generation later. To verify the correlation of video frame and to obtain the modeling parameter, we obtain the frame-to-frame correlation of the video traffic. Figure 9 is an example using our video trace, which shows correlation is present up to 20 seconds apart.

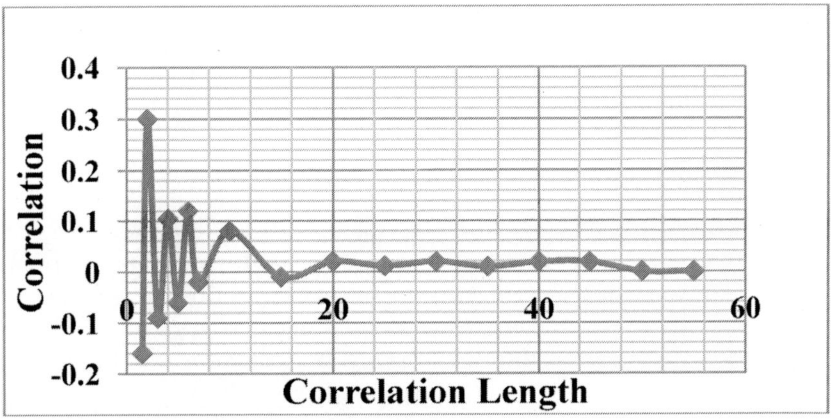

Figure 9. Correlation length of driving video.

We have used the Pareto distribution to characterize the general correlation of "action" video frame duration in wireless video streaming as well as the strong correlation between a cluster of byte loss and/or duplication caused by the air interface. The Pareto distribution is a long-tailed distribution with the following pdf (probability density function) $g(x)$ for the consecutive I-frame duration, where the edge activity level is high. Note that x here is not the frame size but the group length rather.

$$g(x) = c\alpha^{c} / x^{c+1} \qquad \alpha \leq x < \infty \tag{1}$$

where $\alpha > 0$ is the location parameter and $c > 0$ is the shape parameter. The location parameter value can be obtained from the mean correlation length E(x) of the trace where E(x) = cα/(α − 1). On the other hand, the shape parameter has to be obtained via the Hurst parameter. That is,

$$H = \frac{1}{2}(3-c) \Rightarrow c\text{=}3\text{-}2H \tag{2}$$

Note that the Hurst parameter is a useful parameter to reflect the invariance according to the entropy conservation property [26]. Since our video is highly compressed with little loss of information, the entropy/uncertainty remains the same. Therefore, we can determine c from Equation (2).

An indirect but easy way to obtain the Hurst parameter value is via the *slope* of the IDC (Index of Dispersion for Count) curve as a function of the level of aggregation. Here IDC is defined to be normalized variance of aggregated variables [26], and the level of aggregation refers the logarithm of the number of variables base-10 (therefore level-0 has 1 variable, level-1 has 10 variables, level-2 has 100 variables and so on). Mathematically, the relationship is given by [26]

$$H = \frac{1}{2}(1 + slope) \tag{3}$$

The slope of the curve is usually measured from the first point to the last point on the graph. For example, Figure 10gives the IDC of the video trace we use. From this figure, the slope is measured to be 0.33. Hence the Hurst parameter H is 0.67, and the shape parameter is $c = 1.66$.

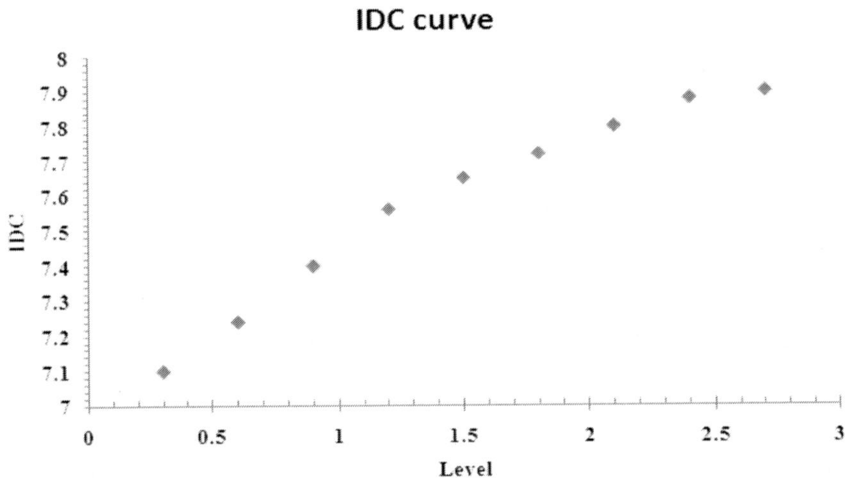

Figure 10. Entire trace IDC curve.

Once we obtain the pdf $g(x)$ to characterize the activity duration (via the correlation of I-frames), we shall next determine the packet (frame) size distribution $f(x)$, which is not Pareto in general. Furthermore, unlike the traditional video (e.g., video conference) with the moving part in the middle, our driving video has the moving part on the edge. Whereas the traditional video has a normal distribution in the middle for its packet size after 2D-DCT (Discrete Cosine Transform), the distribution for driving video is at the edge, which becomes very hard to model analytically to match the measured curve. After many trials, we have determined that an empirical model using nine mini-sources laid out in a grid can capture the distribution properly. The surrounding sources will capture the distribution of packets further away from the middle (edges and corners) which are usually moving and which produce large packets. The mini-sources closer to the center will capture the scenes in the middle which are relatively still and that produce smaller packets.

Figure 11 demonstrates the empirical analysis we performed on frame size (horizontal axis) of our traffic trace. For simplicity, here we are using the basic camera configuration, which produces one packet per frame. We use a tool called EasyFit™ [55] to obtain the pdf of the n = 9 video traces. The orange curve in the figure shows that the lognormal distribution is the best distribution to fit the given histogram data.

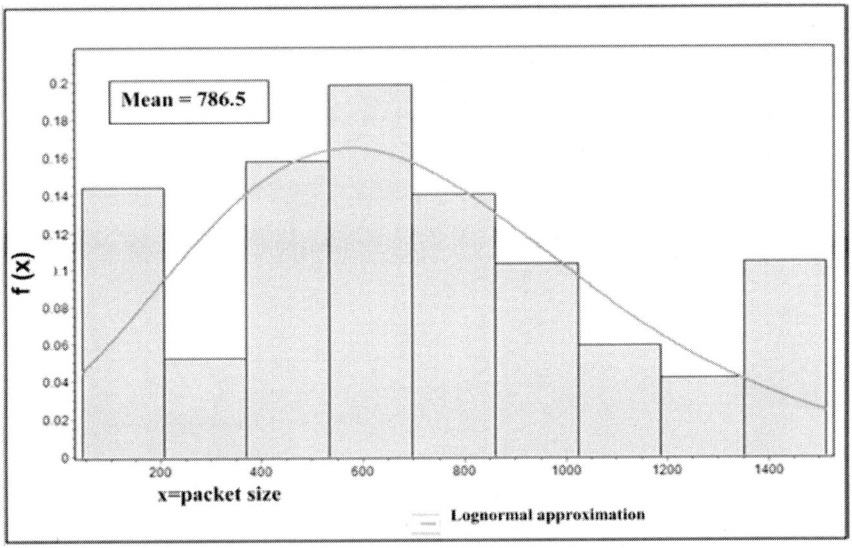

Figure 11. The pdf f(x) of video trace frames.

Finally, we want to determine the mean off-time of each source in order to model the inter-arrival time between each driving scene (such as trees or buildings on the road side). We have determined that the distribution is relatively memoryless, and therefore its pdf is exponential given by

$$a(x) = \begin{cases} \lambda e^{-\lambda x} & x > 0 \\ 0 & \text{otherwise} \end{cases} \quad (4)$$

where $1/\lambda$ is the mean inter-arrival time.

4.3. Driving Video Traffic Generation

Having obtained all the characterization parameters for traffic generation in previous sections, we are ready to emulate our wireless video traffic. Figure 12 shows the schematics of our wireless driving video traffic generation model from the superposition of *n* mini-sources [56]. Each mini-source represents a video traffic stream regulated by a switch to give a long-range dependency. We shall model the on-time switch by a Pareto distribution given in Equation (1) and the off-time by a Poisson process [an exponential distribution as given in Equation (4)].

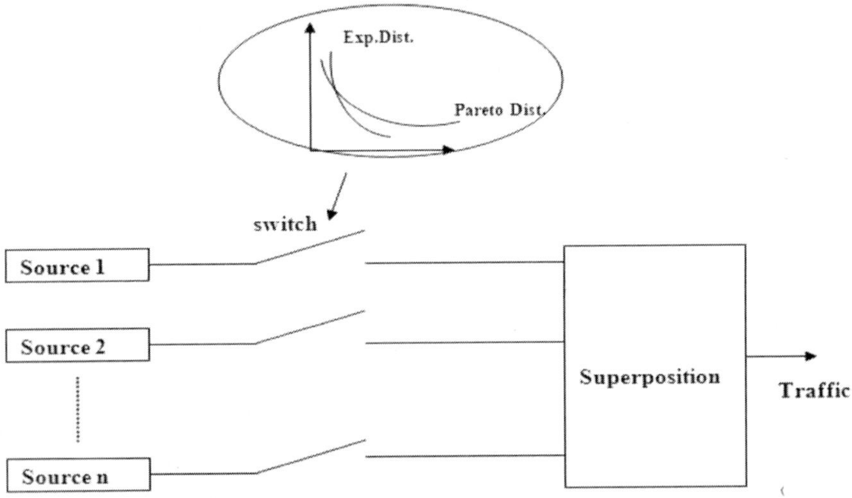

Figure 12. Model description for driving video traffic generation.

Table 4 shows an implementation of using nine mini-sources, each representing one of the 3 × 3 sectors of a camera screen. Here, frame duration is the transmission time of a frame (*i.e.*, frame size divided by bit rate). Assume the camera is facing the front when driving on a road.

The middle is usually relatively still when compared to the sides that see more activities. The left turns, right turns, and uphills or downhills are all different scenes that can lead to special packet size distributions. Big packet size is produced by a fast side view of the camera while the small size is produced by the almost still middle view. In the characterization of each mini-Pareto source in the table, we use the same shape parameter obtained from the Hurst parameter, but the location parameter is different for different packet size bin.

Table 4. Mini-sources with characterization values.

Bins	Mean Off-Time (ms)	Mean On-Time (ms)	Frame Duration (ms)	Mean Packet Size (Bytes)
mini1	7531	195	8	125
mini2	20603	453	18	290
mini3	6911	702	28	450
mini4	5515	960	38	615
mini5	7800	1216	32	779
mini6	10400	1472	39	943
mini7	18200	1723	46	1104
mini8	27300	1984	53	1272
mini9	10400	2232	59	1430

We have also tried other numbers such as $n = 3 \times 4 = 12$ mini-sources to match the horizontal and vertical ratio of the camera. As verified by our experiments, the more mini-sources created, the higher the accuracy. However, the computational complexity also increases due to the more parameters needed to match the trace. This is translated into longer simulation time. So we have chosen $n = 9$ for our model for the best trade-off we found between parsimony and accuracy.

Figure 13 shows the video traffic generated mini-pareto video traffic, which can be compared to the live video traffic in Figure 8. Although not exactly the same, one can verify the simulated traffic captures the level of fluctuation of the driving video traffic.

4.4. OPNET Simulation Setup

Table 5 gives the values of the general parameters we used in our simulations. The terrain has an area of 1300 × 1250 m. The relative position (x, y) on the terrain is used to integrate the VANET mobility model trajectories and obtain the initial positions of the vehicles. Vehicular environment for the path loss parameter is modeled according to the description in the "Radio Tx Technologies for IMT2000" white paper of the ITU [57]. The shadow fading standard deviation was set to

10 dB. The mobility pattern (trajectory) during the simulation is predefined using the *VanetMobiSim* discussed in Section 3.2.1.1.

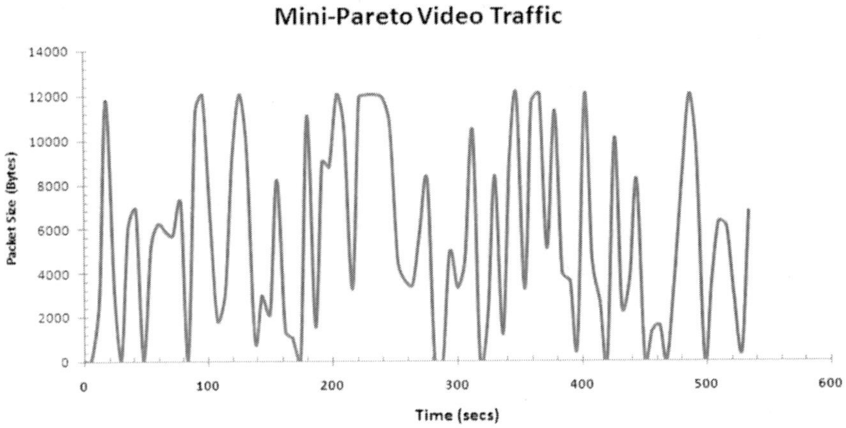

Figure 13. Mini-Pareto video traffic.

Table 5. Simulation parameters.

Parameter	Value	Note
Physical Layer	IEEE802.16e	WiMax
Data Rate	10	Mbps
BS Tx Power	5	W
MS Tx Power	1	W
Antenna Type	Omni-directional	Horizontal
BS Antenna Gain	15	dBi
MS Antenna Gain	9	dBi
Link Bandwidth	20	MHz
Modulation Scheme	16-QAM	Model
Path Loss Parameter	Vehicular Environment	ITU
Number of Vehicles	10	Cars
Mobility Model	VanetMobiSim	Open
Number of RSUs	2	Base
Simulated Time	3600	secs
Seeds	127	random
Terrain Dimensions	1300 × 1250	m^2

We have investigated different scenarios such as highway and residential, and have studied the effect of varying traffic congestion (density), wireless interference and traffic speed limits. Due to space limitation, we shall present the highway scenario for this paper.

In the highway scenario shown in Figure 14, we consider cars moving along the highway with a minimum speed of 60 km/h and a maximum speed of 100 km/h. There is one traffic light, just before the cars enter the highway. The car trajectories are represented by the white lines. We use the free space loss model for our pathloss. Unless otherwise stated, the following are assumptions taken throughout the paper for our simulation study:

1) WiMAX BS is a "stationary" node. This is required due to the limitation of our OPNET model and we need it to act as an intermediate node for packet forwarding to the destination;
2) OFDMA is used by the RSU and there is always a slot available for each SS sending video traffic once the SS is within the communication range;
3) No disruption in a communication channel once the node is allocated a dedicated channel;
4) No obstacle along the LOS between the RSU and the mobile cars to allow the simulation to monitor the vehicles within the range of the RSU;
5) Finite buffer size for each transmitter in order to be more realistic so that the trade-off between buffer size and end-to-end delay can be determined.

5. PERFORMANCE EVALUATION USING OPNET TESTBED

With the simulation platform established, we can now evaluate the performance of a practical controller through measurements of different performance measures using different network parameters such as network size and driving speeds, and different protocol parameters.

There are two network sizes we use to evaluate the scalability of our explicit congestion control algorithm: a small network consisting of 10 cars and 2 RSUs, and a larger network of 30 cars and 2 RSUs. Each car in these networks has a maximum sustainable traffic rate of 384 Kbps. With reference to Figure 2, the link between the RSU and the backhaul network was a DS3 link with a capacity of 44.736 Mbps. Section 4.4 has also provided the values of other parameters.

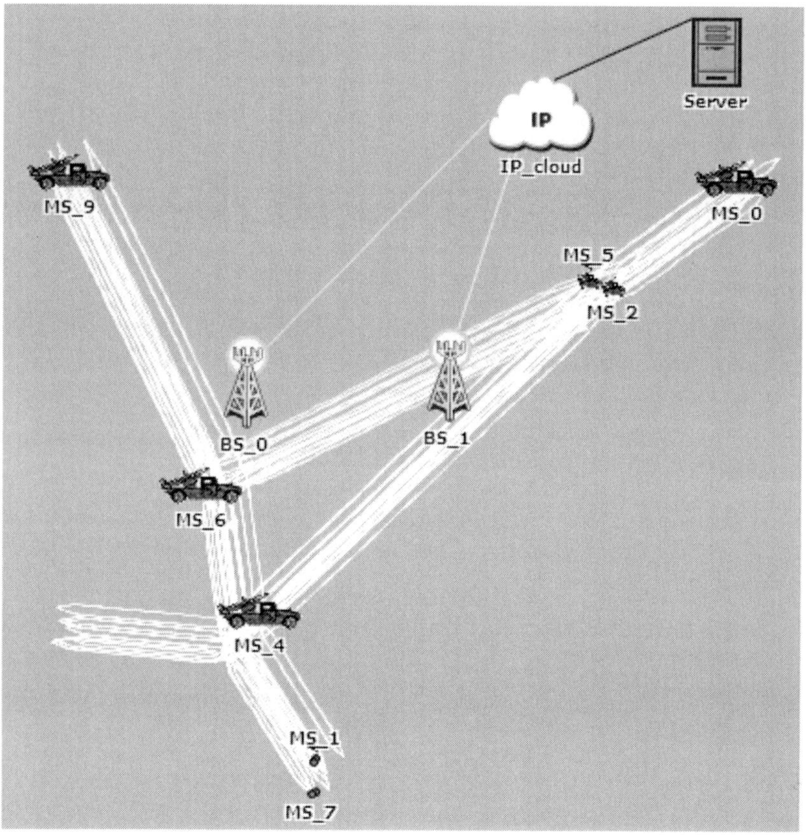

Figure 14. Highway scenario.

Each simulation took 3600 s, which is determined to be a good duration for the performance measures to converge. The following are the definitions of the performance measures we used in our investigation:

1) End-to-End Delay (in seconds): This is defined as the time duration from the instant when a packet is generated at the source node (e.g., the safety camera on board a car) until the time it is received at the destination node. This performance measure presents a wholistic view of the time components in video capture, encoding and network delay before an end user visualizes the images. In real-time traffic, this parameter is very critical as it shows how "current" the information at the end user (e.g., a law enforcement officer) is. Since we track this at the application layer, the end-to-end delay also takes

into account compression delay and all other delays incurred along the communication path and system;

2) Jitter: Jitter is defined to be the variation of end-to-end delay between consecutive packets. If two consecutive packets leave the source node with time stamps *t1* and *t2* and arrive at the destination at time *t3* and *t4* after reassembly and playback, then the jitter will be represented by Equation (5).

$$\text{Jitter} = (t4 - t3) - (t2 - t1) \tag{5}$$

Negative jitter means that the packets where received in different time range *i.e.*, $(t4 - t3) < (t2 - t1)$;

3) Visual MOS Rating: This rating is a subjective parameter that measures the quality of video received by the server, judging the end-user experience. This measure was borrowed from the same parameter used to measure the MOS (Mean Opinion Score) in voice. Using the definition given by the ITU-T recommendation G.107 [58], the score R is given by

$$R = Ro - Is - Id - Ie + A\ , \tag{6}$$

where *Ro* is the SNR (Signal to Noise Ratio); *Is* is the simultaneous impairment factor; *Id* represents impairment caused by delay; *Ie* is the equipment impairment factor as a result of low-bit codecs and packet loss and *A* is the advantage factor that compensates for the loss cause by other factors.

To customize this parameter for video evaluation, we have created a testbed case with all the “ideal” conditions. We allocate one base-station to one car so that there is more than sufficient bandwidth, hence keeping R as high as possible. We obtained a Visual MOS value of 3.6 that we should use as a reference to represent the best visual experience and 1 the worst visual experience, which is plot as the Y-axis in Figure 15.

4) Buffer Overflow Percentage: This measure is the fraction of time during which arriving packets find the buffer at the Subscriber Station full and are not served. This measure implicitly reflects the percentage of time video packets lost due to buffer overflow.

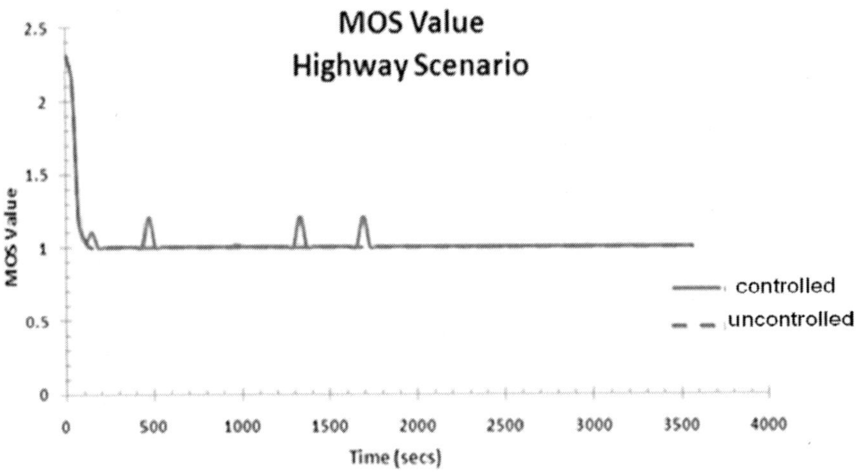

Figure 15. MOS value for a highway scenario.

5.1. Small Network

We only use 10 cars in this small network. After 10 s into the simulation, the WiMAX bandwidth is observed to vary from 125 kHz to 20 MHz (due to the adaptive modulation used as specified in Table 5). At the same time, we observe the video bandwidth also varies randomly with a peak of about 200 kbps and with an average of about 50 kbps at the Subscriber Station. Under this peak to average ratio of 6 dB, we set the controller threshold to 0.1 s in order to keep the controller active most of the time and to verify the operation of our congestion control algorithm. Below are more discussions of various performance measures.

5.1.1. Time Evolution Performance

Figure 16 shows the highly varying end-to-end delay, which can be attributed to the wireless interference and the high speed of the vehicular nodes in the highway. One can see that the controller is always active in reducing the end-to-end delay (blue solid curve) but not always to the minimal point. This is due to the coupling effect of the car speed and periodic feedback so that some packets go "unnoticed", thereby losing it effectiveness.

MOS value for the highway scenario is shown in Figure 15. The score reflects the effect of fluctuations in end-to-end delay on the quality of video seen by the user. The controller tends to keep the visual experience at a constant rate, and improves when the end-to-end delay is reduced substantially.

Figure 17 shows the effect of the controller on the queue size. By controlling congestion in the network, our controller is able to reduce the occasions of buffer saturations and therefore the loss of video quality due to packet loss.

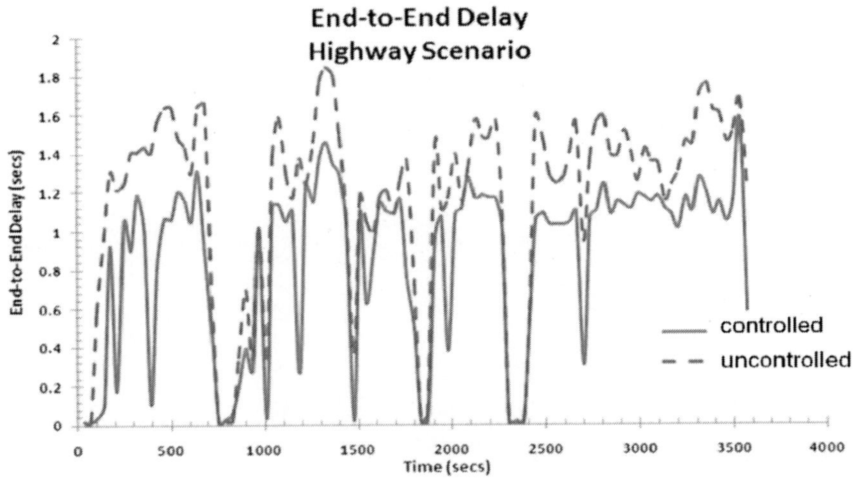

Figure 16. End-to-end delay for a highway scenario.

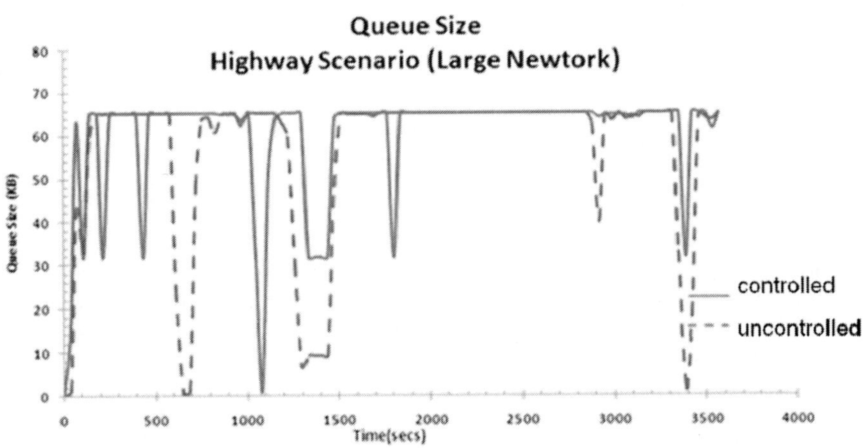

Figure 17. Instantaneous queue size for highway scenario.

The mean end-to-end delay performance for the highway scenario is shown in Figure 18. As expected, as the service rate increases, the end-to-end delay reduces. Increasing the service rate reduces the end-to-end delay and increasing the buffer size increases the end-to-end delay.

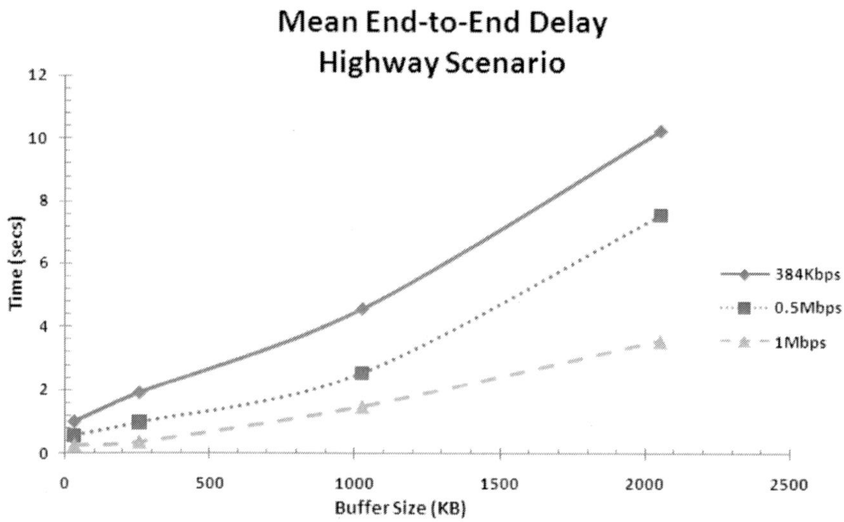

Figure 18. Mean end-to-end delay performance for highway scenario.

5.1.2. Buffer Overflow Percentage

The percentage of buffer saturation of the highway scenario is shown in Figure 19. As expected, the percentage of time for which the buffer is full decreases with respect to increasing buffer size. Note also the larger bandwidth also reduces the percentage as packets can be served faster.

5.2. Large Network

We next study a larger network with 30 cars. All other parameters and scenario remain the same as the small network unless otherwise stated.

5.2.1. Time Evolution Performance

Figure 20 shows the end-to-end delay for the highway scenario in the large network. The solid line shows the end-to-end delay with controller implemented and the dotted line shows the end-to-end delay without the controller. The behavior seen here is similar to what was seen in Figure

16 except that the end-to-end values are much higher in this case due to an increase in the network size (longer path length and queuing delay, *etc.*). The controller again helps to reduce the end-to-end delay in this case, although its effectiveness is influenced by other factors, especially the speed of the car.

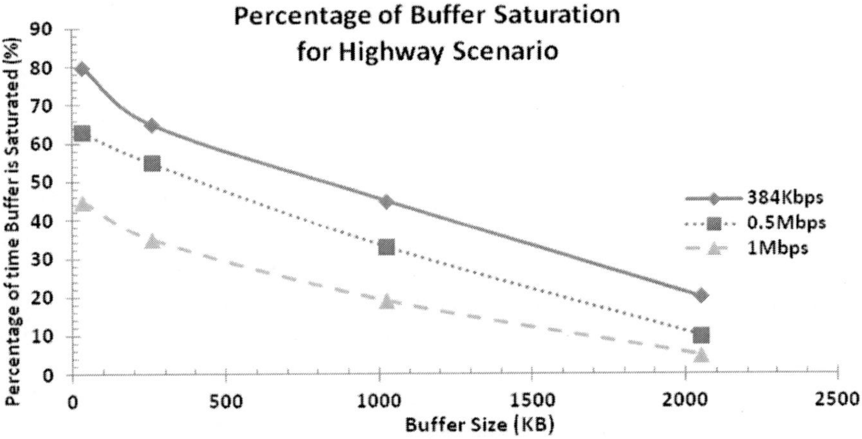

Figure 19. Percentage of buffer saturation performance for highway scenario.

Figure 21 shows the MOS value for the highway scenario for the large network. Similar to the small network, the effect of the controller on the quality of service as seen by the user is not obvious as the end-to-end delay and their fluctuations are still high in this scenario.

Figure 22 shows the maximum queue size is reached more in this case due to the increase in network size. This also contributes to the visual experience discussed earlier.

5.2.2. Mean End-to-End Delay

Figure 23 shows the mean end-to-end delay performance for the highway scenario in the large network for varying buffer sizes and service rates. Observations are similar to those of Figure 18 and hence the same discussion applies, except the mean end-to-end delay is higher in this case due to the increase in network size.

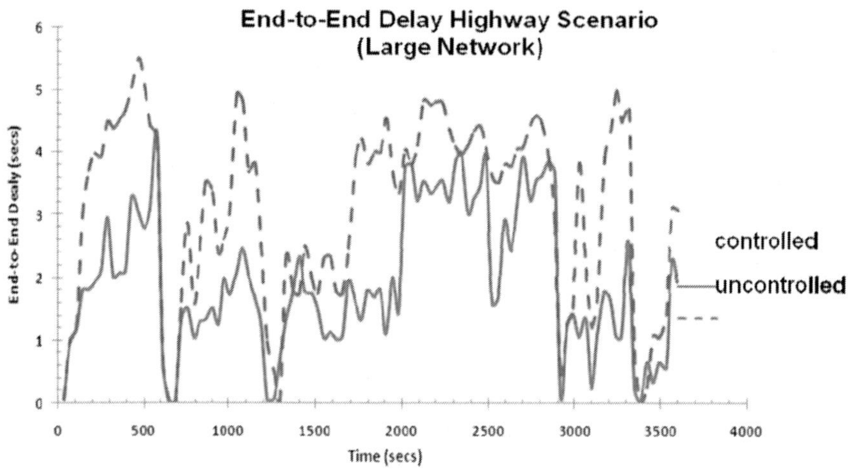

Figure 20. End-to-end delay for highway scenario (large network).

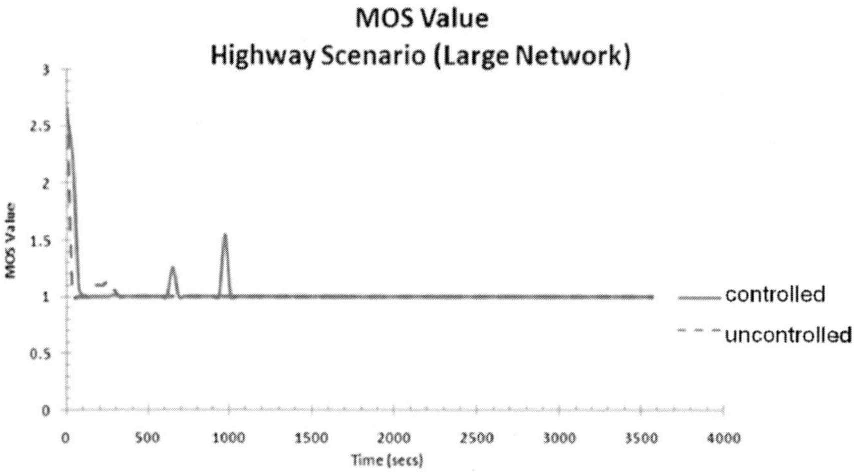

Figure 21. MOS value for highway scenario (large network).

5.2.3. Buffer Overflow Percentage

The percentage of buffer saturation performance curve for the highway scenario is shown in Figure 24 for the large network. It is seen that as the percentage of buffer overflow reduces as the buffer size increases and the service rate increases. This behavior is consistent with what is presented in Figure 19 except that the percentage of buffer saturation is higher in this case since the network size is increased.

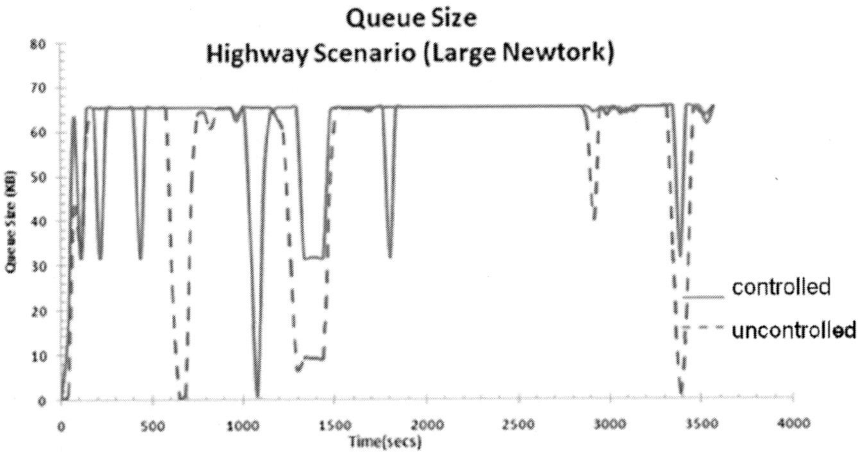

Figure 22. Instantaneous queue size for highway scenario (large network).

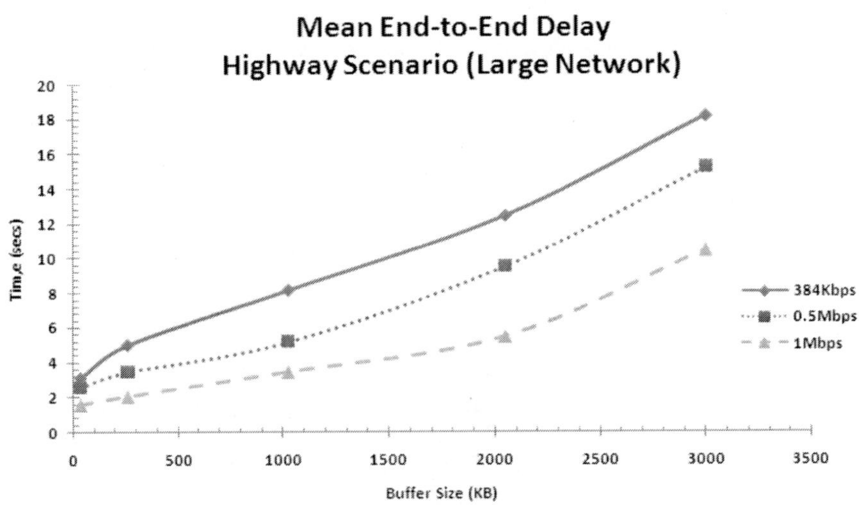

Figure 23. Mean end-to-end delay performance for highway scenario (large network).

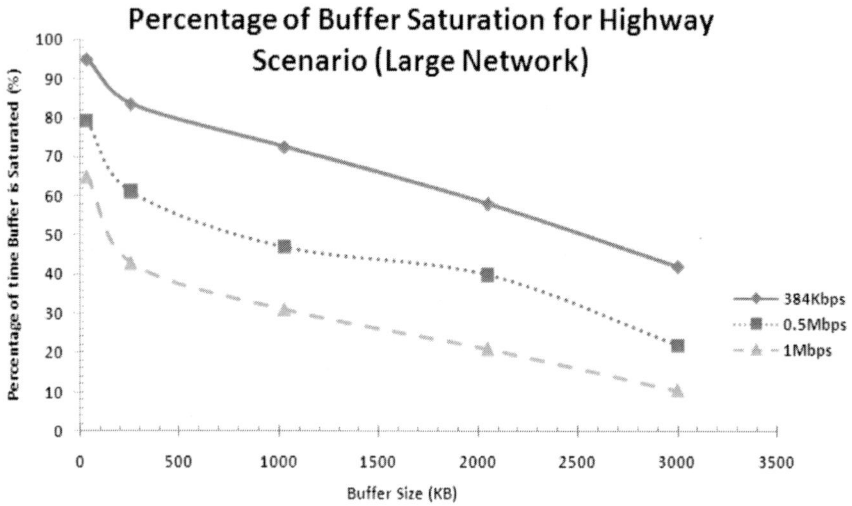

Figure 24. Percentage of buffer saturation performance for highway scenario (large network).

6. CONCLUSIONS

We have created and evaluated an effective driving video VANET simulation platform with which other researchers can develop and test various VANET applications. The platform was built using the OPNET simulation tool to integrate our theoretical driving video model with a VANET model. We have built a simple but practical traffic controller for driving video traffic over RTP applications, and provided a complete tier of communication layers for proper performance analysis.

With the initial work done, there is still a lot of room for improvement and for exploring new model futures. Concurrent simulation using the simulation model and the mobility model would allow the wireless communication to affect the mobility of vehicles more directly so that closer reality results can be obtained. The traffic controller can be improved to keep the end-to-end delay closer to constant in order to reduce the quality impact on the viewers. Others include the comparison of our traffic controller under DSRC, and the validity of the Rician/Raleigh propagation model for moving vehicles.

ACKNOWLEDGMENTS

The research was supported by Auto21 Center of Excellence in Canada. Thanks go to Botao Zhu and Xiaoxiao Liu for reviewing and comments.

CONFLICTS OF INTEREST

The authors declare no conflict of interest.

REFERENCES

1. IEEE P802.16-REVd/D4, Air Interface for Fixed Broadband Wireless Access System. Available online: http://hunter.hosted.pl/tts/Strony_www_TTS_2004.2005/ LMDS_Marcin.Gilewski_Lukasz.Waksmanski/airInterface.pdf (accessed on 17 July 2012).
2. Ramage-Morin, P.L. Motor Vehicle Accident Deaths, 1979 to 2004; Component of Statistics Canada Catalogue No. 82-003-X Health Reports. Statistics Canada: Ottawa, Ontario, Canada, 2008. Available online: http://www.statcan.gc.ca/pub/82-003-x/2008003/article/10648-eng.pdf (accessed on 17 July 2012).
3. Transport Canada. Canadian Motor Vehicle Traffic Collision Statistics: 2007. Available online: http://www.tc.gc.ca/eng/roadsafety/tp-tp3322-2007-1039.htm (accessed on 17 July 2012).
4. Heyman, D.; Lakshman, T. What are the implications of long-range dependence for VBR-video traffic engineering? IEEE/ACM Trans. Netw. 1996, 4, 301–317.
5. Ryu, B.; Elwalid, A. The importance of long-range dependence of VBR video traffic in ATM traffic engineering: myths and realities. ACM SIGCOMM Comput. Commun. Rev. 1996, 26, 3–14.
6. Li, X.; Huang, H.; Shu, W. VStore: Towards Cooperative Storage in Vehicular Sensor Networks for Mobile Surveillance. In Proceedings of the IEEE Wireless Communication and Networking Conference (WCNC), Budapest, Hungary, 5–8 April 2009; pp. 1–6.
7. Huang, J.; Qian, H. Video Encryption for Security Surveillance. In Proceedings of the 41st Annual IEEE International Carnahan Conference on Security Technology, Ottawa, Ontario, Canada, 8–11 October 2007.
8. Jacobson, V.; Braden, R.; Borman, D. TCP Extensions for High Performance. May 1992. Available online: http://www.ietf.org/rfc/rfc1323.txt (accessed on 17 July 2012).
9. Postel, J. User Datagram Protocol. 28 August 1980. Available online: http://www.ietf.org/rfc/rfc768.txt (accessed on 17 July 2012).
10. Balk, A.; Maggiorini, D.; Gerla, M.; Sanadidi, M.Y. Adaptive MPEG-4 Video Streaming with Bandwidth Estimation. In Proceedings of the 2nd International Workshop on Quality of Service in Multiservice IP Networks, Milano, Italy, 24 February 2003; pp. 525–538.
11. Schulzrinne, H.; Casner, S.; Frederick, R.; Jacobson, V. RTP: A Transport Protocol for Real-Time Applications. Available online: http://www.ietf.org/rfc/rfc3550.txt (accessed on 17 July 2012).
12. Liu, B.; Khorashadi, B.; Du, H.; Ghosal, D.; Chuah, C.-N.; Zhang, M. VGSim: An integrated networking and microscopic vehicular mobility simulation platform. IEEE Commun. Mag. 2009, 47, 134–141.
13. Sommer, C.; Dressler, F. Progressing toward realistic mobility models in VANET simulations. IEEE Commun. Mag.2008, 46, 132–137.

14. Wegener, A.; Hellbruck, H.; Wewetzer, C. VANET Simulation Environment with Feedback Loop and its Application to Traffic Light Assistance. In Proceedings of the 2008 IEEE GLOBECOM Workshop, New Orleans, LA, USA, 30 November–4 December 2008; Volume 3, pp. 1–7.
15. Fiore, M.; Harri, J.; Filali, F.; Bonnet, C. Vehicular Mobility Simulation for VANETs. In Proceedings of the 40th Annual Simulation Symposium, ANSS 07. Norfolk, VA, USA, 26–28 March 2007; pp. 301–309.
16. D1.3.1—VanetMobiSim: The Vehicular Mobility Model Generator Tool for CARLINK. Available online: http://carlink.lcc.uma.es/doc/provis/D1.3.1-VanetMobiSim%20The%20vehicular%20mobility%20model%20generator%20tool%20for%20CARLINK.pdf (accessed on 17 July 2012).
17. OPNET. Analyze and Troubleshoot Application Performance from a Network Perspective. Available online: http://www.opnet.com/solutions/brochures/ACE_Analyst.pdf (accessed on 17 April 2010).
18. Tian, L.T. Research on Intelligent Transportation Systems in Taiwan. In Proceedings of the 27th Chinese Control Conference, 16–18 July 2008; pp. 18–23.
19. Laskowski, M.; Friesen, M.R.; McLeod, R.D.; Ferens, K. Rapid Prototyping Vehicle-to-Infrastructure Applications Using the AndroidTM Development Platform. In Proceedings of the 2009 9th International Conference on Intelligent Transport Systems Telecommunications, (ITST), Lille, France, 20–22 October 2009; pp. 273–278.
20. Intel. Intel CTO Rattner Outlines Research Challenges in Home, Car and Network Energy Consumption. Available online: http://www.intel.com/pressroom/archive/ releases/2010/20100413comp.htm (accessed on 17 April 2010).
21. Lalonde, J.; Laganière, R.; Martel, L. Single-View Obstacle Detection for Smart Back-Up Camera Systems. In Proceedings of the 2012 Computer Vision and Pattern Recognition Workshops (CVPRW), Providence, RI, USA, 16–21 June 2012.
22. Hoogendoorn, S.P.; Bovy, P.H. State-of-the-art of vehicular traffic flow modelling. Proc. Inst. Mech. Eng. 2001, 215, 283–303.
23. Zhang, S. Object Tracking in Unmanned Aerial Vehicle (UAV) Videos Using a Combined Approach. In Proceedings of the 2005 IEEE International Conference on Acoustics, Speech, and Signal Processing, Philadelphia, PA, USA, 18–23 March 2005.
24. Harri, J.; Filali, F.; Bonnet, C. Mobility models for vehicular ad hoc networks: A survey and taxonomy. IEEE Commun. Surv. Tutor. 2009, 11, 19–41.
25. Beran, J.; Sherman, R.; Taqqu, M.S.; Willinger, W. Long-range dependence in variable-bit-rate video traffic. IEEE Trans. Commun. 1995, 43, 1566–1579.
26. Hong, S.H.; Park, R.; Lee, C.B. Hurst parameter estimation of long-range dependent VBR MPEG Video traffic in ATM Networks. J. Vis. Commun. Image Represent. 2001, 12, 44–65.
27. Haghani, E.; Parekh, S.; Calin, D.; Kim, E.; Ansari, N. A quality-driven cross-layer solution for MPEG video streaming over WiMAX networks. IEEE Trans. Multimed. 2009, 11, 1140–1147.
28. Krunz, M.; Tripathi, S.K. On the characterization of VBR MPEG streams. ACM Sigmetrics Perform. Eval. Rev. 1997, 25, 192–202.
29. Matrawy, A.; Huang, C.C. MPEG4 Traffic Modeling Using the Transform Expand Sample Methodology. In Proceedings of the 2002 Gaithersburg Proceedings 2002 IEEE 4th International Workshop on Networked Appliances, Gaithersburg, MD, USA, 15–16 January 2002; pp. 249–256.
30. Yang, S.; Daigle, J. A Source Model of Video Traffic Based on Full-Length VBR MPEG4 Video Traces. In Proceedings of the Global Telecommunications Conference, St. Louis, MO, USA, 28 November–2 December 2005; Volume 2, p. 5.
31. Luo, J.; Hubaux, J.-P. A Survey of Inter-Vehicle Communication; EPFL Technical 1618 Report IC/2004/24; École Polytechnique Fédérale de Lausanne: Lausanne, Switzerland, 2004.
32. Gray, D. Mobile WiMAX Part I: A Technical Overview and Performance Evaluation. v2.8. April 2006. Available online: http://www.wimaxforum.org/techno-Logy/downloads/ Mobile_WiMAX_ Part1_Overview_and_Performance.pdf (access on 17 July 2007).

33. Jiang, D.; Delgrossi, L. IEEE 802.11p: Towards an International Standard for Wireless Access in Vehicular Environments. In Proceedings of IEEE Vehicular Technology Conference (VTC) Spring, Singapore, 11–14 May 2008; pp. 2036–2040.
34. Tufano, D.R.; Knee, H.E.; Spelt, P.F. In-Vehicle Signing Functions of an In-Vehicle Information System. Available online: http://www.osti.gov/bridge/ product.biblio.jsp?query_id=3&page=0&osti_id=219502 (accessed on 17 July 2012).
35. Hossain, E.; Chow, G.; Leung, V.; MacLeod, R.D.; Misic, J.; Wong, V.W.S.; Yang, O. Vehicular Telematics over heterogeneous wireless networks: A survey. Comput. Commun. 2010, 33, 775–793.
36. Ghosh, A.; Ghosh, M. Fundamentals of WiMAX: Understanding Broadband Wireless Networking; Prentice Hall: Upper Saddle River, NJ, USA, 2007.
37. Zukerman, M. Back to the future. IEEE Commun. Mag. 2009, 47, 36–38.
38. Tanenbaum, A. Computer Networks; Prentice Hall: Upper Saddle River, NJ, USA, 1996.
39. Hong, Y.; Yang, O. Design of adaptive PI rate controller for best-effort in the internet based on phase margin. IEEE Trans. Parallel Distrib. Syst. 2007, 18, 550–561.
40. Hac, A. Congestion control in a wireless network. Int. J. Netw. Manag. 1999, 9, 185–192.
41. Rath, H.K.; Sahoo, A. Cross Layer Based Congestion Control in Wireless Networks. Available online: http://www.it.iitb.ac.in/research/techreport/reports/8.pdf (accessed on 17 January 2010).
42. Wischhof, L.; Rohling, H. Congestion Control in Vehicular Ad Hoc Networks. In Proceedings of the 2005 IEEE International Conference on Vehicular Electronics and Safety, Xi'an, China, 14–16 October 2005; pp. 58–63.
43. Floyd, F.; Jacobson, V. Random early detection gateways for congestion avoidance. IEEE/ACM Trans. Netw. 1993, 1, 397–413.
44. Jacobson, V.; Karels, M.J. Congestion Avoidance and Control. In Proceedings of the SIGCOMM 88 Symposium on Communications Architectures and Protocols, Stanford, CA, USA, 16–18 August 1988; pp. 314–329.
45. Hassani, M.M.; Tavakolaie, B.H. An Analytical Model for Evaluating Utilization of TCP TAHOE Using Markovian Model. In Proceedings of the International Conference on Networking, Architecture, and Storage, NAS 2007, Guilin, China, 29–31 July 2007; pp. 257–258.
46. Huang, C.; Xu, L. SRC: Stable rate Control for Streaming Media. In Proceedings of the IEEE Global Telecommunications Conference GLOBECOM 03, San Francisco, CA, USA, 1–5 December 2003; pp. 4016–4021.
47. Hanley, M.; Floyd, S.; Padhye, J.; Widmer, J. TCP Friendly Rate Control (TFRC): Protocol Specification. Available online: http://www.ietf.org/rfc/rfc5348.txt (accessed on 17 July 2012).
48. Li, K. IEEE 802.16e-2005 Air Interface Overview; WiMAX Solutions Division Intel Mobility Group: Santa Clara, CA, USA, 2006.
49. IEEE WirelessMan 802.16, The 802.16 WirelessMAN MAC: It's Done, but What is it? Available online: http://ieee802.org/16/docs/01/80216-01_58rl/pdf (accessed on 17 July 2009).
50. Ahmadi, S. Introduction to Mobile Radio Access Technology: PHY and MAC Architecture. Available online: http://vivonets.ece.ucsb.edu/ahmadiUCSB_slides_Dec7.pdf (accessed on 12 December 2009).
51. Ertico. GDF—Geographic Data Files. Available online: http://www.eritco.com/en/links/links/gdf_-_geographic_data_files.htm (accessed on 17 July 2010).
52. U.S. Census Bureau. Topologically Integrated Geographic Encoding and Referencing (TIGER) System. Available online: http://www.census.gov/geo/www/tiger (accessed on 17 February 2010).
53. Huang, J. Presentation for Generalizing 4IPP Traffic Model for IEEE 802.16.3. Available online: http://www.ieee802.org/16/tg3/contrib/802163p-00_58.pdf (accessed on 17 July 2012).
54. WireShark. Available online: http://www.wireshark.org (accessed on 17 July 2013).
55. Easyfit. Available online: http://www.mathwave.com/products/easyfit.html (accessed on 17 July 2009).

56. Gu, H.; Ji, Q. An Automated Face Reader for Fatigue Detection, Automatic Face and Gesture Recognition, 2004. In Proceedings of the Sixth IEEE International Conference, Seoul, Korea, 17–19 May 2004; pp. 111–116.
57. ITU-R, Guideline for Evaluation of Radio Transmission Technologies for IMT-2000. 1997. Available online: http://www.itu.int/dms_pubrec/itu-r/rec/m/R-REC-M.1225-0-199702- I!!PDF-E.pdf (accessed on 17 July 2012).
58. Mehmood, M.A.; Jadoon, T.M.; Sheikh, N.M. Assessment of VoIP Quality over Access Networks. In Proceedings of the First IEEE and IFIP International Conference in Central Asia on Internet, Bishkek, Kyrgyzstan, 26–29 September 2005; pp. 26–29.

CHAPTER 6

Adaptive Region Construction for Efficient Use of Radio Propagation Maps

Vinay B. Ramakrishnaiah, Suresh S. Muknahallipatna*, Robert F. Kubichek

Department of Electrical & Computer Engineering, University of Wyoming, Laramie, WY, USA

ABSTRACT

The efficient construction of contours of a radio propagation map is crucial in using radio propagation maps in a number of real-time communication and network applications. In this research work, we first propose an adaptive region construction (ARC) technique capable of constructing contours of different resolutions of a radio propagation map. Next, the process of implementing the ARC technique for real-time execution on a GPU is presented. The drawbacks of the first implementation using only the global memory are discussed, and optimization techniques to improve the performance are discussed and implemented. Simulations are performed with varying sizes of radio propagation maps, and the suitability of the ARC technique for real-time operation is presented. A speedup of 25× is achieved with the shared version of the GPU compared to the sequential CPU implementation. Also, the contour constructed using the ARC technique is compared to that constructed using the convex hull approach demonstrating the higher accuracy of the contour from the ARC technique.

Keywords: Radio Propagation, Sampling, Parallel, Adaptive, Accelerator, Contours

1. INTRODUCTION

A mobile ad-hoc network (MANET) of nodes (equipped with sensors) can be deployed rapidly in an environment to provide a communication infrastructure for a number of applications like environmental monitoring, rescue and defense operations to mention a few. However, the successful deployment of a MANET is dependent on the ability of neighboring nodes establishing a wireless communication link and provides connectivity across the network. Establishing a communication link is dependent on the availability of radio spectrum, transmission power, interference from neighboring nodes, and the effect of terrain on radio propagation. Depending on the deployment environment, the effect of terrain on radio propagation can be modeled with free space (Omni-directional) or "two-ray" propagation models if the terrain does not have any hills, buildings, and foliage affecting the propagation of radio signals minimally. However, in a realistic environment where MANETs are deployed, the terrain consists of hills, buildings, foliage, etc., causing reflections, diffraction, blocking and unreliable path loss estimates which render free space or two-ray propagation models ineffective in modeling the effect of terrain on radio propagation. Hence, more complex propagation modeling techniques like the Walfisch-Ikegami model (WIM), and 3D ray tracing have to be used to determine the effect of terrain on radio propagation. The effect of terrain on the radio propagation by WIM or 3D ray tracing is quantified as radio propagation map.

Radio propagation maps specify the path loss (or received signal strength) at various distances and directions from the transmitter taking into account the effect of the terrain. The path loss [1] is computed using WIM, 3D ray tracing, and other models. Each modeling offers trade-offs in terms of accuracy and computational complexity. A radio propagation map consists of received signal streng- ths from a transmitter over a geographic region show neither as a heat map or radio contours. Heat maps represent varying signal strengths from a transmitter using distinct colors while in radio contours equal signal strength locations are connected by lines known as contour lines. A heat map can be stored as a pixel image, with pixels representing the signal strength of a location from the transmitter. Radio propagation maps find many applications like the optimum placement of mobile phone base stations for maximum coverage, adjusting the antenna beam patterns for efficient communication based on the terrain, localization of mobile nodes in MANETs, etc.

The application of radio propagation maps in localizing nodes, and antenna beam forming [2] [3] [4] [5] has been demonstrated by the authors of this paper. The first application addressing efficient localization of nodes of a MANET under free space and terrain effects is discussed in references [2] [3] [4] . In reference [3] , the optimal trajectory of a single moving beacon (beacon mounted on a drone or UAV) to localize nodes under free space was presented. Next, the use of high-resolution radio propagation maps [2] to localize nodes in a MANET using a single moving beacon like a drone or unmanned aerial vehicle has been presented.

In the research work [2] , the use of regular geometric shapes known as convex hulls to represent irregular radio propagation shapes constructed using the WIM model has been presented. The paramount reason for representing irregular radio propagation shapes with convex hulls is associated with the localizing algorithm [3] developed for nodes of a MANET. The localization algorithm requires determination of the area of intersection (approximate node position) of two radio propagation maps received by the node. Determining the area of intersection of two radio propagation maps using a simple bit-wise AND operation [4] was demonstrated and found to be impractical due to computational complexity, bandwidth, and storage requirements of each node to use the radio propagation maps. Therefore, to address the issues of bandwidth and storage requirements, the contour of radio propagation maps was constructed as convex hulls using Andrew's Monotone Chain algorithm [6] . Next, the algorithm developed by O'Rourke [7] was used to determine the area of intersection of two radio propagation maps using the constructed convex hulls. The second application consists of using low-resolution radio propagation map for computing antenna beam patterns [5] to reduce the interference by neighboring nodes.

The success rate of the localization algorithm using convex hulls representing the contour of a radio propagation map of the small geographical area was 80% with an accuracy of 1 m. However, with an increase in the size of the geographical area, the performance of the algorithm deteriorated first due to the convex hulls not capturing the contour of the radio propagation map accurately. The second issue was with the nonlinear increase of the computational time for constructing a convex hull of a radio propagation map of the large geographical area (a suburb of a city) with high resolution rendering the localization algorithm not suitable for real-time application.

Hence in this work, we propose an adaptive region construction technique to capture the contour of a radio propagation map of large geographical area accurately and suitable for real-time implementation. We propose the use of a general purpose graphical processing unit (GPGPU) based adaptive region construction (ARC) for constructing multiple convex hulls of a radio propagation map of a large geographical area and combine multiple convex hulls to form regions representing the contour of radio propagation maps accurately.

This paper is organized as follows: In Section 2, a brief discussion of the localization algorithm [2] developed previously is discussed. The error in the intersection area determined using two convex hulls in comparison to the direct use of radio propagation maps is shown. Also, the increase in computational time for constructing convex hulls of large radio propagation maps with high resolution is demonstrated. Section 3 presents a discussion on the related work of capturing contour of radio propagation maps. In Section 4, first, a brief discussion of the sequential Andrew's monotone chain algorithm and divide and conquer approach for constructing convex hulls is presented. Section 5 presents the adaptive region construction technique that merges intermediate convex hulls to form regions. The GPGPU implementation of the ARC using only the global memory of the GPU is presented in Section 6. Section 7, presents the optimizations using the shared memory of the GPU to improve the performance of the algorithms is presented. Results and analysis of the results are presented in Section 8. In Section 9, conclusion and future work are presented.

2. LOCALIZATION IN MOBILE AD HOC NETWORKS

Miles et al. envisioned a single moving beacon mounted on a vehicle capable of moving and broadcasting its position periodically to nodes in its transmission range based on radio propagation models [2] representing a particular urban environment. Using a-priori knowledge of local terrain including average building height and separation, average street width and orientation, etc., the WIM model is used to estimate path loss and transmission range in any direction. The single moving beacon will acquire its geographical position through GPS and broadcast its changing position. Having a single moving beacon broadcasting its changing position is equivalent to multiple stationary beacons broadcasting their different positions. An exchange of a few position messages and acknowledgments between an un-localized node and the moving beacon will allow the moving beacon to compute an approximate area to confine the un-localized node location.

Figure 1 shows an approximate propagation map generated using WIM techniques. The white area in Figure 1 shows the estimated area in which an antenna is capable of receiving a transmission from a transmitter (beacon node) positioned at the centroid of the white area. The possible position of a sensor in a wireless network using WIM transmission maps can be approximated as the centroid of the set given by the intersection of several beacon transmissions as shown in Figure 2. A WIM localization technique [4] suggested by Muralidhara and Kubichek relies on bitwise AND operations between two radio propagation maps for beacon transmissions near an unknown sensor. Depending on the size of the coverage area spanned by the MANET, these maps can be quite large.

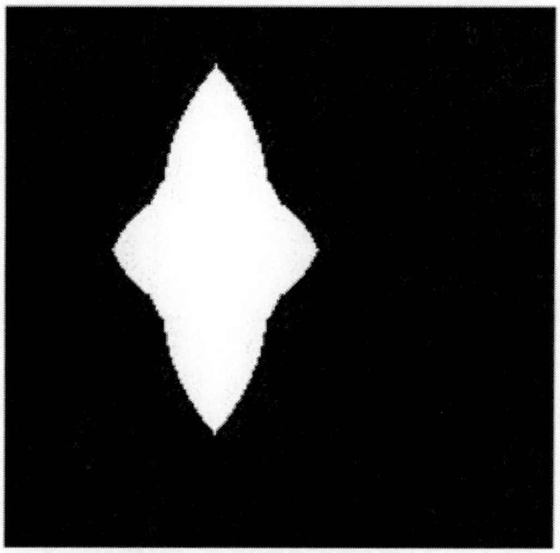

Figure 1. WIM propagation approximation.

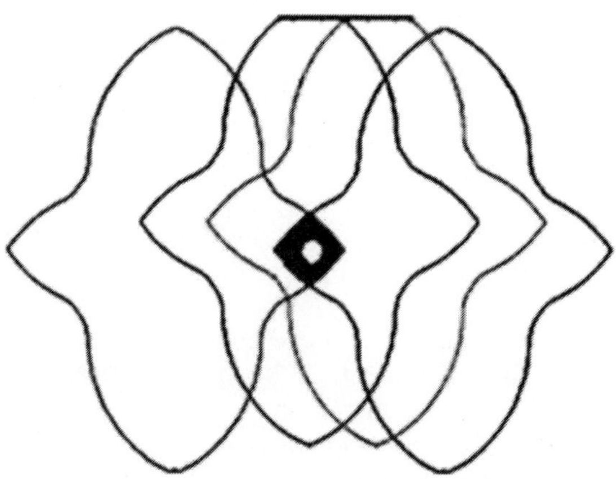

Figure 2. Possible position of a node in MANET using WIM.

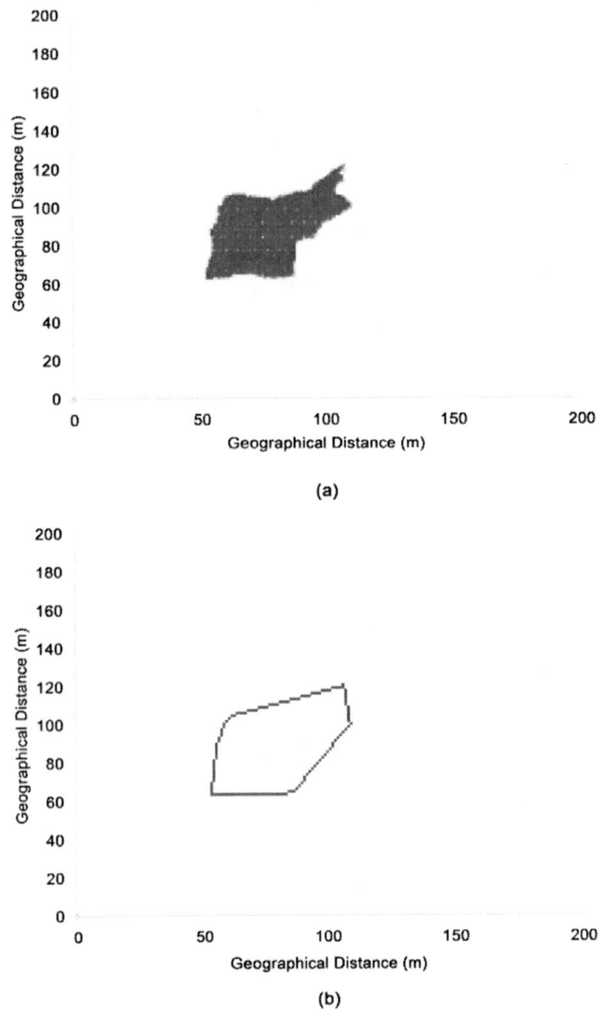

Figure 3. (a) Range map and its corresponding (b) convex hull.

Transmission and comparison of these maps require large bandwidth and computational capability. Also, it is difficult to implement an intelligent localization algorithm based on the shapes of the range maps. The above drawbacks are addressed by using convex hulls to represent the irregular radio propagation shapes with regular geometric shapes [2] . By using the convex hull approach, each radio propagation map can be stored using only a small number of boundary points as shown in Figure 3. Next, the intersection of two convex hulls representing the approximate location of an un-localized node as shown in Figure 4 is determined using the algorithm proposed by O'Rourke [7] .

Even though the use of convex hulls to represent radio propagation maps had reduced the storage requirement and transmission bandwidth, it introduced significant errors in localization and increased the computational burden. In Figure 5, a number of examples of the artifacts introduced in representing radio propagation maps by convex hulls are shown. The first column (a - c) in Figure 5 depicts the radio propagation maps constructed using the WIM model, the second column (d - f) shows the corresponding convex hull, and the third column (g - i) shows the artifacts introduced in representing radio propagation maps by convex hulls. The difference in the area of the convex hull and the area enclosed by the radio propagation contour is the artifact introduced by the convex hull approximation. While using the technique of localization using the intersection of the convex hulls, the artifacts introduce superfluous area, which in turn introduces error in the computed localized position compared to the localization using the intersection of radio propagation contours as shown in Figure 6. In Figure 6, with the actual radio propagation maps, the position is close to the real position, whereas for the convex hulls it is the centroid of the intersection area of the two hulls, which is far away from the real position. As an example, a convex hull was constructed to represent the radio propagation map of size 2.5 km by 2.5 km. The difference in area due to the artifact introduced between the contour of the radio propagation map and the corresponding convex hull was approximately 0.4 km^2, which is about 1/15th of the original area. This difference in the area can be even more significant when considering radio propagation maps of large urban areas. Along with the introduction of artifacts, the computation of convex hulls of very large geographic areas is a computationally intensive problem. Even though efficient algorithms [7] are available to compute convex hulls with the computational complexity of (O(nlog(n))), the computational complexity is an issue when computing convex hulls of large cities sequentially.

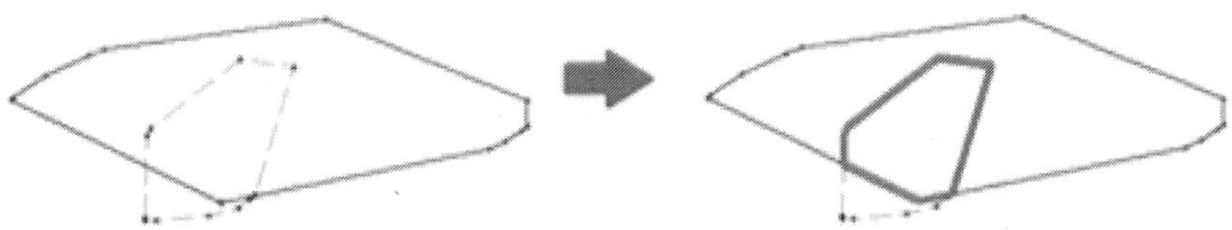

Figure 4. Intersection of two convex hulls.

The time taken to compute a convex hull sequentially on an Intel Xeon Sandy Bridge processor using the best sequential algorithm for different resolutions is shown in Figure 7. From Figure 7 we can see that the execution time required to compute convex hulls using sequential algorithms is not suitable for real time applications, especially when high resolution radio propagation maps are used.

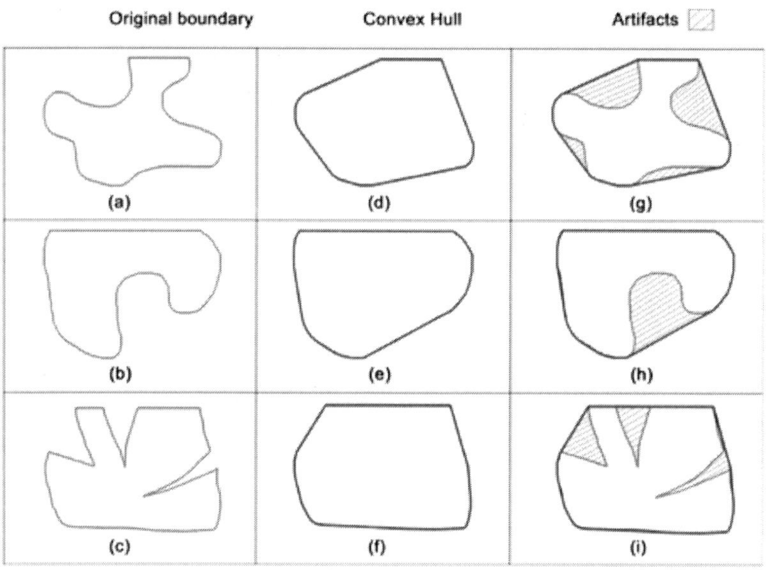

Figure 5. The original boundary, convex hull, and the artifacts introduced by convex hulls.

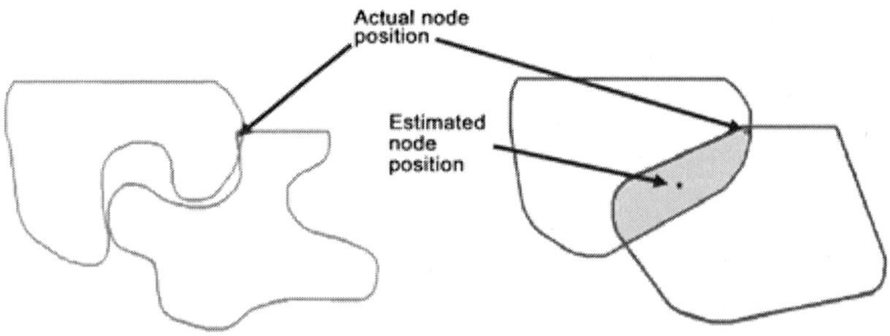

Figure 6. Estimated node positions using the boundary of radio propagation map compared to the estimated position using convex hulls.

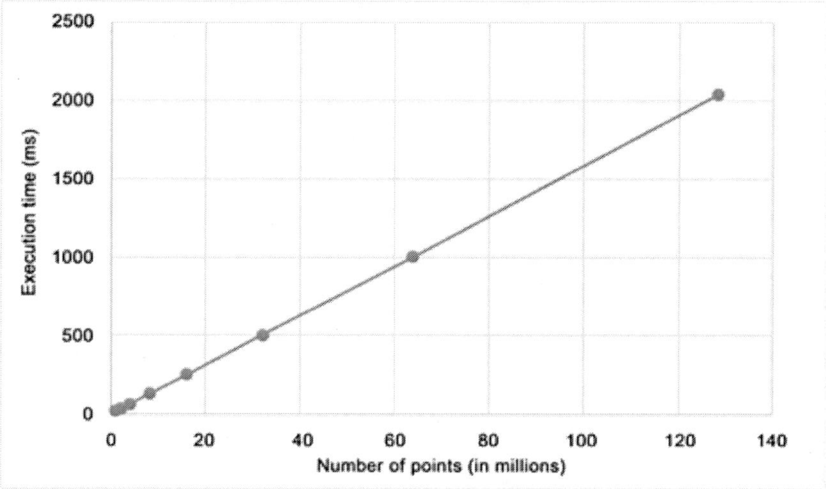

Figure 7. Time taken to compute convex hulls using Andrew's monotone chain algorithm.

In this research work, we propose a new method to assist computation of contours of a radio propagation map known as the Adaptive Region Construction (ARC) technique. The ARC technique first reduces the superfluous area introduced by the use of convex hulls representing radio propagation maps and thereby reduces the localization error. Second, the ARC technique is implemented using the general-purpose computing on graphic processing units (GPGPU) to reduce the computational time and make use of radio propagation maps in real-time applications feasible.

3. PREVIOUS WORK

Curve simplification algorithms like the Ramer-Douglas-Peucker algorithm [8] [9] are used to approximate radio contours by representing the sequence of points as line segments. The simplified curve consists of a subset of the original set of points, and the algorithm tries to minimize the distance between the original curve and the simplified curve. This algorithm does a crude simplification of joining the first and the last vertices of a polyline with a single edge, which can result in over-simplification of the details. Furthermore, using these algorithms directly on large data sets is not suitable for real time applications due to increase in computational complexity.

Many computer vision applications make use of convex hulls to approximate blobs and shapes in images. The authors of [10] use convex hulls to categorize shapes of leaves. Convex hulls are constructed to represent the contours of leaves and are categorized by finding the variations between the interior angles at each control point. However, if two distinct leaves have the same contour constructed as convex hulls, the method fails to categorize distinct leaves. This idea has been extended to represent radio contours using convex hulls in [2] .

The authors of [11] propose using convex hulls for a simplified representation of "building footprints" on radio propagation which is a crucial step in wireless communication. Footprint reduction is crucial for reducing prediction time and controlling prediction accuracy in radio communication. They identify that such reductions often affect the accuracy of results as simplification error constrains the efficiency that can be achieved. In other words, the prediction accuracy can be improved by better footprint reduction techniques. This analysis helps in better understanding of the trade-off between the precision of the building database and the accuracy of predictions generated by ray-tracing based radio propagation prediction systems.

The authors of [12] construct convex ray paths to simplify radio propagation ray path calculations. Multiple reflections are modeled by their equivalent convex hull. This is a good approximation for calculating signal strengths at a given location from the transmitter but can result in errors if the propagation path of radio waves through the topography is complex, which cannot be modelled using simple convex hulls. They also propose using the ordinary graphics card and specialized algorithms to achieve extremely fast radio wave propagation predictions. They show that their implementation of the COST-Walfisch-Ikegami model can efficiently calculate 200 predictions per second, whereas a CPU implementation of the same COST-Walfisch-Ikegami models needs slightly less than a minute for a single prediction.

Cheng et al. [13] proposes a method to improve wireless connectivity in ad hoc networks using a partitioning technique based on the conductance of a network. They use convex optimization to maximize the number of connections between the communicating nodes on different sides of the partition. The optimization is used to find the precise location of the relay node, which is within the convex hull defined by the radio transmission ranges of all the nodes that can connect the relay node. This process can be improved by accurately defining the radio propagation maps for each transmitter positions.

Liu et al. [14] focus on identification of non-line-of-sight (NLOS) signal propagation, which is the dominant source of localization error in wireless network nodes. They present a theoretical analysis of mobile user localization involving one or more NLOS beacons and show that if the mobile user is within the convex hull region formed by the underlying beacons, localization involving NLOS is likely to be largely inconsistent. However, if the mobile user is outside the convex hull region, localization involving NLOS could be performed consistently. They argue that relying on existing methods to identify NLOS would lead to a great chance of underestimating the potentially serious errors in localization involving NLOS.

Most of the research work discussed above requires contour and points internal to the contour to represent the radio propagation maps. However, for localization and other applications, accurate representations of the radio propagation map to reduce the storages and bandwidth requirements, which are suitable for real time applications that are required. Hence in our work, we present the adaptive region construction (ARC) technique capable of aiding the construction of an accurate contour representing the shape of the radio propagation map. The ARC technique described in this paper can define the given radio propagation map contour more accurately compared to a convex hull. Even though our algorithm is developed for approximating radio propagation maps, it can improve the accuracy of many applications that make use of sample approximations and demand real-time/near real-time performance. Our algorithm is computationally less complexity and is parallelizable, which makes it suited for real-time applications.

4. REVIEW OF CONVEX HULLS

To review, by definition, a set, C, is convex [15] if and only if for any $x_1, x_2 \in C$ and any θ where $0 \le \theta \le 1$ the following condition holds: $\theta x_1 + (1-\theta)x_2 \in C$.

In simple terms, this means that a set is convex if the direct path between any two points in the set is entirely included in the set. Figure 8 shows a convex set. Note that the line between two elements within the set is, itself, completely encompassed in the set. If a set bounded by the edges of the white area in Figure 1 is used, it is easy to see that there are direct paths between elements of the set that do not lie completely within the set as in Figure 9(a). A convex hull of a set, C, is the minimum convex set that contains the set C. Figure 9(b) represents the convex hull of the set shown in Figure 9(a). As the figure indicates, all paths between points within the convex hull are now completely encompassed in the set.

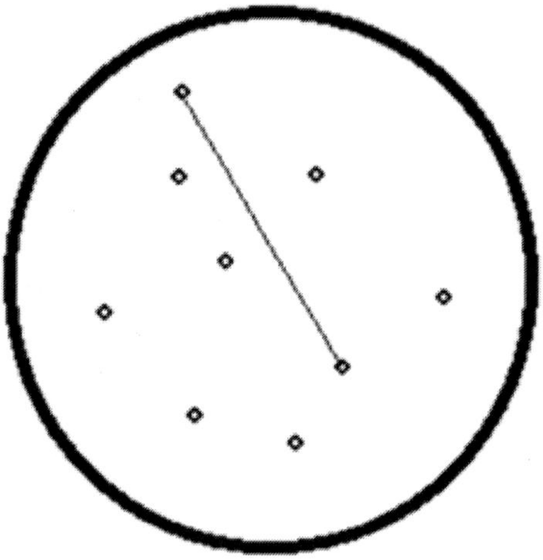

Figure 8. A convex set of points.

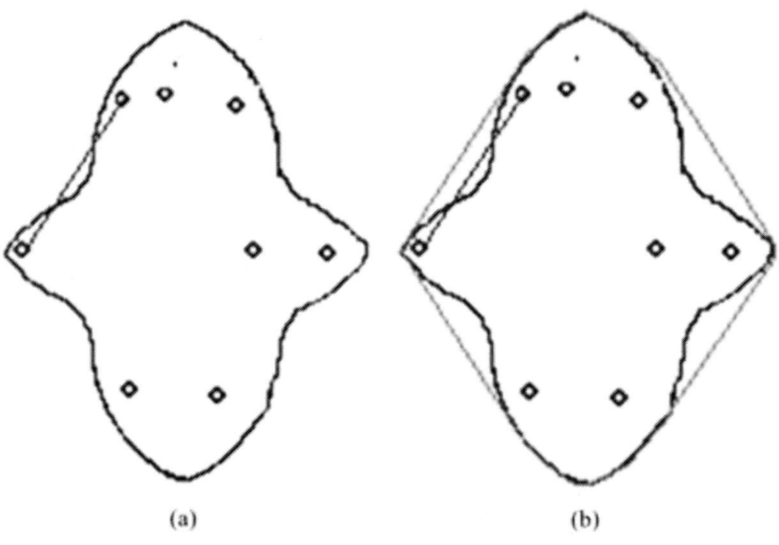

Figure 9. Convex hull of a non-convex set of points.

By constructing a convex hull of a range map, the storage and transmission bandwidth requirements can be greatly reduced. This results from the fact that only a small number of boundary points are required to represent the convex hull, which approximates the actual radio propagation map. This will serve as a lossy compression technique for the localization method.

Another benefit of the convex hull is that it can be used to make intelligent movement decisions more easily as the computation of the intersecting area only requires the use of the boundary points of the intersecting convex hulls instead of the entire radio propagation maps.

4.1. Overview of Andrew's Monotone Chain Convex Hull Algorithm

The Andrew's monotone chain convex hull algorithm [6] can find the convex hull of a set of points in O(n logn) time. One particular advantage of this algorithm is that it can find the convex hull in O(n) time if the points are already sorted in ascending order from left to right and top to bottom, which is the case for the data in the radio propagation maps used in this work. This algorithm computes the upper and lower convex hulls of a monotone chain of points. The flowchart in Figure 10 illustrates the mechanism by which this algorithm computes the convex hull.

The upper hull is computed in a similar fashion, and the two hull sets are joined to find the final convex hull. Essentially, the algorithm works by comparing points to lines formed between previous points starting from left to right to make the upper hull, and then from right to left to make the lower hull. The algorithm makes its decision on which point belongs in the hull by computing the curl between the vector composed of the previously selected point and the second to last point in the hull and vector between the current point and the second to last point in the hull. Figure 11shows a set of points in the early stage of hull construction. The curl, Crl, between the vectors $P_{minmax,1}$ and $P_{minmax,2}$, computed from Equation (1) will result in a positive number, indicating that the point P_2 lies to the relative interior if the line between P_{minmax} and P_2.

$$Crl = P_{\min\max,1} \times P_{\min\max,2} \tag{1}$$

In order to satisfy Equation (1), the points included in the hull must be located to the relative exterior of all points included in the hull, and in line with all points included in the hull. In the case illustrated in Figure 11, the point, P_1 will be discarded from the hull and replaced, by P_2. Then the algorithm proceeds by checking points to the right until it reaches the right-most point. Then it begins moving back to the left computing the lower hull in a similar fashion. Figure 12 shows the result of the algorithm for a set of points.

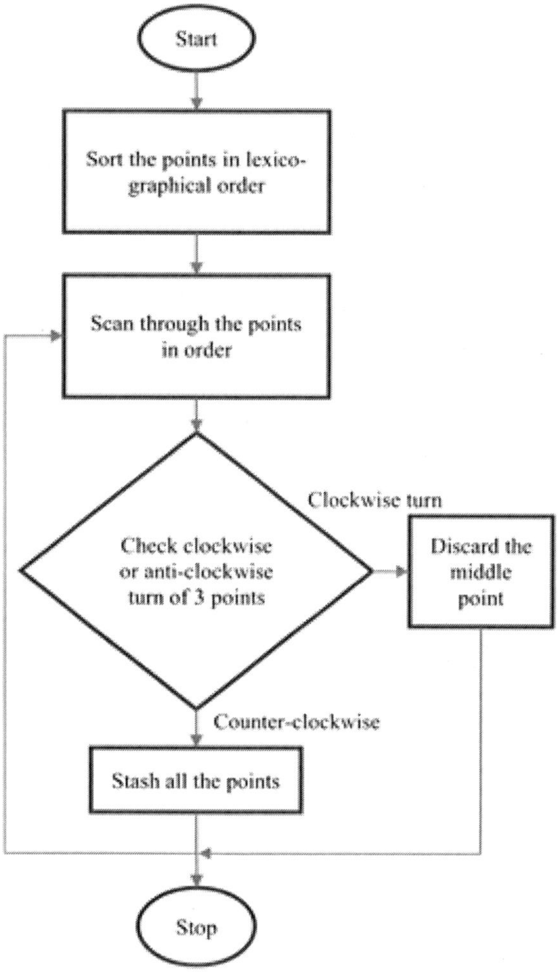

Figure 10. Flow chart of the sequential Andrew's monotone chain convex hull algorithm.

4.2. The Divide and Conquer Approach for Constructing Convex Hulls

The divide and conquer approach was developed by [16] as an efficient algorithm for computing convex hulls in three dimensions if the points are sorted in lexicographical order. The points are divided into two sets A and B, containing the left half and the right half of the points respectively as shown in Figure 13. Convex hulls are computed recursively on these two sets, and the sets are merged by computing the union of the convex hulls. The division of points into left and right sets is continued recursively until the number of points, n, in each set is less than or equal to three. This algorithm assumes non-collinear points, which makes the smallest convex hull either a triangle (if n = 3) or a straight line (if n = 2). Therefore, majority of the computational effort involved in this algorithm is with the merge step.

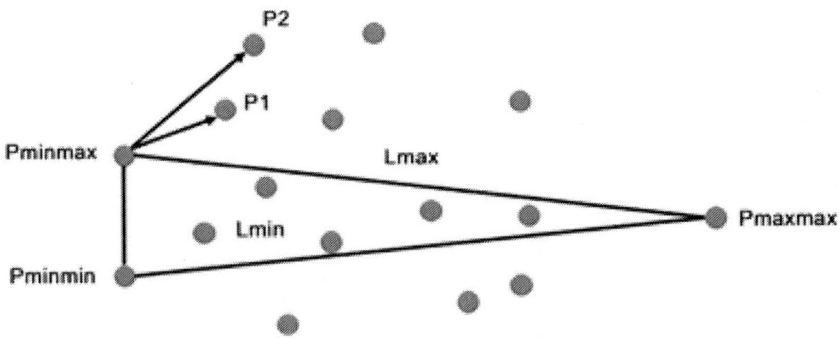

Figure 11. Set of points in the early stage of hull computation.

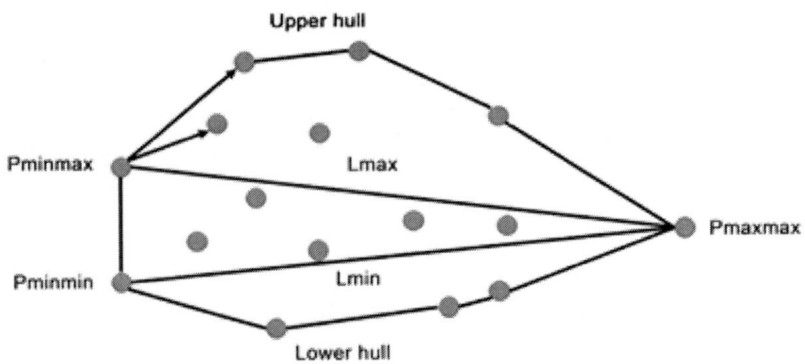

Figure 12. Resulting convex hull.

To merge the convex hulls, common tangents are constructed between two consecutive convex hulls and the convex hulls are merged hierarchically. In Figure 13, the numbers represent the steps of the tangent determination process. In order to construct the tangents, a line is drawn between the rightmost point of the left hull and the leftmost point of the right hull. The left end of the line is fixed, and the right end is moved on the convex hull until it becomes a tangent to the right hull (Step 1 in Figure 13). Now the right end of the line is fixed, and the left end is moved until it becomes a tangent to the left hull (Step 2 in Figure 13). This process is repeated until a common tangent is attained as shown in Figure 13.

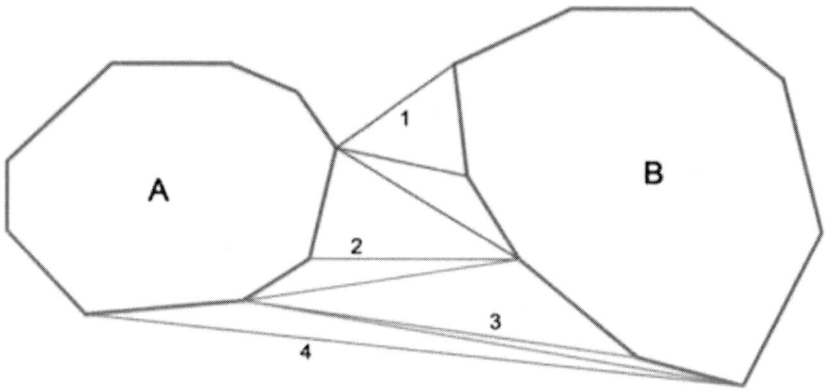

Figure 13. Constructing the lower tangent to merge two consecutive hulls.

5. ADAPTIVE REGION CONSTRUCTION

This section describes the process of adaptive region construction (ARC). This approach is developed to represent the radio propagation characteristics like signal strength at a spatial location in an efficient way. The procedure described here combines the ideas from the Andrews's monotone chain convex hull algorithm [6] and the divide and conquer approach [17] to implement ARC. ARC provides more details about a contour of a radio propagation map when compared to a convex hull approximation. ARC constructs the contour of a radio propagation map by constructing intermediate convex hulls to fit the given radio propagation map contour and combining them consecutively. This process also requires points to be sorted in lexicographical order. A number of parallel sorting algorithms like the CUDA Dynamic Parallelism (CDP) quicksort, CUDA quicksort [18] , etc., can be used. Furthermore, if the radio propagation map is constructed using WIM, the data points are sorted in the Cartesian coordinate system, thereby eliminating the need to sort the data set. The given data is divided into smaller segments and operated in parallel on individual segments of data to exploit data level parallelism. Andrew's monotone chain convex hull algorithm is used on each segment of data to construct intermediate convex hulls. Later, the individual convex hulls are combined by constructing common tangents to the consecutive convex hulls in parallel. The resulting set of points tries to preserve the shape of the radio propagation map in general. The boundary of ARC compared with the convex hull of the corresponding radio propagation map is exemplified in Figure 14. This set obtained using the process described above includes points that are not in the final convex hull for the given set of points. The result at the end of this step is the adaptively constructed region as illustrated in Figure 15. The ARC process is a combination of Andrew's monotone chain algorithm and the divide and conquer approach of computing convex hulls, and both have a worst case computational complexity of O(nlog(n)). Therefore, the inherently parallel process of constructing adaptive regions has a computational complexity of the order

$$O\left(\underbrace{\frac{n}{m}\log\left(\frac{n}{m}\right)}_{\text{Andrew's monotone chain}}+\underbrace{\frac{n}{m}\log\left(\frac{n}{m}\right)}_{\text{Divide \& Conquer}}\right)=O\left(2\frac{n}{m}\log\left(\frac{n}{m}\right)\right),$$

where n is the total number of points in the dataset, m is the number of processes or threads that can execute simultaneously, and $n/m \geq 3$ as at least three points are required to compute a convex hull. This shows that having many processes running in parallel reduces the computational complexity of the algorithm.

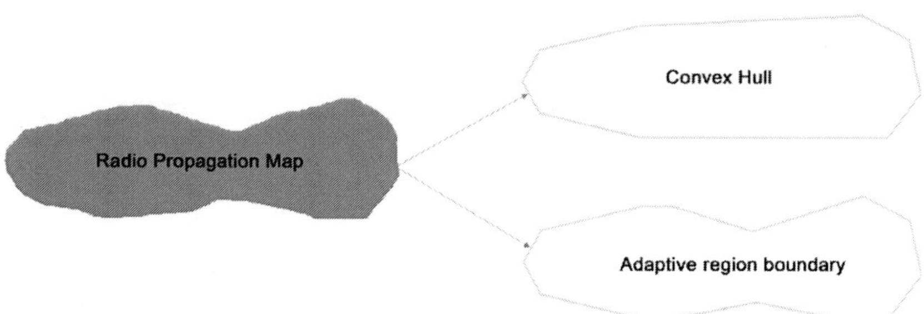

Figure 14. Radio propagation map represented using convex hull and adaptive region construction.

6. GENERAL PURPOSE GPU IMPLEMENTATION

Heterogeneous computing is the approach of using accelerators/co-processors in conjunction with Central Processing Units (CPUs) to solve computationally intensive problems. Accelerators can be vector processors; many core processors like Graphics processing units (GPUs) and Intel Xeon Ph is that improve the performance of applications by utilizing parallelism. GPUs are specialized hardware designed to handle the intensive operation of the rendering of image frames for output to a display device. With the emergence of programmable shaders, researchers started using GPUs to solve problems involving matrices and vectors to achieve performance improvement by making use of parallelism. When GPUs are used for computations in non-graphics related problems, it is known as general purpose GPU (GPGPU) computing. Initial efforts of programming GPUs involved refactoring the problems to use graphics primitives provided by the graphics application programming interfaces. NVIDIA's Compute Unified Device Architecture (CUDA) [19] is an attempt to ameliorate the cumbersome process of programming GPUs. CUDA provides simple language extensions to programming languages like C/C++, FORTRAN, and Python to expose fine and coarse grained parallelism in applications. NVIDIA has introduced several hardware architectures with CUDA support to improve the performance of parallelized programs.

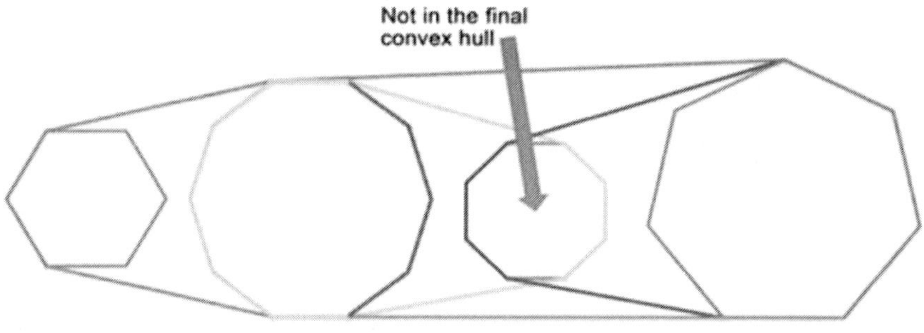

Figure 15. Illustration of adaptive region construction. Adaptive region construction includes the octagon which is not a part of the final convex hull.

The generalized hardware hierarchy in NVIDIA GPUs consists of multiple arithmetic and logic units (ALUs), and they are called CUDA cores as shown in the right-half of Figure 16. A fixed number of these cores are grouped along with control hardware and memory to form units known as Streaming Multi-processors (SMs). The entire device constitutes of several SMs, providing a large number of processing cores. This hierarchy in hardware is matched in the software hierarchy shown in the left-half of Figure 16 by the CUDA programming model. It provides a software hierarchy of threads, thread blocks, and grids, which have an affinity to

CUDA cores, SMs, and the device correspondingly as shown in the left half of Figure 16. The threads in a thread block can be arranged in 1D, 2D, or 3D fashion and in a similar fashion, the thread blocks can be arranged in a grid. The total number of threads spawned in a thread block is fixed, hence is the load handled by each SM.

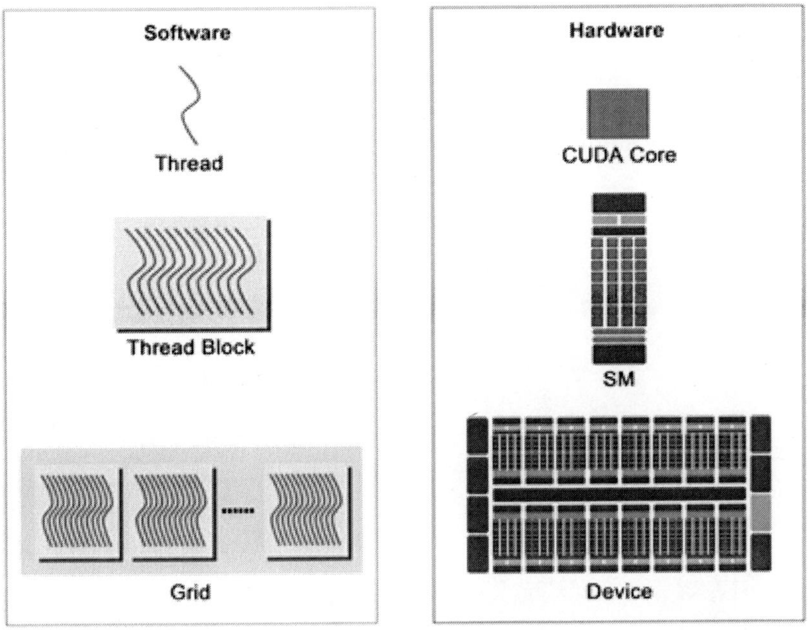

Figure 16. The software (left-half) and hardware (right-half) hierarchy correspondence in NVIDIA GPUs (Image source [21]).

GPU memory can be classified into 3 categories namely the registers, shared memory, and global memory as shown in Figure 17. Some GPU architectures, in addition to the shared, global, and register memory also have texture and constant memory that are read-only memories for GPUs with optimized cache access. Each CUDA thread has limited private registers which are the fastest form of memory available on a GPU. Threads within a block have access to the shared memory through which they can exchange data, while all the threads in the device have access to the global memory. The memory access latency increases exponentially from registers to global memory as we move away from the processing core and so does the size of memory. In other words, GPUs have a memory hierarchy similar to any modern-day vector processor. Like any other modern computer, GPUs are also benefited by the efficient use of memory bandwidth.

NVIDIA GPUs follow the single program, multiple threads (SPMT) execution model of parallel computing. This means a group of threads execute the same set of instructions in lock-step, though conditional branches in the algorithm can violate the lock-step execution of instructions contributing to an increase in computational time. The SMs in NVIDIA GPUs always execute instructions with a granularity of 32 threads known as a warp. A SM has multiple warp schedulers allocating hardware resources to each thread/ warp and scheduling the concurrent execution of multiple warps based on the requested shared resources per thread.

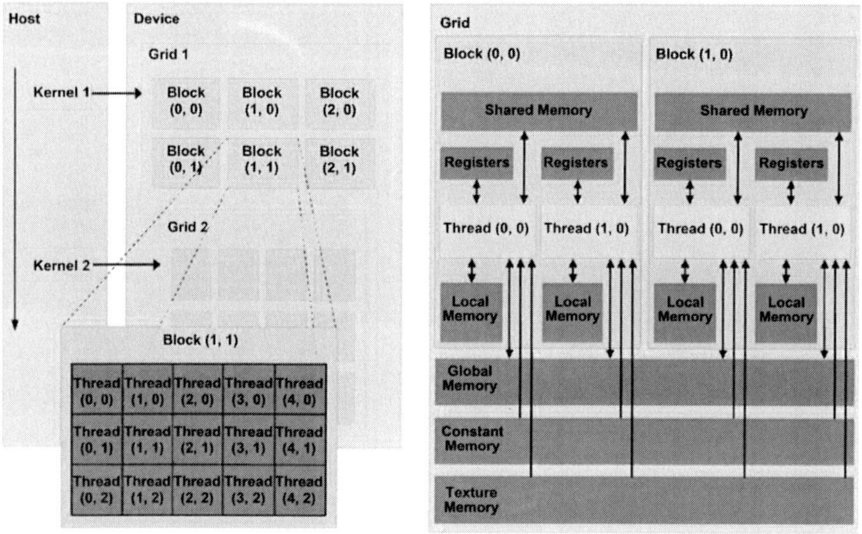

Figure 17. NVIDIA's representation of CUDA execution model and the memory hierarchy in GPUs.

The CUDA programming model can be exploited to implement both data level and task level parallelism in the implementation of ARC. The given data is divided into smaller segments and Andrew's monotone chain convex hull algorithm is used on individual segments to construct intermediate convex hulls. Each CUDA thread operates on a segment of data and computes one convex hull. CUDA has the capability to spawn a large number of threads to compute several convex hulls in parallel. Once the intermediate convex hulls are constructed by individual threads, each thread next considers two consecutive convex hulls at a time and constructs common tangents to merge the two hulls. This process is shown in Figure 18. If the number of intermediate convex hulls is N, then N-1 threads are required for to merging these hulls in parallel. The resulting set of points may not form a convex hull as we do not combine the intermediate convex hulls hierarchically but consecutively as explained in Section 5. One of the important observations is that the computations on the upper half are independent of the lower half computations, thereby allowing concurrent computations on the upper and lower half. The CUDA streams approach is used to compute the upper and lower hull in parallel and exploit task level parallelism.

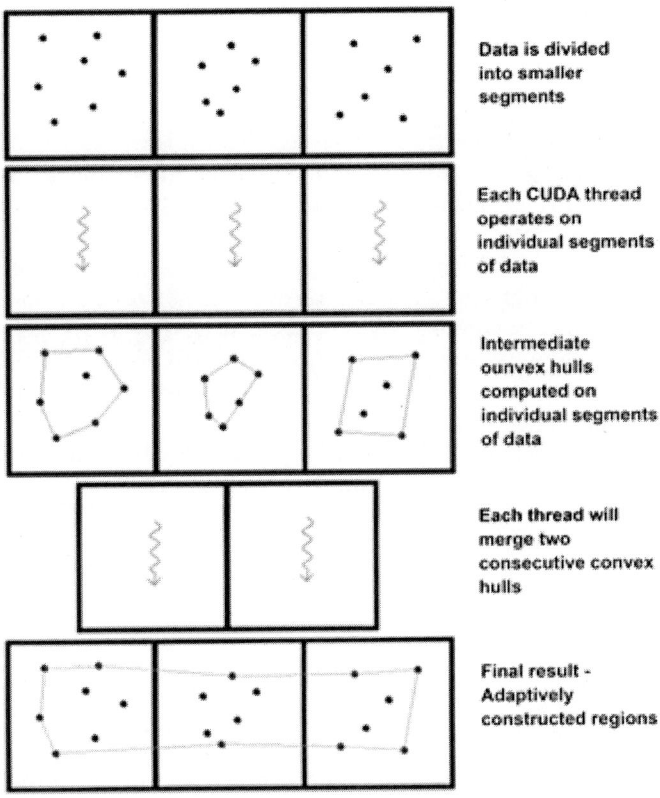

Figure 18. Scaled down illustration of data level parallelism in our implementation.

An initial version of the algorithm utilizing both data level and task level parallelism was implemented on a NVIDIA Tesla K40c accelerator and hence forth known as the naïve version. For the naïve version, the number of points processed by each thread was fixed at a value of 4 and the kernel execution time of the naive version is shown in Figure 19. Comparing the execution time of the naïve and the sequential versions of Andrew's monotone chain convex hull algorithm (Figure 7) shows a 60% improvement in performance. Even though 60% improvement in performance is significant for many applications, the naïve version is still not suitable for real time applications, especially when handling large data points (64 million points take 650 ms for computation of ARC). To improve the performance of the naive version, refactoring the program to the GPU hardware and software architectures is necessary. Therefore, as a first step, the naïve version code is profiled using the NVIDIA visual profiler [19] .

6.1. Profiling Analysis of Naive Version

The NVIDIA Visual Profiler [20] is a cross-platform performance analysis tool that provides guidance for optimizing CUDA applications. It helps in the identification of performance bottlenecks and delivers a graphical visualization of the bottlenecks. The profiling results of the naive version are shown in Figure 20. The naïve version consists of 4 kernel functions: 2 kernels to construct upper/ lower intermediate convex hulls and 2 kernels to merge the intermediate convex hulls consecutively. As we can see in Figure 20 timeline, the memory transfer time from the host (CPU) to the device (GPU) and vice versa is significantly greater than the computational time, and also the memory transfers are not contiguous. This indicates that the program performance is bottlenecked by the bandwidth of the Peripheral Component Interconnect Express (PCIe) bus. Also, the computations of the kernel functions that operate on the upper/lower halves of data are not perfectly overlapped. This is mainly due to the GPU being stalled as it waits for all the data required by the kernel to be transferred before starting the computations.

Furthermore, the profiler also identifies additional performance bottlenecks which are summarized below:

- Low warp execution efficiency due to divergent branches

The profiler indicates low warp execution efficiency for the kernel functions signifying the inefficient use of GPUs for computation. The compute resources are best utilized when all the threads in a warp are active. The algorithm is implemented with different control statements that result in branching, and the profiler recognizes 33.2% and 93% divergence in the kernel function that computes intermediate convex hulls and the kernel function that merges the hulls respectively. The number of active threads in an SPMD execution model can be improved by having less divergent branches executing different instructions within the same warp.

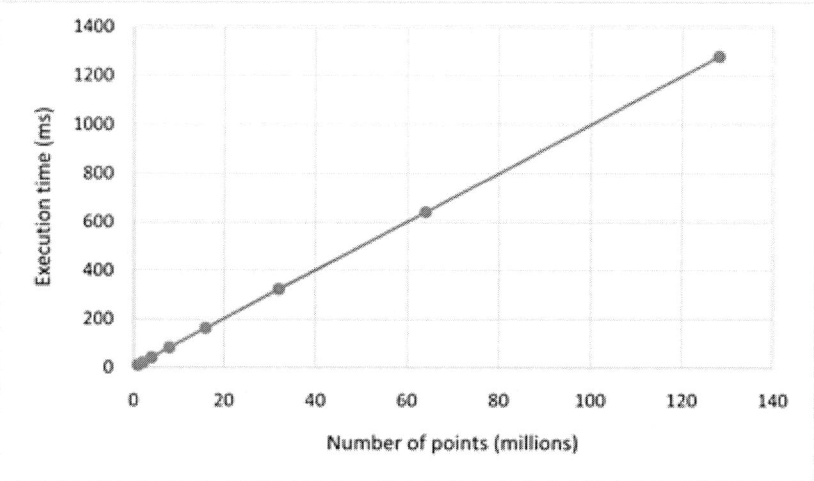

Figure 19. Execution time of the naive version of ARC.

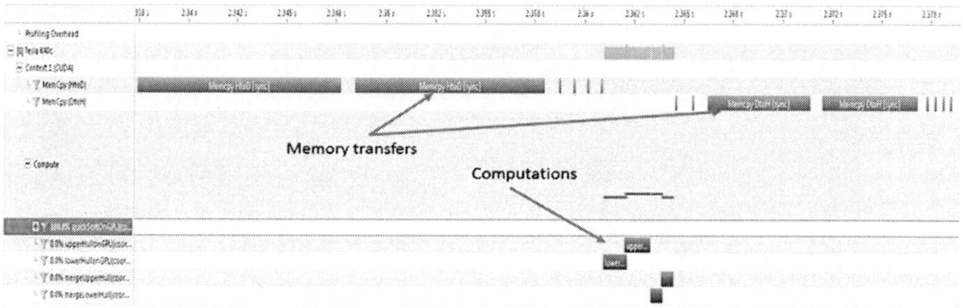

Figure 20. Execution timeline generated by the NVIDIA visual profiler.

- Global memory alignment and access pattern

The profiler identifies inefficient use of memory bandwidth due to misaligned global memory access patterns. As the instructions are issued per warp in an SPMD execution model, 32 threads in a warp cooperatively request a single memory access, which is serviced by one or more memory transactions. Un- aligned and non-coalesced memory access due to warp divergence or the pattern of memory addresses requested by each thread can result in inefficient memory accesses. For uncached global memory accesses, the data always flows through the L2 cache, and it performs four 32-byte transactions in a single memory cycle. In ARC, redundant loads of data occur if the threads in a warp access data points such that N mod (128) ≠ 0, where N is the total number of data points accessed by the threads in a warp as shown in Figure 21. Redundant loads could be avoided by making N an integer multiple of 32, however, for efficient utilization of memory bandwidth N must be an integer multiple of 128.

- L2 cache access latency

The profiler records 2.7 million global memory loads performed at a rate of 155.852 GB/s and 5.3 million reads from the L2 cache. The L2 cache reads are higher because the algorithm reuses spatially adjacent data in computations, benefitting by both temporal and spatial locality of data. As an example, we have the arrays that store the size of intermediate convex hulls and the convex hulls themselves accessed repeatedly within the same kernel function and therefore are cached. However, the L2 cache located outside the SMs has significant memory access latency of 100 clock cycles, and this latency can be reduced by moving data that is reused to a cache closer to the SMs. The cache closer to the SMs which can be programmatically controlled in the GPUs is known as the shared memory which has a latency of 12 to 32 clock cycles.

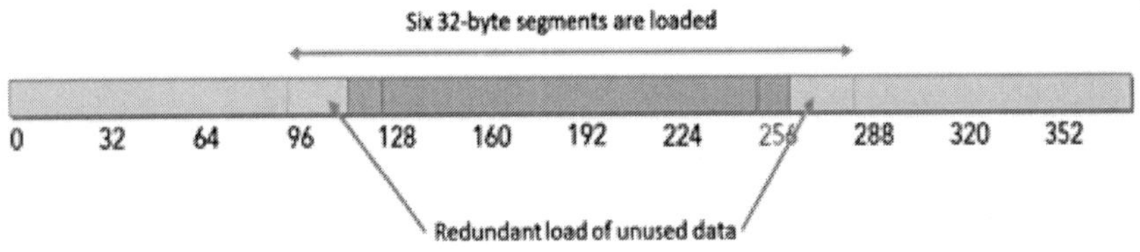

Figure 21. Inefficient use of memory bandwidth due to redundant loads.

Table 1. CGMA for different kernel functions.

Kernel functions	CGMA
lower Hull On GPU	1/2
upper Hull On GPU	1/2
merge Lower Hull	8/15
merge Upper Hull	8/15

GPUs use DDR5 memory, which is a high bandwidth memory but has latency [21] of 400 - 800 cycles resulting in large memory access latency compared to 10 - 20 cycle latency for arithmetic operations. The memory access latency is hidden due to the multiple threads executing the job at the same time, but it is still necessary to access the memory efficiently. To analyze the memory access efficiency, the compute-to-global memory access ratio (CGMA) for the naive version is determined. CGMA is defined as:

$$CGMA = \frac{\text{Number off loating point operations}}{\text{Number of global memory accesses}}. \quad (2)$$

If CGMA is significantly greater than 1, the GPU spends more time performing computations rather than fetching data from memory. These types of problems are called compute bound problems. On the other hand, if the CGMA is less or close to 1, the problem is memory bound indicating that the GPU spends most of the time fetching data from the memory rather than computing. Table 1 shows the CGMA of different kernel functions of the naïve version. The CGMA of all the four kernels is significantly less than 1, making the naïve version memory bound. The performance of memory bound problems is limited by the memory bus bandwidth and memory clock speed, which makes it difficult to improve the performance.

In order to improve the performance, we have to increase the CGMA for our implementation. Considering Equation (2), we can either increase the numerator to improve CGMA or decrease the denominator. Increasing the numerator is not a feasible option because increasing the number of floating point operations translates to artificially introducing the computational complexity of the existing algorithm. Therefore, we consider the second option, which is to decrease the value of the denominator. This can be done by reducing the number of global memory accesses and specifically multiple accesses to the same data either on the global memory or L2 cache. We use shared memory, which is a user controlled cache to store chunks of data from global memory. Later, we use the data in the shared memory to perform the computations. This reduces the memory access latency due to multiple accesses of the data on global memory and L2 cache.

7. OPTIMIZATIONS

The profiler analysis of the naïve version along with the CGMA computations provides insights about the possible approaches that can improve performance. This section discusses the various optimization approaches used to improve the performance of the naïve version.

7.1. Shared Memory to Reduce Global Memory Access

To improve L2 cache access latency by reusing on-chip data, and reduce the global memory bandwidth required by the kernels we make use of shared memory. Assuming each thread performs only one iteration of the algorithm, the kernel function that computes convex hulls of one half of the given set of points have to access the global memory 16 times, and the kernel function that combines two consecutive convex hulls has to access the global memory 30 times in the naïve version. The shared memory latency being 12 to 32 cycles is about 50 times lower than the uncached global memory latency [22] and three times lower than the L2 cache. Therefore, a program accessing shared memory instead of global memory or L2 cache performs better. To reduce the number of global memory accesses, we load the data from global memory to shared memory and perform the computations. Later, the result is written back into global memory.

In the kernel function that computes either the upper half or lower half of intermediate convex hulls, the data seen by each thread block is loaded into the shared memory. Each thread computes convex hulls by considering a small number of elements. The number of elements processed by each thread is calculated as the ratio of the total number of points to the total number of threads. Copying the data from the global memory to the shared memory and performing computations using the copied data on the shared memory is shown in Step 1(a) and 1(b) of Figure 22. Once all the threads in a block have finished computing the convex hulls, the resulting points are written back into the global memory. This is illustrated in Step 2 of Figure 22. As discussed previously, two consecutive convex hulls are combined together by constructing common tangents between them.

To reduce the number of global memory accesses while constructing tangents, the convex hulls seen by each thread block along with one convex hull from the next thread block is loaded into the shared memory (Figure 23: Step 1). For a given pair of consecutive convex hulls, only the indices to increment the right hull and the indices to decrement the left hull are stored in registers local to each thread (Figure 23: Step 2). These indices point to the data points that form a common tangent to the two consecutive convex hulls. The indices are written into the global memory after each thread completes its operation (Figure 23: Step 3).

We also use shared memory as a scratchpad memory to store the size of intermediate convex hulls and also enabled L1 caching (16 KB) along with the shared memory (48 KB) to cache global memory transactions.

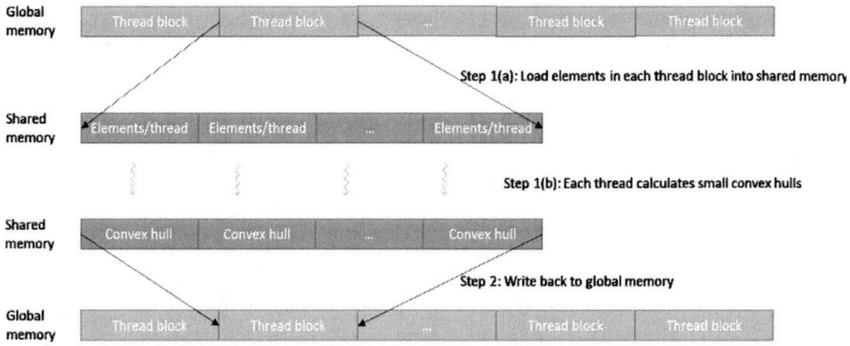

Figure 22. Shared memory implementation of constructing one half (upper/lower) of the convex hulls.

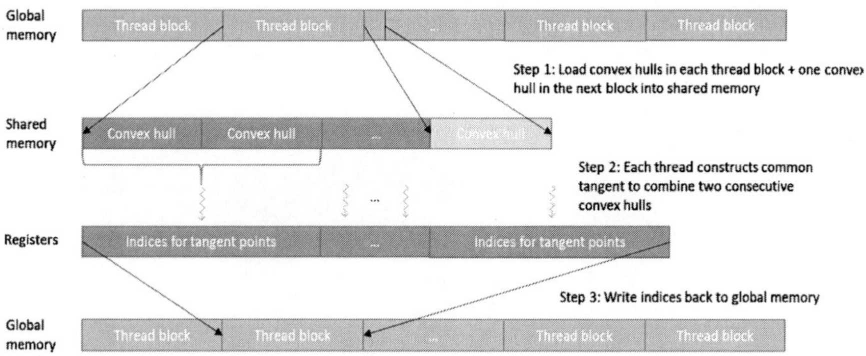

Figure 23. Shared memory implementation of combining two convex hulls by constructing common tangents.

7.2. Avoiding Warp Divergence

While loading the data into shared memory for combining two consecutive convex hulls, each thread loads one convex hull into the shared memory. But the threads at the end of each thread block (except for the last block) must load two convex hulls, one at the end of thread block and the other from the beginning of the next thread block. This can be easily achieved by using simple control statements on a traditional CPU based computing system. CPUs have complex hardware with advanced branch prediction mechanisms to implement control statements. On a CPU, there are pipelines for each program flow of the control statement. If the predicted branch is false, a CPU can quickly switch to the other pipeline and continue with the execution flow, eluding any significant performance penalty.

On the other hand, GPUs are simple devices with no branch prediction mechanisms requiring all the 32 threads in a warp execute in a synchronous fashion. If different threads in a warp execute different instructions, the GPU flushes the execution pipeline each time to load new instructions resulting in the sequential execution of each branch of the control statement. Also, since all threads in a warp execute in parallel, some of the threads in a warp will be idle and will become active during the upcoming sequence that will make the previously executing threads in that warp idle as shown in Figure 24.

To avoid warp divergence, we loaded both the flow paths of the control statements into the same branch by making use of multiple if statements instead of if-else chains as exemplified in Figure 25. In this way, both the conditional instructions are loaded into the execution pipeline, and only the statements with conditions resulting to true will be executed by the threads.

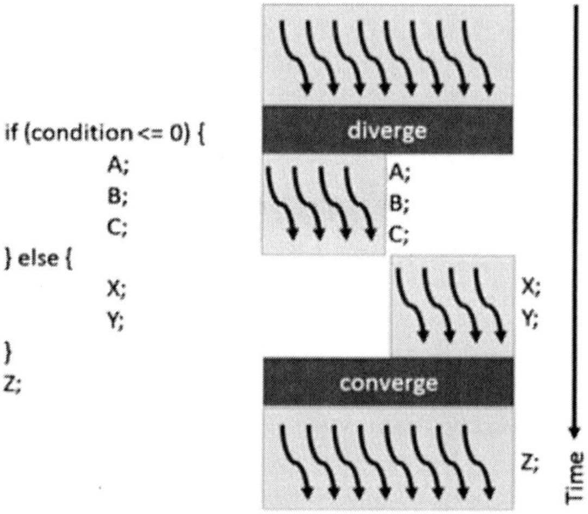

Figure 24. Warp divergence due to if-else statements.

7.3. Optimized Memory Access

While accessing global memory, the data has to pass through L2 cache by default, and four 32-byte transactions are performed to fetch 128 bytes of single precision data for the threads in a warp. On enabling the L1 cache, a 128-byte transaction request is used to load single precision data for a warp. In other words, NVIDIA GPUs has a L1 cache line granularity of 128 bytes and an L2 cache line granularity of 32 bytes. The memory fetches from the global memory is a major performance bottleneck, and it is necessary to keep the number of load transactions to a minimum. One way to keep the load transactions to a minimum is to load only the required data by a warp and avoid redundant data loads. Figure 26 shows an example where a warp requests 128 bytes of data and the GPU performs four 32-byte transactions to load 128 bytes, and the data is accessed within the same 128-bytesegment (aligned to the 128-byte boundary). This is very efficient when compared to the unaligned redundant load shown in Figure 21, where the data requested by a warp requires six 32-byte transactions in three 128-byte segments, and all the data that is loaded is not used by the warp.

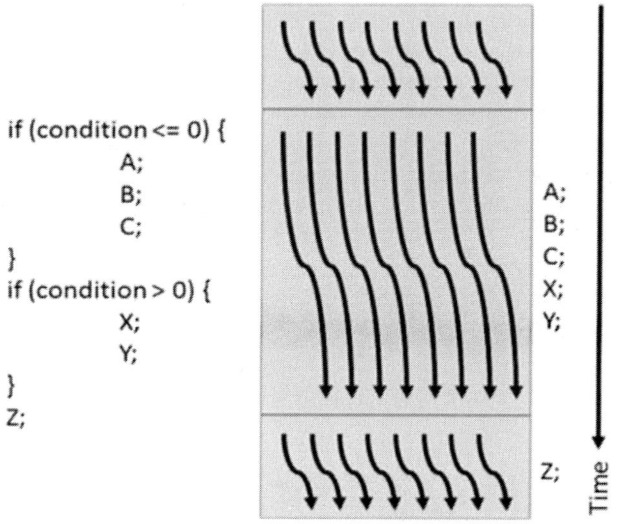

Figure 25. Warp divergence due to if-else statements.

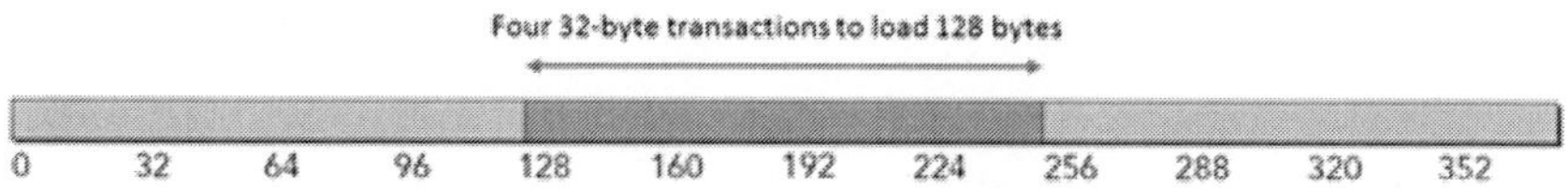

Figure 26. Optimized memory access with L1 caching disabled.

We adjust the number of points seen by each thread to construct intermediate convex hulls such that the data requested by a warp is a multiple of cache line granularity depending on the problem size, thereby minimizing redundant loads of data. NVIDIA also reports [23] that the effective bandwidth is poor for strided memory access with strides greater than 8 as the hardware cannot combine the accesses that are far apart in the physical memory. Therefore, adjacent threads in our program access contiguous data points to construct adjacent intermediate convex hulls and do not perform strided access.

7.4. Reducing Host to Device Data Transfer Latency

The transfer of data from the host to the device takes place over the PCIe bus. Even though it is not possible to increase the speed of data transfer due to hardware limitations, it is possible to reduce the time that the GPU spends waiting for data. Data is allocated on the CPU memory as pageable memory. Pageable memory can be swapped into the secondary storage by the operating system to give an illusion of additional main memory than available. Since the GPU does not have control over the paging operation, it takes more time for the data to be transferred from pageable memory to GPU memory. To decrease the data transfer time from CPU memory to GPU memory, we used pinned memory on the CPU. Pinned memory or page-locked memory is a non-swappable memory allocation on the CPU random access memory (RAM) preventing the operating system from swapping the allocated memory to secondary storage. This allows the data transfer between CPU and GPU through the PCIe bus at a higher bandwidth.

8. RESULTS AND ANALYSIS

We implemented the ARC technique on a NVIDIA GPU using the CUDA C programming model. The hardware platform consists of an Intel Xeon E5-2620-0 (Sandy Bridge) processor for implementing the sequential Andrew's monotone chain convex hull algorithm and NVIDIA Tesla K40c for implementing the ARC technique.

Sets of random points with a normal distribution to test and compare the optimized implementation of ARC technique with the sequential Andrew's monotone chain convex hull algorithm were generated. Figure 27 shows the execution times of the sequential Andrew's monotone chain convex hull algorithm and the parallel ARC technique kernels of the naïve and advanced versions using the shared memory with the number of elements processed by each thread held constant. The results shown in Figure 27 correspond to the load being equally distributed among CUDA threads with each thread operating on 4 data points to construct the intermediate convex hulls and excludes the memory transfer time over the PCIe bus for the parallel implementations. We can see from Figure 27 that the computation of adaptive regions for 16 million data points takes place in about 14 ms in contrast to 306 ms for the sequential implementation, indicating near real time performance. Figure 28 shows the overall execution time for the same three cases indicated previously and the result includes the data transfer time over the PCIe bus. The naïve parallel version had a larger execution time in comparison to the sequential version due to significant time spent on memory transfers from host to device and vice versa. The considerable time for memory transfers is due to a redundant data transfers required in the naïve version. The memory transfer time was improved by eliminating redundant data transfers and making use of pinned memory in the advanced version, which shows significant improvement in performance. In Figure 29, the speedup between the naïve kernel and sequential version and the advanced kernel and sequential version is presented. The advanced version kernel on an average has a speedup of 21.6× while the naïve version kernel had only a speedup of 2×. The higher speedup of the advanced version clearly demonstrates the effectiveness of the optimizations applied to the naïve version. Taking into account the memory transfer time for the advanced versions, the average speedup achieved is 9.3× as shown in Figure 30.

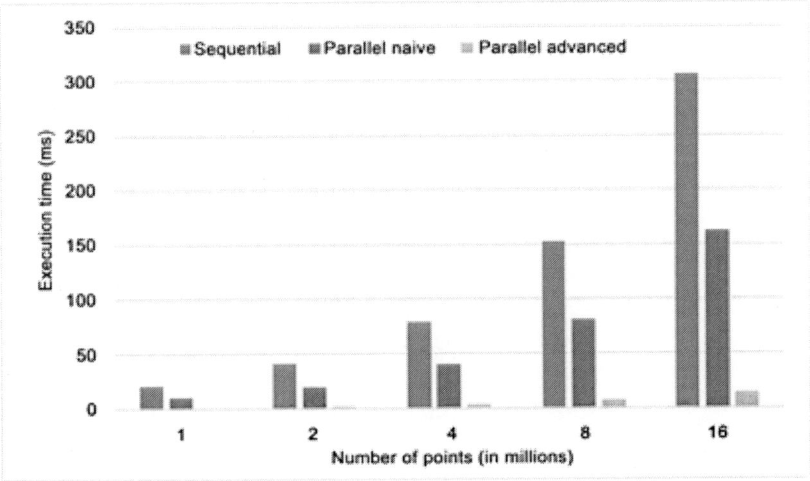

Figure 27. Execution times of sequential, naive parallel kernel, and advanced parallel kernel implementations for computing contours.

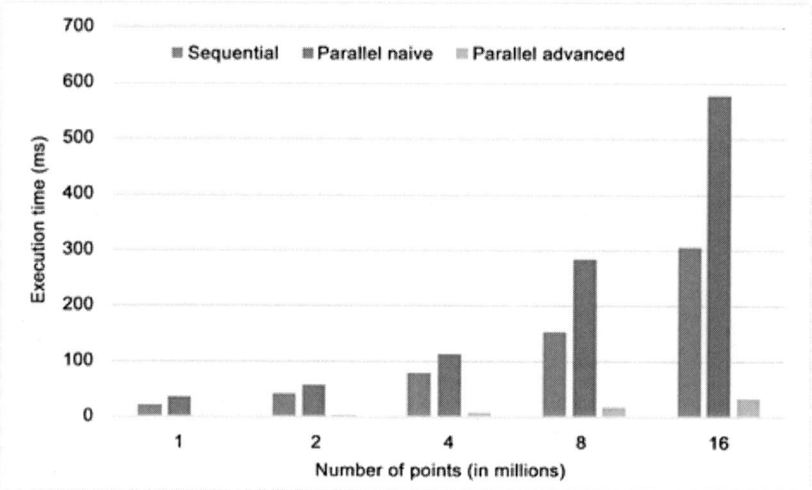

Figure 28. Overall execution times of sequential, naive parallel and advanced parallel implementations for computing contours.

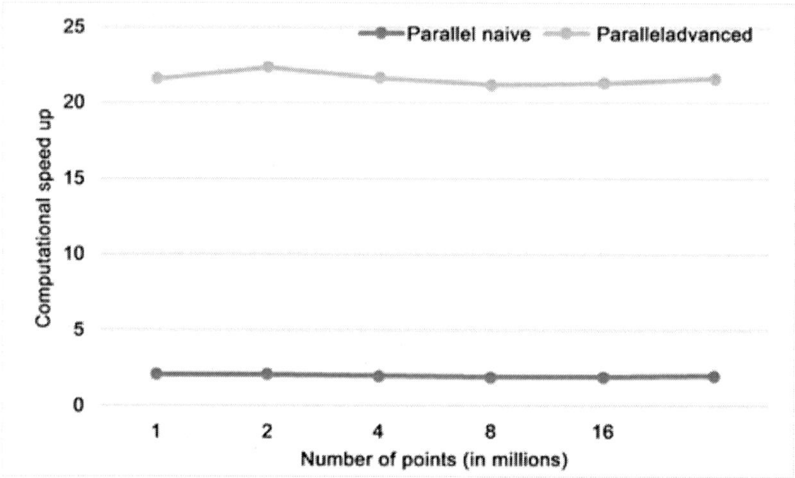

Figure 29. Computational speedup of naive and advanced parallel versions.

The overall improved speedup of the advanced version can be attributed to the use of pinned memory instead of the paged memory in the naïve version in addition to the use of shared memory. Even though an overall 9.3× speedup has been achieved, the speedup remains constant with increasing number of points as depicted in Figure 30indicating weak scaling of the problem. As the number of points in increased, correspondingly, the number of threads is also increased as the number of points per thread is held constant. However, the number of cores or processors in a GPU is constant. According to Gustafson's law [24] , the workload is scaled up to maintain a fixed execution time as the number of processor increases; the speedup increases linearly. Since the number of GPU cores is not increasing with increasing workload, the speedup has to remain constant or decrease with increasing workload.

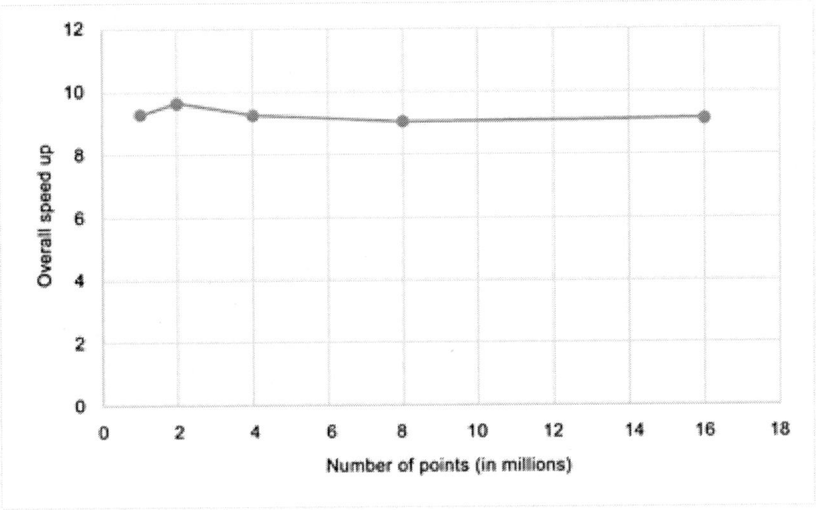

Figure 30. Overall speedup of the advanced parallel version.

The second goal for using the ARC technique was to eliminate the artifacts present in the contour of a radio propagation map determined using the convex hull approach. Given a set of points, the ARC technique can either construct a convex hull or a set of points, which is not a convex hull representing the contour of a radio propagation map accurately. If the ARC technique is forced to use a single thread, i.e., a sequential construct, the set of points obtained using ARC will match the convex hull. However, by varying the number of threads, the result can be a non-convex hull with varying levels of granularity. The resulting set of points obtained using ARC is selected by computing a number of intermediate convex hulls to fit the given set of points. These intermediate convex hulls are merged consecutively in order to obtain the resulting set. In other words, the number of intermediate convex hulls constructed represents the "resolution" or detail with which the radio propagation map is approximated. In our implementation, since each thread constructs one intermediate convex hull, the resolution of approximation will depend on the number of threads. Decreasing the number of threads decreases the number of intermediate convex hulls, and degrades the application performance as the load handled by each thread increases. ARC does not result in the contour of a radio propagation map directly but also includes points inside the contour that are eliminated using simple techniques [25] if a contour is desired. In Figure 31, the original radio propagation map, convex hull based, and ARC based contours are shown for increasing number of points. We can see that the contours generated based on the ARC technique has eliminated the artifacts present in the convex hull based contour and also accurately represent the contour of the original radio propagation map.

9. CONCLUSIONS

The technique of adaptive region construction is a low complexity approach that can represent the given contour with varying degrees of details. Adaptive region construction technique provides the capability to construct the contour of a radio propagation map efficiently. The implementation of the adaptive region construction technique on a GPU using the CUDA programming model has been demonstrated. The GPU implementation provides good application performance (speedup) for high resolution representation of contours but is not suitable for low resolution representations. By applying optimization techniques to the naïve version, a 21× improvement in computational performance for large data sets was achieved. As most of the applications that use radio propagation maps are benefited by the detailed representation of radio propagation maps, the ARC technique fulfills the necessity for a fast algorithm. The ARC technique is not only suitable for real-time operation but also avoids artifacts in contrast to the contours determined using the convex hull approach.

In addition to using the ARC technique for determining the contour of a radio propagation map, it is also possible to approximate other spatial data. Using the ARC, multi-resolution representation of the spatial data is possible. The multi-resolution representation of large spatial data sets allows improved processing time and lower storage requirements.

The ARC technique as mentioned previously is inefficiently operating on low resolution radio propagation maps. Also, with large resolution, special attention has to be paid to the memory transfers between the CPU and the GPU. However, with the newer versions of the NVIDIA GPU equipped with the NVlink technology, the latency due to memory transfers is significantly reduced.

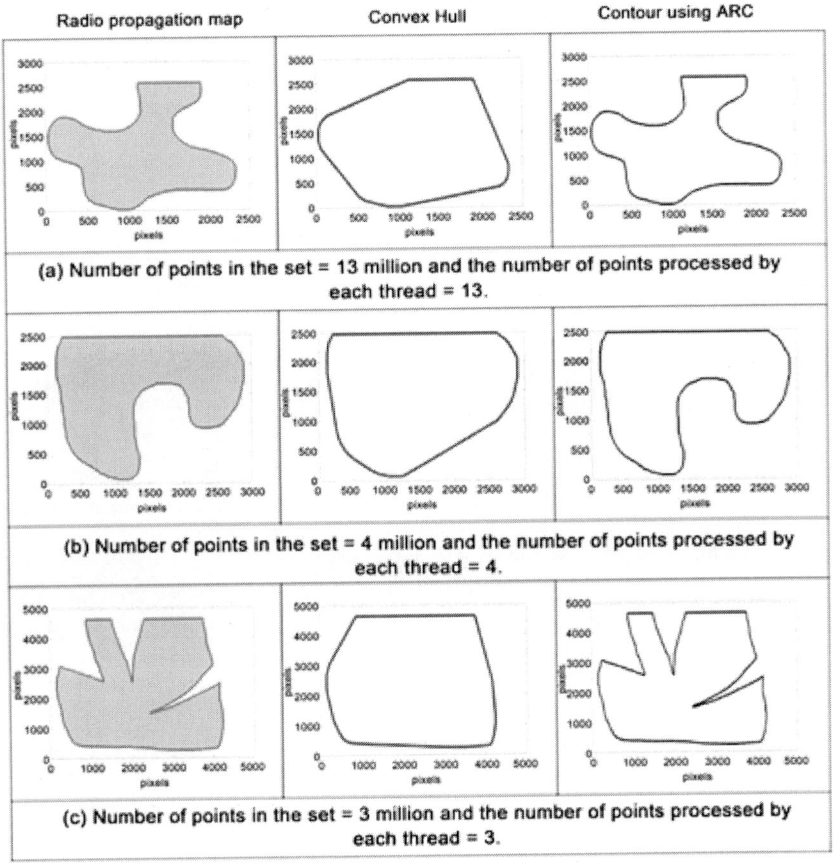

Figure 31. Contours of radio propagation map using ARC.

REFERENCES

1. Haslett, C. (2008) Essentials of Radio Wave Propagation. Cambridge University Press, Cambridge.
2. Miles, J., Muknahallipatna, S., Kubichek, R.F., McInroy, J. and Muralidhara, H. (2014) Use of Radio Propagation Maps in a Single Moving Beacon Assisted Localization in MANETs. 2014 International Conference on Computing, Networking and Communications (ICNC), Honolulu, 3-6 February 2014, 871-877.

3. Miles, J., Kamath, G., Muknahallipatna, S., Stefanovic, M. and Kubichek, R.F. (2013) Optimal Trajectory Determination of a Single Moving Beacon for Efficient Localization in a Mobile Ad-Hoc Network. Ad Hoc Networks, 11, 238-256.
4. Muralidhara, H. and Kubichek, R. (2011) MANET Localization Using Non-Circular Overlapping Range Maps. International Conference on Wireless Networks, Las Vegas, 18-21 July 2011, 8-12.
5. Ramakrishnaiah, V.B., Kubichek, R.F. and Muknahallipatna, S.S. (2015) Optimization of Antenna Beam Pattern in Ad Hoc Networks for Optimal Global Performance. 2015 IEEE 58th International Midwest Symposium on Circuits and Systems (MWSCAS), Fort Collins, 2-5 August 2015, 1-4.
6. Andrew, A.M. (1979) Another Efficient Algorithm for Convex Hulls in Two Dimensions. Information Processing Letters, 9, 216-219.
7. O'Rourke, J. (1993) Computational Geometry in C. Cambridge University Press, Cambridge.
8. Douglas, D.H. and Peucker, T.K. (1973) Algorithms for the Reduction of the Number of Points Required to Represent a Digitized Line or Its Caricature. Cartographical: The International Journal for Geographic Information and Geovisualization, 10, 112-122.
9. Ramer, U. (1972) An Iterative Procedure for the Polygonal Approximation of Plane Curves. Computer Graphics and Image Processing, 1, 244-256.
10. Prakash, N. and Sarkar, A. (2015) Development of Shape Based Leaf Categorization," IOSR Journal of Computer Engineering (IOSR-JCE), 17, 48-53.
11. Chen, Z., Delis, A. and Bertoni, H.L. (2004) Building Footprint Simplification Techniques and Their Effects on Radio Propagation Predictions. The Computer Journal, 47, 103-133.
12. Catrein, D., Reyer, M. and Rick, T. (2007) Accelerating Radio Wave Propagation Predictions by Implementation on Graphics Hardware. IEEE Vehicular Technology Conference, Dublin, 22-25 April 2007, 510-514.
13. Cheng, M.X., Ling, Y. and Sadler, B.M. (2014) Wireless Ad Hoc Network Connectivity Assessment and Relay Node Deployment. 2014 IEEE Global Communications Conference, Austin, 8-12 December 2014, 399-404.
14. Liu, D., Lee, M.-C., Pun, C.-M. and Liu, H. (2013) Analysis of Wireless Localization in Nonline-of-Sight Conditions. IEEE Transactions on Vehicular Technology, 62, 1484-1492.
15. Boyd, S. and Vandenberghe, L. (2004) Convex Optimization. Cambridge University Press, Cambridge.
16. Preparata, F.P. and Hong, S.J. (1977) Convex Hulls of Finite Sets of Points in Two and Three Dimensions. Communications of the ACM, 20, 87-93.
17. Preparata, F.P. and Shamos, M.I. (1985) Computational Geometry. Springer, Berlin.
18. Manca, E., Manconi, A., Orro, A., Armano, G. and Milanesi, L. (2016) CUDA-Quicksort: An Improved GPU-Based Implementation of Quicksort. Concurrency and Computation: Practice and Experience, 28, 21-43.
19. NVIDIA (2017) NVIDIA Developer Zone—CUDA Toolkit Documentation. http://docs.nvidia.com/cuda/index.html#axzz4fZgKptTq
20. NVIDIA (year) NVIDIA Visual Profiler. https://developer.nvidia.com/nvidia-visual-profiler
21. Cheng, J., Grossman, M. and McKercher, T. (2014) Professional CUDA C Programming. John Wiley & Sons, Indiana.
22. Harris, M. (2013) Using Shared Memory in CUDA C/C++. https://devblogs.nvidia.com/parallelforall/using-shared-memory-cuda-cc/
23. Harris, M. (2013) How to Access Global Memory Efficiently in CUDA C/C++ Kernels. https://devblogs.nvidia.com/parallelforall/how-access-global-memory-efficiently-cuda-c-kernels/
24. Gustafson, J.L. (1988) Reevaluating Amdahl's law. Communications of the ACM, 31, 532-533.
25. Nitzberg, M., Mumford, D. and Shiota, T. (1993) Filtering, Segmentation and Depth. Springer-Verlag New York, Inc., Secaucus.

CHAPTER 7

Model of a Context-Aware Middleware for Mobile Workers

Esraa Moustafa, Gaëtan Rey, Stéphane Lavirotte, Jean-Yves Tigli

Université Côte d'Azur, Centre National de la Recherche Scientifique (CNRS), I3S, Nice, France

ABSTRACT

With the development of Internet of things and Web of things, computing becomes more pervasive, invisible and present everywhere. In fact, in our environment, we are surrounded by multiple devices that deliver (web) services which meet the needs of the users. However, the mobility of these devices as the users has important repercussions that challenge software design of these applications because the variability of the environment cannot be anticipated at the design time. Thus, it will be interesting to dynamically discover the environment and adapt the application during its execution to the new contextual conditions. We therefore, propose a model of a context-aware middleware that can address this issue through a monitoring service which is capable of reasoning and observation channels capable of calculating the context during the runtime. The monitoring service evaluates the pre-defined X-Query predicates in the context manager and uses Prolog to deduce the services needed to respond back. An independent observation channel for each different predicate is then dynamically generated by the monitoring service depending on the current state of the environment. Each channel sends its result directly to the context manager which consequently calculates the context based on all the predicates' results while preserving the reactivity of the self- adaptive system.

Keywords: Auto-Adaptation, Context-Awareness, Middleware, Reasoning Engine

1. INTRODUCTION

Nowadays, the world has nearly 13 billion connected devices in use and it's estimated that by 2020, this number will increase to reach more than 29 billion connected devices [1] . Pervasive Computing, aka Ubiquitous Computing, was once a vision of Mark Weiser. He predicted that technologies would weave themselves into the fabric of everyday life until they were indistinguishable from it [2] .

Despite the huge number of connected devices, pervasive computing is challenged by the constant change in the environment. People (along with their on- body sensors) are constantly moving; objects might get displaced and sensors might fail. These changes are impossible to predict at applications' design time. Thus, we need to discover the environment (context) dynamically and adapt the applications in the runtime accordingly through a Context-Aware Middleware.

This paper is organized as follows. Section 2 provides a discussion about related works. In Section 3, we introduce CONTINUUM project and the motivation behind our research. In Section 4, we discuss our contribution to the impro- vement of CONTINUUM. In Section 5, we introduce our model of a context- aware middleware from the conceptual and implementation perspectives. We also highlight our proof of concept. Finally, we conclude our work in Section 6.

2. RELATED WORK

Many researchers proposed Context-Aware Middleware. In [3] , Context-Aware- ness is defined as an "Opportunistic Situation Identification". A phone-centric middleware is proposed which uses a hybrid learning approach for reasoning that combines pre-computed models and imputed models. This middleware tackles multiple challenges specially the constant movement of the users but it's limited by the phone constraints such as the battery life and the local storage capacity. In [4] , middleware architecture for a context-aware system in smart home environment is proposed. Web

Ontology Language (WOL) is used to model the context and a rule-based algorithm is used for reasoning. A conducted survey on context aware middleware architectures [5] compared multiple recent projects such as FlexRFID [6] , Context Awareness for Internet of Things (CA4IOT) [7] and Octopus [8] . Each project has a different modelling and reasoning approach. The survey pointed some limitations such as the need to handle the users' security, increase the degree of context awareness and ensure standardization. However, these middleware architectures are either based on predefined rules only and thus can't handle unknown situations or they use a specific language such as OWL which makes it hard for the users to define new situations without the engagement of developers.

3. CONTINUUM

CONTINUUM [9] Project offers architecture to evaluate the context in the runtime through a three-tiered adaptation middleware and observation channels that monitor the environment as shown in Figure 1. This architecture is based on Rasmussen's model of human cognitive behavior [10] .

- Reflexive Behavioral Adaptation: The first tier can make the adaptation of the application according to the devices present in the environment and the rules of adaptations activated within a very short period of time hence the name "reflexive". This corresponds to human behaviors based on reflexes.
- Contextual Tactics Adaptation: The second tier identifies the current state among a set of known states specified at the design through a knowledge base and a context manager. This corresponds to human behavior based on sets of rules learned with experience.
- Strategic Adaptation to Unknown Contexts: This layer proposes mechanisms to adapt the application to unknown states. This corresponds to human be- havior based on knowledge. This involves developing an action plan to respond to an unknown situation.

3.1. Terminology

In the next sections, we'll be describing our work using below terms:

All the objects, people and computer systems are included in the environment.

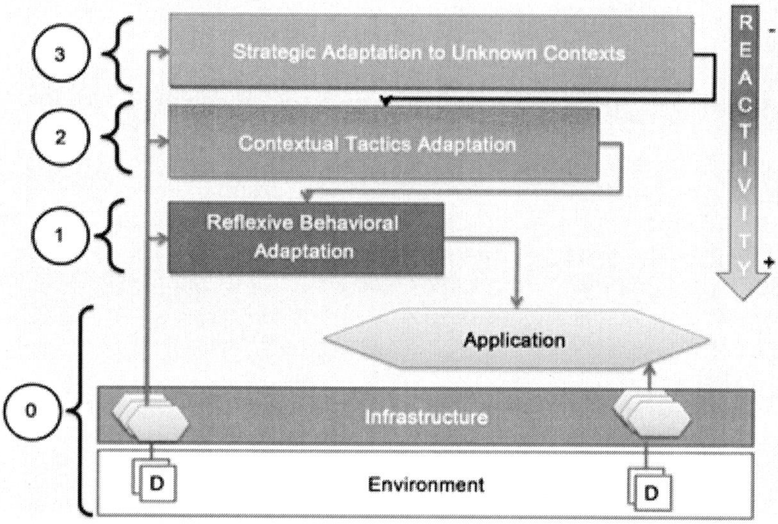

Figure 1. The architecture of CONTINUUM based on Rasmussen's model of cognitive behavior [4] .

The observables are the data of the devices (sensors) which make it possible to describe the attributes of the entities of the world (user, physical object ...). These observables serve to characterize the entities of the world (at the design time) and to identify them (at the runtime).

Predicates are Boolean functions based on entities. From a set of verified predicates, we find the current state of the context (usually named situation). It is for this reason that from n predicates, we will obtain 2^n possible states. For each state, we define one or more adaptation rules.

3.2. Scenario

To better illustrate the importance of a context-aware middleware for mobile workers, let's look at below scenario.

Raoul is a technician at the combustion turbine. Every morning, he makes a round to take measurements of some equipment in different sites. Each site has a different security level. There are 2 types of security:

- Building Security which indicates the level of authorization of the worker to access the site.

- Worker Security indicating if he is sufficiently equipped to access the site.

In this example, the goal is to identify the authorized and equipped worker to access any site. If this is the case, the time spent at the site is calculated, and an optimized itinerary service is offered to the technician, in order to increase the number of items he can inspect during his round. In case an issue occurred and the sound sensors, temperature or pressure exceeded a certain threshold, then an alert service notifies the technician to take the necessary measures. For simplicity purpose, we will limit ourselves to the pressure sensors in the scenario. In case there is an intruder, the system will launch an alarm.

In other words, with the notions defined in 2.1, we get the following:

For the security preoccupation context, we have the following predicates, states, and rules:

Predicates:

P1 is Zone Secured.

P2 is Authorized/Equipped Worker.

P3 Pressure Exceeded Threshold.

Rules:

R1 starts an alarm.

R2 calculates past time.

R3 shows route/itinerary service.

R4 shows Alert Service.

Since for each n predicates, we have 2^n possible states. We thus distinguish 8 possible states.

States 1 and 2

If Raoul enters either a secured or unsecured area, if he is authorized and equipped and the pressure sensor has exceeded the threshold, then the 3 rules (R2, R3 and R4) should be applied as in (1).

$$P1, P2, P3 / !P1, P2, P3 \rightarrow R2, R3, R4. \tag{1}$$

States 3 and 4:

Same as states 1 and 2 except that the pressure doesn't exceed the threshold, R2 and R3 should thus be applied as in (2)

$$P1, P2, !P3 / !P1, P2, !P3 \rightarrow R2, R3. \tag{2}$$

States 5 and 6:

If Raoul is unauthorized to enter a secured zone, an alarm should be started as in (3).

$$P1, !P2, P3 / P1, !P2, !P3 \rightarrow R1. \tag{3}$$

States 7 and 8:

Same as states 5 and 6 except that Raoul is unauthorized to enter the unsecured zones as in (4):

$$!P1, !P2, !P3 / !P1, !P2, P3 \rightarrow R1. \tag{4}$$

3.3. Motivation

Our research was driven by the results of CONTINUUM specifically by the 2nd tier. In fact, in this tier, the adaptation is performed in 3 steps [11] as shown in Figure 2.

1) Observation: The purpose of this step is to provide numerical observables. It relies on both digital and analogue sensors and converts their data into a format compatible with the next step.
2) Transformation: This step transforms numerical observables into semantic observables.
3) Identification: this stage makes it possible to identify the current situation from the semantic observables.

To make this happen, a Knowledge Base (KB) and a Context Manager (CM) were implemented [12] .

The KB [13] is part of the Transformation step. It aims to maintain a model of the environment using ontology based RDFS language.

It receives the values and events of the sensors as well as their appearance and disappearance and thus, it keeps an image of the entire system.

The CM is part of the identification step. It mainly interrogates the KB through queries to verify the different predicates.

Field experiments were performed with the help of mobile workers to evaluate CONTINUUM which showed very promising results [14] . On the other hand, some limitations were identified which can be summarized in below points:

1) The Knowledge Base (KB) is a centralized module and thus it's a single point of failure on which the system depends. In addition to that, it doesn't en sure high availability nor scalability.
2) The Context Manager (CM) depends on the model of the KB. In CONITI-NUIUUM, the KB stores all the sensors' data using RDFS Ontology, consequently the predicates in CM must use the same ontology as the KB to be able to communicate with it. This limits the possibility of adding different reasoning engines.

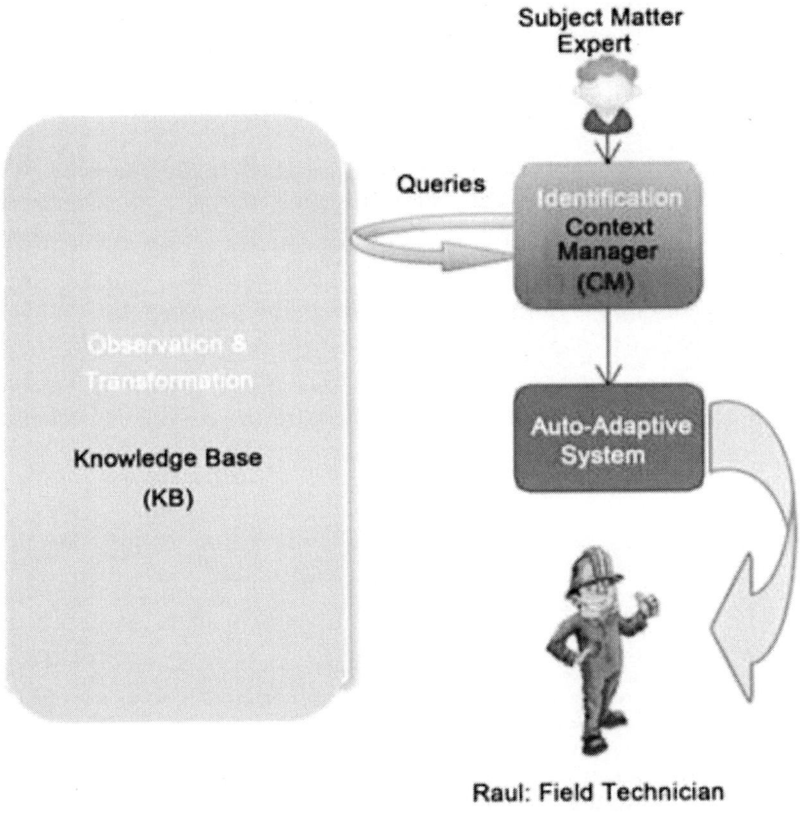

Figure 2. "Contextual tactics adaptation" Tier in CONTINUUM.

4. IMPROVING CONTINUUM

To start tackling these limitations, we divided our work into 3 parts:

1) Study of Predicates and its possible alternatives.
2) Study of the possible languages to use.
3) Study of the path between the observables and the predicates.

4.1. Study of Predicates and Its Possible Alternatives

In continuum, as explained above, situations are identified by evaluating the answer of the predicates for a given Preoccupation. But are these predicates sufficient to identify all possible situations for all the preoccupations?

To answer this question, we studied below possibilities:

1) Using continuous functions and operators to transform the output into Boolean.

   For instance, a function can be used to transform the temperature data from the sensor into Fahrenheit degrees and then transform these values into Boolean values to decide if it's hot or not (Bayesian Networks can be used in this case).

2) Using continuous functions and operators to transform the output into discrete values.

   If we take the same temperature example, the only difference would be to use fuzzy logic for instance to transform the continuous values into discrete ones.

3) Using predicates only.

   Predicates offer a finite number of possibilities to identify the current situation since for n predicates we have 2^n states.

   Also, it will be easier for an expert to express his rules associated to specific predicates.

   Since our model is intended for experts not developers, we opted for the predicates approach.

4.2. Study of the Possible Languages to Use

Defining a language is essential to expressing the users' needs through predicates. This language must be independent of the reasoning techniques used.

In addition, we must take into consideration that the context is dynamic, that objects can be moved, people enter and leave rooms, temperatures fluctuate, and activities begin and end [15] . Also, we opt for a distributed approach to overcome continuum's limitations.

We found that Contextual Query Language (CQL) can be classified into 5 categories [16] :

SQL

The SQL works well with the relational model and therefore a SQL query only returns tabular data. However, the structure of a sensor network is hierarchical, so we need a query language that can traverse in a tree-like manner [17] .

Ontology

We have found several context models based on OWL (Web Ontology Language) ontologies. OWL is much more expressive compared to other ontologies languages like RDFS and it allows semantic interoperability to exchange and share knowledge of the context between different systems in various domains [18] . On the other hand, their query language is specific and not generic.

Programming language

Programming languages can address various recursive queries, but they require the development of complex algorithms to handle queries [16] . We have eliminated it because it requires developers to write predicates and thus it will not be suitable for experts.

Graphic

We found a language called "chiromancer" [19] that is a Visual Query Language (VQL) based on a "Query by Browsing" paradigm. This paradigm is based on the questioning of a relational schema using familiar concepts of the desktop user interface paradigm. This is done by representing both the schema and the query as a folder hierarchy.

XML

Among the XML-based CQLs, the one that has most interested us is called "X-Query" because it is a flexible language by nature and it can query tabular and hierarchical data and is therefore adapted for the networks of Sensors. Moreover, it allows scalability and it meets our criteria of independence between the technology of the implementation of the reasoning and that of the writing of the requests. Moreover, it is easy for an expert to learn such a language.

4.3. Study of the Path between the Observables and the Predicates

This task consists in studying how predicates will be evaluated using the current observables in the environment. To do this, we studied the different types of reasoning to identify situations [20] . In fact, there are 2 approaches to reasoning.

The specification-based approach consists of reasoning according to predefined rules and predicates. For example, in the mobile worker scenario, if the pressure exceeded a certain threshold, an alert service will be activated.

This approach has the advantage that it is direct and easy to use by experts but its disadvantage is that it does not allow the identification of unknown situations and it is frustrating in cases where it is necessary to define many rules.

The learning-based approach consists in using learning techniques with the advantage of identifying unknown situations or better adapting to a given concern. For example, the user's mood is among the contexts extremely difficult to detect [21] . It is difficult to write rules to predict the mood of the user, since each user is different. That is why in this case, it is better to use learning techniques. These techniques learn to identify the situations from a training period in which one or more people define situations according to the sensor data (Supervised Learning). There are also other learning algorithms that can do clustering but do not label them (Unsupervised Learning). Consequently, the major disadvantage is that learning can take a lot of human effort and time (several months [22]).

Since both approaches have advantages and disadvantages, the best is to use a hybrid approach [21] .

5. PROPOSED MODEL

In the first part, we will present the conceptual model that we propose to answer the problem. Then, we will detail how to implement such a model. Finally, we present the proof of concept that we implemented.

5.1. Conceptual Model

Our model, as shown in Figure 3, is based on the model defined in continuum. It contains the context manager whose purpose, is to modify the list of adaptive rules (AR) activated in the self-adaptive system. The list of activated ARs is calculated per the current situation itself calculated according to the predicates.

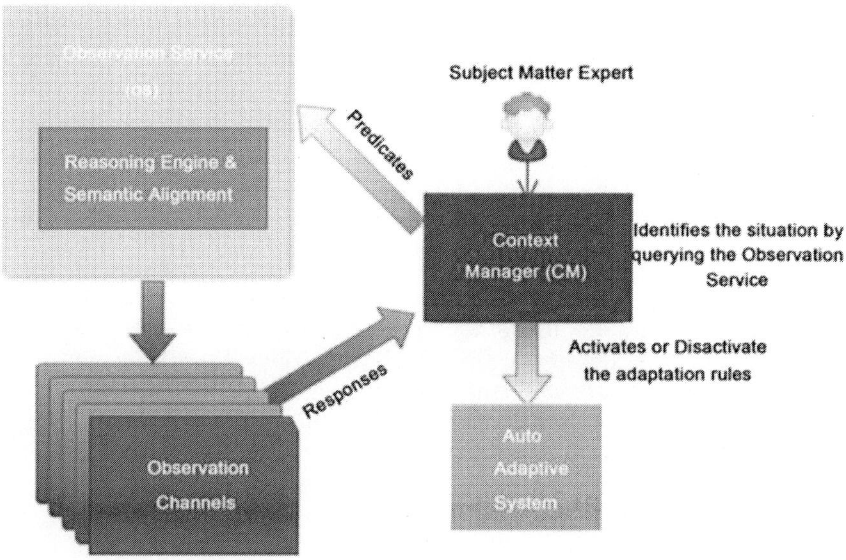

Figure 3. Conceptual model.

To evaluate each of the predicates, the CM relies on observation channels. It will therefore start by looking for an observation channel corresponding to the predicate it's evaluating. If it does not find such a channel, it will ask its creation to the observation service.

Our model again introduces 2 essential components:

1) OBSERVATION SERVICE (OS) which receives the predicate from the Context Manager. This service is responsible for:

    - Semantic alignment which is one of the scientific challenges of today. In fact, let us imagine that to express the first predicate of the scenario "is Zone Secured", we expressed it with another equivalent word, that is to say that we re placed the word "zone" by "site" or "factory" or "place", the system will not know that it is the same predicate! This is why the system must take into consideration these equivalences; it must be able to discover correspondences between two different ontologies. This issue is currently attracting the attention of researchers in web semantic. We did not handle it as it was out of our scope.

- The reasoning needed to answer the predicate. In fact, this service contains a reasoning engine composed of 2 elements. The first is an observation base that keeps a model of the environment containing the description of existing business services or services from devices typically sensors or communicating objects. This database is updated automatically when a service appears or disappears. The second element is a set of inference rules. These rules are used to deduce the services needed to respond to predicates. Let us take the example of the third predicate "Pressure exceeded threshold", as soon as the engine receives it, it passes by the rules of inferences and it will thus return all the pressure sensors that exist and the methods necessary to identify the thresholds.

2) OBSERVATION CHANNEL (OC) created by the Observation Service for each predicate. Following the reasoning, the OS indicates the services needed to respond to the predicate. Then the OS generates an Observation Channel so that it is responsible for the assembly of the services and thus the calculation of the predicate. Once the string has finished the calculation, it sends the Boolean response to the CM to begin the calculation of the situation.

Advantages of the model:

1) The semantic alignment makes it possible to directly generate or re-use the observation channels for the same predicates expressed in a different way instead of repeating the reasoning.

2) Our model, unlike that of continuum based on a KB, separates well the reasoning (establishment of the CO) from the observation of the context (calculation of the predicates with the data of the sensors).

3) The language dependency between reasoning and observation has been removed.

5.2. Implementation Model

In this part, we will describe the model from the implementation point of view as shown in Figure 4.

The Observation Service contains:

1) Cache system connected to the system database.

2) It stores each predicate P with the result of the semantic alignment associated with it and the result of the assembly of services that it needs.

3) It thus keeps the triple (P, P', Assembly of Services).

4) It is responsible for verifying the existence of the services in the environment via the database since it is connected to the observatory.

5) The observatory has a major role to maintain a model of the world, i.e., in our case, the list of available services and their descriptions. It is also responsible for automatically updating the reasoning engine observation database and the system database when a new service appears or disappears.

6) Semantic alignment responsible for finding the equivalence of predicate expressions. As this issue is outside our scope, we have not studied how to implement it.

7) Reasoning engine made in Prolog which seemed to us the most interesting because it allows deducing the services necessary to answer the predicates without the intervention of the user.

8) This engine contains mainly:

- Observation Base that contains the services currently present in the environment. Its main role is to observe new services that appear or disappear so that it is updated automatically.
- Inference rules defined by the developer to describe the relationships between predicates and services in the environment.
- Deployment responsible of generating the observation channel from the re- sults of the engine. It will instantiate the container WComp which will be our channel of observation. WComp [23] is a prototyping and dynamic execution environment on which the Auto-Adaptive system is based. WComp is composed of an application container which manages components (like beans). This components composition describes the application and can be modified dynamically to adapt the application. Other tools are added to complete the WComp framework (some tools to detect services and devices available in the environment, some others to adapt the application according to rules and observations on the environment. In our case, we use WComp as an Auto Adaptive System (Figure 3) but also as support to implement our Observation Channels. The use of WComp is not an obligation for either of these uses. Another platform could be used to replace WComp. The choice of this platform is only due to the technical mastery of it and the ease of interfacing with it.
- Observation Channel which corresponds to a container WComp created by the SO in 2 cases:
- After the SO completes the reasoning and provides the necessary names and methods.

- If the predicate was found in the cache system, then the SO will directly create the container without going through the reasoning engine.

This channel has the role of calculating the predicate to respond to the CM. It assembles the services to generate the boolean response. Hence we have N channels of observations for N predicates.

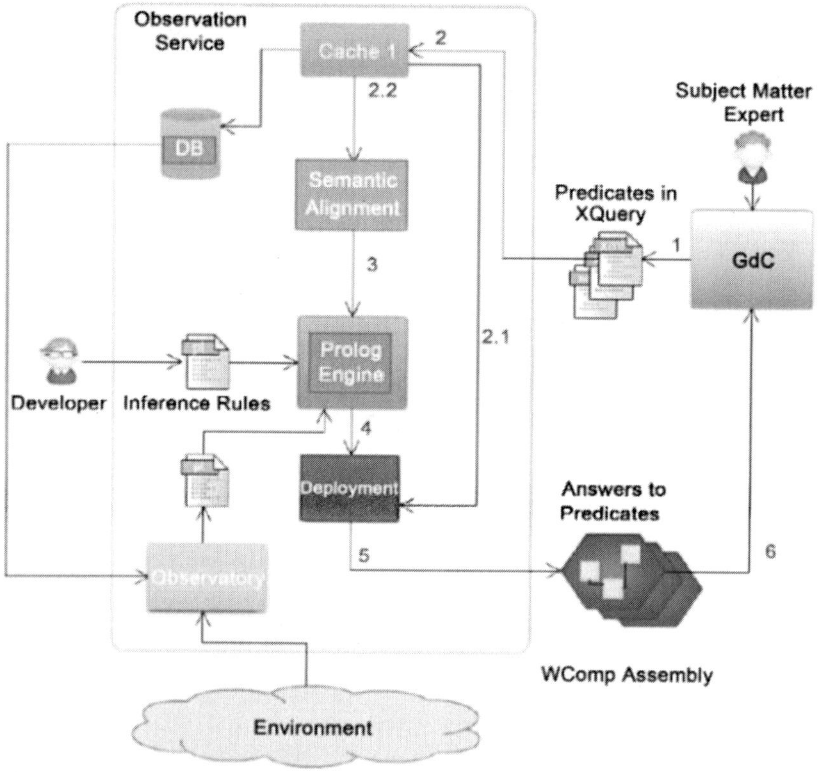

Figure 4. Implementation model.

Advantage:

1. Time saving

We believe that the cache system will save us time. In fact, if we assume that:

- P1 is the probability of finding the predicate in the cache.

- P2 is the probability of needing to reason.
- T_C is the time spent in the cache.
- T_{AS} is the time spent in semantic alignment.
- T_M is the time spent in the reasoning engine.
- T_D is the deployment time needed to generate the WComp container.

We'll have gain in time as per (5).

$$T_{AS} + T_M + T_D > \left(P_1 T_C + P_2\left(T_C + T_{AS} + T_M\right)\right)T_D. \quad (5)$$

Knowing that Tc is a small time compared to T_M because the cache searches in a list (order of n) and verifies the presence of services associated with the predicate while the engine can make a reasoning that takes a considerable amount of time. In fact, T_M depends on the complexity of the predicate.

However, it remains to verify whether we have a significant time saving in cases where we have only one CM. In fact, once a predicate is analyzed by the SO and its corresponding channel of observation is deployed, there will mostly be no need to repeat this operation.

In spite of this, if we have several applications, each having their own CM that interrogates a single SO, the interest of a cache system is reinforced. The probability of the SO must deploy the same predicate increases. This saves time with a cache system.

2. The system allows high availability since if the SO becomes unavailable, the CM can continue to use the OCs already in place to calculate some of its predicates.

Work sequence:

In below part, we explain how the system works. We have two possible paths:

1. CM sends predicate P to SO.

2. The cache system receives it and verifies initially that the assembly of services associated with the predicate P exists.

2.1. If yes, the cache communicates with the BD to verify the existence of the services in the environment. If this is the case, the cache sends the assembly directly to Deployment to create the container that will then send the response to the CM. If the verification has failed, proceed to Step 2.2.

2.2. If not, the cache sends P to the semantic alignment.

3. The result of the semantic alignment produces P' and sends it to the Prolog engine.

4. When the assembly of components corresponding to the predicate P' has fi- nished being computed in the engine of Prolog, it is transmitted to the deployment service.

5. The deployment creates the WComp container and instantiates in it the com- ponents and connectors corresponding to the assembly of the predicate P'.

6. The container can now calculate the predicate P' and transmit the result to the CM.

5.3. Proof of Concept

During our research, we developed a proof of concept to answer a simple predicate the 3rd predicate of the scenario which was "Pressure exceeded Thresholds". To better explain our evidence, we would like to follow a bottom-up approach. We will thus begin by zooming on the WComp container responsible for calculating the predicate to send the response to the CM. Then we will detail each block implemented.

1) WComp container

WComp in general contains a library of ready-to-use components. Each of these components issues events to inform others of an internal state change or to invoke a method of another component. These components are called "Beans". In addition, it is possible to add new beans in WComp or new services in the environment called "UPnP Proxies". These are the representatives of the services in the container. So thanks to beans and proxies, we can do the assembly of services with the methods that suit us to calculate the response of the predicate.

In our case, to respond to P3, we need to assemble the service of the pressure sensor with a bean called "Threshold" and to link these two components with an "is Reached" method that will return a Boolean value to CM to determine if the sensor has exceeded the threshold.

2) Observatory

To observe the changes in the environment, we use the UPnP Wizard Designer which is one of the essential bricks of the WComp middleware. In fact, this brick allows the automatic generation or degeneration of proxies for the services that appear or disappear in the environment at the time of execution. We also added a bean to update the Prolog database as well as the cache system.

3) Deployment

This block is made in C # or the WComp container is compatible with this programming language. It integrates the libraries of SWI Prolog and UPnP open Tools so that it can act as the bridge between the reasoning engine and the chain of observation.

4) The reasoning engine in Prolog

To do this, we began by studying the language of Prolog as well as these two major components: the observation base and the rules of inference.

Rules of inferences:

We have developed generic rules that deduce the beans and services needed for predicates in the following form:

1. Threshold Reached (name of the sensor) typically for our example it is a pressure sensor. This rule associates the threshold bean with the service found in the observation base with a name identical to the name of the sensor. And so we do a matching to find the suitable service.

2. Is Bigger (service 1, service 2), the aim being to use comparison operators (≤, ≥, !, <, >, =) with service values. We also find a rule for each operator that returns the service names and comparisons beans as well as their methods.

3. And (service 1, service 2), the aim being to use the logical operators (and, or, no and, xor ...). Similarly we have one rule per operator that returns the names of services and comparisons beans as well as their methods.

The observation base is written in prolog by the observatory. It contains a bean that updates the facts when changing services in the environment.

5) The database

It can correspond to any type of database. A strong point of our system is that it is independent of the technology of the database. To make it simple, we imple- mented our database tables in C #.

6) The CM

It was provided by the team. We have made some modifications to adapt it to our system so that it sends the predicates to X-query.

7) Semantic Cache and Alignment System

We did not handle them in our proof of concept as it's out of our scope.

6. CONCLUSIONS

The objective of our research was to propose a model of a Context-Aware Middleware. In an environment undergoing frequent changes due to the mobility of devices and users, it becomes increasingly difficult to adapt the application at runtime, hence, the need to dynamically discover the environment (context) and to self-adapt the application to these new contextual conditions.

The study of the CONTINUUM project aimed at ensuring continuity of service in ambient intelligence led us to identify some limitations such as the fact that it relied on a Knowledge Base which did both the reasoning and the Observation of the context. Moreover, there is a language dependency between the reasoning and the observation.

So we started the research with these limitations in mind. We started by studying the predicates and their languages and we found that the predicates written in X-Query corresponded perfectly to our criteria. Then we moved on to another objective, which was to create and automate independent observation channels. To do this, we have separated the reasoning of the observation such that the reasoning is included in an observation service responsible for making the semantic alignment as well as generating the lists of services needed to respond to the predicate while the observation is represented by observation channels or WComp containers generated by the SO. To optimize the system, we have implemented a cache system responsible for verifying the existence of services associated with predicates. Finally, we have developed a proof of concept based on the scenario explained earlier in 2.2. However, further development and testing are still to be performed to accurately evaluate our middleware.

REFERENCES

1. IDC (2015) Worldwide Internet of Things Forecast, 2015-2020. Doc No. 256397.
2. Weiser, M. (1991) The Computer for the Twenty-First Century. Scientific American, 265, 94-104.
3. Yang, K., Wang, J., Bao, L., Ding, M., Wang, J. and Wang, Y. (2016) Towards Future Situation-Awareness: A Conceptual Middleware Framework for Opportunistic Situation Identification. Proceedings of the 12th ACM Symposium on QoS and Security for Wireless and Mobile Networks, Malta, 13-17 November 2016, 95-101.
4. Kim, H., Robiul Hoque, M., Seo, H. and Yang, S.-H. (2016) Development of Middleware Architecture to Realize Context-Aware Service in Smart Home Environment. Computer Science and Information Systems, 13, 427-452.
5. Li, X., Eckert, M., Martinez, J.-F. and Rubio, G. (2015) Context Aware Middleware Architectures: Survey and Challenges. Sensors, 15, 20570-20607.

6. Khaddar, M.A.E., Chraibi, M. and Harroud, H. (2015) A Policy-Based Middleware for Context-Aware Pervasive Computing. International Journal of Pervasive Computing and Communications, 11, 43-68.
7. Perera, C., Zaslavsky, A., Christen, P. and Georgakopoulos, D. (2012) Ca4iot: Context Awareness for Internet of Things. Proceedings of the 2012 IEEE International Conference on Green Computing and Communications, Besancon, 20-23 November 2012, 775-782.
8. Firner, B., Moore, R.S., Howard, R., Martin, R.P. and Zhang, Y.Y. (2011) Poster: Smart Buildings, Sensor Networks, and the Internet of Things. Proceedings of the 9th ACM Conference on Embedded Networked Sensor Systems, Seattle, 1-4 November 2011, 337-338.
9. Rey, G., Tigli, J.-Y., Lavirotte, S., Ferry, N., Fathallah, S., Coutaz, J., Fontaine, E., Jouanot, F., Benyelloul, A., Rousset, M., Renevier, P., Pinna-Dery, A. and Hourdin, V. (2010) Modélisation du contexte et Adaptation dans CONTINUUM.
10. Rasmussen, J. (1983) Skills, Rules, and Knowledge: Signals, Signs, and Symbols, and Other Distinctions in Human Performance Models. IEEE Transactions on Systems, Man, and Cybernetics, SMC-13, 257-266.
11. Rey, G. (2005) Contexte en Interaction Homme-Machine: Le contexteur. Communication Langagière et Interaction Personne-Système. Fédération IMAG, Université Joseph Fourier.
12. Rey, G., Tigli, J.-Y., Lavirotte, S., Ferry, N., Fathallah, S., Coutaz, J., Fontaine, E., Jouanot, F., Benyelloul, A., Rousset, M., Renevier, P., Pinna-Dery, A. and Hourdin, V. (2010) Modélisation du contexte et Adaptation dans CONTINUUM. D2.1 and D2.2. https://continuum.unice.fr/_media/livrables:t2.1_2.2_modelisation_du_contexte_et_adaptation.pdf
13. Jouanot, F., Rousset, M., Morin, G., Johar, A. and Benyelloul, A. (2012) Conquer, gérer l'hétérogénéité. D3.2 and D3.3.
14. Synyukov, L., Russo, A., Colombi, T., Lavirotte, S., Rey, G. and Bourgeois, H. (2012) Retour d'évaluation terrain. D6.1 and D6.2.
15. Heer, J., Newberger, A., Beckmann, C. and Hong, J.I. (2003) Liquid: Context-Aware Distributed Queries. 5th International Conference, Seattle, 12-15 October 2003, 140-148.
16. Haghighi, P., Zaslavsky, A. and Krishnaswamy, S. (2006) An Evaluation of Query Languages for Context-Aware Computing. 17th International Workshop on Database and Expert Systems Applications, Krakow, 4-8 September 2006, 455-462.
17. Meena, B., Jain, N. and Singh, C. (2013) A Heterogeneous Middleware Architecture for Wireless Sensor Network. International Journal of Applied Information Systems, 5, 36-41.
18. Gu, T., Wang, X., Pung, H. and Zhang, D. (2004) An Ontology-Based Context Model in Intelligent Environments.
19. Polyviou, S., Evripidou, P. and Samaras, G. (2004) Context-Aware Queries Using Query by Browsing and Chiromancer.
20. Yea, J., Dobsona, S. and McKeever, S. (2012) Situation Identification Techniques in Pervasive Computing: A Review. Pervasive and Mobile Computing, 8, 36-66.
21. Ranganathan, A. and Campbell, R.H. (2003) A Middleware for Context-Aware Agents in Ubiquitous Computing Environments. Proceedings of the ACM/IFIP/U-SENIX 2003 International Conference on Middleware, Rio de Janeiro, 16-20 June 2003, 143-161.
22. Kofod-Petersen, A. and Aamodt, A. (2006) Contextualised Ambient Intelligence Through Case-Based Reasoning. 8th European Conference, Fethiye, 4-7 September 2006, 211-225.
23. http://www.wcomp.fr/

CHAPTER 8

Cybersecurity Investment Guidance: Extensions of the Gordon and Loeb Model

Scott Farrow[1], Jules Szanton[2]

[1]*Department of Economics, UMBC, Baltimore, USA*

[2]*Center for Health and Homeland Security, University of Maryland, Baltimore, USA*

ABSTRACT

Extensions of the Gordon-Loeb [1] and the Gordon-Loeb-Lucyshyn-Zhou [2] models are presented based on mathematical equivalency with a generalized homeland security model. The extensions include limitations on changes in the probability of attack, simultaneous effects on probability and loss, diversion of attack, and shared non-information defenses. Legal cases are then investigated to assess approximate magnitudes of external effects and the extent they are internalized by the legal system.

Keywords: Cybersecurity, Investment, Externality, Log-Convexity, Law

1. INTRODUCTION

The most pressing cyberthreats once came from emailed viruses, but today's cyberattacks increasingly take the form of massive identity and intellectual property thefts and the potential for physical damage to critical infrastructure. As cyberattacks have proven to be increasingly disruptive to the economy, a growing body of scholarship examines how much firms should invest in protection and what are appropriate roles for governments. Gordon and Loeb, GL [1] , and later, Gordon, Loeb, Lucyshyn and Zhou, GLLZ [2] , are leaders in examining the optimal level of spending that organizations should optimally invest in cybersecurity. Their approach uses an unconstrained expected profit maximization model where cybersecurity investments are separable from other activities of the firm. The benefit to the firm from a cybersecurity investment is a cost reduction; the remaining probability of a security breach (S(z)) times the loss (L), which can be altered based on investing in cybersecurity, z. GL analyzed direct (private) damages while GLLZ extended the model to include external damages.

GL and GLLZ investigate the implications of their model in some detail after first deriving the condition that the optimum (interior) investment is found where the incremental benefits of information security equal the incremental costs. As the optimal investment is shown to be increasing in damages (losses), including external damages increases the optimal level of investment. As with standard models of investment, an organization that only considers private losses in its optimization is correct if there are no external losses; but if external losses exist then optimum social expenditures increase. By investigating several functional forms for the security breach function, GL and later researchers showed that it is not uncommon for investments to have a maximum of about 37 percent of expected losses although this result is conditional on the specification.

This paper proceeds by investigating extensions to the GL and GLLZ models implied by a general investment model for homeland security expenditures. A review of legal cases involving cybersecurity breaches is then used to assess the implications of including external costs in the optimal investment model.

2. EXTENSIONS OF THE GL AND GLLZ MODELS USING A HOMELAND SECURITY MODEL

While GL and GLLZ examine how much an individual firm should invest in preventing a cyberattack, related work by Farrow [3] investigates a set of expected, constrained cost minimization models for homeland security expenditures. The models were originally conceived to support Government performance audits in the US Government Accountability Office. The GL, GLLZ and Farrow models make similar simplifying assumptions about the relevance of expected value decision-making, continuity and derivatives of key functions[1]. The core similarities and differences are investigated below followed by several extensions presented in Farrow. The extensions illustrate modifications to investment rules where there are different types of constraints, interactions, and investment alternatives.

A summary of the definitions for the general homeland security investment model based on Farrow [3] is below. The "organization" referred to was originally modeled as the government, since governments are expected to consider both direct and external effects and assumed to select the socially optimal outcome. The organization could also be a firm or consumer. However, these organizations are typically modeled as having different objective functions. While the government is concerned with minimizing overall social costs, a self-interested firm or consumer will not consider the external effects of its choices unless there is some feedback mechanism, such as legal liability, which incentivizes the firm or individual to internalize the costs it creates for others.

Define:

e_i: organizational security expenditures on site i.

$\bar{E}$: an aggregate expenditure constraint over all sites and pathways.

$P(e_i)$: probability of an event. $P' < 0$; $P'' > 0$ where P' is the partial derivative and functions are assumed to be twice continuously differentiable. This assumes some behavior or reaction function on the part of the attacker such that expenditures could alter their choice of targets or the expenditures could lead to capture prior to an attack.

$S(e_i)$: additional costs incurred as a result of the investment expenditure whether for the expending organization or third parties such as time in security lines or changes in productivity which are not part of the budget constraint, expect $S' > 0$.

$C(e_i)$: social cost given an event happens, $C' < 0$; $C'' > 0$, which includes direct costs to the organization, $C^D(e_i)$ and costs external to the organization (external costs) $C^E(e_i)$. Note that the constrained expenditure amount e_i is always assumed to be obligated and spent whether or not an attack occurs. It is the social cost, C, that is conditional on the event occurring.

The organization's investment problem is stated as choosing the level of expenditure at each site ($e_i^* \geq 0$) in order to minimize expected social cost:

Min

$$\sum_{i=1}^{N} P(e_i)\left[C(e_i)+e_i+S(e_i)\right]+\left[1-P(e_i)\right]\left(e_i+S(e_i)\right)$$

Subject to:

$$\sum_{i=1}^{N} e_i = \overline{E}$$

$$e_i \geq 0$$

The unconstrained minimization form of the problem is that used by Baryshnikov [5] in his extension of the underlying mathematical properties of the GL model and by Gordon, Loeb and Lucyshyn [6] . The GL and GLLZ models can be seen as the dual of the Farrow model prior to the inclusion of constraints—maximizing cost reductions is the dual of minimizing costs for an interior solution [6] .

GL and GLLZ do not consider a budget constraint, although they note that conflict between the Chief Information Officer and the Chief Executive Officer may affect the derivation of the optimal amount. In many instances, a budget constraint may be a more realistic decision context. In the budget constrained problem, a budget larger than the optimum expenditure yields the unconstrained solution (the constraint is not binding) while a binding constraint implies a shadow price affecting the expenditure allocation. At the same time, the parameterization in GL adds greater interpretation to the Farrow results.

The notation changes and constraints to place the GL model in the Farrow notation are as below (Table 1).

Farrow investigated several cases which can be considered extensions of the GL and GLLZ models[2]. Security and investment concerns modeled by these extensions include:

1) Multiple sites with a budget constraint: The primary difference compared to GL and GLLZ is inclusion of the shadow price of the constraint. First order conditions require that the marginal (incremental) benefit of the investment equal the marginal cost at each site where the marginal cost takes into account the shadow price associated with the binding constraint. Further, marginal expected social costs avoided—the benefits—are to be equated across sites. Where such equality cannot occur, some sites have zero optimal investment. In application, GL appear to follow such an approach for multiple information sets [7] .

2) Probability and consequence reductions: Investments may reduce not only the probability of an attack but the loss from the attack. When these impacts are separated, investments should occur until the incremental return per dollar invested is the same across the

probability and consequence domains. Recent cybersecurity approaches echo this conclusion by extending cybersecurity beyond protecting access to actions designed to limit internal and external damage.

3) Attacker diversion: Investments in defense by one organization may divert attacker effort to another site. If larger firms are better protected than smaller firms, whether in the defense industry or elsewhere; the probability of attack may increase at less defended sites.

4) Continuous asymmetric focus or advanced persistent attack: Limitations on ability to defend a site or consequences of an attack may lead to optimal inequality of defense across sites and information sets as security may not be reducible to the level desired in the absence of such persistent attacks.

5) Shared filtering or defenses: The benefit of the investment includes the sum of benefits across all units to the extent that defensive activity reduces damages at other sites through positive external effects. This may occur for example if government or the private sector provides centralized hacker detection. The centralization may protect a number of sites and returns to scale may exist such that there is a low marginal cost to protect more users. (Note that the potential for external public bads of a security breach are included in the social cost of the base model). Game theoretic models for firm decision-making with free-riding or probability of a breach elsewhere in the network typically lead an individual firm to underinvest in shared information or individual defenses [6] [8] .

6) All hazards and/or false negative and false positive outcomes: As with most applications of uncertainty, there is often a chance of incorrectly applying a defensive method; or of failing to apply a defensive method. For instance, as cybersecurity defense may move from "signature" identification of problematic sites or malware toward "behavioral" identification based on the actions of software; it may be that the probability of a "false positive" increases. A false positive in this case is when an action is indeed appropriate, but the behaviorally based software identifies the action as inappropriate. There is a cost associated with such false positives, even if the focus is often on the costs of the false negatives-those actions that are indeed "bad" but are not identified as being bad. The investment model extends naturally to include the additional probabilities and costs associated with this broader set of actions. A similar concern may occur if a cyber expenditure reduces the hazard of a cyber-physical system breach but increases the probability of a false (positive) signal to the cyber-physical system.

Table 1. Notation changes and equivalencies.

Underlying concept	GL original notation	Farrow notation	Note
Sites or information set; unit of analysis	One unit	Multiple sites i	$i = 1$ for equivalence
Investment (expenditure) in cybersecurity	Z	e	Equivalent
Probability of successful attack given an investment level	$S(z)$ Security breach function	$P(e)$ Terrorism event function	Equivalent (but modified initial limits of prob. not incorporated in Farrow)
Conditional cost or loss of an event	L Initially, L; later $L^P + L^E$ for private and external	$C(e)$ Includes both direct and external. C^P and C^E $C = L^P + L^E$	GL is constant GL start with L^P, Farrow starts with $C = C^P + C^E = L^P + L^E$ and as a function of expenditures

[2]See [3] for the formal model statements, derivations and further discussion.

These extensions of the cybersecurity model and their resulting optimum conditions are summarized below (Table 2).

3. MAXIMUM CYBERSECURITY INVESTMENTS

Expected value optimization models generally bound investments to lie between zero and the expected value of losses based on the boundary conditions of the problem. An important analysis in GL was the additional step of considering specific functional forms for the security breach function, S. Their rather dramatic conclusion was that for the forms investigated, the optimal security investments would not exceed about 37 percent (1/e) of the initial expected loss. This conclusion has been the subject of additional research by Willemson [9] , Hausken [4] and Baryshnikov [5] indicating that while a significant class of functional forms (log convex with independent security effects of additional investments) follows the 1/e limit; other forms, such as linear, extend the full range of possible investment up to the value of the expected loss.

Recent work on log convexity and log concavity by Bagnoli and Bergstrom [10] informs the sensitivity of log convexity to functional form. Starting with S, the security breach probability in GL and GLLZ; it represents the remaining probability of a breach (or break) after an investment z. A statistical interpretation is that it represents a reliability function (or exceedance function), the complement of a cumulative distribution function. The initial probability of a breach, v, would then be the initial reliability which can range between zero and one. The difference between v and S is the increase in reliability or conversely the decrease in the probability of a breach. Bagnoli and Bergstrom [10] investigate the log-concavity and convexity of numerous reliability functions (after investigating the implications of various transformations). They catalog a large number of common probability and cumulative density, and reliability functions. Log-concavity appears to dominate but some distributions are log-convex in their density functions and log-concave in other functions. The conclusion drawn by this author is that the functional form of the security breach function is an empirical question with numerous candidate forms implying the range of loss, in the expected value model, is from zero to the expected loss. This is consistent with the discussion in GL and GLLZ, that specification matters. Quantification of any expenditure bounds in the Farrow model are expected to follow those of the GL model given the equivalent mathematical structure.

Table 2. Optimality conditions for extensions of the GL model.

Issue/model	Summary of Socially Optimum Condition
Allocating a Total Defensive Expenditure among Multiple Independent Sites.	Equate the marginal expected social costs avoided (MESCA) across sites; possibly no protection at some sites.
Advanced Persistent Threat: Technological or Behavioral Constraint on Probability or Cost Reduction.	Technological or behavioral constraints can result in an optimal inequality among sites even where investment occurs.
Allocation of Expenditures Across Damage and Probability-Reducing Activities.	Equate the marginal social cost avoided of each type of expenditure where expenditures are positive (some may be below threshold).
Public Goods, Border control and Positive Interdependencies.	Invest until the sum of their marginal damage cost avoided equals the individual site MESCA.
Site Interdependencies Due to Displacing the Probability of Attack.	Determine the net MESCA, net of probability increasing effects at other sites; sites of attack may be spread but social costs reduced.
Multiple Sources of Probability (All Hazards) and Cost, as with false positives and false negatives from behavioral controls.	The form of the allocation decision is the same (e.g. equate MESCA), but all costs and probabilities should be taken into account.

4. EXTERNAL EFFECTS: A LEGAL ANALYSIS

Optimal security expenditures increase as expected damages increase [1] . Because GLLZ include external damages in their calculation of expected damages, they find that the socially optimal expenditure on cybersecurity increases without bound as external damages increases. However, the 1/e (~37%) rule applies to the external losses as well as private losses with a log-convex specification with independent security effects[3]. While optimal investment with externalities may be unbounded, GLLZ established a reference point by analyzing "How large must external losses be as a proportion of private losses in order for optimal investment to equal expected private losses?" Through a numerical example they establish that an external loss that is 180% of private losses would imply an optimal investment approximately equal to the expected private loss of the firm. The exact reference proportion (and percent if multiplied by 100) is a constant that can be derived from the GLLZ model as e – 1, or ~1.718 (172%). GLLZ call an external loss exceeding the reference point of ~180% of expected private losses as being "extremely large", implying that a firm may often be acting in society's best interest when it spends less on cybersecurity than its expected private cost.

A legal approach is taken here to inform the empirical magnitude of external losses. The investigation focuses on the magnitude and extent to which an attacked firm is liable for damages to additional parties, the external costs. Although the attacked firm is itself a victim, the incentives the firm faces to undertake defensive actions reflects in part the losses it may incur through legal action (or through insurance payments reflecting the potential for legal action).

A close look at several data breaches shows that an external cost of more than 180% of the private cost is not unusually large for some types of attacks indicating optimal social expenditures in excess of private expected losses[4]. While larger expenditures are consistent with GLLZ, this finding indicates that the reference point of expected private losses may not be particularly relevant. Firms face risks of many different sorts of data breaches. Some data breaches target consumers' financial information, others target a firm's intellectual property, while other breaches target connections between cyber and physical infrastructure. Each type and incidence of breach may have different private and external costs. Yet in many of the cases discussed below, external costs are much larger than private costs, and the legal system is unable to assign legal liability to data-storing firms in a manner that effectively internalizes the external costs of a data breach.

4.1. Personal Identity Theft

Personal identity (PI) theft is one of the more visible breaches of cybersecurity when attackers gain personal information from human resource departments, stored billing information or other databases. In PI cases, the perpetrator of a data breach generally seeks information about third-parties (e.g. customers), not information about the company whose servers are breached. Not surprisingly, these data breaches have the potential to create high levels of external costs.

When there are external costs of a personal information data breach, third-parties who lose money (including customers, their financial institutions, and their credit card companies) often sue the directly attacked firm. These plaintiffs have enjoyed varying degrees of success in the legal system. In some cases, plaintiffs have recovered a portion of their costs from legal settlements. When a plaintiff receives a settlement from the directly attacked firm, the external cost from the data breach is reduced and the private cost as defined by GL increases. In other cases, plaintiffs were not able to recover because they were unable to show standing, were prevented from recovering due to the economic loss doctrine, or faced some other legal or practical barrier to recovery. In these cases, the plaintiffs' external costs remain external costs and are not expected to enter the private benefit- cost calculation as discussed by GLLZ.

The Heartland Payment Systems data breach is an example of third parties recovering some of the external costs of a data breach, but still losing more the reference point of 180% of the private cost. Heartland Payment Systems is a major payment processing company [12] . In 2007, malware was implanted in Heartland's servers leading to the theft of 130 million customers' credit card. Heartland faced five lawsuits from third parties: a class-action suit from consumers; suits from Visa, MasterCard, and American Express, each of which filed the suits together with affiliated card-issuing financial institutions; and a suit from financial institutions that sued independently from the credit card companies.

In settling four of the suits, Heartland partially internalized the external costs that the breach had imposed on financial institutions and consumers. Heartland paid a total of $105 million to VISA, MasterCard, American Express, and financial institutions that issued credit and debit cards through these companies. This appears to be far less than the full damages suffered by the plaintiffs. As Graves, Acquisti, and Christin [13] showed, between 60% and 90% of compromised credit cards are reissued by financial institutions after a data breach. The same study showed that when second-order costs are considered, an issuer does not save money by not reissuing the cards. Therefore, a data breach costs the card issuer roughly the same amount regardless of whether the issuer reissues the cards or not.

Crosman [14] estimated the cost of reissuing credit cards ranges from $2.70 to $11 per card, while the cost of reissuing debit cards ranges from $2.99 to $12.75 per card. The cost depends on the size of the financial institution; large banks can reissue for less than smaller community banks and credit unions. The theft of 130 million records from Heartland, implies that the credit card companies and affiliated financial institutions lost between $350 million (assuming a loss of $2.70/card) and $1.7 billion (assuming $12.75). The $105 million in settlements that the financial institutions received in settlements was a fraction of their external costs. Assuming that the entire settlement went to the financial institutions (in reality, some of it was consumed in legal expenses) the financial institutions' uncompensated losses would be somewhere between $250 million and $1.6 billion.

Consumers also lost money in the Heartland Security breach and filed a class-action suit against Heartland. Heartland settled the suit for $3 million. Under the terms of the settlement, consumers were eligible for up to $175 in compensation if they could show, by a preponderance of the evidence, that they had lost time or money cancelling a credit card or as the result of unauthorized credit cards. Consumers were also eligible for up to $10,000 if they could show that they had suffered identity theft as a result of the breach. Only 11 consumers successfully qualified for relief, and they received a combined total of just $1925. The rest of the $3 million settlement was spent on legal fees, administrative costs, and a cy pres payment to a non-profit focused on information security [12] . While the settlement increased Heartland's private costs by $3 million, it only compensated consumers' external costs by $1925. It is difficult to believe that $1925 represents the socially optimal expenditure to avoid external costs for the 130 million consumers.

Heartland has estimated its private cost from the data breach as $140 million, a figure that includes the $108 million in settlements ($105 million to the financial institutions, and $3 million to the consumers), plus legal fees and other expenses [15] . It is challenging to put an exact figure on the external losses, but it is clear that they are greater than $250 million, which would be 180% of Heartland's private costs. As shown above, the external cost to financial institutions—after subtracting the $108 million in legal settlements—is likely between $250 million and $1.6 billion. (Without the $108 million in settlements, the financial institutions would have lost between $350 million and $1.7 billion.) Since the external cost to consumers is not negligible (though hard to value) the combined external cost to consumers and financial institutions appears to be extremely large.

While external costs in the Heartland data breach substantially exceeded private costs, the discrepancy would have been even greater had Heartland's legal settlements not decreased the external costs and increased the private costs. In other major data breaches, courts have thrown out lawsuits against directly attacked firms. In these data breaches, external costs as a percentage of private costs can be even greater than in Heartland.

Third parties who incur costs as the result of a data breach have struggled to show standing (a sufficient legal basis on which to file suit) since the Supreme Court's decision in Clapper v. Amnesty International [16] . A requirement for standing in a federal court is that a plaintiff must have suffered an "injury in fact," which is "concrete and particularized" instead of "merely speculative" as in Lujan v. Defenders of Wildlife [17] . In Clapper, the Court held that the "injury in fact" must be something that either already happened or is "certainly impending," not something that might happen in the future. Furthermore, a plaintiff cannot "manufacture" standing by "incurr[ing] certain costs as a reasonable reaction to a risk of [future] harm" [16] . In a data breach case, a consumer will often wish to sue before becoming the victim of identity theft. Similarly, a financial institution may wish to reissue credit cards before the credit or debit cards are misused. Under the rule announced in Clapper, the legal system may be unable to reimburse third-party data breach victims for these costs likely increasing the external component of losses.

The Zappos data breach [18] , which occurred in 2012, is an example of a data breach in which the legal system has done little to turn external costs into private costs. The perpetrators of the breach stole 24 million customers' names, email addresses, billing and shipping addresses, phone numbers, the last four digits of payment card numbers, and encrypted passwords. No credit card numbers were compromised, so financial institutions did not sue. A class-action suit from Zappos consumers alleged that they faced an increased risk of identity theft. In addition to facing an increased risk of identity theft, the consumers asked to be compensated for credit monitoring purchases that they had made. The United States District Court for the District of Nevada cited Clapper [16] in dismissing the suit, holding that the consumers did not suffer the sort of injury that could confer standing in federal court. Judge Jones wrote that his court "realizes that [dismissing the suit] is a frustrating result where Plaintiffs' fears of identity theft and fraud are rational, and it recognizes that purchasing monitoring services is a responsible response to a data breach. Nevertheless, costs incurred to prevent future harm is not enough to confer standing, even when such efforts are sensible" [18] . While the consumer litigation was dismissed,[5] Zappos settled a separate lawsuit with nine state attorneys general for $106,000. But aside from this payment, none of the data breach's external costs were converted to private costs and so the external costs are likely to be an extremely large proportion of private costs.

Third parties who suffer external costs in personal information data breaches can also be prevented from recovering by the economic loss rule. In some—but not all—states, the economic loss rule prevents plaintiffs from recovering for negligence when they have only lost money as a result of the alleged negligence. In these states, financial disputes can only be adjudicated through contract law. If a plaintiff cannot show that the defendant breached a contract, then she cannot recover for negligence. The economic loss rule prevented recovery for employees of the University of Pittsburgh Medical Center. These employees were unable to sue their employer for negligence when the hospital lost their personal information when a court found that the employees' only losses had been financial [19] .

4.2. Intellectual Property Theft

In cases of intellectual property (IP) theft, the relation between external and private losses is likely to be reversed compared to the previous cases: external losses but not private losses are likely to be low at least in the short-term. Some intellectual property data breaches are committed by insiders: employees—often departing ones—who steal records from their employer. These insider breaches of intellectual property are likely to have considerable private costs, although companies that are the victims of these incidents have been fairly successful at using the legal system to reduce those losses. In contrast, American companies impacted by foreign intellectual property attacks—like the Chinese military's Unit 61398—have generally been unsuccessful at using the legal system to reduce their private costs. Yet in either case, there may be little external cost at least in the short- term. For example, when a departing bank employee steals a list of customers who have applied for loans, the customer loses little. In fact, the customer may actually benefit from the data breach. If, for example, the departing employee uses the stolen information to offer the customer a lower interest rate, the external cost of the data breach could actually be a positive benefit to the individual although a private loss to the original firm. In the long run, however, intellectual property theft could create external costs by increasing the cost of information security and decreasing the overall competitiveness of American firms, an external cost to the country.

The 2011 litigation over an intellectual property data breach at Huntington National Bank [20] illustrates the fact that these sort of data breaches can have low (or no) external costs, and private costs that are generally recoverable through litigation. The Huntington breach occurred when employees of Huntington National Bank— loan officers and their administrative assistants—left Huntington for MVB Bank, a rival financial institution which (like Huntington) issued mortgages. Huntington accused the employees of downloading records from 200 loan applications before leaving Huntington for MVB. Huntington alleged that as a result of the ex-employees' conduct, they suffered damage to their reputation and goodwill in the marketplace, lost customers, and lost rights of exclusive possession in their intellectual property. The United States District Court for the Northern District of West Virginia issued a temporary injunction preventing the defendants from using any proprietary information obtained from Huntington National Bank for any business purpose. After the court issued its injunction, the two sides settled. The settlement obligated the ex-employees to refrain from using the proprietary information, to return the documents from Huntington National Bank, and not to contact Huntington customers with whom the ex-employees worked. As stated above, this sort of conduct creates little short-term potential for external costs, since the 200 customers probably would have benefited from MVB offering a more attractive mortgage than the one offered to them by Huntington. This sort of data breach also offers little potential for large private costs, since Huntington obtained a consent decree which prevented MVB from accessing any records the employees might have taken from Huntington, or even contacting any customers the employees worked with at Huntington.

It is harder for American companies that suffer intellectual property data breaches from perpetrators outside the United States to use the legal system to recover their private costs. Westinghouse, an American nuclear power company, suffered several data breaches when hackers from Unit 61398 of China's People's Liberation Army (PLA) broke into the company's network and stole information about the company's strategy for negotiating with a Chinese counterpart [21] . As with the data breach at Huntington National Bank, this theft created almost no short-term external costs. In fact, third-parties might have even benefitted if Westinghouse's Chinese competitors were able to use the stolen information to generate power more inexpensively. The breach likely did create substantial private costs, especially if Westinghouse ended up at a disadvantage in its negotiations with the Chinese firm, or if the company lost market-share to a Chinese competitor with lower costs. A grand jury at the United States District Court for the Western District of Pennsylvania indicted five officers of Unit 61398 for their role in data breaches against Westinghouse and other American firms. This indictment is unlikely to reduce Westinghouse's private costs, since China will almost certainly not extradite the indicted officers. In fact, Westinghouse's private costs could actually increase as a result of its stepping forward and identifying itself as a victim of Unit 61398, since China could retaliate against the company's Chinese interests to punish the company for accusing the PLA unit [21] .

Speculation exists that longer term, macroeconomic external effects may occur with large scale intellectual property thefts [22] . A loss of macro-level comparative advantage, for instance in technologically advanced areas, could affect the welfare of the US labor force as well as affecting US based shareholders.

4.3. Critical Infrastructure Cyberattacks

A cyberattack that targeted critical infrastructure could create external costs that greatly exceed private costs. The Critical Infrastructures Protection Act [23] , a federal law that is part of the USA Patriot Act, defines critical infrastructure as "systems and assets, whether physical or virtual, so vital to the United States that the incapacity or destruction of such systems and assets would have a debilitating impact on security, national economic security, national public health or safety, or any combination of those matters." The Obama Administration has designated 16 sectors of the economy as critical infrastructure.[6]

Like data breaches that target personal information or intellectual property, cyberattacks on critical infrastructure (CI) involve an attacker exercising control over a computer network to which they do not have authorized access or authority. There are, however, important differences between cyberattacks on CI and data breaches that target PI or IP. Perpetrators of PI and IP data breaches primarily attempt to steal information for economic benefit. Perpetrators of CI cyberattacks, on the other hand, are typically motivated by strategic or political goals.

The United States has never experienced a successful, large-scale cyberattack on critical infrastructure, but other countries have. The Russian government is widely believed[7] to have conducted cyberattacks on critical infrastructure in both Estonia and Georgia. Estonia experienced cyberattacks in 2007 as the Baltic nation was engaged in a dispute with Russia about a monument to Soviet war dead [25] . Many Estonians viewed the monument as a reminder of the Soviet occupation of their country, while Russians viewed the memorial as expressing respect to Soviet soldiers who fell in battle during World War II. On April 26, 2007—one day before the Estonian government was to move the statue from the center of Tallin to a military cemetery—many Estonian websites experienced denial-of-service attacks. The websites of Estonian banks, government agencies, and media outlets were overwhelmed with traffic, causing them to crash. On April 27, the statue was moved as planned, but the attacks continued, reaching their peak on May 9. Desperate to stop the attacks, the Estonian government took the comprehensive action of blocking all internet traffic from outside the country. By May 19, 2007, the attacks ended.

Georgia experienced similar denial-of-service attacks during its war with Russia in the summer of 2008 [26] . Hackers targeted the websites of Georgia's national and local governments, as well as news websites. The National Bank of Georgia's site was also briefly targeted [27] . The cyberattacks appeared to be coordinated with Russia's military operations: the attacks escalated as Russian troops crossed the Georgian border, and targeted websites of specific regions of Georgia as Russia bombed those areas. The cyberattacks were also coordinated with Russia's strategic objections in the war. Just as Russia damaged areas around Georgia's strategic Baku- Ceyhan oil pipeline but did not actually destroy the pipeline, the Russian hackers targeted government and media websites, but declined to target Georgia's electric grid or attack the National Bank's site in a more sustained manner. The impression is that Russia could have done worse damage later if it wanted.

Both of these cyberattacks demonstrated that an attack on critical infrastructure can produce external costs that are significantly higher than the private costs. A leaked American diplomatic cable [28] estimated that Hansabank, the bank whose website was most disabled by the cyberattack, spent ?0 million (roughly $14 million, in 2007 dollars) as a result of the attack. ?0 million is a suspiciously round number, and reflects the challenge of reaching an accurate estimate. The New York Times reported at the end of May 2007 (after the last wave of cyberattacks) that Hansabank had spent $1 million so far fending off the so-called "bots" that were overwhelming its servers [29] . Yet both these estimates only reflect private costs to Hansabank. The bank also lost significant business during the three weeks when its website was either nonoperational or closed off to traffic from outside of Estonia.

Assessing the external cost of the cyberattacks on Estonian banks and other websites is more difficult. Estonia is one of the most technologically sophisticated countries in the world, and by 2007, over 96% of Estonian banking transactions took place online [30] . When Estonian bank websites were either non-operational or closed off to foreign traffic, the Estonian economy was significantly constrained. Yet the damage to the Estonian economy was not catastrophic, and not as bad as it could have been had the cyberattack been marginally more aggressive. The same leaked American diplomatic cable noted that the damage to the Estonian economy could have been significantly worse had the "second wave" of attacks targeted the "poorly-defended" websites of the logistics firms that transport food and gasoline around the country [31] . One indication of the cyberattacks' potential high external cost is the lengths to which the Estonian government has gone to prevent another wave of cyberattacks. Since 2007, Estonia has become a world leader in defending against cyberwarfare, and has played a crucial role in NATO and EU efforts to respond to cyberattacks. In 2008, largely in response to the attacks on Estonia, NATO created a Brussels-based Cyber Defense Management Authority and an Estonia-based Cooperative Cyber Defense Centre of Excellence [32] .

Because the cyberattacks against Georgia occurred in the context of a conventional war and were coordinated with war objectives, it is hard to isolate the private and external costs specific to the cyberattack. Hollis [26] explains how the cyberattacks were integrated into Russia's war strategy:

Russian-oriented hackers/militia took out news and local government web sites specifically in the areas that the Russian military intended to attack in the ground and air domains. The Federal and local Georgian governments, military, and local news agencies were unable to communicate with Georgian citizens that were directly affected by the fighting. ...[The cyberattacks] created panic and confusion in the local populace, further hindering Georgian military response [26] .

The cyberattacks didn't just cost Georgia money; they weakened Georgia's ability to fight. The external cost was military, not just financial.

Russia's goal in launching the cyberattacks against Georgia and Estonia was presumably strategic, not economic. Russia sought to assert its power throughout the former Soviet Union. To accomplish that goal, Russia did not need to cause massive damage to the economy of Georgia or Estonia; it just needed to demonstrate its capability. Simply by demonstrating the power to disable crucial elements of its rivals' economies, Russia increased its ability to deter its neighbors from defying it. Today, it is likely that when countries in the former Soviet Union (including Estonia and Georgia) consider taking some action that would displease the Kremlin, they consider the possibility that a cyberattack could damage their economy. Some countries may minimize their risk of a Russian cyberattack by making political concessions, or refraining from adopting policies likely to anger Russia. This is an external cost as well.

If the United States experienced a cyberattack on critical infrastructure, the external losses could greatly exceed the private costs. The costs would, of course, depend on what sort of critical infrastructure was attacked. One threat that looms particularly large is the threat of a cyberattack on the electric grid. In 2014, NSA Director Admiral Mike Rogers warned Congress that China and at least one other country had the potential to disrupt large sections of the American power grid. Rogers warned that other countries were already conducting "reconnaissance" to figure out how American electric networks operated, and how they could be shut down online [33] . According to a 2015 report from the University of Cambridge Centre for Risk Studies and the Lloyd's of London insurance market [34] , a cyberattack that targeted electricity supply could create huge costs to the American economy. The report models several different attacks. In each one, the external cost of a cyberattack to the economy as a whole greatly exceeds the costs borne by individual electric companies. For example, in a scenario where the U.S. economy loses $1.024 trillion as the result of a catastrophic interruption in the power supply, power companies would only lose $4.21 billion in lost revenue. In a scenario where the economy loses $243 billion, the power companies would only lose $1.15 billion [34] . Because a catastrophic power outage would be extremely disruptive to the economy as a whole, external costs could exceed private costs by two orders of magnitude.

The American legal system may be able to transfer some of the external cost of a critical infrastructure data breach onto the company that suffered the attack. It is difficult, but sometimes possible, to successfully sue a power company for failing to prevent a power outage. In nearly every state of the country, power companies are allowed to limit their liability for an electric outage to cases of "gross negligence," as opposed to the sort of ordinary negligence for which most companies are held liable [35] .[7] In New York, for example, a public utility can limit its liability to "gross negligence" or "willful misconduct," and exempt itself from being sued for ordinary negligence [37] . In Maryland, a public utility is allowed to limit its liability to "willful neglect" or "willful default," which is a similar standard [38] .

Customers who experience losses as the result of a power outage sometimes are able to show "gross negligence" and recover from electric companies. After the 1977 blackout in New York City, for example, a grocery store successfully recovered from the Con Edison power company when it showed that Con Edison failed to take a number of safety precautions that could have prevented or limited the damage caused by the blackout [37] . Similarly, after Hurricane Sandy, Con Ed reached a settlement with homeowners who lost power in the storm. The power company paid $17 million, and agreed to cancel a $40 million rate increase [39] . It is possible that a third-party victim of a cyberattack on an electric company could sue the electric company, effectively turning the third-party's external costs into the company's private costs. The electricity sector is subject to binding cybersecurity regulation [40] . If an electric company was grossly negligent in failing to meet these cybersecurity standards, it could face liability which would convert its customers' external costs into company private costs.

Despite this thin reed of legal opportunity, third-parties who suffer losses in a critical infrastructure cyberattack are unlikely to recover much of their losses by filing a lawsuit for gross negligence. Occasional successes notwithstanding, it is generally very difficult to show that a public utility was grossly negligent [41] . Furthermore, in a truly catastrophic critical infrastructure cyberattack, an affected company may not have enough money to compensate all the third-party victims. Recognizing that the tort system was a poor means of protecting consumers from cyberattacks, Congress passed the Support Anti-Terrorism by Fostering Effective Technologies Act (SAFETY Act) of 2002 [42] . The SAFETY Act protects companies from liability in the event of a physical or cyberattack, on the condition that the companies employ technology that the Department of Homeland Security finds can be effective at preventing the attack from occurring. Technologies can be certified by the Department of Homeland

Security if they comply with the best practices in counterterrorism, and if certified, they are protected from legal liability [42] . The SAFETY Act seems to assume that government and the legal system are better situated to prevent attacks in the first place than to adjudicate liability in the event of an attack.

5. LARGE LOSSES AND RISK AVERSION

GL explicitly focused on small losses and used a risk neutral model [1] . Some, although not all, cybersecurity breaches could entail large losses such that private or public decision-makers may be risk averse. For instance, a loss of intellectual property that is the primary asset of a firm, or a breach that endangers a linked cyber-physical system such as the power grid, water, or some transportation modes. In such instances private sector decision- makers are routinely modeled as being risk averse instead of risk neutral. In general, risk aversion implies a willingness to invest to avoid a risky outcome (for instance, a security breach) that exceeds the expected loss in contrast with risk neutrality, as above, where the investment is limited by the expected value [43] . While this result also occurs in the cybersecurity literature, Huang, Hu and Behara [44] demonstrate that the willingness to invest has an upper bound of conditional loss even with risk aversion while investments can be less than the expected loss depending on the nature of the asset being threatened, for instance, it if is “irreplaceable” [45] .

Economists have considered whether national level, public decision-makers should be risk neutral or risk averse. Influential work by Arrow and Lind presented a model that such decision-makers “should” be risk neutral when, in fact, public decisions are often made where the costs of control appear larger than the expected value implying risk averse decision-making [46] . Stewart, Ellingwood and Mueller [47] have contrasted expected value and risk averse decision-making for the increases in security expenditures since the 9/11 attacks, and in Stewart and Mueller [48] applied that analysis to the Transportation Security Agency. They used a specific functional form for utility and solved for a break-even risk aversion parameter given their estimates of probability. In general, a large degree of risk aversion was necessary to be indifferent between the prior and current security expenditures. In two examples discussed by Stewart, Ellingwood, and Mueller [47] , the chosen defensive investment incorporating risk aversion exceeds the expected monetary loss by factors of 2.97 and 125 respectively, noting that with small probabilities the expected loss can be a small fraction of the conditional loss.

The specific point in the context of the GL two outcome model is that expenditures with risk aversion can significantly exceed expected losses in a discrete outcome model.

However, the result for a continuous state model is more ambiguous. While the general point remains that a risk averse decision-maker will expend more than a risk neutral decision-maker, the difference need not be large. In a continuous state setting, damage functions and probability are both varying. If damages are rising faster than the probability is declining, it is possible that no mean value exists. In contrast, for a concave damage function investigated for flooding [49] ; the mean values using a risk neutral and a risk averse utility function, and a weighting based on cumulative prospect theory were not substantially different. In part, the large losses where risk aversion can have a significant effect were associated with sufficiently small probabilities that the distinction was small between the mean values using a risk neutral or a risk averse utility function. Like the finding for the security breach function, the importance of risk aversion is an empirical question involving the structural form of damages, probabilities and the utility function.

6. CONCLUSIONS

GL thoroughly developed an influential model of cyber-security investment with important implications on the size of cybersecurity investment. As with the history of economic modeling, if one is fortunate enough to get clear initial results; then such results often get extended and qualified. Such is the main theme here. The key issues and conclusions identified here are:

- Consideration of externalities is a primary concern for government policy. Although GLLZ imply that externalities are unlikely to be large; evidence from past data breaches and cyberattacks suggests that externalities may be large, and that the legal system often fails to significantly internalize external costs by allocating risks to the original target. Such allocation may or may not be viewed as fair. This conclusion is relatively clear for personal identity theft and infrastructure attacks while the external effect of intellectual property attacks is less well documented in legal findings. These findings can imply significantly larger cybersecurity expenditures than those based solely on internalized, private sector damages.

- While an expected value (risk neutral) decision-maker will not spend more than expected losses and may spend significantly less, the results depend on the empirical functional form for the security breach function.

- When risk neutral investment considerations include: a) multiple datasets or sites, b) public defenses that protect many sites (as opposed to sharing of information), or c) an ability to invest in reducing damages, then the optimal (constrained) level of cyber investment changes and typically requires an optimal security investment based on the equivalency of marginal expected social cost avoided to the extent technologically possible.
- When additional modeling of the (dis)utility of uncertainty is added, whether in the form of irreversible losses or risk aversion; models commonly exist in which investments exceed expected losses.

The overall conclusion drawn here is that while there may be useful rules of thumb for decision-making, those behavioral rules may be incorrect depending on the empirical context of a specific problem including the behavior of attackers. To the extent that government policies and investments tend to focus on cyber issues with larger externalities, make use of public defenses, or be subject to advanced persistent threats, then the socially optimal investment decisions may be larger and differ significantly from those of the private sector.

ACKNOWLEDGEMENTS

Appreciation is extended to Larry Gordon, Anupam Joshi, Marty Loeb, Markus Rauschecker, Matt Shabat and an anonymous referee for comments and to Andrew Naviasky for research assistance; to the University of Maryland Center on Health and Homeland Security for coordination of the legal research and to the Department of Homeland Security Cyber Security and Communications division for short term space. Funding was provided by the Department of Homeland Security National Center on the Risk and Economics of Terrorism Events (CREATE).

REFERENCES

1. Gordon, L. and Loeb, M. (2002) The Economics of Information Security Investment. ACM Transactions on Information and System Security, 5, 438-457.
2. Gordon, L., Loeb, M., Lucyshyn and Zhou, L. (2015) Externalities and the Magnitude of Cyber Security Underinvestment by Private Sector Firms: A Modification of the Gordon-Loeb Model. Journal of Information Security, 6, 4-30.
3. Farrow, S. (2007) The Economics of Homeland Security Expenditures: Foundational Expected Cost-Effectiveness Approaches. Contemporary Economic Policy, 25, 14-26.
4. Hausken, K. (2006) Returns to Information Security Investment: The Effect of Alternative Information Security Breach Functions on Optimal Investment and Sensitivity to Vulnerability. Information Systems Frontiers, 8, 338-349.

5. Baryshnikov, Y. (2012) IT Security Investment and Gordon-Loeb's 1/e Rule. Proceedings of the 11th Workshop on the Economics of Information Security (WEIS), Berlin, 25-26 June 2012.
6. Gordon, L., Loeb, M. and Lucyshyn, W. (2003) Sharing Information on Computer Systems Security: An Economic Analysis. Journal of Accounting and Public Policy, 22, 461-485.
7. Gordon, L. and Loeb, M. (2011) You May Be Fighting the Wrong Security Battles. Wall Street Journal, September 26.
8. Kunreuther, H. and Heal, G. (2003) Interdependent Security. Journal of Risk and Uncertainty, 26, 231-249.
9. Willemson, J. (2010) Extending the Gordon and Loeb Model for Information Security Investment. 2010 International Conference on Availability, Reliability and Security, Krakow, 15-18 February 2010, 258-261.
10. Bagnoli, M. and Bergstrom, T. (2005) Log-Concave Probability and Its Applications. Economic Theory, 26, 445-469.
11. Cohen, M.A. (2000) Measuring the Costs and Benefits of Crime and Justice. In: Duffee, D., Ed., Measurement and Analysis of Crime and Justice, Criminal Justice 2000, Vol. 4, National Institute of Justice, Washington DC, 263-316.http://www.ncjrs.org/criminal_justice2000/vol_4/04f.pdf
12. Heartland Payment Systems, Inc., Customer Data Security Breach Litigation (2012) 851 F. Supp. 2d 1040 (S.D. Tex.).
13. Graves, J., Acquisti, A. and Christin, N. (2014) Should Payment Card Issuers Reissue Cards in Response to a Data Breach? WEIS: Workshop on the Economics of Information Security, Pennsylvania State University, State College, 23-24 June 2014. http://www.econinfosec.org/archive/weis2014/papers/GravesAcquistiChristin-WEIS2014.pdf
14. Crosman, P. (2014) How Much Do Data Breaches Cost? Two Studies Attempt a Tally. American Banker. http://www.americanbanker.com/issues/179_176/how-much-do-data-breaches-cost-two-studies-attempt- a-tally-1069893-1.html
15. Silver-Greenberg, J. and Schwartz, N. (2012) MasterCard and Visa Investigate Data Breach. The New York Times, 31 March 2012. http://www.nytimes.com/2012/03/31/business/mastercard-and-visa-look-into-possible-attack.html?_r=0
16. Clapper v. Amnesty International (2013) 133 S. Ct. 1138.
17. Lujan v. Defenders of Wildlife (1992) 504 U.S. 555, 560-61.
18. Zappos.com, Inc., Customer Data Sec. Breach Litig. (2015). No. 3:12-cv-00325-RCJ-VPC, (D. Nev.).
19. illett, B. (2015) Employees Can't Sue Hospital for Negligence, Breach of Contract, After Personal Data Breach. Reed Smith Technology Law Dispatch, 12 June 2015.
20. The Huntington National Bank v. Kokoska, et al. (2011) Docket No. 1:11-cv-00063 (N.D. W. Va. Apr 25).
21. Schmidt, M. and Sanger, D. (2014) 5 in China Army Face U.S. Charges of Cyberattacks. The New York Times, 19 May 2014. http://www.nytimes.com/2014/05/20/us/us-to-charge-chinese-workers-with-cyberspying.html
22. Andrijcic, E. and Horowitz, B. (2006) A Macro-Economic Framework for Evaluation of Cyber Security Risks Related to Protection of Intellectual Property. Risk Analysis, 26, 907-923.
23. Critical Infrastructures Protection Act (2001) 42 U.S.C. § 5195c(e).
24. Miller, C. (2009) Russia Confirms Involvement with Estonia DDOS Attacks. SC Magazine, 12 March 2009. http://www.scmagazine.com/russia-confirms-involvement-with-estonia- ddos-attacks/article/128737/
25. Tanner, J. (2007) Estonia Moves Soviet Statue to Cemetery. The Associated Press, 30 April 2007. http://www.washingtonpost.com/wp-dyn/content/article/2007/04/30/ AR2007043000478.html
26. Hollis, D. (2011) Cyberware Case Study: Georgia 2008. Small Wars Journal, 6 January 2011. http://smallwarsjournal.com/blog/journal/docs-temp/639-hollis.pdf
27. Markoff, J. (2008) Before the Gunfire, Cyberattacks. The New York Times, 13 August 2008. http://www.nytimes.com/2008/08/13/technology/13cyber.html?_r=0

28. Keizer, G. (2010) Estonia Blamed Russia for Backing 2007 Cyberattacks, Says Leaked Cable. Computer World, 9 December 2010. http://www.computerworld.com/article/ 2511704/vertical-it/estonia-blamed-russia-for-backing-2007-cyberattacks --says-leaked-cable.html
29. Landler, M. and Markoff, J. (2007) Digital Fears Emerge After Data Siege in Estonia. The New York Times, 29 May 2007. http://www.nytimes.com/2007/ 05/29/ technology/ 29estonia.html?pagewanted=all
30. Richards, J. (2009) Denial-of-Service: The Estonian Cyberwar and Its Implications for US National Security. International Affairs Review, 18. http://www.iar-gwu.org/node/65
31. Hobemagi, T. (2010) Price of Cyberattacks to Hansabank: 10 Million Euros. Baltic Business News, 12 August 2010.http://balticbusinessnews.com/article/ 2010/ 12/08/Price-of-cyberattacks-to-Hansabank-10-million-euros
32. Herzog, S. (2011) Revisiting the Estonian Cyber Attacks: Digital Threats and Multinational Responses. Journal of Strategic Security, 4, 49-60.http://scholarcommons.usf.edu/c gi/viewcontent.cgi?article=1105&context=jss
33. Crawford, J. (2014) The US Government Thinks China Could Take Down the Power Grid. CNN.com, 21 November 2014. http://www.cnn.com/2014/11/20/politics/nsa-china-power-grid/
34. Lloyd's of London (2015) Business Blackout: The Insurance Implications of a Cyber Attack on the US Power Grid. Lloyd's Emerging Risk Report-2015. https://www. lloyds. com/~/media/files/news%20and%20insight/risk%20insight/2015/business %20blackout/business%20blackout20150708.pdf
35. Liptak, A. (2003) The Blackout of 2003: Lawsuits; Plaintiffs to Face Hurdles Proving Liability. The New York Times, 15 August 2003. http://www.nytimes.com/2003/ 08/15/us/the-blackout-of-2003-lawsuits-plaintiffs-to-face-hurdles- proving-liability.html
36. Garrison v. Pac. Nw. Bell (1980) 608 P.2d 1206, 1211.
37. Food Pageant, Inc. v. Consol. Edison Co. (1981) 429 N.E.2d 738, 740.
38. Singer Co., Link Simulation Sys. Div. v. Baltimore Gas & Elec. Co. (1989) 558 A.2d 419, 428.
39. Frankel, A. (2012) Can Customers Sue Power Companies for Outages? Yes, But It's Hard to Win. Reuters.com, 9 November 2012.http://blogs.reuters.com/alison-frankel/2012/11/ 09/can-customers-sue-power-companies-for-outages-yes -but-its-hard-to-win/
40. Zhang, Z. (2013) Cybersecurity Policy for the Electricity Sector: The First Step to Protecting Our Critical Infrastructure from Cyber Threats. Boston University Journal of Science and Technology Law, 19, 319-366.
41. Wei, L., Debaise, C. and Bray, C. (2003) Blackout Exposes Power Companies to Potential Lawsuits. Dow Jones Newswires New York, 18 August 2003. http://www.oandb.com/ blackoutexposes.html
42. Venable LLP (2014) The SAFETY Act: Providing Critical Liability Protections for Cyber and Physical Security Efforts.https://www.venable.com/files/Publication/6c0b031e-c2c5-4029-9ac7-13cb1d8c0d07/Presentation/ PublicationAttachment/e81d24a3-fc57-4ece-8e1f-179418baf994/The_SAFETY_Act_Providing_ Critical_Liability_Protections_for_Cyber_and_Physical_Securi.pdf
43. Eeckhoudt, L., Gollier, C. and Schlesinger, H. (2005) Economic and Financial Decisions under Risk. Princeton University Press, Princeton.
44. Huang, C.D., Hu, Q. and Behara, R.S. (2008) An Economic Analysis of the Optimal Information Security Investment in the Case of a Risk-Averse Firm. International Journal of Production Economics, 114, 793-804.
45. Cook, P. and Graham, D. (1977) The Demand for Insurance and Protection: A Case of Irreplaceable Commodities. Quarterly Journal of Economics, 92, 143-156.
46. Lucas, D. (2014) Rebutting Arrow and Lind: Why Governments Should Use Market Rates for Discounting. Journal of Natural Resources Policy Research, 6, 85-91.
47. Stewart, M., Ellingwood, B. and Mueller, J. (2011) Homeland Security: A Case Study in Risk Aversion for Public Decision Making. International Journal of Risk Assessment and Management, 15, 367-386.

48. Stewart, M. and Mueller, J. (2013) Aviation Security, Risk Assessment, and Risk Aversion for Public Decisionmaking. Journal of Policy Analysis and Management, 32, 615-633.
49. Farrow, S. and Scott, M. (2013) Comparing Multi-State Expected Damages, Option Price and Cumulative Prospect Measures for Valuing Flood Protection. Water Resources Research, 49, 2638-2648.

NOTES

[1]Hausken [4] investigates some of the assumptions noting how the skills of the attackers may affect the convexity (leading to an interior solution), or the concavity (leading to a corner solution) of the problem. Game theoretic concerns about the assumptions may be somewhat abated by noting that the initial probability of a breach is not constant across sites but reflects the interests of the attacker, and that the change, if any, in probability of a security breach empirically reflects the behavioral response of the attacker.

[2]See [3] for the formal model statements, derivations and further discussion.

[3]For purposes of this section, the "private cost" of a data breach is the cost incurred by the directly attacked firm, and the "external cost" of a data breach is the cost incurred by the rest of society. This conception of "external cost" is narrower than the definition employed by Cohen [11] in the crime literature, who defines the "external cost" of a crime as "a cost imposed by one person onto another, where the latter person does not voluntarily accept the negative consequence." For the purpose of this section, however, the "external cost" excludes the cost to the directly-attacked firm.

[4]Several cases were selected as being large and identifiable, others as setting important legal precedents, and others chosen at random from the data breach data base at the Privacy Rights Clearinghouse (www.privacyrights.org/).

[5]The case was dismissed without prejudice, allowing the consumers to submit the suit again if they could show an injury in fact.

[6]The 16 sectors are: chemical; commercial facilities; communications; critical manufacturing, dams, defense industrial base, emergency services, energy, financial services, food and agriculture, government facilities, healthcare and public health, information technology, nuclear reactors, materials, and waste; transportation systems; and water and wastewater systems.

[7]Russia has never claimed responsibility for the attacks on Georgia, although (as explained below) the cyberattacks appeared to be coordinated with the movements of conventional Russian military forces. A Russian

official did, however, eventually confirm the participation of a Russian government-sponsored youth group in the denial-of-service attacks on Estonian websites [24] .

[8]See for example [36] “Courts are virtually unanimous that provisions limiting a public utility’s liability are valid so long as they do not purport to grant immunity or limit liability for gross negligence.”

CHAPTER 9

Governing the "Digital Shadows": Public Policy and Information Communication Technology (ICT) Acquisition and Utilization in Africa

Ebenezer Olatunji Olugbenga

Department of Political Science, Ekiti State University, Ado-Ekiti, Nigeria

ABSTRACT

This paper examines the challenges of appropriating the benefits of the Information Communication Technology (ICT) revolution by African states, against the backdrop of the realities of globalization and the role that ICT plays in global power relations. Built on the foundations of Jurgen Habermas' public sphere, it weaves a conceptual framework around the ideas of a "cyber-square" and "cyberspace policy" to argue for an African perspective to the adoption, acquisition and utilization of Information Communication Technology (ICT) to meet the specific needs of sub-Saharan African countries. It argues that, in spite of the challenges of ICT development in Africa, it is a lifeline that African states should embrace determinedly through purposeful public policy. It argues this deliberately to underscore the importance of purposeful ICT policy making to meet Africa's needs for social and economic revival and the promotion of the numerous national and continental interests that straddle the broad spectrums of the African political, cultural and economic landscapes. Through the use of secondary data, the author gives evidences for these by drawing examples from African countries. The paper recommends a multi-stakeholder approach to ICT policy development that reigns in not only African governments but also other stakeholders in Africa's ICT revolution. This, it argues, will help Africa evolve acceptable, adaptable and beneficial ICT policies capable of galvanizing and sustaining positive development to move Africa to its next stage of development.

Keywords: "Digital Shadows", Public Policy, Information Communications Technology (ICT), "Cyber-Square", Cyberspace, Collaborative Policymaking, Africa

1. INTRODUCTION

The rapid development and global spread of Information Communications Technology (ICT) is a reality that has caught up with human societies in the twenty-first century. Whereas technological research, knowledge production, dissemination and transfer now drive international politics to a reasonable extent, states rank differently in terms of technological knowhow and Information Communications Technology (ICT) capabilities. Today, ICT capabilities can advance or hinder the attainment or otherwise of national political, economic and cultural objectives, goals or values of states. Indeed, a country's ICT capability can affect the extent to which a country can pursue and attain her national values of cultural preservation and advancement, achieve socio-political stability as well as economic recovery and advancement, depending on which side of the global technological movement the nation finds itself.

Adopting a combination of the "cybersquare" and "cyberspace policy" as conceptual framework, the paper interrogates the significant question of African states' engagement with the ICT revolution as a requirement for continental political, economic and socio-cultural renaissance. It identifies the challenges, opportunities and strides taken by African states in ICT capability and development, arguing that taking advantage of the opportunities offered by ICT is the next golden opportunity for Africa to break away from its past experiences of poverty, socio-economic exploitation and underdevelopment.

Section one introduces the paper while Section two examines the state of the ICT revolution in Africa. Section three explicates briefly, the significance of the research while Section four focuses on the conceptual framework that weaves the concepts of "cybersquare" and "cyberspace policy" into Habermas' public square to explain the relevance of ICT to the African development process. Section five presents an historical trajectory of globalization, ICT and Africa. It argues that since telecommunications serve as a catalyst for overall development by activating and making available relevant data and information for development, ICT development in Africa must necessarily be policy driven for specific ends. Thus, it presents the case for an African renaissance through ICT but warns this can become a reality soon if African governments and other stakeholders develop the capacity and exhibit the willingness to implement acceptable, people-oriented policies. Section eight highlights the major contributions of the study to scholarship and policy, its innovations and limitations. Section nine concludes the study and suggests areas for further study.

2. THE STATE OF INFORMATION COMMUNICATIONS TECHNOLOGY (ICT) REVOLUTION IN AFRICA

For many African countries, the global technological movement and technological relations among states has yielded different types of outcomes as they relate and negotiate with countries of the North, who have been the main custodians and propagators of modern, western technology and culture that have attained global relevance, acceptability and dominance.

Thus, just as there is economic differentiation and diversity between countries of the global North and South (which includes Africa), there are differences between the "technologically advanced" countries of the North and the "technologically backward" countries of the South. This is not surprising since technological knowhow and advancement has become one of the major indices of development. Countries of the North are the main producers or generators of modern technology (even if not "originators" in the strict sense of the word). This development is traceable to historical factors including "brain drain" that has evacuated much human talent and expertise from countries of the South to those of the North in search of better living and fulfillment. Thus, many (with a few exceptions like South Korea and several "Asian Tiger" countries of the South) are mainly recipients or, in the strict sense of the word, "users" of modern, Western technology.

Many African economies that display aspects of western development are merely ramparts of western capitalism mostly with assembly plants and "showrooms" for western technologies. In some African countries like South Africa and to some extent, Ghana and Nigeria, these shadows of technological advancement have altered the structure of the economy by creating two types of economies, namely the "skilled" and the "unskilled" out of the co-existence of the pre-existing (traditional) and new (mainly information technology dependent) economic structures.

In South Africa, for instance, Mbeki [1] notes that technological knowhow and technological relations have created two separate but co-existing economies: a first world or "new" (technologically driven) economy that is "advanced, sophisticated... based on skilled labour... (and is) becoming more globally competitive". The other is a "third world economy" that is mainly "informal, marginalized unskilled... populated by the unemployed and those unemployable in the formal sector". This is largely reflective of the situation in many African countries.

Taking Ghana as another example of one of the most foreign technology dependent countries in Africa, research findings indicate that, along with financial services, transport, construction and mining, communications contributed a fifth of the total increase in total factor productivity of Ghana between 1991 and 2005 [2] [3] and [4] . However, Ghana achieved that high total productivity factor temporarily in those years by changing the sectoral composition of employment away from agriculture, one of the main areas where Ghana has comparative advantage and thrived in the 1960s, to the high-tech sectors (including communications) which are mainly dependent on foreign technology.

Nigeria's experience with oil and associated technologies is also instructive. Since the discovery and exportation of crude oil shortly before Nigeria's independence, the country's development planning has revolved around oil for which purpose the country relied on foreign technology, having no indigenous technology for oil exploration, extraction, refinement and even transportation. This was at the expense of agriculture that was the backbone of the economy prior to the discovery of oil. Many African countries experienced dependency in different areas of development including technology. A knowledging Africa's situation of all-round (including technological) dependency as a possible contributory factor to the declining fortunes of the continent, The World Bank [5] noted that "by the 1990s, it was clear that Africa was being marginalized in the world economy, with declining world export shares, falling terms of trade, and rising indebtedness". Also, Kiely [6] also affirms this fall in Africa and Latin America's share of world trade in spite of the globalization of production. In essence, this meant that globalization had not been working in the favour of Africa.

Since information communications technology is a major global driver of overall development, it becomes important to inquire about the state of ICT development in Africa today. As the second largest but least computerized continent with a population of over 500 million, Africa was in the past left out of the "global information society" and has been described as the "lost continent" [7] . One should question how easy it would be for Africa to develop if the estimation is true that a minimum of 90% of data on Africa may reside on databases in the West? [8] . Thus, although the embrace of ICT has brought several benefits to the continent so that it plays an important part in its process of development, ICT in Africa still suffers a myriad of problems relating to procedures, purpose and most importantly, policy objectives and direction. Odedra, Lawrie, Bennet and Goodman [7] have identified these to include lack of coordination that has resulted in uneven development of Africa's IT sector; poor infrastructure and inadequate IT literacy that has promoted over-dependence on expatriate personnel for many IT solutions ranging from systems analysis, programming, maintenance, consulting for business and for e-governance to the high cost of IT equipment and lack of high speed internet connectivity in many countries. There are also the challenges of vandalization of the little available equipment.

Then, there is the overarching influence of ICT on the security of Africa's many weak, economically and technologically dependent states because in the technological age, information is power which now resides not with strong- willed tyrants and sit-tight rulers (not leaders) that dot Africa's political landscape but with the owners and custodians of technology. Thus, it can be safely said that as far as ICT in Africa is concerned, real power resides not within but outside the continent in the twenty-first century. Herein lays the importance of purposive public policy both to direct and midwife ICT development to address the specific needs of Africans rather than the economic, cultural, security and political interests of the owners and originators of ICT in Africa.

Since Africa's development efforts are currently dominated by foreign ideas and technology, many African economies experience growth without development. But there are more serious consequences for Third World countries that depend excessively on foreign technology. In African and many other Third World countries, there are several national political and cultural values which protection and preservation are affected by the "technological progress" which the embrace if ICT has helped to mediate.

While the economies of the developed countries are often formal, ICT based, sophisticated, based on skilled labour and are global leaders in science, technology and industry, the bulk of Third World economies are characteristically informal, un-skilled, marginalized and mainly populated by the unemployed and those who are unemployable in the formal sector. For these reasons, the embrace of ICT and new skills has given birth to a "first-world" or "new" economy in Third World countries that has been polarizing their labour markets [9] [10] and [11] . According to Pejout [12] , labour market polarization in Africa is explained by the skill-based technology that characterizes the "new economy" for which majority of existing labour forces in African countries are not prepared in terms of knowledge and skills. This happened at the point of embrace of ICT, the fifth historical phase of capitalist development and a follow-up to the Structural Adjustment Programme (SAP) which ended in the early 1990s.

Pejout [12] argues further that the typical relationship between the old and the new economies in Africa are sub-optimal, varying between "disconnection and a trickle-down effect". This is not surprising, given that the technological market by countries of the North is "closed" against Third World countries, because countries of the North are very reluctant to transfer technology to countries of the South, Africa inclusive. At best, they are willing to enter into economic alliances with certain countries of the South only to serve as distribution hubs for Western technology; the so-called ramparts of imperialism.

The mass media which are also products of Western technology also helps to perpetuate imperialism through dependency of developing countries on the technologically advanced countries of the North. Although this second level of imperialism has been going on for a long time, some developing countries try to work collectively to resist this using several means that include global institutions such as the United Nations Educational, Scientific and Cultural Organization (UNESCO). For example, Smith argues that:

Through UNESCO, Third World Countries try to act collectively to resist the pressures from Westernized mass media, and the cultural, educational and scientific imperialism which introduces inappropriate technology and educational values into their societies [13] .

Smith argues further that the struggle to rid Third World countries of this second level of imperialism through collective action by affected countries constitutes an aspect of the anti-imperialist alliance by such countries against colonialism, neo-colonialism and racialism [9] . Yet, since many Third World countries relate with the Information Communication Technology (ICT) world mainly as recipients rather than producers or originators of technology, the extent and outcomes of ICT control within such recipient countries will be limited. For instance, although there is no proof of its correctness, western media's portrayal of Satan as a black personality and of God and His angels as white promotes in people an involuntary association of black with evil and white with good [14] .

The Information Communication Technology (ICT) revolution is affecting African countries in several other ways. These include promotion and deepening of cultural, educational and scientific dependency in Africa through neglect and promotion of other cultures at the expense of African cultures, value systems and orientations.

Also, the (ICT) revolution is threatening political stability in Africa by rendering African states vulnerable to the activities of violent non-state actors who have access to modern, "virtual weapons" of technology in addition to physical arms and ammunition with which they effectively contest the political space with government. Such groups have the capacity to unleash on the state what Madayan [15] describes as "a worldwide franchise of terror". They do so to weaken the economies of their target states by attacking major governmental and economic installations; by discouraging foreign direct investments and by diverting resources (including hard-earned foreign exchange) away from development projects to investment in arms and ammunition that are required to successfully engage such groups in campaigns for state security, stability, survival and economic prosperity.

When such actors or groups with ethnic or religious agenda contest the political space with governments of weak, heterogeneous states (and they are common in Africa), such countries may easily become ethnically polarized, religiously divided and politically vulnerable and unstable with catastrophic outcomes for such states and their citizens. This is because projections of national cohesion are affected with consequences for national security. African examples of such technology-bolstered groups include the Al-Shabab operations in East Africa, particularly Somalia and Kenya and the Boko Haram insurgency in West Africa. It is instructive that Somalia did not have a central government for some time due partly to such challenges. There are many examples of the breakdown of state power and authority in the Middle East due to the activities of technology-bolstered terrorist groups such as the Islamic State in Syria (ISIS) and the Levant (ISIL), among others.

National values of social cohesion are very important to the average African state. This is because in many cases, such states are composed of multiple ethnic nationalities resulting from the ways by which colonial powers created many African states by fiat, often without consultation or thought for the effects of heterogeneity on the socio-political stability and development of such states. This is why Madayan [15] argues "in the Third World countries, the issue of (political) stability (has come) to be as important as the issue of democratic change". An untamed mass media and uncontrolled use of ICT (where, for instance, there is no respect for human rights or the sanctity of the state and its government on-line) can easily become detrimental to national political, socio-cultural and economic goals and visions of the state.

ICT also affect African states by discouraging neglect of the primary sectors of the economy where they have comparative advantage such as agriculture while concentrating huge investments in high-tech sectors (such as telecommunications) that are controlled by foreign countries who own and control ICT technology. ICT affect African economies by sharply polarizing them and labour markets into the skilled and unskilled; "the employables" and "the unemploy- ables" in the high-tech dominated sectors of the economy which are becoming more popular in Africa. The experiences of South Africa and Ghana that were cited above are instructive.

Information Communication Technology (ICT) has been linked to globalization, which objectives include:

To throw the national economy, now marketized, wide open to the international market which is seen as a global open field for equal players... the globalization campaign sees the world market as confined by many prison walls. Among these are self-reliance, production for the development of the home market and for the consumption of millions of persons rather than for export, any act aimed at protecting the value of the national currency, state trading which is usually not on capitalistic free market terms, any restriction on foreign capital investment, any act aimed at encouraging industrialization in developing countries (such acts being regarded as hostility to agriculture), any tax on agricultural export goods, and any protection of domestic activity by almost any form of trade restrictions-tariff or non-tariff [16] .

Paraphrasing Strange [17] , Smith aptly summarizes the over-arching negative influences of globalization and ICT on states and governments, particularly Third World states. He argues:

Globalization has social and cultural dimensions... Global communications networks have far-reaching consequences for businesses, governments, educational institutions, voluntary bodies and community groups... The nation state is ...undermined by these forces... Transnational networks of production, trade and finance relegate national governments to "transmission belts" for global capital. World market forces are more powerful than state actions both domestically and in the international arena, so that while state intervention may have increased, the state's effectiveness in providing what markets do not-security, financial stability, law and order, and public goods such as infrastructure—has declined. Global capital imposes a discipline on states, leaving governments only with policy choices that are consistent with a free market. National sovereignty has been displaced by global and regional institutions... [13] .

The worst affected states in the scenario painted above are the developing or Third World countries, Africa inclusive. This paper seeks to explore the extent to which public policy can be used as an instrument for regulating and controlling the use of telecommunications by African countries such that state sovereignty would not be unduly compromised and the cultural and economic interests of the people would not be jeopardized through the adoption, deployment and utilization of ICT by African countries.

3. SIGNIFICANCE OF THE RESEARCH: PUBLIC POLICY DRIVEN ICT DEVELOPMENT IN AFRICA

The major significance of this research lies in its attempt to explore the utility of public policy as an instrument both for strengthening and straightening the path of ICT development in pursuit of African values; to strengthen its capacity to serve the purpose of lifting the continent out of its present quagmire; and to assure a brighter future for Africa's younger populations. A public policy-driven ICT development is possible because public policy is what governments choose to do or not to do in the pursuit of specific public goals or purposes be they re-direction, regulation, rejection, renewal, development, consolidation, etc. Thus Dye [18] , for instance, argues "public policies may regulate behaviour, organize bureaucracies, distribute benefits, or extract taxes-or all these things at once". Kwankam and Ningo [19] therefore notes that many African countries have not been exploring the possibilities of public policy to address the numerous challenges facing their societies, states and governments to the fullest. In their words:

Policy issues are central to most development efforts, ... (but) in most (African) countries there is a policy vacuum in IT, with only inadequate coverage (if any) being provided from related areas such as telecommunications and the computer industry. The policy aspects of IT therefore need to be addressed, in terms of formulation, dissemination, and implementation. In the absence of clear and enforceable policy, the industry is likely to evolve in a haphazard manner in reaction to uncoordinated external motives, thus allowing improper practices that would impair the growth of enthusiasm for IT... the prospect of a technology with such potential as IT evolving totally unchecked within our (African) countries is disquieting... The rational transfer and application of this technology requires that some guidelines be set down for service providers, distributors of equipment, and end users alike.

This paper aims to help African governments and the African Union, the private sector, policy makers, non-governmental organizations and other stakeholders see the many possibilities for using public policy as an instrument for addressing the challenges and harnessing the opportunities presented by the adoption and utilization of ICT in Africa for the benefit of the continent.

4. CONCEPTUAL FRAMEWORK: "CYBER SQUARE" AND CYBERSPACE POLICY

The concept of "cyber square" is conceived in this paper to indicate the almost inescapable presence and importance of the internet and associated technologies that promote the convergence of ideas and discourses that underlie relationships in modern personal, corporate and public lives and governance. It is comparable to the direct democracy of the Greek city-state's public square or city-centre, where issues of state or public importance were discussed in such a manner that every citizen had the opportunity to make contributions to how the city was governed. "Cyber square" is an idea for which "e-governance" in today's public realm and discourse can be a close substitute or at least, a variant. This is because both concepts which today, are becoming clearer as realities in the public realm, opportunes wide strata of the citizenry to affect, or at least, contribute to modern governance.

According to Habermas [20] and Arendt [21] , the public sphere which arose with the rise of the capitalist economy and the bourgeoisie in the eighteenth century provided a melting point for reconciling the differences between public authority and civil society. For Raiti [22] , it is surprising that Habermas' "public sphere seldom appears in ICT for development (ICT4D) literature even though the notion of democratization in Africa is nearly ubiquitous" and "technology has been considered a gateway toward a global public sphere". In spite of its many criticisms, Habermas' nostalgic attachment [20] to the debates at French public salons of the early 19th Century has survived and re-echoed as "talk shows" by Livingstone and Lunt [23] , as "new ICTs" by Sparks [24] and by Raiti [22] as "the efficacy of mobile telephony" in empowering citizens to contribute to their governments globally including sub-Saharan Africa. Calhoun [25] argues this will lead to rational debate capable of facilitating political deliberation. But the uneducated and property-less classes were ostracized from this bourgeois public sphere which later transformed into a realm of what Arendt termed "tangible freedom", the "site of speech".

In line with the above, Irele has argued that:

The public sphere ... embodied the ideas of a group of people coming together as equals in a private forum, which was distinct both from the public authority of the state and the private realm of the civil society and family life, and was capable of shaping public opinion and opinion and tastes through logical argument, critical analysis and persuasive language. The idea of the public sphere embodied what Habermas calls a principle of "publicness" or "publicity", that is, the opinion of private individuals could evolve into a public opinion through the rational-critical arguments of a group of public-spirited citizens, which was open to everyone as well as free from domination [26] .

Just like the determinants of "publicness" and "privateness" that were identified by Benn and Gaius [27] , the "cyber square" and its operations can be said to be characterized by access, agency and interest. While access is a description of the level or extent of restriction that can be placed on an activity (an activity that cannot be restricted is public while it is otherwise private), agency seeks to answer the question on whose behalf the action is undertaken or the extent of autonomy of an action. Interest attempts to pinpoint or describe who benefits from an action-the individual, the group involved, the state or some other actors. It is a measure of the degree of altruism or selfishness involved in an action.

In reality, access to cyberspace is relatively unrestricted, guaranteeing the widest access to anyone that wishes to utilize cyber technology for specific ends. The cost of entry is also cheaper than other traditional means of engagement with target audiences. Comparing traditional civil disobedience with "cyber civil disobedience", Crosston argues that:

Traditional civil disobedience is a "performance" via visual and physical mediums, while cyber disobedience is essentially a digital performance with difficulty in attributing true ownership of the act... But this new space also has a low cost of entry and regimes will find it difficult to physically control (it). Another distinction is how actors intending to cause wide-scale state damage are a very real cyber threat, while cyber disobedience that does not intend to fundamentally damage the state from cyber-attacks that aspire to is incredibly important but has proven elusive within formal cyber policy [28] .

Like the public sphere described above, the "cyber square" of today represents a major domain for a worldwide virtual franchise of ideas on almost every subject that affects the welfare of the global citizen including governance, representation, economy, human rights, livelihoods and a host of other issues that have become relevant to humanity. The "cyber square" does not recognize any physical, social, spatial, political or territorial boundary as it operates in free space and in a world of its own, limited only by technological knowhow and availability of equipment. It is a domain where no ruling tyrant can easily command obedience or impose limits on entry or circumscribe the freedoms of expression that individuals can enjoy for selfish ends without earning public opprobrium.

Therefore, the "cyber square" is gradually becoming a threat to unpopular governments and so-called tyrants who can be easily criticized and made to listen to opposing ideas which they would ordinarily silence through soldiers, guns, bayonets and imprisonment if the contest and the battles were physical. The Arab Spring in North Africa and parts of the Middle East proved this at the end of the first decade of the twenty-first century. This happened most notably in Libya where the use of the internet helped bring Mouamar Ghaddafi's regime to an end. It also happened in Egypt where sustained exchange of information using different modes of telecommunication amongst citizens helped mobilize popular actions that brought Hosni Mubarak's three-decade old government to its knees in less than three weeks in February 2011. Similar actions in 2011 also forced former Tunisian leader Zine Ben Ali to relinquish power and flee the country. Although several governments have now cultivated the habit of blocking or severing internet connectivity to their citizens at critical periods in their countries' histories, this is only a temporary unpopular measure that cannot continue as governments now rely on the Internet and other products of communications technology to conduct official government business through "e- governance".

The concepts of "cyber square" and cyber space are applicable to this study because many media of telecommunication exist and operate in and through space, which makes them somehow autonomous and, barring temporary governmental clampdowns, affords free entry and exit to whoever has the equipment and technical knowhow to access and utilize them. Also, they are domains that afford larger, almost unlimited extents of freedom and opportunity to individuals and groups to free themselves from the shackles of fellow men, oppressive governments and institutions through self-expression and the definition of identity, whether they are political, economic, cultural, etc in nature. The "cyber square" and cyber space affords today's global citizens the power of virtual existence to give and to receive information (for example, through the information superhighway) that cannot be easily circumscribed. It provides enormous informational powers and opportunities to individuals, groups, states and societies to maximize their opportunities. This is the world to which Africa is welcome.

5. AFRICA, GLOBALIZATION AND ICT

Research and development of new technology is a major characteristic of globalization while Information Communications Technology (ICT) is one of its major features and platforms for its propagation. Today, ICT and globalization have become realities that any country can hardly avoid or do without. As the timeframe for attainment of the Millennium Development Goals (MDGs) ended in 2015, they have been replaced by the new United Nations Sustainable Development Goals (SDGs) for the future, which highlights the importance of ICT to human development and the need to provide humans with universally affordable access to the Internet.

The new SDGs contain the following six ICT-related indicators:

- Proportion of schools with access to computers for pedagogical purposes and proportion of schools with access to the Internet for pedagogical purposes (target 4.a-upgrade education facilities);
- Proportion of youth/adults with ICT skills, by type of skills (target 4.4-pro- mote relevant skills);
- Proportion of individuals who own a mobile phone, by set (target 5.b-en- hance technologies to empower women);
- Percentage of the population covered by a mobile network, by technology (target 9.c-increase access to ICT);
- Fixed Internet broadband subscriptions, by speed (17.6-enhance cooperation on science, technology and innovation); and
- Proportion of individuals using Internet (17.8-enhance the use of enabling technologies, particularly ICT [29] .

In the reckoning of International Telecommunications Union, the above specifics are attributable to the fact that, while data are often available to measure ICT infrastructure and adoption, data on other topics, such as ICT in education, skills, and gender equality is, where available, are often less substantial [29] . This is true of Africa where data availability, gender and religious biases still affect development research.

Although the world is now a global village, the question of a country or region's strength and ability to harness the gains of globalization and appropriate its benefits for development depends on several factors which include access to and versatility of its citizens in ICT. Relating the above to Africa, one can safely infer that ICT in Africa have come with mixed outcomes or results.

The ascendancy of ICT and its strategic relevance to the continent's economic recovery from centuries of exploitation and marginalization is regarded as Africa's "fourth industrial revolution". There are high expectations based on the rising ICT profiles of some African countries like South Africa, Nigeria, Morocco, Egypt and Kenya and the overall bright continental outlook. Taking Nigeria, the most populous black nation worldwide as an example, with government's political will that resulted in the licensing of three GSM operators in 2001, a fourth in 2002 and the privatization of the incumbent parastatal NITEL in July 2006, Nigeria passed Egypt and Morocco in 2004 to become second to South Africa in mobile market coverage and more than fifty (50) companies providing fixed telephony services in addition to privatized NITEL, the second national operator (SNO) [29] . Yet, the country only reached just a quarter of its estimated market potential. Internet services are also booming in different countries with fixed telephony services and a vibrant young population in most African countries. As Wentworth [30] explains, internet connectivity across the continent grew from around 7% of the population with Internet access in 2008 to over 20% with Internet access in 2015.

In spite of the above, however, the benefits have not been generalized or evenly distributed across African countries and regions. For example, the figures cited by Wentworth [21] above showed that about 80% of the African populations were yet to enjoy Internet services as at the time. The Internet Society [31] summarized the overall picture succinctly. According to it:

Internet penetration levels are about 20% and rising. Mobile subscriptions are just shy of 70%, and mobile broadband access accounts for more than 90% of Internet subscriptions. But the aggregate indicators mask glaring disparities. At the high end of the spectrum, countries such as Morocco enjoy penetration rates above 50%, but at the other end are countries with penetration rates of below 2%, and the majority of countries have internet penetration of less than 10% (well below the 20% threshold that has been found to be critical for countries to reap the economic benefits of broadband investment).

The above shows that ICT have not led to the same outcomes in different African countries. Next, we take a brief look at the benefits and challenges of ICT adoption in Africa.

6. INFORMATION COMMUNICATION TECHNOLOGY (ICT) POLICIES IN AFRICA

A national information communications technology policy can be defined as an integrated set of principles, norms and ideals that are meant to guide ICT objectives, development, adoption, content and usage within a state. Because every state has historically specific conditions and needs which must have been agreed upon by the people (something like directive principles of state policy), a state's ICT policy should locate its raison d'etre within the historical, political, economic and cultural situations in which it is to be adopted and the challenges it is to address.

The first and arguably the most critical challenge confronting the development of ICT in Africa, which also has a bearing on other problems of ICT development in the continent is the relevance of Africa's national ICT policies to the African situation. For example, ICT policies of African states should interrogate the objectives of ICT adoption and utilization at this critical historical junction where Africa is confronted with the realities of unrestrained capitalist globalization with its negative implications for weak economies such as those of Africa. African ICT policies should question the level or degree of political will that African governments demonstrate in making ICT serve the political, economic and cultural needs of Africans; and they should enquire into the possibilities of creating digital cultural spaces through ICT to promote African cultures, values and ways of life rather than those of the creators (or manufacturers) of ICT technologies which have little or no respect for African values and worldview but rather disparage or seek to subvert them.

Lasswell [32] demonstrates that in many post-colonial states including Africa, the development of national communication structures and organizations in the immediate post-independence era did not encourage political inclusion but pursued a psychology of political exclusion against numerous ethnic nationalities estranged from political power. Many of Africa's political leaders misused communication to emphasize the primacy of political power, to further the "strategy of awe" to their political opponents and to transmit a "deliberate and unpremeditated message of modernity, determination and self-confidence" [32] to those for whom the image of their society had been tarnished by alien colonial and imperial subjugation [33] . They also failed to utilize communication to entrench and deepen the democratic culture, ethos and ideals of national integration or broad-based political development. No wonder many of such governments fell to military rule for various reasons.

Given that many African countries failed to maximize the benefits of communication for national development in the immediate post-independence era, they should not repeat that error with a second opportunity provided by ICT. For this reason, we now attempt to conduct a simple assessment of ICT adoption in Africa by examining its consequences or outcomes of its adoption by African states. Thereafter, we prognosticate on how African states can leverage on ICT for their next stage of development with the aid of purposeful ICT policies.

7. BENEFITS AND CONSTRAINTS OF ICT ADOPTION IN AFRICA

The embrace of ICT in Africa has contributed to the spread of ideas that have re-shaped and are still reshaping the political, economic, business and governmental landscapes as well as the security architecture of Africa.

Whether for good or bad, it may be said that the embrace of ICT will ensure that Africa cannot be the same old continent again. ICT have brought several salutary results to Africa.

First, ICT have succeeded in linking the continent to the rest of the world through high bandwidth submarine fibre optic cables linking Africa (from Nigeria and other countries) to Europe through a 7000 kilometre-long distance from Portugal. This put an end to decades-long isolation of Africa from other continents [34] . It is expected to affect positively, every facet of African life.

Second, ICT has contributed towards deepening and entrenching democracy in Africa by providing media for citizen actions to stand up against authoritarian and autocratic governments. The governments of such countries characteristically shut down communication networks at critical periods in their countries' histories, sometimes for selfish political reasons. Examples of countries where this happened include Uganda, Chad, Republic of Congo, Zimbabwe, DRC, Burundi and even Ghana with its democratic credentials that makes it to be regarded as a model of democracy on the continent [35] . Others in this category include Tunisia under former President Zine Ben Alli and Egypt's Mubarak who imposed media blackouts in the wake of the Arab Spring in 2011 but were removed by popular actions powered mainly through the use of ICT. Similar incidents also occurred in several countries of the Middle East at the end of the first decade of the twenty-first century. In spite of governments' actions, activists utilized the internet and social networks to inform and mobilize people for the defence of democracy in such countries, thus bringing to pass Raiti's [22] expectation that African tele-centers could become sub-Saharan Africa's versions of the French salons.

In order to appropriate the benefits of ICT to the fullest, however, there is a need for education and literacy, and Habermas was also emphatic on this point. In making the point that the literature often overlooks these requirements for ICT usage, Raiti [22] becomes suspicious that most western and some African literature on democratization (such as Berger, 2002) [36] may be merely an extension of academic and political imperialism even as Africa struggles to stabilize and consolidate her tottering democracies. Therefore, Raiti queries whether democracy is an end goal in itself or a means to an end? He queries the ethical foundations of the desire of corporations and their shareholders to reap financial benefits especially from rural Africa by making telephony and ancillary services available to the rural poor without fulfilling the requirements for doing so. These include the "critical junctures" of literacy and growing education. Thus, more than education without ICT can induce "schooling without learning", the provision of ICT to the rural folk without literacy, education and nationalistic orientation can induce misguided zeal. This scenario has escalated the threat of terrorism globally and especially in Africa as ICT devices become increasingly available to dispossessed, disenfranchised, displaced, disoriented and disgruntled individuals and groups. Both are potentially catastrophic and unfortunately, represent the reality in Africa today. Interrogating these issues is directly related to ICT for development on the continent.

Third, if current growth rates are sustained and built upon, ICT will likely help to raise Africa's productivity factor in the near future. Projections by GSMA, an association of mobile telephone operators suggest that by 2020, there will be in Africa more 700 million smart-phones in Africa, more than twice the projected number for North America and close to the projected figure for Europe. Mobile telephony is expected to contribute 8% to Africa's GDP by 2020 while the Internet could potentially contribute 10% of GDP to African countries by 2025 [37] .

Fourth, ICT is already helping to contribute to the ease of doing business in Africa, thus bringing more investors into the continent provided the issues of corruption and the power sector are well handled and government policies create investor-friendly environments in Africa. Already, e-commerce is growing while mobile financial services are on the rise, showing signs of a better business environment in Africa. Within these, there is the probability of finding better markets for Africa's resources, finding better uses for their raw materials as well as greater capabilities to turn them into semi-finished products with higher values. Overall, digitization efforts will bring more businesses and governments online in Africa and the economy will improve.

In spite of the benefits, however, there are numerous challenges confronting the development of ICT which may affect the continent's chances of reaping maximum benefits from its development in Africa.

First is the challenge of the relevance of Africa's national ICT policies to the African situation. As Momoh [38] argues, "to combat an endemic psychology of "under-developed man and culture", should be one of the main thrusts of an informed national communication policy in an African country". He opined further that "it is indeed crucial that any enlightened national communication policy in an African society ought to have the goal of decolonization as its central focus". Another observer makes the point more clearly and more forcefully when he argues that:

If, in the process of acquisition of modern technology and scientific outlook that goes with it, people of developing countries acquire and perpetuate a sense of inferiority and loss of confidence vis-à-vis current sources of technology, the gap between developing and developed nations will continue to widen [39] .

This is a warning to African countries and their governments not to see the embrace of ICT as an end in itself or a solution to the many problems of Africa and its peoples. Rather, African countries should see it as a means to the end of dependency on the West for virtually everything. This includes but is not limited to technologies for exploiting Africa's natural resources, cultural resuscitation and renewal, entrenchment and consolidation of democracy as well as urban planning, growth and development. The critical question is "what are the goals and objectives of Africa's ICT policies?" and "who is and who is not consulted in their drafting and approval?" ICT policy drafting and adoption in Africa should not be the exclusive preserve of government, the bourgeoise capitalist entrepreneurs and representatives of foreign capital alone. It should adopt a bottom-up process involving collaborative governance that is reminiscent of the new network society that we now live in.

Second, although African governments have adopted the multi-stakeholder approach towards ICT governance and is yielding result, they should demonstrate greater commitment to ICT development through greater funding, more collaboration with stakeholders, better regulation that recognizes no sacred cow (of operators) and other oversight functions to stabilize the sector for sustained growth and benefits. African governments will need more political will, commitment and practical action to meet the needs of the continent's growing ICT market that is populated mainly by young people. According to the Internet Society [31] , "Africa needs a coherent strategy for capacity development at all levels, and this strategy needs to look first at ICT as a discipline and secondly as a cross-cutting enabler of other disciplines".

Third, there is the challenge of increased cybercrimes and privacy concerns but this is a global rather than an exclusively African problem. As Serracino-In- glott [40] and Crosston [28] inform, there has been a remarkable lack of consensus on establishing unified norms of cyber behaviour and the global political system is seen as having utterly failed to protect civilians from cyber crimes, attacks and abuses of human rights online. In a development that shows the weakening powers of the state globally, cyber vigilantes acting self-righteously within self-imposed boundaries of morality and operating outside of the law now take upon themselves the duty of cyber protection and cyber crime fighting.

Fortunately in a show of determination and solidarity, the African Union (AU) has developed a Convention on Cyber Security and Personal Data Protection aimed at committing member states to establish legal frameworks for e-transactions, data protection and punishment of violators [31] . The AU is also involved in AXIS and dot Africa projects to combat cyber abuses while it is including the control of cybercrimes and privacy concerns in the continent's fifty-year plan, 2063 Agenda to secure the cyberspace. The continental organization also has an African Internet Governance Forum to address several cyber security related issues [40] . However, since experience shows that many international protocols and agreements are breached at will once there is no monitoring organ to enforce compliance and there are no penalties for default, it is recommended that the AU should empower a committee to monitor compliance and impose fines on defaulters.

Fourth is the challenge of flagrant abuse of human rights on digital media platforms such as face book, twitter, whatsapp, etc especially when contested political, social and economic prizes and value allocations such as elections are involved. Although digital media platforms have the capacity to serve positive purposes such as checkmating dictatorial tendencies in political leaders (such as happened during the Arab Spring around year 2011), several developments have combined to raise the issue of control of digital media platforms to the front burner of public discourse using the instrumentality of the United Nations to advance common understanding and solutions to online abuse of human rights. Examples include the use of online media to discredit political opponents and spread hatred in speech and action during the Nigerian presidential elections of 2015. That election was eventually lost by the Peoples Democratic Party (PDP) that had ruled the country for four unbroken terms totaling sixteen years.

However, human rights abuses online are being addressed at the continental level through an aggregation of concerned organizations who launched the African Declaration on Internet Rights and Freedoms in 2014. Its objectives include the promotion of online respect for human rights in Africa; openness in Internet and ICT policy making and implementation in Africa [40] . Again, there is need for collaborative efforts by all stakeholders including network operators, network engineers, industry players, civil society, individual and corporate end users. Governments must be involved because they have the instruments of ensuring compliance, redress and punishment in cases of breach. However, governments, intelligence agencies, criminals and corporations are also involved in cyber surveillance; hence the need for a collaborative approach to cyber-right watch in order to have an Internet of opportunities rather than of apprehension. How that can be achieved can be the subject of another research.

Other challenges to ICT utilization in Africa include inadequate and aging infrastructure that causes congestions; the need for funding to upgrade equipment to desired levels; lack of basic infrastructure like access roads and electricity to drive the ICT revolution and the high cost of ICT services that raises the challenge of affordability for Africa's teeming poor populations. On cost, for instance, the Internet Society [40] reports that "currently ... users in Africa pay up to 30 or 40 times more for Internet access than their peers in developed countries". Although Africa currently has over 30 Internet exchange points (IXPs), each country and each of the five geographical regions should have at least one to catalyze the build-out of terrestrial infrastructure in order to make access to the Internet faster and cheaper for everyone [40] . Achieving this is a question of funding.

The African ICT space is dominated by foreign competitors whose practices may not promote the national and indigenous values of their host countries such as local language content. And African governments sometimes shut down ICT facilities for punitive political purposes or values. Given that many African investors shy away from the ICT sector, there is therefore the challenge of how to rein in Africa's entrepreneurs so they can invest in ICT as this may help drive the objectives of national ICT policies faster. There is also a need to bring into the ICT threshold many Africans who currently operate in the informal sector.

Many of the challenges of ICT adoption and utilization in Africa can be addressed through dedicated national ICT policies, especially if the drafting and implementation of such documents follow the collaborative, bottom-up model of public policy making and implementation. The collaborative or multi-stake- holder model has prospects for group thinking (or "thinking together") with unlimited capacities for problem-solving among stakeholders in a mutually-rein- forcing manner. Although the challenges are enormous, the collaborative model has a capacity to throw up useable new heuristics that may lead to problem-solving as individuals and groups work and think together over common problems. For example, the ICT industry in Kenya is now practicing the infrastructure-sharing policy that allows several networks to use a single mast [41] , a practice that can be experimented in other countries.

Different African countries have various qualities and features several high performers in the ICT, e-commerce and e-entertainment and ICT funding sectors whose experiences can be leveraged upon to promote Africa's ICT development. For instance, while Nigeria has the best ICT market potential in the continent, South Africa has the best ICT infrastructure and education while Kenya has a very good ICT policy. Again, some high performers in Africa's ICT and allied sectors include South Africa's MTN and M Pesa mobile money; Nigeria's Globacom and the Jumia Group; Kenya's iHub and Tanzania's Savannah Fund Investment. African must leverage on the experiences and strengths of these and many other continental players not only to develop the ICT sector further in Africa, but also to indigenize or "Africanize" it. However, this cannot happen in a vacuum.

To achieve the above, Pejout [12] has outlined four priorities while there is a gender perspective [42] to the enhancement, acceleration and "Africanization" of the second new economy in the continent. An expansion of Pejout's priority areas in line with current realities would possibly include the following:

1) Building and enhancement of appropriate telecom/IT (to widen and improve coverage) and other basic infrastructure (like electricity, access roads, etc) without which ICT cannot thrive;

2) Building of appropriate institutions to facilitate fair competition among players; a strong and efficient regulatory regime to curtail operator abuses and excesses; and the democratization of access by building more Internet public access and training points. This can be achieved through collaboration with local, national and international stakeholders;

3) By deliberately creating a "second new economy" or ICT industry plan to improve Africa's broadband infrastructure network and to inculcate the digital culture into Africa's educational systems. The New Partnership for Africa's Development, governments at various levels and the philanthropic private sector and non-governmental organizations took up this challenge in the past and got results; now the challenge is to build on its achievements for future expansion. Also, the e-schools initiative is succeeding as many pupils in Africa are already computer literate. Already, there are many e-learning programmes in Africa's schools while many examination bodies like Nigeria's Joint Admissions and Matriculation Board (JAMB) are gradually shifting to e-examinations. In light of the ICT revolution, Babalola [43] argues, it has become clear that without ICT/digi- tal education, Africa's children may get schooling without learning. Such an education would not prepare its beneficiary for gainful employment;

4) Consequent upon the polarization of Africa's labour market by the ICT revolution, there is a need to prevent unemployment from rising higher by facilitating multi-layered skills development strategies to enable many Africans (even with the basic skills) to find opportunities for gainful employment in the new, ICT-led economy, from which they can develop their skills further;

5) Telecommunication serves as a catalyst in human and social development by providing timely access to data and information. Therefore, access to ICT can be regarded as a determinant feature of gender relations, women's empowerment [42] and productivity. Given that women constitute over 50% of Africa's 1.2 billion population [32] and that they are an indispensable force for economic advancement in many African cultures, the gender perspective must be brought to bear on ICT planning and development in Africa in order to reap its fullest benefits;

6) Finally, Africa's ICT development must be public policy-driven for several reasons. These include the need to direct it towards meeting African rather than foreign needs in terms of acquisition, domestication, financing, costing and democratization for the sake of sustainability, application or utilization to address Africa's high impact development priority areas rather than attempt to catch up with the developed world who in any case, are not waiting for any region to catch up with them. Policy must also address regulation, local control and ownership, coordination, harmonization (or at least, integration) and encouragement of synergy in ICT development between the public and private sectors of African economies. While the public sector can provide mainly the legal and regulatory environments for ICT development in Africa to address the continent's unique challenges, the private sector can provide funding and expertise to drive the process of ICT development smoothly with an eye for quality service, affordability and guided control to avoid inefficiencies as much as possible.

8. RESEARCH CONTRIBUTIONS, INNOVATION AND LIMITATIONS

The major contribution of the research is its emphasis on the many ways in which all stakeholders in ICT development in Africa can cooperate not only to "domesticate" ICT adoption and usage but also to enhance its benefits to Africa using the instrument of public policy. Its innovation lies in its conceptual framework using ideas of the "cyber-square" and "cyberspace policy" and linking these with the modern utility and reality of Jurgen Habermas' concept of the public sphere and its significance for liberal, representative democracy that most nations practice today. It is particularly relevant to the African political enterprise where sit-tight regimes continue to hold sway in many countries ostensibly with an air of invincibility. The deployment of ICT in the cyber-square extends the frontiers of political communication in liberal democracies with the increasing use of electronic and digital media to register political dissent, embark on cyber protests and to influence voters during electoral campaigns. This means governments alone no longer hold all the aces where political expression is concerned.

The main limitations to the study are its limited tri-disciplinary foundations (limited as it is to political science, public policy and philosophy) rather than a multidisciplinary approach to the development of ICT for development (ICT4D) which Raiti [22] canvasses. However, research is continuous and this effort can be improved upon by introducing fresh perspectives from other disciplines like sociology, mass communication and security studies. Such new perspectives may constitute areas for further research into ICT and Africa. The second limitation is its greater reliance on secondary than primary data. On the first limitation, the research can be seen as an improvement on existing monolithic However, this does not impact negatively on the findings of the study because the author had many opportunities to cross-check facts and data that were used for the study.

9. CONCLUSION

This paper has examined the challenges and prospects of the Information Com- munications Technology (ICT) revolution against the historical backgrounds to globalization in Africa. It identifies the ICT revolution as a consequential extension of capitalist development that no country can ignore. It therefore argues that in spite of the disadvantaged historical political and economic positioning of Africa vis-à-vis the developed world who are the custodians of most forms of modern technology, African countries can still latch on to the ICT revolution to take an economic leap forward in the historical future. The paper recommends several means of achieving this including the adoption of collaborative synergy in ICT policymaking and implementation at the local, national and international levels. This means such approach must necessarily involve all stakeholders in order to reap the fruits ICT for Africa's economic, political and cultural leap forward.

REFERENCES

1. Mbeki, T. (2003) Characteristics of South Africa's First and Third World Economies. In: Padayachee, V., Ed., A Political Economy of Africa, Routledge, London and New York, 231-244. https://books.google.com.ng/books?isbn=1136989072
2. Baudry, P. and Sowa, N.K. (1994) Labour in an Era of Adjustment: The Case of Ghana. In: Killick, T., Ed., Development and Economics in Action: A Study of Economic Policies in Ghana, 2nd Edition, Routledge, London and New York, 234-287.
3. World Bank (2007) Ghana: Meeting the Challenge of Accelerated and Shared Growth. Volume I, World Bank Report No. 40934-GH, World Bank, Washington DC. http://documents.worldbank.org/curated/en/200461468031469957/pdf/Pages0from040915403volumes0ER01GH13.pdf
4. Killick, T. (2010) Development and Economics in Action: A Study of Economic Policies in Ghana. 2nd Edition, Routledge, London and New York, 234-287.
5. The World Bank (2004) Strategic Framework for Assistance to Africa: IDA and the Emerging Partnership Model. The International Bank for Reconstruction and Development/The World Bank, Washington DC, 6.
6. Kiely, R. (2010) Rethinking Imperialism. Palgrave Macmillan, New York, 184.
7. Odedra, M., Lawrie, M., Bennett, S. and Goodman, S. (1993) Sub-Saharan Africa: A Technological Desert. Communications of the ACM, 36, 25-29.

8. Zwangobani, E. (1987) Communications for Development: A Developing Country Perspective. Conference Proceedings of Africom 87, Computer Society of Zimbabwe, Harare.
9. Brender, A. and Pisani, F. (2004) La Nouvelle Economie Americaine. Economica, Paris. http://www.cepii.fr/PDF_PUB/em/2010/em2010-02.pdf
10. Milkman, R. and Dwyer, R.E. (2002) Growing Apart: The "New Economy" and Job Polarization in California, 1992-2000. University of California Institute for Labour and Employment, e Scholarship Repository, University of California, Oakland. http://escholarship.org/uc/item/9k208732
11. Artus, P. (2000) Nouvelle Economic, Nouveaux Problems. In: Le Cercle des Economists, Esperances et Menaces de la Nouvelle Economie, Descartes and Cie, Paris, 21-42.
12. Pejout, N. (2010) Africa and the "Second New Economy": How Can Africa Benefit from ICT for a Sustainable Socio-Economic Development? In: Padayachee, V., Ed., The Political Economy of Africa, Routledge, Oxon and New York, 231-244.
13. Smith, B.C. (2009) Understanding Third World Politics: Theories of Political Change and Development. 3rd Edition, Palgrave Macmillan, Hampshire and New York, 102.
14. Fashek, M. A Nigerian Reggae Music Star Sang This over Two Decades Ago.
15. Madayan, R. (2014) The New Al-Qaeda in the Levant and North Africa: The Rebirth after Bin Laden's Elimination. The 13th International Conference of Africanists with the Theme "Society and Politics in Africa", Moscow, 27-30 May 2014, 8.
16. Toyo, E. (2000) Background to Globalization. The Academic Staff Union of Universities Educational Publication Series No. 2, Ibadan, 18.
17. Strange, S. (1996) The Diffusion of Power in the World Economy. Cambridge University Press, Cambridge.
18. Dye, T.R. (2005) Understanding Public Policy. 11th Edition, Pearson Education Inc., Pearson, 1.
19. Kwankam, S.Y. and Ningo, N.N. (1997) Information Technology in Africa: A Proactive Approach and the Prospects of Leapfrogging Decades in the Development Process.
20. Habermas, J. (1989) The Structural Transformation of the Public Sphere: An Inquiry into a Category of Bourgeois Society (Trans. by Burger T. with the Assistance of Lawrence F.). Polity Press, Cambridge, 161.
21. Arendt, H. (1958) The Human Condition. The University of Chicago Press, Chicago, 50-58.
22. Raiti, G.C. (2006) The Lost Sheep of ICT4D Research. Massachusetts Institute of Technology Information Technologies and International Development, Vol. 3, 1-7. [Citation Time(s):5]
23. Livingstone, S. and Lunt, P. (1994) Talk on Television: Audience Participation and Public Debate. Routledge, London.
24. Sparks, C. (1998) Is There a Global Public Sphere? In: Thussu, D., Ed., Electronic Empires: Global Media and Local Resistance, Arnold, London, 108-124.
25. Calhoun, C. (1992) Introduction: Habermas and the Public Sphere. In: Calhoun, C., Ed., Habermas and the Public Sphere, MIT Press, Cambridge, 1-50.
26. Irele, D. (1999) The Public Sphere and Democracy. Viewpoint: A Critical Review of Culture and Society, Vol. 1, 52-64.
27. Benn, S. and Gauss, G. (1983) Public and the Private: Concepts and Action. In: Benn, S. and Gauss, G., Eds., Public and Private in Social Life, St. Martin's Press, New York, 7-11.
28. Crosston, M. (2017) The Fight for Cyber Thoreau: Distinguishing Virtual Disobedience from Digital Destruction. In: Korstanje, M.E., Ed., Threat Mitigation and Detection of Cyber Warfare and Terrorism Activities, IGI Global, Hershey, 198-219.
29. International Telecommunications Union (ITU) (2016) Sustainable Development Goals and the Internet: Measuring the Information Society Report. Internet Platform/Digiwatch in Partnership with Internet Society, Geneva. https://digitalwatch. giplatform.org/processes/sustainable-development-goals
30. International Telecommunications Union (ITU) (2016) ICT Facts and Figures 2016. http://www.itu.int/en/ITU-D/Statistics/Documents/facts/ICTFactsFigures2015.pdf https://www. Internetworld stats.com

31. Wentworth, S.S. (2015) The Internet Needs Africa as Africa Needs the Internet—A Speech to the African Union.
32. Internet Society (2015) Internet Development and Internet Governance in Africa. http://www.internetsociety.org/doc/internet-development-and-internet-governance-africa
33. Lasswell, H.D. (1977) Building Political Communication: The Signature of Power and Environment. In: Daniel, L. and Lyle, M.N., Eds., Communication Research: A Half Century Appraisal, The University Press of Hawaii, Honolulu, 280-294.
34. Nnaemeka, T. (1989) Issues in National Communication Policy: Parameters of Theory and Experience. In: Nnaemeka, T., Uvieghara, E. and Uyo, D., Eds., Philosophy and Dimensions of National Communication Policy, Vol. 1, Centre for Black and African Arts and Civilization, Lagos, 1-9.
35. The Guardian (2016) Africa's Top 10 Tech Pioneers: "We Have Become an Internet-Consuming Culture". http://www.africaontherise.com/2016/07.africa's-top-10-tech-pioneers-we-have-become-aninternet-consuming-culture/
36. Berger, G. (2002) Theorizing the Media-Democracy Relationship in Southern Africa. Gazette: The International Journal for Communication Studies, 64, 21-45.
37. The Guardian (2016) Can the Internet Reboot Africa? https://www.theguardian.com/world/2016/jul/25/can-the-internet-reboot-africa
38. Momoh, T. (1989) A Framework for National Communication Policy. In: Nnaemeka, T., Uvieghara, E. and Uyo, D., Eds., Philosophy and Dimensions of National Communication Policy, Vol. 1, Centre for Black and African Arts and Civilization, Lagos, 10-23.
39. Banani, A. (1977) Towards a National Communication Policy for Iran. In: Teherania, M., Hakimzadeh, F. and Marcello, L.V., Eds., Communications Policy for National Development, Routledge and Kegan Paul, London, 279.
40. Serracino-Inglott, P. (2013) Is It OK to an Anonymous? Ethics and Global Politics, 6, 220.
41. Ekiti State of Nigeria (2011) Ekiti State Gender and Development Policy. BIGIF/ Kingdom of the Netherlands, Ado-Ekiti, 11.
42. Babalola, J. (2010) Transition from Chalkboard to Digital Whiteboard: Keeping pace with Challenges of 21st Century Learning Technologies in a Developing Economy. His Lineage Publishing House, Ibadan, 5.
43. Worldstat (2017) Sex Ratio in Africa. http://en.worldstat.info/Africa

CHAPTER 10

A Review of Security Concerns in Internet of Things

Engin Leloglu

R&D Department, Vestel Electronic Inc., Manisa, Turkey

ABSTRACT

The Internet of Things (IoT) represents a technologically optimistic future where objects will be connected to the internet and make intelligent collaborations with other objects anywhere, anytime. Although it makes appreciable development, there are still uncertainties about security concepts of its usage that is usually considered as a major concern in the design of IoT architectures. This paper presents a general survey of all the security issues in IoT along with an analysis of IoT architectures. The study defines security requirements and challenges that are common in IoT implementations and discusses security threats and related solutions on each layer of IoT architecture to make this technology secure and more widespread accordingly.

Keywords: Internet of Things, IoT, Security Requirements, Security Challenges, Security Threats, Security Solutions

1. INTRODUCTION

Although Internet of Things (IoT) is a well-known term and a rising trend in IT arena, there has been no agreed definition by the world community of users until now. In fact, there are many different groups in industry and standardization organizations that formulate similar ideas but in different forms and based on different components or aspects of an IoT system.

The best definition for the Internet of Things would be defined by ITU-T Y.2060:

"Global infrastructure for the society, enabling advanced services by interconnecting (physical and virtual) things based on existing and evolving interoperable information and communication technologies."

IoT is such a system that supplies connectivity and interactive communication for anything. Even though "being connected" is usually used in term of electronic devices in our daily life, physical objects that have hardware such as sensors or actuators, connect to the Internet with unique addresses. Data of physical object are transmitted continuously through wired/wireless networks to platforms where it will be interpreted. Physical objects are capable of understanding complexity of the environment and reacting due to their feature of sense and communication. The revolutionary advance in this case is that physical objects begin to be deployed and adopted widely. In addition, most of them begin to work properly without human intervention [1] .

In future, every object in our daily life will be connected to Internet. Mobile phones will be used as the center point or the remote control for all objects in the physical world commonly called as IoT [2] . According to Gartner [3] , it is expected that the number of Internet-connected devices will increase from around 25 billion to 50 billion by 2020. Prevalence of such a big network induces new security risks that can allow attackers to steal even more personal information about the users or the organizations that are connected to such an IoT system.

Emphasizing security issues surrounding IoT is the main goal of this paper. Security is an important concern for IoT technology because of following reasons [4] :

- IoT is accepted as an extended version of some different technologies such as Wireless Sensor Networks, Mobile Broadband and 2G/3G Communications Networks which are already under threat because of various security flaws.
- Every device is connected to Internet in IoT technologies and Internet is an unsecured environment naturally. There are many evil-minded

people who are on the lookout for various system breaches and remote code executions.

- Objects in IoT communicate with each other; hence, there is a possibility that privacy and security can be hindered.

This study presents a general survey of all the security issues in IoT along with an analysis of IoT architectures. The paper describes security requirements and challenges that are usually faced in IoT implementations and mentions security threats and related solutions on each layer of IoT architecture to make this technology secure and more widespread.

The paper is organized as follows. In Section 2, IoT scope and recommended architecture are described. Section 3 studies security requirements and challenges for IoT implementations. In Section 4, security threats plaguing the Internet of Things are surveyed in such a way that all these threats are categorized based on layers of IoT architecture. Section 5 discusses security solutions and research directions on each layer and finally Section 6 concludes this study.

2. IOT SCOPE AND ARCHITECTURE

IoT purposes to enable things to be connected anyplace and anytime using any service/network [5] . Having this purpose of IoT in mind, it is stated that a correct and easy implementation of an IoT system mainly depends on identifying the right principles regarding the proper discovery, identification, configuration and manipulation of interconnected devices and sensors [6] .

In the study of Uma Mahesh et al. [7] , a classification is proposed that helps in defining the various elements of IoT from a higher level perspective;

1) Hardware: Sensors, central units and built-in communication hardware are included in this level. Since a sensor has limited hardware, it is usually utilized in sensor networks that multiple sensors are linked together. A central unit that is a source of centralized services in IoTs, has a capable of storing, processing, and delivering data to users.

2) Middleware: It consists of storage and calculation tools for data analytics. Cloud computing is given as an example in this section.

3) Cloud computing is the integrity of several traditional technologies such as hardware virtualization, service-oriented architecture, load-balancing, distributed computing, grid computing, utility computing and autonomic computing. It can be considered as a natural step forward from the grid-utility model [8] . This style of computing relies

on sharing of resources are provided as a service over the Internet to achieve coherence and economy of scale.

4) Presentation: There are visualization and interpretation tools in presentation level. These tools are designed for various applications and can be accessed from any platform.

From the network point of view, the opportunity of accessing information through tagged object by browsing on Internet primarily inspired the idea of IoT. Bringing objects into the digital world and identifying them by using their Internet addresses are supplied with different tagging technologies such as RFID, NFC and QR Codes [9] . RFID, intelligence embedded technology, sensor technology and nano-technology are pioneer technologies for the development of IoT. Radio frequency identification (RFID) is the foundation and networking core of the construction of IoT among them [10] . Kevin Ashton who was a pioneer of IoT underlines this issue in his article that RFID and the sensor technology strengthen traditional computers and gain them some significant features such as observation, identification and understanding the world of sensor data [11].

Wireless sensor network (WSN) is another type of data collection technology of the IoT that has some features to maintain the control over many nodes through wireless communication such as multi-hopping and self-organization. A WSN system contains a central unit that provides wireless connectivity back to the wired world and distributed nodes [12] . Each node is equipped with a sensor to detect physical phenomena such as light, heat, pressure, etc. [13] . Cooperative sensing, collecting and processing sensor information are purposes of this network model. The system can execute data collection and quantification, pro- cessing fusion and transmission application [14] .

According to Jian An et al. [15] , the architecture of IoT should be an open architecture, using open protocols to support a variety of existing network applications. Likewise, it should additionally incorporate security, adaptability and semantic representation middleware to promote data world integration with Internet. In consideration of these ideas and some related studies [1] [16] [17] [18] [19] [20] , the architecture in Figure 1 is proposed to guide theoretical research.

1) Perception Layer: The sensor technology, intelligence embedded technology, nano technology and tagging technology are located in this layer. Main purpose of the layer is the identification of unique objects and the collection of information from the physical world with the help of its sensors [21] .

2) Network Layer: It contains WSN, optical fiber communication networks, broad television networks, 2G/3G communications networks, fixed telephone networks and closed IP data networks for

each carrier. Transfer of collected information from sensors, devices, etc., to an information processing system is under the responsibility of this layer.

3) Support Layer: The layer involves information processing systems which takes information in one form and processes (transforms) it into another form. This processed data is stored in a database and will be available when there is a demand. This layer works very closely with applications. Therefore, researchers prefer to place it in application layer [22] .

4) Application Layer: In this layer, there are practical and useful applications which are developed based on user requirements or industry specifications such as smart traffic, precise agriculture, smart home, mining monitor, etc.

3. SECURITY OF IOT

3.1. Existing Requirements and Challenges of Security

Hui Suo et al. [18] refer that IoT extends the term of 'internet' through corresponding technologies such as traditional Internet, mobile networks, sensor networks and so on. Every "thing" is connected to this "Internet" and these "things" communicates with each other. According to Rolf H. Weber [23] , these kinds of systems imply great potential for flexibility and scalability, but they have the risk of having security problems too. There are many issues about its wide adoption and without offering relevant solutions for the newly posed threats; it looks like it cannot be a practically applicable technology in close future.

Security requirements are examined in studies [21] [16] [18] [24] [19] [25] [26] in different dimensions. The requirements addressed in many studies can be summarized under five headings in Table 1.

In order to fulfill these requirements in Table 1, there are several challenges [21] [6] [16] [17] [27] [19] [26] [28] that must be handled in Table 2.

3.2. Existing Security Threats in IoT Systems

In this section, existing threats in IoT systems are examined in four categories based on IoT architecture which have been addressed in Section 2. The examination is summarized in Figure 2.

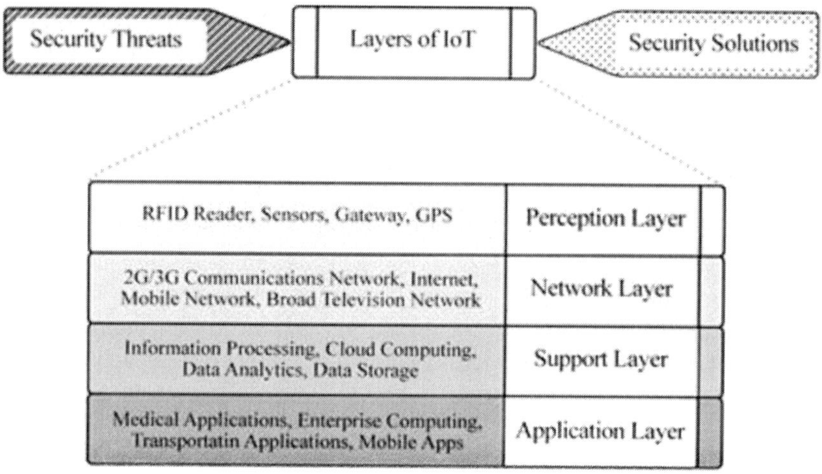

Figure 1. IoT Architecture.

Table 1. Security requirements.

Authenticity:	Only legal users should be allowed to access the system or sensitive information [16].
Authorization:	The privileges of device components and applications should be limited as so they are able to access only the resources they need to do their addressed tasks [25].
Confidentiality:	Information transmission between the nodes should be protected from intruders [18].
Integrity:	Related information should not be tampered [19].
Availability and Continuity:	In order to avoid any potential operational failures and interruptions, availability and continuity in the provision of security services should be ensured [26].

3.2.1. Threats of Perception Layer

Sensor and intelligence embedded technologies including RFID readers, sensors or GPS are under threat because of various security flaws. Main threats are discussed below:

Spoofing: It is initiated with a fake broadcast message sent to sensor network by the attackers. It makes it to assume its originality falsely which makes it appearing from the original source [29] . It is quite often that this scenario is results in the attacker obtaining full access to the system making it vulnerable.

Table 2. Security challenges.

Interoperability:	Relevant security solutions should not prevent the functionality of interconnected heterogeneous devices in IoT network system [27].
Resource constraints:	In IoT architecture, most of nodes lack of storage capacity, power and CPU. They generally use low-bandwidth communication channels. Hence, it is unable to apply some security techniques such as frequency hopping communication and public key encryption algorithm. Setup of security system is very difficult under these circumstances [6].
Data volumes:	Although some IoT applications use brief and infrequent communication channels, there are considerable number of IoT system such as sensor-based, logistics and large scale system that have potentials to entail huge volume of data on central network or servers [28].
Privacy protection:	Since a great number of RFID systems are short of suitable authentication mechanism, anyone can tracks tags and find the identity of the objects carrying them. Intruders can not only read the data, but can also modify or even delete data as well [21].
Scalability:	The IoT network consists of a large number of nodes. The proposed security mechanism on IoT should be scalable [19].
Autonomic control:	Traditional computers need users to configure and adapt them to different application domains and different communication environments. However, objects in IoT network should establish connections spontaneously, and organize/configure themselves for adapting to the platform they are operating in. This kind of control also involves some techniques and mechanisms such as self-configuring, self-optimizing, self-management, self-healing and self-protecting [27].

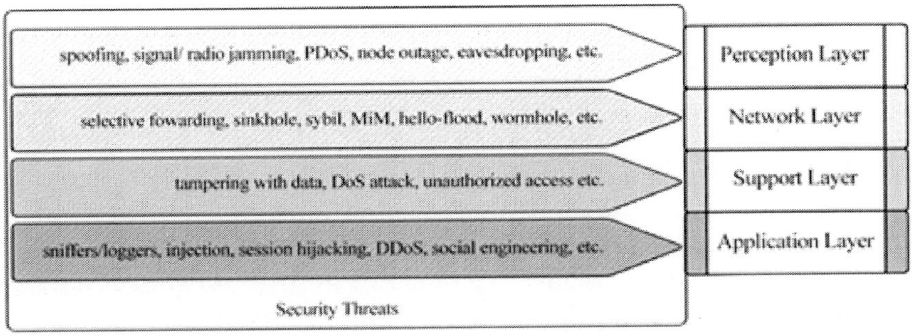

Figure 2. Threats on layers of IoT.

Signal/Radio Jamming: It is a type of DoS attack that it occupies the communication channel between the nodes and hinders them from communicating with each other [30] .

Device-tampering/Node-capturing: The attacker captures the sensor node physically replaces the node with their malicious node. This type of attack usually results in the attacker gaining total control over the captured node and harms the network [31] .

Path-based DoS Attack (PDoS): In this type of DoS attack, the attacker overpowers sensor nodes a long distance away by flooding a multihop end-to-end communication path with either replayed packets or injected spurious packets [32] . Diminished system availability and exhaustion in batteries of nodes are impacts of this physical attack.

Node Outage: The attack is applied logically or physically to the network and it stops the functionality of network components. Node services such as reading, collecting and initiating operations are stopped because of this attack [31] .

Eavesdropping: Wireless characteristics of RFID system make it possible that attacker sniffs out the confidential information such as password or any other data flowing from tag-to-reader or reader-to-tag making the system vulnerable [21] [33] .

Various kinds of perception layer attacks are listed below with related risks on security mechanisms of IoT in Table 3.

3.2.2. Threats of Network Layer

Network layer which is known as the next-generation network are exposed to many kinds of threats. Related threats that come from this layer are listed below:

Selective Forwarding: In such attacks, malicious nodes do not forward some messages and selectively drop them, ensuring that they cannot propagate later on. The attacker who is responsible for suppression or modification of packets originating from a select few nodes can sometimes forward the remaining traffic not to reveal her wrongdoing. There are different types of selective forwarding attacks. In one type, the malicious node can selectively drop the packets coming from a particular node or a group of nodes. This situation poses a risk of DoS attack for that node or a group of nodes. Another type of selective forwarding attack is called Neglect and Greed. In this type of attack, the subverted node arbitrarily skips routing some messages [34] .

Table 3. Attacks and related risks on security mechanisms of IoT.

Attacks	Risks
Spoofing	Authenticity, integrity and confidentiality.
Signal/Radio Jamming	Availability and integrity.
Device-tampering/Node-capturing	Availability, integrity, authenticity and confidentiality.
Path-based DoSAttack	Availability and authenticity.
Node Outage	Availability and authenticity.
Eavesdropping	Confidentiality.

Sybil Attack: It is clarified as a malicious device illegitimately taking on multiple identities [35] . Sybil attack [36] , an attacker can "be in more than one place at once" as a single malicious node. It presents multiple identities to other nodes in the network reducing the effectiveness of fault tolerant schemes.

Sinkhole Attack (Blackhole): The sink hole is defined in [37] by intense resource contention among neighboring nodes of the malicious node for the limited bandwidth and channel access. It results in congestion and can accelerate the energy consumption of the nodes involved. With sink holes forming in a sensor network, it is vulnerable to several other types of denial of service attacks [38] [37] [39] .

Wormhole: This form of DoS attack induces relocation of bits of data from its original position in the network. This relocation of data packet is carried out through tunneling of bits of data over a link of low latency [39] .

Man-in-the-Middle Attack: This attack is described as a form of eavesdropping in which the unauthorized party can monitor or control all the private communications between the two parties hideously. The unauthorized party can even fake the identity of the victim and communicate normally to gain more information [21] .

Hello-flood Attack: High traffic in channels is the main disrupting effect of this attack which congests the channel with an unusually high number of useless messages. Basically, a single malicious node sends a useless message which is then replied by the attacker to create a high traffic [30] .

Acknowledgement Flooding: Routing algorithms in sensor-based systems need acknowledgements from time to time. In this type of DoS attack, a malicious node sends false information to destined neighboring nodes by the help of these acknowledgements [30] .

3.2.3. Threats of Support Layer

Target of threats in support layer are mainly data storage technologies. These threats are discussed below:

Tampering with Data: The attack appears when a person from the inside tampers the data for personal benefits or commercial benefits of any 3rd party companies. The data can be extracted and modified easily on purpose from the inside [17] .

DoS Attack: Similar effects of DoS attacks that are discussed in previous layers are seen in this layer, too; e.g. it shuts down the system which results in unavailability of the services.

Unauthorized Access: The attacker can easily infiltrate into the system and damage the system by preventing the access to the related services of IoT or deleting sensitive data. Hence, an unauthorized access can be fatal for the system [21] .

3.2.4. Threats of Application Layer

The personalized services based on the needs of the users are included in the application layer; e.g. the interface that user can control devices in IoT [4] . Threats in this layer mainly target these services as mentioned below:

Sniffer/Loggers: Attackers can introduce sniffer/logger programs into the system that take important information from the network traffic. The main goal of the sniffer is to steal passwords, files (FTP files, E-mail files), and E-mail text. Many protocols are prone to sniffing [40] .

Injection: Attackers may enter code directly into the application that is executed on the server. This is a very common attack, easy to exploit, and can cause some bad results such as data loss, data corruption and lack of accountability [41] .

Session Hijacking: This attack reveals personal identities by exploiting security flaws in authentication and session management. This type of attack is very common and effects of attack are really important. With the identity of someone else, attacker can do anything the real user can do [41] .

DDoS (Distributed Denial of Service): Its working principle is the same as the traditional Denial of Service attack. However, it is executed by multiple attackers at the same time [21] [30] [41] .

Social Engineering: A serious threat for application layer where attackers can obtain information from users via chats, knowing each other etc. [4] .

3.3. Recommended Solutions and Research Directions with Respect to Security in IoT

Recommended solutions and research directions with respect to security in IoT are examined in three categories: security of perception layer, security of network layer and security of support and application layers. The examination is summarized in Figure 3.

3.3.1. Security of Perception Layer

Taking security measures for the perception layer dates back times before IoT.

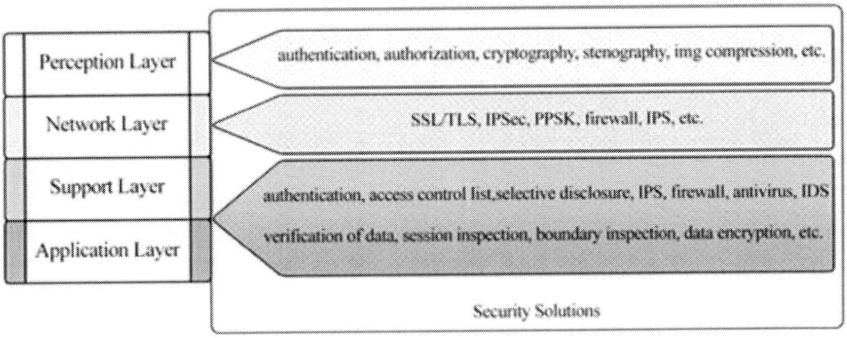

Figure 3. Security solutions on layers of IoT.

Table 4. Cryptograhic algorithms.

Type	Algorithm	Purpose
Symmetric Encryption	Advanced encryption standard (AES)	Confidentiality
Asymmetric Encryption	Rivestshamir Adelman (RSA)/Elliptic curve cryptography (ECC)	Digital Signatures, Key Transport
Asymmetric Key Agreement	Diffie-hellman (DH)	Key Agreement
Hashing	SHA-1/SHA-256	Integrality

Equipments such as RFID readers, sensors, gateways, GPS and other devices require to be secured efficiently. OWASP has identified poor physical security in the top 10 IoT vulnerabilities [42] . The first step is to ensure that only authorized people can have access to sensitive data produced by physical objects, that's why a physical identity and access management policy need to be defined [43] . Authentication and authorization requirements from IoT are satisfied in this similar fashion.

Data collection is an important issue for this layer. In [44] , this issue is examined in two separate headings. In one heading which is presented as multimedia data collection, there are some recommended security techniques such as multimedia compression, stenography, water marking, encryption, time session and intellectual property. The second heading is image data collection, to use security in images as image compression, and CRC.

Cryptographic processing is one of the main tasks in security mechanisms for sensor data on IoT. These operations that are often used in order to guarantee privacy of data include encryption and decryption, key and hash generation, and sign and verify hashes. Table 4 gives some frequently used cryptographic algorithms and their use purposes in Internet security protocols based on studies [18] and [45] .

Wander et al. [46] compare two asymmetric algorithms in Table 4, RSA and Elliptic Curve Cryptography (ECC) [47] , on sensor nodes and prove that ECC is more efficient than RSA, and asymmetric cryptography is applicable for resource-constrained hardware. Hence, researchers focus on reducing complexity of asymmetric cryptographic algorithms and key distribution protocols. Wood et al. [48] and Hu et al. [49] present hardware cryptographic solutions for smart objects in their study. Key distribution mechanism of Liu et al. [50] and Chung et al. [51] are demonstrated in order to use in lightweight communication channels in resource-constrained networks. These improvements make cryptographic mechanisms in the context of WSNs more applicable. However, unique customized solutions are created and still there has been no standardized way of implementing services [52] .

Risk Assessment is a fundamental of IoT security which determines the extent of the potential threat and the risk associated with an IoT system. The output of this process helps to identify appropriate controls for reducing or eliminating risk during the risk mitigation process. A number of organizations have developed guidelines for conducting risk assessment such as the U.S. National Institute of Standards and Technology (NIST) [53] [54] ; the International Standards Organization (ISO) and the International Electrotechnical Commission (IEC) [55] .

3.3.2. Security of Network Layer

The security of network layer can be examined in two main sub-layers; wireless and wired. One of the initial actions in wireless security sub-layer is the development of protocols for authentication and key management [56] . For example; SSL/TLS is developed to encrypt the link in the transport layer, and IP security protocol (IPSec) is developed to keep the network layer secure. They can provide authenticity, confidentiality and integrity in the each layer [18] . Also, using PPSK (Private Pre-Shared Key) for each sensor or device connected to the network provides another security measure for IoT system. By providing different unique keys, the access domain for each type of device can be defined easily. Moreover, disabling guest and default passwords in network devices such as routers and gateways should be done immediately upon installing a new network device. This includes strong password policies, password management and periodic change of passwords [43] .

The wired security sub-layer is concerned with devices, which communicate with other devices on the IoT system using wired channels. Common security techniques are applied in wired type networks are firewalls and Intrusion Prevention System (IPS). If the network has firewall or IPS, it can inspect network packets deeply that are destined towards the destination. However, existing IoT has no ability in terms of packet inspection and packet filtering. There is an ongoing research on this issue where security researchers try to design a low resource-hungry firewall for IoT to provide the ability of packet inspection [4] .

All information about the security of network layer that is discussed above is summarized in Table 5.

3.3.3. Security of Support and Application Layers

Devipriya et al. [44] claims that this topic contains two sub-layers. In one sub- layer, there are local applications and related middleware functions which should be secured with various techniques. For example, intelligent transportation systems can use encryption techniques, while smart home/smart metering systems uses steganography techniques. The second sublayer corresponds to national applications and their security systems, ensuring that sent and received data are secure. Therefore, various security techniques are applied in these systems based on the scope of each system such as authentication, authorization, access control list, selective disclosure, intrusion detection, firewall, and antivirus.

According to Farooq et al. [21] , authentication mechanism preventing the access of intruders is applied in support and application layer by integrated identity identifications. This identity security mechanism is exactly similar to that in the network layer. The difference is that these layers focus on authentications by some certain cooperating services which means users can even choose the associated information to be shared with the services.

Table 5. Security of Network Layer on IoT.

Sub-layers	Security Techniques	Purposes
Wireless	TLS/SSL	Authenticity, Confidentiality, Integrity
	IPSec	
	PPSK	
Wired	Firewall	
	IPS	

Data security is another issue on these layers [57] . There are various precautions taken by security system on IoT such as:

- Safe programming and anti-virus software testing against malicious code injections and service loopholes,
- Verification of data and developing temporary cache against malicious operations,
- Session inspection mechanism to stop attacks of hijacking and redo sessions,
- Boundary inspection, data encryption mechanism and resource access control to avoid leakage of privacy.

The IoT is vulnerable to a number of attacks that are mentioned in previous sections to disrupt the whole system, thus intrusion detection is a crucial concept for IoT deployments in real world such as industrial automation, building automation, smart metering and smart grids [58] . Attacks against a system are detected during analysis of actions in the system by a security mechanism broadly termed as Intrusion Detection System (IDS). When an attack is detected, IDS may log information about it and/or report an alarm. There are different existing intrusion detection techniques such as anomaly detection [59] , data mining techniques [60] [61] , statistical analysis [62] etc.

4. CONCLUSIONS

IoT is an emerging technology that has attracted a considerable number of researchers from all around the world. There have been major contributions making this technology adapted into our daily life. However, there are lots of key issues addressing security concerns of IoT and they need more research effort to be solved.

In this paper, security concepts of IoT were reviewed substantially. Requirements and challenges of security measures in IoT were analyzed and collected under different headings. All kinds of security threats that may be critical in the development and implementation of IoT in different fields have been discussed and classified with respect to layers of IoT architecture: perception layer, network layer, support layer and application layer. Finally, the recent solutions have been provided for these threats and research directions with respect to security concerns have been introduced such as cryptographic mechanisms and firewalls.

REFERENCES

1. Madakam, S., Ramaswamy, R. and Tripathi, S. (2015) Internet of Things (IoT): A Literature Review. Journal of Computer and Communications, 3, 164-173.
2. Tyagi, S., Darwish, A. and Khan, M.Y. (2014) Managing Computing Infrastructure for IoT Data. Advances in Internet of Things, 4, 29-35.
3. Gartner Inc. Press Release (2014) http://www.gartner.com/newsroom/id/2905717
4. Gupta, J., Nayyar, A. and Gupta, P. (2015) Security and Privacy Issues in Internet of Things (IoT). International Journal of Research in Computer Science, 2, 18-22.
5. Yehia, L., Khedr, A. and Darwish, A. (2015) Hybrid Security Techniques for Internet of Things Healthcare Applications. Advances in Internet of Things, 5, 21-25.
6. Arseni, S.C., Halunga, S., Fratu, O., Vulpe, A. and Suciu, G. (2015) Analysis of the Security Solutions Implemented in Current Internet of Things Platforms. IEEE Grid, Cloud & High Performance Computing in Science, Romania, 28-30 October 2015, 1-4.
7. Chandrakanth, S., Venkatesh, K. and Mahesh, J.U. (2014) Internet of Things. International Journal of Innovations & Advancement in Computer Science, 3, 8.
8. Shawish, A. and Salama, M. (2014) Cloud Computing: Paradigms. Inter-Cooperative Collective Intelligence: Techniques and Applications, Studies in Computational Intelligence 495, Springer-Verlag, Berlin, Heidelberg.
9. Briseno, M.V., Hirata, F.I., Lopez, J.D.S., Garcia, E.J., Cota, J.N. and Hipolito, J.I.N. (2012) Using RFID/NFC and QR-Code in Mobile Phones to Link the Physical and the Digital World. InTech.
10. Li, B.A. and Yu, J.J. (2011) Research and Application on the Smart Home Based on Component Technologies and Internet of Things. Procedia Engineering, 15, 2087-2092.
11. Ashton, K. (2009) That "Internet of Things" Thing. RFID Journal. http:// www.rfidjournal.com/articles/pdf?4986
12. National Instruments (2016) What Is a Wireless Sensor Network? http://www.ni.com/white-paper/7142/en/
13. IEC Market Strategy Board (2014) Internet of Things: Wireless Sensor Networks. http://www.iec.ch/whitepaper/pdf/iecWP-internetofthings-LR-en.pdf
14. Wang, R., Wang, J. and Wang, N. (2015) Analysis of Key Technologies in the Internet of Things. 3rd International Conference on Material, Mechanical and Manufacturing Engineering, Guangzhou, 27-28 June 2015, 938-941.
15. An, J., Gui, X.L. and He, X. (2012) Study on the Architecture and Key Technologies for Internet of Things. Advances in Biomedical Engineering, 11, 329-335.
16. Huang, X., Craig, P., Lin, H. and Yan, Z. (2015) SecIoT: A Security Framework for the Internet of Things. Security and Communication Networks, 9, 3083-3094.

17. Cloud Security Alliance (2015) Security Guidance for Early Adopters of the Internet of Things (IoT). https://downloads.cloudsecurityalliance.org/whitepapers/ Security_Guidance_for _Early_Adopters_of_the_Internet_of_Things.pdf
18. Suo, H., Wan, J., Zou, C. and Liu, J. (2012) Security in the Internet of Things: A Review. IEEE International Conference on Computer Science and Electronics Engineering, Hangzhou, 23-25 March 2012, 648-651.
19. Nguyen, K.T., Laurent, M. and Oualha, N. (2015) Survey on Secure Communication Protocols for the Internet of Things. Ad Hoc Networks, 32, 17-31.
20. Yang, X., Li, Z., Geng, Z. and Zhang, H. (2012) A Multi-Layer Security Model for Internet of Things. Springer International Workshop on Internet of Things, Vol. 312, Changsha, 17-19 August 2012, 388-393.
21. Farooq, M.U., Waseem, M., Khairi, A. and Mazhar, S. (2015) A Critical Analysis on the Security Concerns of Internet of Things (IoT). International Journal of Computer Applications, 111, 1-6.
22. Qian, X. and Zhang, J. (2010) Study on the Structure of "Internet of Things (IOT)" Business Operation Support Platform. IEEE International Conference on Communication Technology, Nanjing, 11-14 November 2010, 1068-1071.
23. Weber, R.H. (2010) Internet of Things—New Security and Privacy Challenges. Computer Law and Security Review, 26, 23-30.
24. Chen, M., Wan, J.F. and Li, F. (2012) Machine-to-Machine Communications: Architectures, Standards and Applications. KSII Transactions on Internet and Information Systems, 6, 480-497.
25. Wind River Systems (2015) Security in the Internet of Things. http://www.windriver.com/whitepapers/security-in-the-internet-of-things/wr_security-in-the-internet-of-things.pdf
26. European Commission. IoT Privacy, Data Protection, Information Security. http://ec.europa.eu/information_society/newsroom/cf/dae/document.cfm?doc_id=1753
27. ITU-T. Y.2060: Overview of the Internet of Things. http://www.itu.int/rec/T-REC-Y.2060-201206-I
28. Mattern, F. and Floerkemeier, C. (2010) From the Internet of Computers to the Internet of Things. In: Sachs, K., Petrov, I. and Guerrero, P., Eds., From Active Data Management to Event-Based Systems and More, Springer, Berlin Heidelberg, 242-259.
29. Mitrokotsa, A., Rieback, M.R. and Tanenbaum, A.S. (2009) Classifying RFID Attacks and Defenses. Information Systems Frontiers, 12, 491-505.
30. Borgohain, T., Kumar, U. and Sanyal, S. (2015) Survey of Security and Privacy Issues of Internet of Things. International Journal of Advanced Networking Applications, 6, 2372-2378.
31. Anwar, R.W., Bakhtiari, M., Zainal, A., Hanan, A.A. and Qureshi, K.N. (2014) Security Issues and Attacks in Wireless Sensor Network. World Applied Sciences Journal, 30, 1224-1227.
32. Deng, J., Han, R. and Mishra, S. (2005) Defending against Path-Based DoS Attacks in Wireless Sensor Networks. ACM Workshop/Security of Ad Hoc and Sensor Networks, Alexandria, 7 November 2005, 89-96.
33. Khoo, B. (2011) RFID as an Enabler of the Internet of Things: Issues of Security and Privacy. IEEE International Conferences on Internet of Things, and Cyber, Physical and Social Computing, Dalian, 19-22 October 2011, 709-712.
34. Sharma, P., Saluja, M. and Saluja, K.K. (2012) A Review of Selective Forwarding Attacks in Wireless Sensor Networks. International Journal of Advanced Smart Sensor Network Systems, 2, 37.
35. Pooja, M. and Singh, Y. (2013) Security Issues and Sybil Attack in Wireless Sensor Networks. International Journal of P2P Network Trends and Technology, 3, 7-13.
36. Douceur, J.R. (2002) The Sybil Attack. Springer International Workshop on Peer-to-Peer Systems, Cambridge, 7-8 March 2002, 251-260.
37. Ahmed, N., Kanhere, S.S. and Jha, S. (2005) The Holes Problem in Wireless Sensor Network: A Survey. ACM SIGMOBILE Mobile Computing and Communications Review, 9, 4-18.

38. Kalita, H.K. and Kar, A. (2009) Wireless Sensor Network Security Analysis. International Journal of Next-Generation Networks, 1, 1-10.
39. Karlof, C. and Wagner, D. (2003) Secure Routing in Wireless Sensor Networks: Attacks and Countermeasures. Ad Hoc Networks, 1, 293-315.
40. Kulshrestha, A. and Dubey, S.K. (2014) A Literature Review on Sniffing Attacks in Computer Network. International Journal of Advanced Engineering Research and Science, 1, 2.
41. Hermes Engineering. Security in Web Applications. http://www.hermes-ecs.com/en/page/59/documents
42. OWASP, Internet of Things Project. https://www.owasp.org/ index.php/OWASP_Internet_of_Things_Top_Ten_Project
43. Zolanvari, M. and Jain, R. (2015) IoT Security: A Survey. http://www.cse.wustl.edu/~jain/cse570-15/ftp/iot_sec/index.html
44. Sujitha, R., Raghavan, N.V., Suganya, K.S. and Devipriya, A. (2014) A Novel Survey on Internet of Things, Security and Its Application. International Journal of Advanced Information and Communication Technology, 1, 8.
45. Polk, T. and Turner, S. (2011) Security Challenges for the Internet of Things. http://www.iab.org/wp-content/IAB-uploads/2011/03/Turner.pdf
46. Wander, A.S., Gura, N., Eberle, H., Gupta, V. and Shantz, S.C. (2005) Energy Analysis of Public-Key Cryptography for Wireless Sensor Networks. IEEE International Conference on Pervasive Computing and Communications, Kauai Island, 8-12 March 2005, 324-328.
47. Miller, S.D. and Venkatesan, R. (2009) Expander Graphs Based on GRH with an Application to Elliptic Curve Cryptography. Journal of Number Theory, 129, 1491-1504.
48. Wood, A. and Stankovic, J. (2006) AMSecure: Secure Link-Layer Communication in TinyOS for IEEE 802.15.4-Based Wireless Sensor Networks. ACM Conference on Networked Embedded Sensor Systems, Boulder, 31 October-3 November 2006, 395-396.
49. Hu, W., Corke, P., Shih, W.C. and Overs, L. (2009) SecFleck: A Public Key Technology Platform for Wireless Sensor Networks. Springer European Conference on Wireless Sensor Networks, Cork, 11-13 February 2009, 296-311.
50. Liu, D., Ning, P. and Li, R. (2003) Establishing Pairwise Keys in Distributed Sensor Networks. ACM Conference on Computer and Communications Security, Washington DC, 27-30 October 2003, 52-61.
51. Chung, A. and Roedig, U. (2008) DHB-KEY: An Efficient Key Distribution Scheme for Wireless Sensor Networks. IEEE International Workshop on Wireless and Sensor Networks Security, Atlanta, 29 September-2 October 2008, 840-846.
52. Raza, S. (2013) Lightweight Security Solutions for the Internet of Things. No. 139, Malardalen University Press Dissertations. http://www.diva-portal.org/smash/get/diva2:619066/FULLTEXT02.pdf
53. The U.S. National Institute of Standards and Technology (NIST) (2012) Guide for Conducting Risk Assessments. http://nvlpubs.nist.gov/ nistpubs/Legacy/ SP/nistspecialpublication800-30r1.pdf
54. The U.S. National Institute of Standards and Technology (NIST) (2002) Risk Management Guide for Information Technology Systems. http://csrc.nist.gov/publications/ nistpubs/800-30/sp800-30.pdf
55. The International Standards Organization (ISO) (2009) The International Electrotechnical Commission (IEC). ISO/IEC 31010:2009 Risk management—Risk Assessment Techniques. http://www.iso.org/iso/catalogue_detail?csnumber=51073
56. Jara, A.J., Ladid, L. and Skarmeta, A. (2013) The Internet of Everything through IPv6: An Analysis of Challenges, Solutions and Opportunities. Journal of Wireless Mobile Networks, Ubiquitous Computing, and Dependable Applications, 4, 97-118.
57. Zhang, W. and Baosheng, Q. (2013) Security Architecture of the Internet of Things Oriented to Perceptual Layer. International Journal on Computer, Consumer and Control, 2, 2.
58. Raza, S., Wallgren, L. and Voigt, T. (2013) SVELTE: Real-Time Intrusion Detection in the Internet of Things. Ad Hoc Networks, 11, 2661-2674.

59. Verwoerd, T. and Hunt, R. (2002) Intrusion Detection Techniques and Approaches. Computer Communications, 25, 1356-1365.
60. Patel, J. and Panchal, K. (2015) Effective Intrusion Detection System Using Data Mining Technique. International Journal of Emerging Technologies and Innovative Research, 2, 6.
61. Nguyen, H.A. and Choi, D. (2008) Application of Data Mining to Network Intrusion Detection: Classifier Selection Model. Springer Asia-Pacific Symposium on Network Operations and Management: Challenges for Next Generation Network Operations and Service Management, Beijing, 22-24 October 2008, 399-408.
62. Waskita, A.A., Suhartanto, H., Persadha, P.D. and Handoko, L.T. (2013) A Simple Statistical Analysis Approach for Intrusion Detection System. IEEE Conference on Systems, Process & Control, Kuala Lumpur, 13-15 December 2013, 193-197.

CHAPTER 11

Using Converging Strategies to Reduce Divergence in Intercultural User Interface Design

Rüdiger Heimgärtner

Research & Development, Intercultural User Interface Consulting (IUIC), Undorf, Germany

ABSTRACT

This chapter starts with an introduction illuminating the theoretical background necessary for taking culture into account in HCI design. Definitions of concepts used are provided followed by a historical overview on taking culture into account in HCI design. Subsequently, a glimpse of the current state of research in culture-centered HCI design is derived from secondary literature providing the gist of the structures, processes, methods, models and theoretic approaches concerning the relationship between culture and HCI design ("converging" strategies). After presenting controversies and challenges, a short discussion of results from empirical studies and design recommendations for culture-centered HCI design lead to implications and trends in future intercultural user interface design research to close the knowledge gap (the "divergence") regarding the relationship between culture and Human-Computer Interaction (HCI), i.e. converging the divergence to reach the convergent divergence.

Keywords: Culture, HCI, Cross-Cultural, Design, Intercultural, Culture-Centered, Methods, Tools, Standards, Overview, State of Research, Cultural Differences, Communication, Understanding, Empathy, Intercultural Communication, Intercultural HCI Design, Divergence, Convergence, Wave, Process, Cycle

1. INTRODUCTION AND PROBLEM DISCUSSION

It's a natural result of the media convergence we've seen happening for decades, that companies are now starting to converge to offer a new model and to enjoy the same benefits. Therefore, also in intercultural user interface design (IUID), it is reasonable to look for ideas that are deeply connected to culture, which can align with societal changes and can help to stay lean, focused and as profitable as possible without compromising on quality. Cultures are melting together permanently-implicitly e.g. by the process of globalization and explicitly e.g. by doing IUID. Divergence in IUID is represented by the different perspectives in applying IUID concerning objectives, strategies and processing including pro- cesses, methods, and tools. This divergence in IUID is reduced to the extent cultures converging implicitly and converging strategies in IUID are applied explicitly.

1.1 Relationship between Convergence and Divergence in Intercultural User Interface Design and Related Problems

Up to know, there is still a remarkable knowledge gap (a divergence) regarding the relationship between culture and Human-Computer Interaction (HCI). This gap as well as the gap between developer and other culturally imprinted end- users (i.e. another-different-divergence) must be closed by using "converging" strategies that should ensure to yield successful intercultural user interface design (IUID). Today, such strategies contain at least the method of culture oriented HCI design applying intercultural variables (cf. [1]), user interface characteristics (cf. [2]), and intercultural usability engineering (cf. [3]) as well as using HCI dimensions (cf. [4]). These approaches are used to support the design process which finally should lead to good user interfaces of high usability provoking excellent user experience. However, the successful application of these approaches strongly depends on the successful intercultural communication which again depends on the personal ability to mutually understand the web of belief of the others using empathic capabilities (cf. [5]). Experienced designers are aware of this. Young designers have to acquire the experience first. Thereby, several "waves" of diverging and converging emerge, gathering knowledge (converging) and distributing knowledge (diverging). These kinds of ups (converging) and downs (diverging) in processes can be determined also in the overall perspective of designing HCI for the world. Localization (divergence) led to internationalization and UI4All (user interfaces for all) (convergence), which in turn recently dissolved again in indigenous perspectives and designed for the wild (divergence) (cf. [6]). In addition, this can be observed in the wavelike behavior within the HCI design process from top (abstract-convergence) to the bottom (concrete-divergence) and vice versa, which is iterative design, i.e. traversing the phases in circles. In this chapter, the mentioned "waves of divergence and convergence" in this sense are elucidated in detail in the cultural context to derive implications and recommendation for adapting; optimizing and possibly extending (e.g. by using universals (cf. [7])) the existing "converging" strategies in the field of intercultural user interface design.

2. METHOD: LITERATURE STATE OF THE ART/LITERATURE REVIEW

To capture the paradigms and newest aspects regarding methodology, technology transfer and the diffusion of innovation, one has to browse through the literature up to now to get an impression about what the most important tasks in intercultural HCI research can, should or must be in the future. The publications compiled by the author within this field of research connecting culture and HCI serve to determine the current state of research in this area and to categorize the main research topics in culture-centered HCI design. The most prominent results of this collection process by the author are presented in the following.

2.1. Terminology

There are several concepts of "culture". According to the cultural anthropologist Edward T. Hall, culture co-occurs with communication. Culture is a "silent language" or "hidden dimension" which steers people unconsciously (cf. [8]). Difficulties in communication with members of other cultures arise from that. If one is not conscious of one's own motives, which are culturally influenced, one cannot understand the motives and actions of others (cf. [5]). The position that is taken in this paper is that culture is a set of facts (structural conditions) representing an orientation system established by collective programming of the mind (cf. [9]) within a group of individuals. Cultural models describe the cultural distance, i.e. the differences between cultures and allow the comparison of them with each other (cf. [10]). One of the best-known cultural models is the iceberg model of culture (cf. [11]). Only 10% of the attributes of a culture are visible and conscious. The rest is invisible and unconscious and hence, difficult to investigate. Cultural models help to overcome this methodological gap using cultural standards and dimensions to look beneath the water surface, i.e. to probe the unconscious areas of culture. The organizational psychologist Alexander Thomas established the concept of "cultural standards", which expresses the normal, typical and valid attributes for the majority of the members of a certain culture regarding the respective kinds of perception, thought, judgment and action (cf. [12]): 112). Cultural standards serve as an orientation system for the members of a group and regulate action. The individual grows into its culture by assuming and internalizing these cultural standards. This process encompasses learning basic human abilities in the social arena, control of one's own behavior and emotions, the satisfaction of basic needs, worldview, verbal and nonverbal communication and expectations of others as well as the understanding of one's role and scales for judgment. Another key concept for describing a cultural system is that of "cultural dimension", which can serve as a basis for the identification of cultural standards (cf. [13] : 38). According to Hofstede, cultural dimensions are quantitative models to describe the behavior of the members of different cultures allowing the analysis and comparison of the characteristics of different groups quantitatively (cf. [9]) because the cultural imprint of cultural groups can be measured using quantitative questionnaires (cf. [14]). This should also be done for all other cultural dimensions. They represent an aspect of a culture, which is measurable in relation to other cultures. Hence, cultural dimensions can be used to classify kinds of behavior between cultures. Cultural dimensions are indicators showing tendencies in the interaction and communication behavior of members of cultures.

There are similar concepts taking cultural aspects in HCI design into account. At least the following concepts exist:

Ÿ Intercultural HCI design [3] [15] [16] [17] .

Ÿ Cross-cultural HCI design [18] [19] .

Ÿ Culture-oriented HCI design [1] .

Ÿ Culture-centered HCI design [20] .

Their connotations are different, which predisposes the concepts to be applied differently in diverse contexts. Intercultural HCI design means the process of HCI design in the cultural context (cf. [21]). Intercultural HCI design describes the user and culture oriented design of interactive systems and products taking the cultural context of the user into account with respect to the respective tasks and product usage (cf. [1] [22]). This approach has grown in academic literature from 1990 to 2000 and emerged from the processes of globalization, internationalization and localization of products. Localization (L10N) means the adaptation of the system to certain cultural circumstances for a certain local market, for example the adaptation of the look and feel of the user interface or the internal data structures to the cultural needs of the user (cf. [23]). Internationalization (I18N) of a product means that the product will be prepared for its usage in the desired (in the best case for all) countries (cf. [24]). The internationalization of a software product delivers a basic structure on which a later cultural customization (localization) can be carried out. Globalization (G11N) encompasses all activities with regard to the marketing of a (software) product outside a national market (including I18N and L10N software). The objective is to run successful marketing in one or several regional markets by taking into account the technical, economic and legal conditions there [25] . Marcus requested additionally that cross-cultural HCI design should account for dimensions of cultures relating them to user interface characteristics (cf. [18]). Several researchers established the culture-centered HCI design process on research on cross-cultural interface design (cf. [1] [20] [26]) and thereby applying iterative analysis to take the target users and their cultural needs into account. Therefore, the topic of intercultural HCI analysis is particularly interesting from the information sciences point of view since this can yield new knowledge, new requirements and goals for the design of information processing systems involving software engineering, software ergonomics and usability engineering.

2.2. History

"Intercultural research in Information Systems is a relatively new research area that has gained increasing importance over the last few years [...]" ([27] : 17). Using the key words "cross-cultural HCI" when searching the ACM digital library reveals an exponential rise of publications in this area since 2000 (cf. Figure 1).

There are several papers in the literature review concerning the usage of information systems in their cultural context. Two of the first important books regarding internationalization of HMI are "Designing User Interfaces for International Use" [28] and "International User Interfaces" [29] . Another very good introduction to the study of cross-cultural of HCI is [30] reviewing the research methodology, the technology transfer and the diffusion of innovation to shed light on the cross-cultural study of human-computer interaction. Another overview of culture and its effects on HCI is given in [31] . There is also activity investigating the trends in intercultural HCI (cf. [32]). A review of culture in information systems research to postulate a shift to a theory of information technology culture conflict is presented in [33] . The relationship between culture and computers can be illuminated by a re-view of the concept of culture and implications for intercultural collaborative online learning [34] . An overview of a decade of journal publications about culture and HCI can be found in [35] .

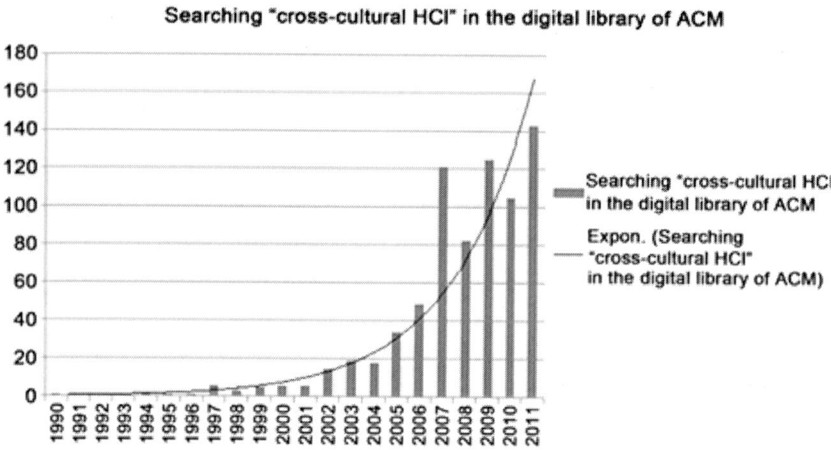

Figure 1. Approximating exponential rise of publications regarding cross-cultural HCI design in the ACM digital library.

From this, several "hypes" can be identified in this area. The first one happened in the early 1990ies. The next one was around 2000 and since about 2010 research in intercultural HCI design has steadily increased. In these "hypes" the number of publications is high indicating high research interest and effort:

Ÿ Before 1990: almost no publications available relating "culture" and "HCI".

Ÿ 1990-1999: pioneers [11] [29] [36] [37] .

Ÿ 2000-2004: basic systematic work [1] [3] [18] [38] [39] [40] [41] .

Ÿ 2005-2010: evaluating the new field and the systematic work [20] [42] [43] [44] [45] .

Ÿ Since 2010: strongly driving research in this field [17] [46] [47] [48] [49] .

Another kind of categorization of the field represents the TLCC model which was derived from the analysis of the history of examining the cultural aspects in HCI design and contains four levels of depth and thereby takes cultural aspects in HCI design into account [50] . This model shows the historical growth of internationalization and localization steps in HCI design represented by its four levels: technical affairs (T), language (L), culture (C) and cognition (C). At the lowest level, certainly adequate programming languages, representation forms and character sets (Unicode), etc. must be used (cf. [51]). Technical aspects have to be adapted so that the products can be used in every country (for example, power supply). Adapting software to Unicode is an example of a precondition to process Asian languages at the language level. Adaptation at cultural level concerns country-specific aspects including format, currency, colors, modality, me- nu structure, content of the menu, help, number of messages, length of texts, number of hints, degree of entertainment or ratio of information to entertainment. At the highest level, cognitive styles that describe types of human thinking such as problem solving or making conclusions can be taken into account (cf. [52] [53]). These processes strongly effect not only the functionality and the user interface of the product (i.e., monitor, keyboard, soft and hard keys, control buttons, speech dialogs, within a graphical (GUI) or speech (SUI) user interface, etc.) but also interactive behavior. In cross-cultural HCI design cultural and cognitive aspects must be taken into account in addition to technical and linguistic aspects of localization, in any case. However, in industry, the usage of internationalization concepts beyond the technological and language level has only recently been initiated (cf. e.g., [54] [55]). Thereby, it has been suggested how to cross-culturally implement information systems [56] . Today, in industry at least technical and linguistic aspects are taken into account in designing products for other cultures. In contrast, the academic approach is predominately concerned with cultural and cognitive aspects.

3. RESULTS: METHODOLOGIES & APPROACHES FOR CONVERGING DIVERGENCES IN INTERCULTURAL USER INTERFACE DESIGN

To bridge the divergence represented by the gap in the knowledge of the differences in intercultural HCI design, converging methods and approaches to reduce this divergence are presented in the following.

3.1. Intercultural Variables and Method of Culture-Centered Design

Intercultural variables describe the differences in HCI design regarding the preferences of the users of different cultures [22] . "Intercultural" variables represent knowledge that can be obtained only by observing at least two cultures and their differences, i.e. doing intercultural research (cf. [57]) to obtain relevant knowledge for internationalization of software and system platforms (cf. Table 1).

Hence, "intercultural variables" are referred to in cases where the intercultural research character for obtaining the values of the variables is meant and "cultural variables" are denoted, when mainly the usage of the values of the variables themselves (concerning a specific culture) is important. However, they can also be called simply "cultural" variables, because the values of those variables re- present knowledge for a specific culture (relevant for system and software localization). There are "direct" and "indirect" cultural variables affecting HCI parameters either directly (e.g., interaction, information presentation or language) or indirectly (e.g., via maintenance, documentation or technical surroundings). Direct cultural variables are the most important, because they have direct and essential influence on the design of HCI. Direct variables can be divided into

Table 1. Intercultural variables according to [22] : 97 et. seqq. (estimated values regarding the difficulty to recognize the variables are added by the author).

Intercultural variable	Level of localization	Relation to HCI design	Perceivability of the variables	Estimated difficulty to recognize [0 (easy) - 10 (difficult)]
Dialog design	Interaction	Direct	Hidden/Over long time and deep analysis	10
Interaction design	Interaction	Direct	Hidden/Over long time and deep analysis	9
System functionality	Function	Indirect	Visible/Immediately	8
Service (Maintenance)	Function	Indirect	Visible/Immediately	7
Technical documentation	Function	Indirect	Visible/Immediately	6
Information presentation	Surface	Direct	Visible/Immediately	4
Language	Surface	Direct	Visible/Immediately	2
General system design	Surface	Indirect	Visible/Immediately	0

"visible" variables concerning surface levels and "hidden" variables affecting interaction levels, together mirroring the concept of the iceberg metaphor [22] . Both kinds of variables have strong influences on the design and determination of the usability and acceptance of the system. Visible intercultural variables concern presentation (colors, time and date format, icons, font size, window size, form, layout, widget position like the position of navigation bar) and language (font, direction of writing, naming) level of a product (appearing above "water surface" in the iceberg metaphor). They can be recognized very easily because they are directly accessible and less determined by cultural context. Non-visible or "hidden" intercultural variables (below the "water surface") affect dialog design (menu structure and complexity, changing of dialog form, layout, widget positions, information presentation speed, frequency of changing dialogs, screen transitions) and interaction design (navigation concept, system structure, interaction path, interaction speed, usage of navigation bar, etc.) which have strong correlations to the cultural context. These variables concern the interaction and dialog level of a product and need high research priority (e.g. using special tools as suggested by [58]). Cultural variables can be used to develop an approach for the design of intercultural human-machine systems using the "method of culture-oriented design" (MCD) according to [22] : 108 as presented in Figure 2.

The MCD integrates factors from established concepts of culture-oriented design into existing concepts of HMI design. Thereby, knowledge about cultural differences is integrated into existing methods.

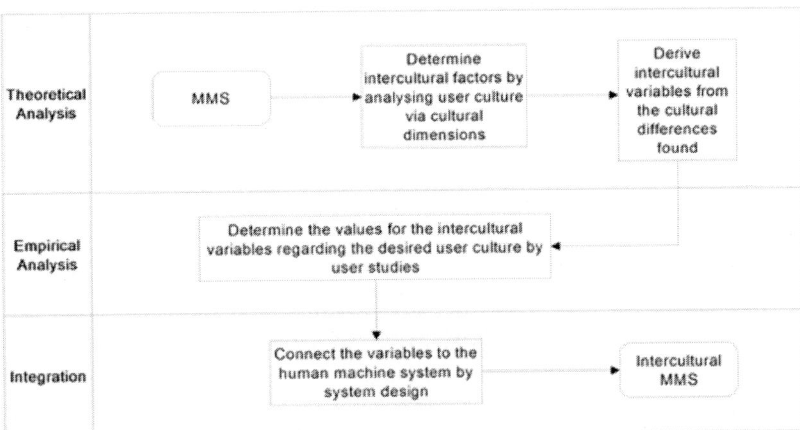

Figure 2. Simplified version of the Method of Culture-oriented Design (MCD) (Source: [17] : 66).

To include intercultural aspects in human-machine interaction, a simplified version of this method will be applied in this work.

3.2. User Interface Characteristics

To make cultural dimensions available for user interface design, [18] developed characteristic factors for user interfaces and gives examples that can have an effect on user interface design. The user interface characteristics “metaphor”, “mental model”, “navigation”, “interaction” and “presentation” are connected to the five cultural dimensions of Hofstede. However, Marcus used a purely deductive approach to obtain these connections. Many possible recommendations for web design have been derived by [59] mainly from Hofstede’s knowledge without empirical foundation of all connections. Therefore, this formulated model still needs empirical validation (even if, meanwhile, there is some empirical work from Marcus himself, cf. [26]). For instance, according to [18] and [60] , Chinese people (and hence users) are rather relationship and family oriented based on traditional powerful social hierarchical structures. In contrast, German users are described as event oriented regarding acts, tools, work, jobs and competition. Some tendencies regarding cultural differences can be used for the intercultural user interface design and further reflections and research. Table 2 shows a sum- mary of general recommendations for intercultural user interface design based on [22] .

3.3. HCI Dimensions

Based on the work of [9] [61] [62] and own studies [17] [58] [63] [64] [65] [66] , the author introduced the concept of HCI dimensions to support the determination of the relationship between culture and HCI [17] . HCI dimensions (HCIDs) describe the “style of information processing” and the “interactional characteristics” of the user with the system. HCIDs are derived from the basic physical dimensions of space and time as well as from their sub-dimensions frequency, speed, duration, density and order) (cf. Table 3).

HCIDs represent the characteristics of HCI by describing the HCI style of the user, i.e. the path of information processing and the interaction style exhibited by the user based on the concepts of “information” and “interaction” according to HCI dialogs that are characterized by transmitting pieces of information during user system interaction (cf. [67]).

Table 2. Summary of recommendations for intercultural HCI design according to the user interface characteristics regarding China and Germany (summarized by the author in accordance to table 6-3 in [22] : 138 as well as to [22] : 305-317).

User Interface Characteristics	China	Germany
Metaphor	Use clear hierarchy and representation instead of abstraction	Use representation instead of abstraction
Mental model	Use many references without sequence of relevance, simple mental models, clear articulation, limited choice and binary logic	Use few references with sequence of relevance and fuzzy logic
Navigation	Use limited and predefined choice and navigation	Use open access and arbitrary choice and unique navigation
Interaction	Use personalized but team-oriented systems giving direct error messages, guided help and providing face-to-face interaction	Use distant but supportive (error) messages providing open and flexible interaction with the system (e.g., full text search)
Presentation	Use formal speech providing high contextual relationship-oriented information as well as feminine colors	Use informal speech providing low contextual task-oriented information as well as masculine colors

Table 3. HCI Dimensions.

Derived physical sub-dimensions [basic physical dimension]	Information related HCI dimension	Interaction related HCI dimension
Frequency [Time]	Information frequency	Interaction frequency
Speed [Time]	Information speed	Interaction speed
Sequentiality/Priority/Order [Time and Space]	Information order/Information parallelism	Interaction order/Interaction parallelism
Density/Quantity [Time and Space]/Context [Time and Space]	Information density	

Frequency, density, order and structure are concerned particularly during information processing; frequency and speed are concerned during interaction behavior. HCI dimensions can be regarded as the main factors relevant for HCI design, because they denote the basic classes for variables useful in HCI design. The view of space, time and mental aspects is strongly culture dependent (cf. [8]). HCI is, therefore, also culture dependent, because HCI dialogs, interaction, information presentation and with that HCI generally are strongly linked with time (interaction, communication) and space (layout, structure) as well as with mental aspects (relations, thoughts) (cf. [3] [68] [69]). At least one potential indicator as a measurement variable is necessary to constitute the specifics of an HCI dimension. Table 4 shows examples of indicators for some HCI dimensions.

Table 4. HCI Dimensions represented by Specifics and Indicators.

HCI dimension	Specifics	Indicator(s)
Interaction frequency	Number of interactions per time unit	Mouse clicks and mouse moves per second or per session
Information density	Number of information units per space unit	Numbe of words per message or on the display
Information/Interaction parallelism/order	Sequence of appearance of information units	Number and sequence of dialog steps (e.g. number of message boxes used to indicate one system error)

For example, the indicator "number of information units per space unit" belongs to the HCI dimension "information density" and can be expressed by the number of words displayed on the screen. The HCI dimension "interaction frequency" contains the variable "number of interactions per time unit" represent- ed by the number of mouse clicks per second.

3.4. Usability Engineering

The usability of a system strongly depends on how the user can cope with the system. This knowledge can be obtained "simply" by ob-serving and asking the user during his interactions with the system. In this case the user articulates his desires and hence his needs regarding the usability of the system. This is trivial and easy, but unfortunately, this method is applied far too little in industrial HCI design even today. This is critical because, if that knowledge is missing in the final product, it will not be wanted by the user: the customer (user) cannot use it because important features are missing or it takes too long to do a certain task using this system because of wrong design.

The preconditions for intercultural usability engineering are knowledge about the cultural differences in HCI and its considerations in product design and product realization (cf. [3] [63] [69]). In addition to the common misunderstandings between developers and users, which lead to different product design, there are also misunderstandings because of cultural conditions. There is not only a different comprehension of the requirements of the product but also culturally dependent perspectives and views of them (cf. [70]). Hence, the developer needs much intercultural knowledge to understand a user from another culture. Furthermore, he needs competency regarding intercultural communication to enable the exchange of information with the user and to know exactly which product the user is likely to have (cf. [71] [72]). With this in mind, [21] presented an empirical study for the development of a framework for the elicitation of cultural influence in product usage to take into account culture and context in HCI design. [73] investigated the impact of culture and gender on web sites. [74] studied the influence of culture in global software engineering by thinking in terms of cultural models. [75] did an empirical study concerning the organizational, cultural and technological use in a developing country.

"Intercultural" usability engineering is a method for designing products of good usability for users from different cultures [3] . The term "intercultural usability engineering" is commonly used by German usability engineers [16] . "Intercultural" in this context refers to the special methods that are necessary to do usability engineering for different cultures [57] . Bad or lacking intercultural usability engineering within the development process of the product increases the development and maintenance costs through requests for change. Detailed analysis of product requirements can save up to 80% of maintenance and implementation costs of such requests for change [76] . Therefore, intercultural HCI design must already begin with the analysis of requirements before starting the design in order to avoid a reduction of the fit between user and product if products of one culture are used in another (cf. [77] [78] [79]). At the collection of culture specific user requirements and culture specific assessment of the concepts used, it must be determined how far approved methods of usability engineering are suitable. The existing cultural models should be taken into account in the process of product design in the context of intercultural usability engineering. First, the product developers must be sensitized to the difficulties of cultural influences on product development and product use. Then cultural factors influencing HCI must be provided to the developers and integrated into the product. Finally, the procedures, which serve to capture the knowledge acquired in concrete product design, must be institutionalized.

After the pioneer research of [79] , several researchers have invested a great deal of effort to determine the best methods and settings to test the usability and user experience in cultural contexts. There is research to study cross cultural think-aloud usability testing to make some suggestions for an experimental paradigm [42] . Moreover, usability constructs are investigated by doing a cross- cultural study of how users and developers experience their use of information systems [80] . The differences in usability testing in three countries as well as the interaction design and usability from an Indian perspective was described by [81] . In addition, the influence of cultural background on non-verbal communication in a usability testing situation was investigated [82] and [83] interpreted cross-cultural usability evaluation based on a case study of a hypermedia system for rare species management in Namibia. The situating media in the transfer of rural knowledge in Africa to enfranchise indigenous rural people is research by [84] . Most of these results of the mentioned research were discussed at a workshop in the frame of the conference "Interact 2011" [46] . The results of the workshop on the international comprehension of usability the application of usability methods were published by [85] . Finally, there is the trend to work on methods to take cross-cultural differences into account in design in general [86] .

3.5. Research Directions, Related Work and Empirical Studies

The number of studies supporting the importance of taking cultural aspects into account in user interface design has been growing steadily since about 2000 (e.g., [87] [88]). However, there is relatively little literature and there are few guidelines for intercultural dialog and design for interaction (cf. [88] [27]) and very few especially for driver navigation systems (e.g., [90]). Most studies concern the presentation of information on web pages (e.g., [91] - [98]). Even though there are already the first pragmatic guidelines for intercultural web design [59] or intercultural HCI design [1] , there are none for intercultural user interface design in specific domains such as driver navigation systems that could be used easily and effectively by HCI designers in this area. This is also supported by the overview of [99] as well as [100] presenting many activities and models for intercultural website design. There are little insights regarding interactive design, as the overview of [45] regarding intercultural information design shows? even if, for a short time, there have also been studies examining stand-alone systems and applications other than web applications (e.g., [27] [89] [101] [102]).

The cultural influences on the values of visible cultural variables of HCI is proven empirically in the literature on internationalization and partly implemented in products (cf. [28] [103]) regarding surface level (presentation of information, speech and general design of machine) and functional level (machine functions, service and technical documentation) of localization. Most of these studies concentrate on "visible" cultural variables such as colors (NASA standard for colors (cf. [104] [105]), icons (use of pictorial or abstract icons, cf. [22] : 135), date and time, phone numbers and address formats, spelling, typography, reading and writing directions, sorting methods (cf. [106] : 23-24), extension of texts, text processing, number of characters (cf. [107] : 77) and multimedia [108] . Also the cultural prescription and user perception of information architecture for a culture centered website was contrasted by [109] by doing a case study on Muslim online users. It was asked by [110] why social media can cross seas but not nationalisms while doing a cross-cultural comparative study of user interface in social media. The proverb "talk is silver, silence is golden" in some cultural context was confirmed by [111] via a cross cultural study on the usage of pauses in speech. A cross-cultural evaluation of the facial expressions of avatars designed by Western designers was performed by [112] . In contrast, [113] concentrated on cross-cultural differences and information systems developer values. In addition, [114] investigated culture and its effects on human interaction design with emphasis on cross-cultural perspectives between Korea and Japan. Hence, in the area of intercultural HCI design there is much research regarding the design of cross-cultural web pages and research of international product design (cf. international workshops of internationalization of products and systems (IWIPS)) as well as many guidelines regarding the visible areas of graphic user interfaces for the internationalization and localization of software.

In contrast, some cultural variables have not been thoroughly investigated so far. Study of the literature does not reveal much about research on hidden intercultural variables at the interactional level. Cultural influence on HCI at the interactional level, for example with respect to navigation, system structure and mental models or varying functionality has not yet been investigated in detail to develop optimal products for the specific culture. In addition, there is still little literature about the connection between visible cultural aspects and hidden intercultural variables for HCI design. The investigation of cultural differences in the information seeking process by [115] also supported the path to guidelines that available on building IT architecture [116] . Regarding different kinds of thinking, [117] proposed that the thought patterns of East Asians and Westerners differ greatly (holistic vs. analytic). Holistically minded people have a tendency to perceive a scene globally; they are more field-dependent. Analytically minded people are more field-independent because they have a tendency to perceive an object separately from the scene and tend to assign objects to categories. The relationship between cognitive styles and webpage perception is analyzed by [118] . Thereby, they studied and presented the culturally different behavior of eye movement. The different viewing patterns of Chinese, Korean and American people suggest that webpage designers should be aware of the cognitive differences existing among holistically minded people and analytically minded people, and that web pages should be designed to match the users' cognitive styles in order to enhance usability. Holistically minded people (e.g., Chinese people) scan the entire page non-linearly. Hence, the design of content should show the whole context of the website and the harmony between the foreground and background as well as the relationship among all the content areas. In contrast, the webpage design should be as clear and simple as possible for analytically minded people (e.g., German people). They tend to employ a sequential reading pattern among areas and to read from the center to the periphery of the page. Hence, the arrangement of all content areas must be considered carefully. Category titles and navigation items should be named as clearly as possible since analytically minded people tend to pay more attention to these items and gain an overall picture of the website from them. [118] also intended to define the relationship between cognitive styles and webpage layout design. This indicates once more that most intercultural studies concentrate on examining web pages. Besides, [49] also investigated cultural dimensions for user experience doing a cross-country and cross-product analysis of users' cultural characteristics. A cross-cultural study on how users and developers experience their use of information systems revealed differences in mobile Internet usage between users from Japan (e.g., high email traffic) and Korea (e.g., many downloads) depending on different value structures in Japan and Korea imprinted by culture [119] . Cultural differences in the understanding of metaphors applied in user interfaces were examined by [120] . Since the real world changes from culture to culture, the metaphors referring to the real world that are used in HCI must also be considered for the localization of user interfaces. Examination has shown that test subjects from different cultures understand metaphors differently and their expectations, which they combine with the metaphors, are also different. Moreover, an explorative study with French and Turkish users on an e-learning site by [121] improved the cross-cultural understanding of the dual structure of metaphorical icons. Hidden cultural variables in HCI design such as information speed, information frequency, and interaction speed and interaction frequency have been touched by [17] (cf. Section 3.3).

However, all these variables can still be regarded as an open field for research in intercultural HCI design because there is just so little empirical evidence for the results in this area. In this respect, much effort must still be invested to investigate and consider hidden cultural variables in intercultural HCI design.

3.6. Models and Theories

The cultural model (iceberg metaphor) as developed by [11] is relevant for international user interface design. The relationship of user interface characteristics to Hofstede's cultural dimensions was elaborated by [122] . In contrast to [123] , who generated a relationship model in cultural usability testing, [124] postulated a three-perspective model of culture, information systems and their development and use. Other authors based their approach on cultural models to study the relationship between culture and HCI. The influences of culture in global software engineering were analyzed by [74] via thinking in terms of cultural models. Based on the results of [17] , the author formulated reflections on a preliminary model of culturally influenced human computer interaction to cover cultural contexts in HCI design which encompass the relationships between cultural and HCI dimensions. According to the results of an empirical study done by the author (cf. [44]), some of the correlations between the cultural dimensions and the HCI dimensions as well as their values were determined (cf. [17]) leading to the concept of HCI style scores, which can be computed for the designated cultural group from the Hofstede's indices. The HCI style score expresses the average degree of information density and frequency as well as interaction frequency and speed the members in the designated cultural group expect according to the model developed by the author. For instance, the lower the normalized HCI style score (ranging from 0 to 100) the lower the expected amount of information and the lower the interaction frequency. The resulting HCI style scores permit the establishment of clusters of countries that have similar HCI scores. According to these cultural clusters identified in the HCI style score continuum it can be expected that these country clusters exhibit a similar HCI style because of their similar cultural characterization defined by power distance index (PDI), individualism index (IDV), masculinity (MAS), uncertainty avoidance index (UAI) and long term orientation (LTO) (cf. Table 5).

These taxonomic results partially resemble the findings of [125] on "Saxonic", "Teutonic", "Gallic" and "Nipponic" styles. However, to generalize the postulated correlations many more studies with other cultural groups are required. To achieve this both the values of the cultural dimensions (using VSM) and the values of the HCI dimensions (such as pieces of presented information per minute, cf. [17]) must be determined for every desired culture. This can be done for indigenous groups as well by exploiting the same use cases and test settings in the arbitrary cultural groups of interest. A test tool developed by the author can be used to support this [58] . However, until there are no other values for the cultural dimensions than Hofstede's at the national level, those must be used to test the model. In addition, to further confirm findings, factor analysis can be applied to statistically calculate the corresponding loadings to the HCI style by clustering Hofstede's indices according to their HCI style score. The findings should refine the currently assumed rules that describe the relationship between cultural imprint and HCI style of a group (with at least 20 members). The explanatory value of this descriptive model still must be worked out.

Table 5. HCI Styles around the world.

HCI style	Cultural characterization	Normalized HCI style score (group averaged)
Asian	PDI high, IDV low, MAS middle, UAI low, LTO high	90
Indian	PDI high, IDV middle, MAS middle, UAI middle, LTO middle	70
African	PDI high, IDV low, MAS middle, UAI middle, LTO low	60
Scandinavian	PDI low, IDV high, MAS low, UAI middle, LTO low	40
Slavic	PDI high, IDV middle, MAS middle, UAI high, LTO low	30
Angle-Saxon	PDI low, IDV high, MAS middle, UAI low, LTO low	20
German	PDI low, IDV middle, MAS high, UAI middle, LTO low	10

In addition to this model, there are several other approaches towards a theory of culturally influenced human computer interaction. An explanatory theory for using management information systems in the Chinese business culture was developed by [126] . Moreover, [127] applied activity theory as a framework for accommodating cultural factors in HCI studies. Integrating activity theory into a usage-centered design approach is the method of [128] to cover environmental contexts, whereas [129] worked towards a HCI theory of cultural cognition. This systematic usage-centered design approach was extended by [130] o also cover cultural contexts by subjoining a cultural model as a new component. A theory of socio-technical interactions was outlined to explain culture by [131] integrating theory, research and application to understand culture. Using activity theory to tackle cultural contexts is very prominent (cf. [52] [128] [132]). ADA and CMU theory was compared in order to derive a theory for cultural usability

[133] . However, until now, there is no final theory that would explain all relevant factors necessary to derive design recommendations for culture-centered HCI design. This still remains a task for the future.

3.7. Processes, Standards and Tools

International standards for HCI and usability have been emerged and commented [134] . The user-centered HCI design process is defined in ISO 9241-210 and the emerging ISO 9241-220. ISO 9241-171 can be used to integrate cultural aspects to cover intercultural HCI design processes. In addition, the working team "quality standards" of the German UXPA (user experience professionals association) carved out a usability engineering process that can be extended by the necessary roles, tasks, methods, documents and work products, which are necessary to take cultural aspects into account and to fit them into any cultural contexts. A company culture audit was serves to improve development team's collaboration, communication and cooperation [135] . The intercultural interaction analysis tool (IIA tool) was developed to determine the cultural differences in HCI at interaction level [58] .

4. DISCUSSION

4.1. Problems and Controversies in Converging Divergences in Intercultural User Interface Design

4.1.1. Methodological Challenges

The methodological problem in researching culture is that the transmission of simple systems is easier than the integration of complex systems, which can only be achieved by human creativity [136] . This applies primarily to cultural questions, which encompass and integrate the complete context of a member of a culture. This problem also confronts intercultural user interface design, which makes it compellingly necessary to deal with the combination or linkage of culture with HCI design. Therefore, along with the common issues and challenges in HCI and in HCI design (cf. [137] [138]) and in the usability engineering process (cf. [139]), problems also arise because they must work in a cultural context (cf. [5] [21] [140] or [141]). Hence, the problems in adapting HCI to the cultural background of the user must be investigated [142] . Many aspects have to be taken into account simultaneously to obtain possible cultural explanations for their effect on HCI. Alternatively, the effects of culture on HCI cannot be explained by only one single aspect but by many different influences due to the complexity of culture. Another problem in cultural research is that one cannot predict how the single parts of the cultural puzzle will fit together (cf. [136] : 130). This has implications for the use of these methods in intercultural HCI design and intercultural usability engineering (cf. [143]).

4.1.2. Different Approaches

Furthermore, different approaches exist for determining intercultural variables and their values. For instance, cultural dimensions arise from cultural studies that can give insight into the diversity of cultures. From cultural dimensions, intercultural factors for HCI design can be derived. The results thus acquired are supported argumentatively and deductively, but not yet confirmed empirically (cf. [59] : 5 et seq.). Furthermore, the connection between cultural dimensions and HCI design has not yet been studied in depth [144] . Either detailed empirical studies must follow or the results can only serve as exemplifications, but not as a scientific foundation for further research. The complement to this deductive approach is the inductive approach: Cultural markers have been determined by empirical studies (e.g., [37] [40] [145]), which are specific for a certain culture and which are preferably used within this certain culture. There is direct influence of cultural markers on the performance of users interacting with the system and hence the connection between culture and usability (confirmed by studies from [37] [40] [41]). However, these results cannot be generalized to be valid for a complete country because the sample sizes are too small and the limited representativeness of the test persons precludes statistical results of high quality.

This is one reason why there are few evident qualitative empirical studies and even fewer purely quantitative studies (cf. [146] as well as [147]) which treat the interaction of culturally different imprinted users with the system.

4.1.3. High Research Effort

Hidden variables are difficult to identify because they are only recognizable over time. Therefore, the reason for the lack of results regarding direct hidden intercultural variables at the interaction level is also grounded in the difficulty of accessing and measuring them. To work against these methodological difficulties in studying hidden variables, it is reasonable, to a certain degree, to regard interaction and dialog design separately. First, the cultural differences in the interaction between user and system must be investigated, and then, how the interaction affects information flow between user and system must be treated.

Finally, how dialog windows should be designed for culturally different users also needs investigation, which should lead to preliminary design recommendations.

4.1.4. Lacking Empirical Confirmation

Not all recommendations have yet been proved empirically ac-cording to the five areas of user interface characteristics, even if there is some research in this area. Röse validated some of the aspects pointed out by Marcus doing qualitative studies in China regarding different layouts for Chinese and German users (cf. [148]). Moreover, regarding metaphors it is the case that in China hierarchical taxonomies and classifying instruments are applied rather than the case in Germany because of the high power distance values. Most of the recommendations presented must be tested and confirmed empirically in detail by additional studies before being suggested as best practices or even useful guidelines, if not already done so. Furthermore, parallel to the research literature, empirical investigations regarding intercultural user interface characteristics are necessary, more specifically by comparing several systems of different cultures (benchmark tests) as well as usability evaluations (usability testing) to determine the usability of different systems.

4.1.5. Usage of Cultural Dimensions

On the one hand, critics of Hofstede claim that the samples drawn from IBM's worldwide employee interview in their original study of 1967-72 are not representative. They do not provide data for actually measuring national culture differences between the countries but rather the differences within the corporate culture of IBM. Furthermore, Hofstede's approach ignores differences within a nation. The model treats a nation like a homogeneous collection of individuals who share the same structure of values. This is not correct in most cases (cf. [149]) and [150]). Some studies show inconsistencies in the values of Hofstede as presented by [151] : Power distance index (PDI) values for Japan, China and USA differ from those found by Hofstede. Furthermore, although much is said about what should be taken into account culturally, little empirical research is available on this topic as also pointed out, for instance, by [151] . In addition, a different behavior does not necessarily mean a different cultural (propositional) attitude, i.e. a different cognitive state in the web of belief. Restricted appreciation and mediation of cultural dimensions and models can lead to ineffective or even restricting action strategies [152] . In this case, a little cultural understanding proves to be just as bad as or even worse than no cultural understanding at all. Therefore, [152] pleads for dimension independent cultural models because they make the derivation of concrete behavior patterns possible whose explanations are founded on concrete manifestations of the culture described in contrast to models that use cultural dimensions. For instance, marrying CIIs with NLP principles as suggested by [17] means "cultural" adaptation at the individual level. The criticism concerning the correctness of Hofstede's cultural dimensions and their indices reduces confidence in them, which then implies that it is probably better or at least advisable not to build an adaptive system based on these but on parameters that represent the immediate behavior of the user with the system.

On the other hand, supporters of Hofstede's theory reject these moves away from Hofstede because numerous independent repetition studies in subsequent years confirmed Hofstede's results. Moreover, Hofstede's results referred to different subgroups of the respective populations and nevertheless showed similar national differences, which agree with Hofstede's dimension values. Furthermore, Hofstede points particularly to the different levels of culture whilst distancing himself from the list of questions (VSM) which was included with his explanations and designed for further use by the readers. According to [153] this is also because one of the consequences of his research and its results (and a starting point for criticism) is the "not reflected" appropriation and assignment of his cultural model which is seen as a useful tool for research (cf. [154]) and a useful starting point to research user interfaces in the cultural context (especially if a well founded theory is the designated goal of the research).

4.2. Research Directions in Converging the Divergence in Intercultural User Interface Design

The trend in research on culture and HCI is to verify preliminary models and theories by doing extensive empirical studies in various cultural contexts. Furthermore, the relationship between culture and HCI design must subsequently be elaborated upon in detail. The focus of investigating cultural differences will shift from the national level to a regional level and even to any other situation to cover all cultural contexts. Thereby, methods, models and theories will be adapted and improved upon in the near future by taking the results from many empirical studies into account to derive and optimize processes for intercultural HCI design and intercultural usability engineering and thereby establish international norms and develop tools that finally augment the international standards of research covering arbitrary cultural contexts in HCI.

4.2.1. Reframing HCI through Indigenous Perspectives

"Reframing" means taking cultural aspects into account at the local level (cultural context/indigeniously) in addition to the national level. For the last years the research and literature accounting for cultural contexts in Human Computer Interaction (HCI) design have grown quickly (cf. [20] [155]). In addition, until recently, culture in HCI was considered a matter of internationalization or localization [156] . As computer use spreads around the world, these traditional approaches to culture and HCI have proven to be seriously insufficient approaches. According to [21] and [69] , successful intercultural HCI design goes far beyond a regular design process by taking into account different mentalities, thought patterns and problem solving strategies that are anchored in culture. Usage patterns differ from culture to culture according to different power structures [9] , for example flat vs. hierarchical ones or problem solving strategies being linear vs. non-linear [148] . Hence, the designer must know exactly what the user needs or wants (e.g. why and in which context [71]). In addition, local designers must adapt general HCI methods to their needs (cf., [84] [85] [157]). Feasible recommendations and guidelines for the conception, design and evaluation of issues when implementing standard HCI perspectives in local contexts, as exemplified by German developers generating products for Chinese people, can be found in [70] . Related work on culture and HCI has been compiled along with [35] [85] [158] and by the author [17] . Within culturally different groups one must also consider dependence on context, situation and experience (cf. [84]). This knowledge can be determined most precisely by using inquiry approaches or methods based on communication like interviews, focus groups or questionnaires [159] . For successful (intercultural) user interface design and (intercultural) usability engineering it is necessary that the developer understands the user [160] , because they have different points of view [161] . Only by taking the perspective of a user by the HCI designer into account in order to grasp their needs depending on their world view, general knowledge, context and purpose of usage can good user interfaces of high usability be achieved. Excellent user experience design should be the result (cf. [135] [162] [163] [164]). However, problems in intercultural communication ensuring empathic access to the user requirements inhibit good usability for system design and the related user experience (cf. [5] [8]). This is because people and groups are shaped by many cultural systems, including religion, language and training as well as gender and life experience (cf. [17] [18]) representing a certain "culture", i.e. being a member of a group representing the same cultural characteristics.

4.2.2. Recommendations and Solutions for Converging Divergence in Intercultural User Interface Design

Several researchers working in this area of taking cultural contexts into account in HCI design have already profited from the results of empirical studies to build well elaborated and comprehensible work products that end in complex but valuable models, theories and tools for further and broader fruitful future research. For instance, the horizontal orientation of menus in layouts for the Chinese population was determined by [165] . A cross-cultural comparative study of users' perceptions of a webpage with the focus on the cognitive styles of Chinese, Koreans and Americans was done by [118] . Finally, [166] developed a culture-sensitive image tagging interface. Another example presents [40] who conducted an exploratory study of cultural markers based on [167] to build a culturally competent corporate multilingual web site. A pilot study in china was performed by [168] to clarify language issues in cross cultural usability testing. Finally, the path to cross-cultural technology design by creating culture-sensitive technology for local users has been augmented by [169] .

In any case, it is important to take cultural context into account in designing HCI. A cross-cultural study on knowledge sharing emerged that saving face and sharing personal information is appropriate depending on the situation [170] . A total of 197 Chinese undergraduate students and 111 American undergraduate students participated in the study. The first finding was that both Chinese and American students were more willing to share personal knowledge with in- group members than with out-group members. Furthermore, the results sho wed that common work experience between group members was more important than common national cultural background in determining a people's attitude towards knowledge sharing. Another interesting finding was that Chinese participants were more willing to share personal information with an American stranger (out-group) than a Chinese stranger (in-group), while American participants showed no such difference. In summary, these findings indicate that a global organization should take both national culture and in-group/out-group factors into consideration to facilitate knowledge sharing.

In addition, personalization and adaptation to the different user needs is necessary: "[...] Internet strategies should be localized or adjusted to unique cultures, since people want different values even from the same services across different cultures. [...] Mobile Internet services need to be personalized to individual users because value structures and usage patterns are influenced by various factors across countries. To develop personalized services, mobile Internet service providers need to segment user groups by cultural, demographical, or socio- economic factors and monitor them, which may enable them to chase users' fast changing needs or values efficiently" ([119] : 237).

5. CONCLUSION

In the area of intercultural user interface design, the difficult investigation of methodological intercultural factors still stands at the beginning where it is acquiring results for phenomena like different habits of interacting with the system, different expectations regarding navigation within hyperspace or different mental models. It is still decisive in the area of intercultural user interface design to bridge the gap between cultural aspects and those specifically for user interface design. This is especially the case with respect to the current lack of research regarding culturally imprinted interaction and dialog design based on empirical studies regarding hidden cultural variables. Even if the research concerning culture-centered HCI design is growing enormously, it is the most important to integrate the results from empirical studies considering cultural contexts in HCI design and thereby, provides the basis of both data to feed models and construct theories and the basis of the graduated measuring rod for their verification representing the path to get the convergent divergence in the field of intercultural user interface design. Even if there is still a long way to go, there are already converging strategies that have to be exploited and developed further to reduce the divergence in intercultural user interface design. One possible approach to this is to reframe HCI by taking cultural aspects into account at the local level (cultural context/indigenously) in addition to the national level up to the approach of designing in the wild. These procedures can be supported by using a mix of IUID methods applying user interface characteristics, human computer interaction dimensions. It is a matter of future research to determine which combination of converged approaches, methods, processes and tools will survive and lead the research paradigm in order to reduce divergence in IUID.

REFERENCES

1. Rose, K. and Zuhlke, D. (2001) Culture-Oriented Design: Developers' Knowledge Gaps in this Area. In: Johannsen, G., Ed., 8th IFAC/IFIPS/IFORS/IEA Symposium on Analysis, Design, and Evaluation of Human-Machine Systems, Kassel, September 18-20 2001, 11-16.
2. Marcus, A. (2007) Global/Intercultural User-Interface Design. In: Jacko, J. and Spears, A., Eds., The Human-Computer Interaction Handbook, Lawrence Erlbaum Associates, Mahwah.
3. Honold, P. (2000) Intercultural Usability Engineering: Barriers and Challenges from a German Point of View. In: Day, D., Galdo, E.D. and Prabhu, G.V., Eds., Designing for Global Markets: 2nd International Workshop on Internationalisation of Products and Systems, 137-147.
4. eimgartner, R. (2014) Intercultural User Interface Design. In: Blashki, K. and Isaias, P., Eds., Emerging Research and Trends in Interactivity and the Human-Computer Interface, Information Science Reference (an Imprint of IGI Global), Hershey, 1-33.
5. Heimgartner, R., Tiede, L.-W. and Windl, H. (2011) Empathy as Key Factor for Successful Intercultural HCI Design. In: Marcus, A., Ed., Proceedings of 14th International Conference on Human-Computer Interaction, Springer Berlin/Heidelberg, 557-566.
6. Chamberlain, A., Crabtree, A., Rodden, T., Jones, M. and Rogers, Y. (2012) Research in the Wild: Understanding in the Wild Approaches to Design and Development. Proceedings of the Designing Interactive Systems Conference, Newcastle Upon Tyne, 11-15 June 2012, 795-796.
7. Schwartz, S.H. (1992) Universals in the Content and Structure of Values: Theoretical Advances and Empirical Tests in 20 Countries. Advances in Experimental Social Psychology, 25, 1-65.
8. Hall, E.T. (1959) The Silent Language. Doubleday, New York.
9. Hofstede, G.H., Hofstede, G.J. and Minkov, M. (2010) Cultures and Organizations: Software of the Mind. McGraw-Hill, Maidenhead.

10. Hofstede, G. (1984) Culture's Consequences: International Differences in Work-Related Values. Sage, Beverly Hills, Calif.
11. Hoft, N.L. (1996) Developing a Cultural Model. In: Del Galdo, E.M. and Nielsen, J., Eds., International Users Interface, John Wiley & Sons, Inc., 41-73.
12. Thomas, A. (1996) Psychologie interkulturellen Handelns. Hogrefe, Gottingen; Seattle.
13. Hodicová, R. (2007) Psychische Distanz und Internationalisierung von KMU: Empirische Untersuchung am Beispiel des Sachsisch-tschechischen Grenzraumes. Duv.
14. Hofstede, G. (1994) VSM94: Values Survey Module 1994 Manual. IRIC, Tilberg, Netherlands.
15. Rose, K., Liu, L. and Zuhlke, D. (2001) Design Issues in Mainland China: Demands for a Localized Human-Machine-Interaction Design. In: Johannsen, G., Ed., 8th IFAC/IFIPS/IFORS/IEA Symposium on Analysis, Design, and Evaluation of Human-Machine Systems, Preprints, Kassel, 17-22.
16. Zuhlke, D. (2004) Useware-Systeme fur internationale Markte. In: Useware-Engineering fur technische Systeme, Springer, Berlin, Heidelberg, 142-164.
17. Heimgartner, R. (2012) Cultural Differences in Human-Computer Interaction. Oldenbourg Verlag. [Citation Time(s):12]
18. Marcus, A. (2001) Cross-Cultural User-Interface Design. In: Smith, M.J.S.G., Ed., Proceedings of the Conference on Human-Computer Interface Internat (HCII), Lawrence Erlbaum Associates, Mahwah, NJ, USA, 502-505.
19. Rau, P.-L.P., Plocher, T. and Choong, Y.-Y. (2012) Cross-Cultural Design for IT Products and Services. Taylor & Francis, Boca Raton, FL.
20. Shen, S.-T., Woolley, M. and Prior, S. (2006) Towards Culture-Centred Design. Interacting with Computers, 18, 820-852.
21. Honold, P. (2000) Culture and Context: An Empirical Study for the Development of a Framework for the Elicitation of Cultural Influence in Product Usage. International Journal of Human-Computer Interaction, 12, 327-345.
22. Rose, K. (2002) Methodik zur Gestaltung interkultureller Mensch-Maschine-Systeme in der Produktionstechnik. Univ., Kaiserslautern.
23. Vdma (2009) Software-Internationalisierung Leitfaden. VDMA Fachverband Software, Frankfurt a.M.
24. DR. International (2003) Developing International Software.
25. Schmitz, K.-D. and Wahle, K. (2000) Softwarelokalisierung. Stauffenburg-Verl., Tubingen.
26. Marcus, A. (2006) Cross-Cultural User-Experience Design. In: Barker-Plummer, D., Cox, R. and Swoboda, N., Eds., Diagrammatic Representation and Inference, Springer Berlin Heidelberg, 16-24.
27. Kralisch, A. (2006) The Impact of Culture and Language on the Use of the Internet Empirical Analyses of Behaviour and Attitudes Berlin.
28. Nielsen, J. (1990) Designing User Interfaces for International Use. Elsevier, Amsterdam.
29. Del Galdo, E.M. and Nielsen, J. (1996) International User Interfaces. Wiley, New York.
30. Day, D.L. (1991) The Cross-Cultural Study of Human-Computer Interaction: A Review of Research Methodology, Technology Transfer, and the Diffusion of Innovation.
31. Cagiltay, K. (1999) Culture and Its Effects on Human-Computer-Interaction. In: Collis, B. and Oliver, R., Eds., Proceedings of World Conference on Educational Multimedia, Hypermedia and Telecommunications 1999, AACE, Chesapeake, VA, 1626-1626.
32. Jetter, H.-C. (2004) Interkulturelles UI Design und UI Evaluation Universitat Konstanz.
33. Leidner, D.E. and Kayworth, T. (2006) Review: A Review of Culture in Information Systems Research: Toward a Theory of Information Technology Culture Conflict. MIS Quarterly, 30, 357-399.
34. Vatrapu, R. and Suthers, D. (2007) Culture and Computers: A Review of the Concept of Culture and Implications for Intercultural Collaborative Online learning. Lecture Notes in Computer Science: IWIC'07 Proceedings of the 1st International Conference on Intercultural Collaboration, Springer-Verlag Berlin, Heidelberg, 260-275.
35. Clemmensen, T. and Roese, K. (2010) An Overview of a Decade of Journal Publications about Culture and Human-Computer Interaction (HCI). Human Work Interaction Design:

Usability in Social, Cultural and Organizational Contexts. IFIP Advances in Information and Communication Technology, 316, 98-112.
36. Aykin, N. (2004) Usability and Internationalization of Information Technology Lawrence Erlbaum Associates Inc.
37. Badre, A. and Barber, W. (1998) Culturabilty: The Merging of Culture and Usabilty. Proceedings of the 4th Conference on Human Factors and the Web AT and T Labs, Basking Ridge, NJ, USA.
38. Hermeking, M. (2001) Kulturen und Technik. Waxmann, Munchen.
39. Rossger, P. and Hofmeister, J. (2003) Cross Cultural Usability: An International Study on Driver Information Systems. Human-Computer Interaction.
40. Sun, H. (2001) Building a Culturally Competent Corporate Web Site: An Exploratory Study of Cultural Markers in Multilingual Web Design. Proceedings of the 19th Annual International Conference on Computer Documentation, Sante Fe, 21-24 October 2001, 95-102.
41. Vohringer-Kuhnt, T. (2002) The Influence of Culture on Usability Freie Universitat Berlin.
42. Clemmensen, T. and Goyal, S. (2004) Studying cross cultural Think-Aloud Usability TESting—Some Suggestions for an Experimental Paradigm. In: Kjeldskov, J., Skov, M.B. and Stage, J., Eds., Proceedings of the Fourth Danish Human-Computer Interaction Research Symposium, Centertryk, Aalborg University, Denmark, 16 November 2004, 25-28.
43. Reinecke, K., Reif, G. and Bernstein, A. (2007) Cultural User Modeling With CUMO: An Approach to Overcome the Personalization Bootstrapping Problem. First International Workshop on Cultural Heritage on the Semantic Web at the 6th International Semantic Web Conference (ISWC 2007), Busan, South Korea.
44. Heimgartner, R. (2007) Cultural Differences in Human Computer Interaction: Results from Two Online Surveys. In: Osswald, A., Ed., Open Innovation, UVK, Konstanz, 145-158.
45. Thissen, F. (2008) Interkulturelles Informationsdesign. In: Weber, W., Ed., Kompendium Informationsdesign, Berlin, Heidelberg, 387-424.
46. Abdelnour-Nocera, J., Kurosu, M., Clemmensen, T., Bidwell, N., Vatrapu, R., Winschiers-Theophilus, H., Evers, V., Heimgartner, R. and Yeo, A. (2011) Re-Framing HCI through Local and Indigenous Perspectives. In: Campos, P., Graham, N., Jorge, J., Nunes, N., Palanque, P. and Winckler, M., Eds., Lecture Notes in Computer Science. Springer-Verlag, Berlin; New York, 738-739.
47. Rau, P.-L.P., Plocher, T. and Choong, Y.-Y. (2012) International Usability Evaluation. In: Patrick Rau, P.-L., Plocher, T. and Choong, Y.-Y., Eds., Cross-Cultural Design for IT Products and Services, CRC Press, 191-200.
48. Sun, H. (2012) Cross-Cultural Technology Design: Creating Culture-Sensitive Technology for Local Users. Oxford University Press, Oxford; New York.
49. Lee, I., Choi, G.W., Kim, J., Kim, S., Lee, K., Kim, D., Han, M., Park, S.Y. and An, Y. (2008) Cultural Dimensions for User Experience: Cross-Country and Cross-Product Analysis of Users' Cultural Characteristics. People and Computers, 1, 3-12.
50. Sturm, C. (2002) TLCC-Towards a Framework for Systematic and Successful Product Internationalization. International Workshop on Internationalisation of Products and Systems, Austin/Texas, USA.
51. Esselink, B. (1998) A Practical Guide to Software Localization: For Translators, Engineers and Project Managers. Benjamins, Amsterdam.
52. Nardi, B.A. (1996) Context and Consciousness: Activity Theory and Human-Computer Interaction. MIT Press, Cambridge, Mass.
53. Norman, D.A. and Draper, S. (1986) User Centered System Design: New Perspectives on Human-Computer Interaction Lawrence Erlbaum Associates.
54. Kersten, G.E., Kersten, M.A. and Rakowski, W.M. (2002) Software and Culture: Beyond the Internationalization of the Interface. Journal of Global Information Management, 10, 86-101.
55. Aykin, N. (2005) Usability and Internationalization of Information Technology. Mahwah, NJErlbaum.

56. Law, W.K. and Perez, K. (2005) Cross-Cultural Implementation of Information System. Journal of Cases on Information Technology, 7, 121-130.
57. Honold, P. (1999) Cross-Cultural or Intercultural-Some Findings on International Usability Testing. In: Prabhu, G.V. and Del Galdo, E.M., Eds., First International Workshop on Internationalisation of Products and Systems (IWIPS 1999), New York, Backhouse Press, Rochester, 107-122.
58. Heimgartner, R. (2008) A Tool for Getting Cultural Differences in HCI. In: Asai, K., Ed., Human Computer Interaction: New Developments, InTech, Rijeka, 343-368.
59. Marcus, A. and Gould, E.W. (2000) Cultural Dimensions and Global Web User-Interface Design: What? So What? Now What?
60. Rose, K., Liu, L. and Zuhlke, D. (2001) Design Issues in Mainland China and Western Europe: Similarities and Differences in the Area of Human-Machine-Interaction Design. In: Smith, M.J. and Salvendy, G., Eds., Systems, Social and Internationalization Design Aspects of Human-Computer Interaction, CRC Press, Boca Raton, 532-536.
61. Schlogl, C. (2005) Information and Knowledge Management: Dimensions and Approaches. Information Research, 10, 10-14.
62. Hall, E.T. and Hall, M.R. (2004) Understanding Cultural Differences: [Germans, French and Americans]. Intercultural Press, Yarmouth, Me.
63. Heimgartner, R. (2005) Research in Progress: Towards Cross-Cultural Adaptive Human-Machine-Interaction in Automotive Navigation Systems. In: Day, D. and Del Galdo, E.M., Eds., Proceedings of the Seventh International Workshop on Internationalisation of Products and Systems (IWIPS 2005), Amsterdam, 97-111.
64. Heimgartner, R. (2007) Measuring Cultural Differences in HCI as Preparatory Work for Cultural Adaptability in Navigation Systems: Results from the Second Online Survey. In: Evers, V. and Mandl, C.S.A.M.A.M.R.A.E.C.M.I.A.T., Eds., Proceedings of the Eighth International Workshop on Internationalisation of Products and Systems, Merida, 28-30 June 2007, Product & Systems Internationalisation, Inc., 43-54.
65. Heimgartner, R. (2013) Reflections on a Model of Culturally Influenced Human Computer Interaction to Cover Cultural Contexts in HCI Design. International Journal of Human-Computer Interaction, 29, 205-219.
66. Heimgartner, R. and Kindermann, H. (2012) Revealing Cultural Influences in Human Computer Interaction by Analyzing Big Data in Interactions. In: Huang, R., Ghorbani, A., Pasi, G., Yamaguchi, T., Yen, N. and Jin, B., Eds., Active Media Technology, Springer Berlin Heidelberg, 572-583.
67. Bernsen, N.O., Dybkjaer, H. and Dybkjaer, L. (1998) Designing Interactive Speech Systems. Springer, London.
68. Preim, B. and Dachselt, R. (2010) Interaktive Systeme—Band I: Grundlagen, Graphical User Interfaces, Informationsvisualisierung. Springer Verlag, Berlin, Heidelberg.
69. Rose, K. (2002) Model of Culture and Their Applicability for Designing User Interfaces. Proceedings of the Conference WWDU 2002—World Wide Work, Berchtesgaden.
70. Heimgartner, R. and Tiede, L.W. (2008) Technik und Kultur: Interkulturelle Erfahrungen bei der Produktentwicklung fur China. In: Rosch, O., Ed., Interkulturelle Kommunikation, Berlin, Verlag News & Media, 149-162.
71. Holzinger, A. (2005) Usability Engineering for Software Developers. Communications of the ACM, 48, 71-74.
72. Honold, P. (1999) Cross-Cultural Usability Engineering: Development and State of the Art. Proceedings of HCI International Conference on Human-Computer Interaction: Ergonomics and User Interfaces, L. Erlbaum Associates Inc., 1232-1236.
73. Simon, S.J. (2000) The Impact of Culture and Gender on Web Sites: An Empirical Study. SIGMIS Database, 32, 18-37.
74. Shah, H., Nersessian, N.J., Harrold, M.J. and Newstetter, W. (2012) Studying the Influence of Culture in Global Software Engineering: Thinking in Terms of Cultural Models. Proceedings of the 4th International Conference on Intercultural Collaboration, Bengaluru, 21-23 March 2012, 77-86.

75. Dasgupta, S. and Gupta, B. (2010) Organizational Culture and Technology Use in a Developing Country: An Empirical Study. Proceedings of SIG GlobDev Third Annual Workshop, Saint Louis, 12 December 2010.
76. Mutschler, B. and Reichert, M. (2004) Usability-Metriken als Nachweis der Wirtschaftlichkeit von Verbesserungen der Mensch-Maschine-Schnittstelle. Proceedings of the IWSM/MetriKon Workshop on Software Metrics (IWSM/MetriKon'04), Konigs Wusterhausen.
77. Plocher, T. and Honold, P. (2000) Culturally-Adapted Product in the Global Market: Dealing with the Naysayers. Proceedings of the Paper Presented at the CHI 2000, The Hague.
78. Beu, A., Honold, P. and Yuan, X. (2000) How to Build Up an Infrastructure for Intercultural Usability Engineering: Ease and Joy of Use for Complex Systems at Siemens. International Journal of Human-Computer Interaction, 12, 347-358.
79. Honold, P. (2000) Interkulturelles Usability Engineering: Eine Untersuchung zu kulturellen Einflussen auf die Gestaltung und Nutzung technischer Produkte. VDI Verl., Dusseldorf.
80. Clemmensen, T., Hertzum, M., Hornbaek, K., Kumar, J., Shi, Q. and Yammiyavar, P. (2007) Usability Constructs: A Cross-Cultural Study of How Users and Developers Experience Their Use of Information Systems.
81. Clemmensen, T. (2010) A Comparison of What Is Part of Usability Testing in Three Countries. In: Katre, D., Orngreen, R., Yammiyavar, P. and Clemmensen, T., Eds., Human Work Interaction Design: Usability in Social, Cultural and Organizational Contexts, Springer Berlin Heidelberg, 31-45.
82. Yammiyavar, P., Clemmensen, T. and Kumar, J. (2008) Influence of Cultural Background on Non-Verbal Communication in a Usability Testing Situation. International Journal of Design, 2, 2.
83. Paterson, B., Winschiers-Theophilus, H., Dunne, T.T., Schinzel, B. and Underhill, L.G. (2011) Interpretation of a Cross-Cultural Usability Evaluation: A Case Study Based on a Hypermedia System for Rare Species Management in Namibia. Interacting with Computers, 23, 239-246.
84. Bidwell, N., Winschiers-Theophilus, H., Koch Kapuire, G. and Rehm, M. (2011) Pushing Personhood into Place: Situating Media in the Transfer of Rural Knowledge in Africa. International Journal of Human-Computer Studies, 69, 618-631.
85. Robig, S., Didier, M. and Bruder, R. (2010) Internationales Verstandnis von Usability sowie Methodenanwendung im Bereich der Usability. In Proceedings of the Grundlagen-Methoden-Technologien, VDI Fachtagung USEWARE 2010 (Baden-Baden 2010), 345-354.
86. Dinet, J., Vivian, R. and Brangier, E. (2011) Towards Future Methods to Take into Account Cross-Cultural Differences in Design: An Example with the "Expert Community Staff" (ECS). In: Marcus, A., Ed., Design, User Experience, and Usability. Theory, Methods, Tools and Practice, Springer Berlin Heidelberg, 53-61.
87. Evers, V. (2003) Cross-Cultural Aspects of User Understanding and Behaviour: Evaluation of a Virtual Campus Website by User from North America, England, the Netherlands and Japan. In: Evers, V., Rose, K., Honold, P., Coronado, J. and Day, D., Eds., Proceedings of the 5th International Workshop on Internationalisation of Products and Systems (IWIPS 2003), University of Kaiserslautern, Berlin, 17-19 July 2003, 189-210.
88. Smith, A. and Chang, Y. (2003) Quantifying Hofstede and Developing Cultural Fingerprints for Website Acceptability. In: Evers, V.R.K.H.P.C.J.D.D., Ed., Proceedings of the 5th International Workshop on Internationalisation of Products and Systems (IWIPS 2003), University of Kaiserslautern, Berlin, 17-19 July 2003, 89-102.
89. Kamentz, E. (2006) Adaptivitat von hypermedialen Lernsystemen: Ein Vorgehensmodell fur die Konzeption einer Benutzermodellierungskomponente unter Berucksichtigung kulturbedingter Benutzereigenschaften Univ., Hildesheim, 293.
90. Rossger, P. (2003) An International Comparison of the Usability of Driver-Information-Systems. In: Evers, V.R.K.H.P.C.J.D.D., Ed., Proceedings of the 5th International Workshop on Internationalisation of Products and Systems (IWIPS 2003), University of Kaiserslautern, Berlin, 17-19 July 2003, 129-134.

91. Hodemacher, D., Jarman, F. and Mandl, T. (2005) Kultur und Web-Design: Ein empirischer Vergleich zwischen Grossbritannien und Deutschland. In: Stary, C., Ed., Mensch & Computer 2005: Kunst und Wissenschaft-Grenzuberschreitungen der interaktiven ART, Oldenbourg Verlag, Munchen, Wien, 93-101.
92. Marcus, A. (2003) Global and Intercultural User Interface Design. The Human-Computer Interaction Handbook: Fundamentals, Evolving Technologies and Emerging Applications.
93. Dormann, C. and Chisalita, C. (2002) Cultural Values in Web Site Design.
94. Baumgartner, V.-J. (2003) A Practical Set of Cultural Dimensions for Global User-Interface Analysis and Design Fachhochschule Joanneum, Graz, Austria.
95. Park, S.J. and Wiedenbeck, S. (2007) Global User-Interface Design: Characteristics of Multinational Corporate Websites Drexel University, College of Information Science and Technology.
96. Stengers, H., Troyer, O., Baetens, M., Boers, F. and Mushtaha, A. (2004) Localization of Web Sites: Is There Still a Need for It? International Workshop on Web Engineering (HyperText 2004 Conference), Santa Cruz.
97. Sun, H. (2001) Building a Culturally-Competent Corporate Website: An Exploratory Study of Cultural Markers in Multilingual Web Design. Proceedings of the 19th Annual International Conference on Computer Documentation (ACM), Sante Fe, 95-102.
98. Callahan, E. (2005) Cultural Similarities and Differences in the Design of University Web Sites. Journal of Computer-Mediated Communication, 11, 239-273.
99. Sturm, C. and Mueller, C.H. (2003) Putting Theory into Practice: How to Apply Cross-Cultural Differences to User Interface Design? In: Rauterberg, M., Menozzi, M. and Wesson, J., Eds., Human-Computer Interaction: INTERACT'03; IFIP TC13 International Conference on Human-Computer Interaction, 1-5 September 2003, International Federation for Information Processing, 1051-1052.
100. Fitzgerald, W. (2004) Models for Cross-Cultural Communications for Cross-Cultural Website Design.
101. Lewandowitz, L., ROSSGER, P. and Vohringer-Kuhnt, T. (2006) Asiatische vs. europaische HMI Losungen von Fahrerinformationssystemen. Useware 2006 VDI, Dusseldorf, 279-287.
102. Braun, B.-M., Rose, K. and Rossger, P. (2007) Localizing for the Korean Market: Actually Being There with a Multi-Method Approach. In: Evers, V., Sturm, C., Alberto, M., Rocha, M., Cambranes Mart\Inez, E. and Mandl, T., Eds., Proceedings of the Eighth International Workshop on Internationalisation of Products and Systems, Merida, 28-30 June 2007, Product & Systems Internationalisation, Inc., 55-62.
103. Evers, V. and Day, D. (1997) The Role of Culture in Interface Acceptance. Proceedings of the IFIP TC13 Interantional Conference on Human-Computer Interaction, 260-267.
104. Currie, N.J. and Peacock, B. (2002) International Space Station Robotic Systems Operations: A Human Factors Perspective. Human Factors and Ergonomics Society.
105. Ou, L.C., Luo, M.R., Woodcock, A. and Wright, A. (2004) A Study of Colour Emotion and Colour Preference. Part I: Colour Emotions for Single Colours. Color Research & Application, 29, 3.
106. Shneiderman, B., Plaisant, C., Cohen, M. and Jacobs, S. (2009) Designing the User Interface: Strategies for Effective Human-Computer Interaction. Addison-Wesley Publishing Company, Boston.
107. Ratzmann, M. (2004) Software-Testing & Internationalisierung. Galileo Press, Bonn.
108. Kromker, H. (2000) Introduction. International Journal of Human-Computer Interaction, 12, 281-284.
109. Emma, N.M.I., Nor, L.M.N. and Shafie, M. (2009) Trust or Distrust in the Web-Mediated Information Environment (W-MIE): A Perspective of Online Muslim Users. Journal of Enterprise Information Management, 22, 5.
110. Tateishi, M. and Toma, T. (2010) A Cross-Cultural Comparative Study of User Interface in Social Media: Why Social Media Can Cross Seas But Not Nationalisms.
111. Endrass, B., Rehm, M., André, E. and Nakano, Y. (2008) Talk Is Silver, Silence Is Golden: A Cross Cultural Study on the Usage of Pauses in Speech. Proceedings of the IUI workshop on Enculturating Conversational Interfaces.

112. Koda, T., Rehm, M. and Andre, E. (2008) Cross-Cultural Evaluations of Avatar Facial Expressions Designed by Western Designers. Lecture Notes in Computer Science, 5208, 245-252.
113. Kankanhalli, A., Tan, B.C.Y., Wei, K.-K. and Holmes, M.C. (2004) Cross-Cultural Differences and Information Systems Developer Values. Decision Support Systems, 38, 183-195.
114. Lee, K.-P. (2007) Culture and Its Effects on Human Interaction with Design: With the Emphasis on Cross-Cultural Perspectives between Korea and Japan.
115. Komlodi, A. (2005) Cross-Cultural Study of Information Seeking. Proceedings of the International Conference on Human-Computer Interaction (HCII 2005). First International Conference on Usability and Internationalization, Springer, Berlin, New York, Las Vegas, Nevada, USA.
116. Koning, H., Dormann, C. and Van Vliet, H. (2002) Practical Guidelines for the Readability of IT-Architecture Diagrams. Proceedings of the 20th Annual International Conference on Computer Documentation, Toronto, 20-23 October 2002, 9099.
117. Nisbett, R.E. (2003) The Geography of Thought: How Asians and Westerners Think Differently ... and Why. Free Press, New York.
118. Dong, Y. and Lee, K. (2008) A Cross-Cultural Comparative Study of Users' Perceptions of a Webpage: With a Focus on the Cognitive Styles of Chinese, Koreans and Americans. International Journal of Design, 2, 2.
119. Lee, Y., Kim, J., Lee, I. and Kim, H. (2002) A Cross-Cultural Study on the Value Structure of Mobile Internet Usage: Comparison between Korea and Japan. Journal of Electronic Commerce Research, 3, 227-239.
120. Evers, V., Kukulska-Hulme, A. and Jones, A. (1999) Cross-Cultural Understanding of Interface Design: A Cross-Cultural Analysis of Icon Recognition. In Del Galdo, E. and Prahbu, G., Eds., Proceedings of the International Workshop on Internationalisation of Products and Systems, IWIPS 1999, Rochester, NY, 173-182.
121. Rizvanoglu, K. and Ozturk, O. (2009) Cross-Cultural Understanding of the Dual Structure of Metaphorical Icons: An Explorative Study with French and Turkish Users on an E-Learning Site. Proceedings of the 3rd International Conference on Internationalization, Design and Global Development: Part of HCI International 2009, San Diego, Springer-Verlag, 89-98.
122. Marcus, A. and Gould, E.W. (2000) Crosscurrents: Cultural Dimensions and Global Web User-Interface Design. Interactions, 7, 32-46.
123. Shi, Q. and Clemmensen, T. (2007) Relationship Model in Cultural Usability Testing. In: Aykin, N., Ed., Usability and Internationalization. HCI and Culture, Springer Berlin/Heidelberg, 422-431.
124. Kappos, A. and Rivard, S. (2008) A Three-Perspective Model of Culture, Information Systems, and Their Development and Use. MIS Q., 32, 601-634.
125. Galtung, J. (1981) Structure, Culture, and Intellectual Style: An Essay Comparing Saxonic, Teutonic, Gallic and Nipponic Approaches. Social Science Information, 20, 817.
126. Martinsons, M.G. and Westwood, R.I. (1997) Management Information Systems in the Chinese Business Culture: An Explanatory Theory. Information & Management, 32, 215-228.
127. Maier, E. (2005) Activity Theory as a Framework forAccommodating Cultural Factors in HCI Studies. In: Auinger, A., Ed., Workshops-Proceedings der 5. fachubergreifenden Konferenz Mensch und Computer 2005. Internationalisierung von Informationssystemen: Kulturelle Aspekte der Mensch-Maschine-Interaktion, Wien, 69-79.
128. Constantine, L. (2009) Human Activity Modeling: Toward a Pragmatic Integration of Activity Theory and Usage-Centered Design Human-Centered Software Engineering, In: Seffah, A., Vanderdonckt, J. and Desmarais, M., Eds., Springer London, 27-51.
129. Faiola, A. (2006) Toward an HCI Theory of Cultural Cognition.
130. Windl, H. and Heimgartner, R. (2013) Intercultural Design for Use-Extending Usage-Centered Design by Cultural Aspects. HCII 2013, Springer, Las Vegas.
131. Wyer, R.S., Chiu, C.-Y. and Hong, Y.-Y. (2009) Understanding Culture: Theory, Research, and Application. Psychology Press, New York.

132. Kaptelinin, V. and Nardi, B. (2006) Acting with Technologie: Activity Theory and Interaction Design. MIT Press Cambridge, Cambridge, MA.
133. Clemmensen, T. (2009) Towards a Theory of Cultural Usability: A Comparison of ADA and CMU Theory. In: Kurosu, M., Ed., Human Centered Design. HCD 2009. Lecture Notes in Computer Science, Vol. 5619, Springer, Berlin, Heidelberg.
134. Bevan, N. (2001) International Standards for HCI and Usability. International Journal of Human-Computer Studies, 55, 533-552.
135. Gould, E. and Marcus, A. (2011) Company Culture Audit to Improve Development Team's Collaboration, Communication, and Cooperation Design, User Experience, and Usability. In: Marcus, A. Ed., Theory, Methods, Tools and Practice, Springer Berlin/Heidelberg, 415-424.
136. Hall, E.T. (1976) Beyond Culture. Anchor Books, New York.
137. Chen, Q. (2001) Human Computer Interaction Issues and Challenges Idea Group Pub., Hershey, Pa.
138. Reiterer, H. (2008) Seminar Reader: Future Challenges and Trends in HCI Human-Computer Interaction Group. University of Konstanz, Konstanz.
139. Holzinger, A. and Weidmann, K.-H. (2005) Empowering Software Quality: How Can Usability Engineering Reach These Goals? 1st Usability Symposium, HCI & UE Workgroup, Vienna, 8 November 2005, Austrian Computer Society.
140. Clemmensen, T., Yammiyavar, P., Orngreen, R. and Katre, D. (2010) Usability in a Cultural Context: A Report on the Scope, Process and Research Results of Cult Usab—The Cultural Usability Project. In: Katre, D., Orngreen, R., Yammiyavar, P. and Clemmensen, T., Eds., Human Work Interaction Design: Usability in Social, Cultural and Organizational Contexts. IFIP Advances in Information and Communication Technology, Vol 316. Springer, Berlin, Heidelberg.
141. Hertzum, M. and Clemmensen, T. (2012) How Do Usability Professionals Construe Usability? International Journal of Human-Computer Studies, 70, 26-42.
142. Rehm, M., Bee, N., Endrass, B., Wissner, M. and André, E. (2007) Too Close for Comfort? Adapting to the User's Cultural Background. Proceedings of the International Workshop on Human-Centered Multimedia, Augsburg, Bavaria, Germany, ACM Press, New York, 85-94.
143. Nielsen, J., Bodker, M. and Vatrapu, R. (2010) Culture and (i)Literacy as Challenges to Scandinavian Cooperative Design. Proceedings of the 3rd International Conference on Intercultural Collaboration, Copenhagen, 19-20 August 2010, 271-274.
144. Cyr, D. and Trevor-Smith, H. (2004) Localization of Web Design: An Empirical Comparison of German, Japanese, and United States Web Site Characteristics. Journal of the American Society for Information Science and Technology, 55, 1199-1208.
145. Dormann, C. (2006) Cultural Representations in Web Design: Differences in Emotions and Values. In Mcewan, T., Benyon, D. and Gulliksen, J., Eds., People and Computers XIX—The Bigger Picture, London, 285-299.
146. Smith, A., Dunckley, L., French, T., Minocha, S. and Chang, Y. (2004) A Process Model for Developing Usable Cross-Cultural Websites. Interacting with Computers, 16, 63-91.
147. Maier, E., Mandl, T., Rose, K., Womser-Hacker, C. and Yetim, F. (2005) Internationalisierung von Informationssystemen: Kulturelle Aspekte der Mensch-Maschine-Interaktion. In Auinger, A., Ed., Workshops-Proceedings der 5. fachubergreifenden Konferenz Mensch und Computer 2005, Wien, 57-58.
148. Rose, K., Zuhlke, D. and Liu, L. (2001) Similarities and Dissimilarities of German and Chinese Users. In Johannsen, G., Ed., Preprints of 8th IFAC/IFIP/IFORS/IEA Symposium on Analysis, Design, and Evaluation of Human-Machine Systems, Kassel, 24-29.
149. House, R.J. and Aditya, R.N. (1997) The Social Scientific Study of Leadership: Quo Vadis? Journal of Management, 23, 409.
150. House, R.J. (2004) Culture, Leadership, and Organizations: The Globe Study of 62 Societies. Sage, Thousand Oaks.
151. Komischke, T., Mcgee, A., Wang, N. and Wissmann, K. (2003) Mobile Phone Usability and Cultural Dimensions: China, Germany & USA. In: Muhlbach, L., Ed., Human Factors in

Telecommunication, Proceedings of the 19th International Symposium on Human Factors in Telecommunication (HFT 03), Berlin.
152. Rathje, S. (2003) Ist wenig kulturelles Verstandnis besser als gar keins? —Problematik der Verwendung von Dimensionsmodellen zur Kulturbeschreibung. Interculture-Online IWK Uni Jena, 20.
153. Hofstede, G. (2006) Culture's Consequences: Comparing Values, Behaviors, Institutions, and Organizations across Nations. Sage Publication, Thousand Oaks.
154. Bryan, N.B., Mclean, E.R., Smits, S.J. and Burn, J. (1994) The Structure of Work Perceptions among Hong Kong and United States IS Professionals: A Multi-dimensional Scaling Test of the Hofstede Cultural Paradigm. Proceedings of the 1994 Computer Personnel Research Conference on Reinventing IS: Managing Information Technology in Changing Organizations: Managing Information Technology in Changing Organizations, Alexandria, 24-26 March 1994, 219-230.
155. Plocher, T., Patrick Rau, P.-L. and Choong, Y.-Y. (2012) Cross-Cultural Design. In Handbook of Human Factors and Ergonomics, John Wiley & Sons, Inc., 162-191.
156. Clemmensen, T. (2009) A Framework for Thinking about the Maturity of Cultural Usability, Copenhagen Business School, C. B. S. Institut for Informatik I. N. F. Department of Informatics I. N. F.
157. Clemmensen, T., Hertzum, M., Hornbaek, K., Shi, Q. and Yammiyavar, P. (2009) Cultural Cognition in Usability Evaluation. Interacting with Computers, 21, 212-220.
158. Marcus, A. and Baumgartner, V.-J. (2004) A Practical Set of Culture Dimensions for Global User-Interface Development. In: Masood, M., Jones, S. and Rogers, B., Eds., Proceedings of 6th Asia Pacific Conference on Computer Human Interaction (APCHI 2004), Rotorua, June 29-July 2 2004, 252-261.
159. Hampe-Neteler, W. (1994) Software-ergonomische Bewertung zwischen Arbeitsgestaltung und Softwareentwicklung. Lang, Frankfurt am Main.
160. Nielsen, J. (2006) Usability Engineering. Kaufmann, Amsterdam.
161. Eigenbrode, S.D., O'rourke, M., Wulfhorst, J.D., Althoff, D.M., Goldberg, C.S., Merrill, K., Morse, W., NIelsen-Pincus, M.A.X., Stephens, J., Winowiecki, L. and Bosque-Pérez, N.A. (2007) Employing Philosophical Dialogue in Collaborative Science. BioScience, 57, 55-64.
162. Heimgartner, R., Windl, H. and Solanki, A. (2011) The Necessity of Personal Freedom to Increase HCI Design Quality. In: Marcus, A., Ed., Design, User Experience, and Usability, Theory, Methods, Tools and Practice (DUXU 2011), Springer, Berlin, 62-68.
163. Maguire, M. (2011) Guidelines on Website Design and Colour Selection for International Acceptance Design, User Experience, and Usability. In: Marcus, A., Ed., Theory, Methods, Tools and Practice, Springer Berlin/Heidelberg, 162-171.
164. Biesterfeldt, J. and Capra, M. (2011) Leading International UX Research Projects Design, User Experience, and Usability. In: Marcus, A., Ed., Theory, Methods, Tools and Practice, Springer Berlin/Heidelberg, 368-377.
165. Dong, J. and Salvendy, G. (1999) Designing Menus for the Chinese Population: Horizontal or Vertical? Behaviour and Information Technology, 18, 467-471.
166. Dong, W. and Fu, W.-T. (2010) Toward a Cultural-Sensitive Image Tagging Interface. Proceedings of the 15th International Conference on Intelligent User Interfaces, Hong Kong, 7-10 February 2010, 313-316.
167. Badre, A. (2000) The Effects of Cross Cultural Interface Design Orientation on World Wide Web User Performance. GVU Technical Report GIT-GVU-01.03, 1-30.
168. Sun, X. and Shi, Q. (2007) Language Issues in Cross Cultural Usability Testing: A Pilot Study in China. Proceedings of the 2nd International Conference on Usability and Internationalization, Global and Local User Interfaces, Springer-Verlag, Berlin, 274-284.
169. Sun, H. (2012) The Case of Facebook Japan: Cross-Cultural Design in Postcolonial Conditions. Proceedings of the 30th ACM International Conference on Design of Communication, Seattle, 3-5 October 2012, 367-368.
170. Zhang, Q., Chintakovid, T., Sun, X., Ge, Y. and Zhang, K. (2006) Saving Face or Sharing Personal Information? A Cross-Cultural Study on Knowledge Sharing. Journal of Information and Knowledge Management, 5, 73-80.

CHAPTER 12

SDN-Enabled Communication Network Framework for Energy Internet

Zhaoming Lu,[1,2] Chunlei Sun,[1,2] Jinqian Cheng,[1,2] Yang Li,[3] Yong Li,[4] and Xiangming Wen[1,2]

[1]*School of Information and Communication Engineering, Beijing University of Posts and Telecommunications, Beijing 100876, China*

[2]*Beijing Laboratory of Advanced Information Networks, Beijing 100876, China*

[3]*China Electric Power Research Institute, Beijing 100192, China*

[4]*Department of Electronic Engineering, Tsinghua University, Beijing 100084, China*

ABSTRACT

To support distributed energy generators and improve energy utilization, energy Internet has attracted global research focus. In China, energy Internet has been proposed as an important issue of government and institutes. However, managing a large amount of distributed generators requires smart, low-latency, reliable, and safe networking infrastructure, which cannot be supported by traditional networks in power grids. In order to design and construct smart and flexible energy Internet, we proposed a software defined network framework with both microgrid cluster level and global grid level designed by a hierarchical manner, which will bring flexibility, efficiency, and reliability for power grid networks. Finally, we evaluate and verify the performance of this framework in terms of latency, reliability, and security by both theoretical analysis and real-world experiments.

1. INTRODUCTION

"Smart grid" applies communication and networking technologies into the power grid to allow for more efficient generation, transmission, distribution, and usage of energy [1], which lead to a sustainable energy generation and consumption. With the increasingly serious situation of energy shortage and environment pollution, DG (distributed generator) has been adopted by more and more countries as renewable and green energy resources. However, compared with the development of distributed renewable energy generations and long distance power transmission technologies like Ultrahigh Voltage (UHV), a series of advanced information technologies, such as smart metering and control, data fusion and mining, smart scheduling, and optimization, are also critical for power grid. Besides, the traditional unidirectional power grid turns into bidirectional power grid with the introduction of DGs. Hence, energy Internet brings an exciting prospect of the future energy utilization containing all phases of novel energy generation, storage, transmission, and distribution [2].

Technically, energy Internet brings three aspects of innovation for power grids. Firstly, more distributed renewable energy terminals, such as wind power and solar power, can be allowed to access the energy Internet through ubiquitous networks. They will considerably improve the proportion of renewable energy usage and reduce greenhouse gas emissions. Secondly, smart grid technologies, such as microgrid technologies, can just support effective energy utilization in local scope, while energy Internet brings about more effective energy utilization in both of small and large scopes by smart communication networks. Thirdly, energy Internet is able to protect the power grid from cascading failure. Cascading failure (also known as blackout) is notoriously known as one of the most devastating forces, which usually results in disastrous damage to modern societies. Independence and isolation are two main reasons for cascading failure. And energy Internet could resist the cascading failure in power grid by extensive interconnecting, which will improve the stability of power systems.

Therefore, energy Internet has attracted increasing attention of government and institutions, such as the US Department of Energy [3], the German Federal Government [4], and the Japan Digital Grid Group [5]. In 2013, Chinese government and the State Grid Corporation of China (SGCC) started the global energy Internet project [6], by which they expected to build a strong smart grid with the support of "Internet+." The energy Internet can adapt to a series of requirements of distributed energy generations and transport renewable energy to all kinds of users flexibly, reliably, and safely. Due to the rigorous requirements of flexibility, latency, reliability, and safety for energy Internet, a lot of work is required to be done in the information and communication system, such as low-latency data interaction, virtual operation, and safe information transmission. Actually, Information and Communication Technologies (ICT) are essentially important components of the underlying infrastructures in energy Internet and play a key role in monitoring, metering, scheduling, and so forth [7–9]. However, as the traditional networks cannot be deployed and managed in an efficient and flexible way, the rigorous and diverse communication requirements of energy Internet have greatly exceeded the capabilities of traditional communication frameworks, and novel communication network framework is urgently required to be designed. Hence, considering that different countries take different strategies in energy Internet and the deployments of power grids also display various characteristics, we just focus on the communication network framework design of energy Internet in China in this paper.

The main contributions of this paper are summarized as follows. Firstly, we proposed an SDN-enabled hierarchical communication network architecture, which satisfies the requirements for information interaction in energy Internet. Besides, the network frameworks of microgrid cluster level and global grid level are designed, respectively. Secondly, performances such as latency, reliability, and security of the proposed communication network framework are analyzed and some available approaches are enumerated, which can contribute to ensuring these performances. Thirdly, one testbed for revealing the feasibility of SDN-enabled networks is constructed and related experimental results are displayed to demonstrate the performance of our proposed framework.

The rest of this paper is arranged as follows. Requirements and related work for communication networks are summarized in Section 2. SDN-enabled hierarchical communication network framework is depicted in Section 3. Application cases of the proposed SDN-enabled communication network framework in the background of Virtual Power Plants (VPPs) and energy e-commerce are described in Section 4. Performance is evaluated by theoretical analysis and experiments, respectively, in Sections 5 and 6. Finally, Section 7 concludes this work.

2. REQUIREMENTS AND RELATED WORKS FOR COMMUNICATION NETWORKS

Smart grid has been studied for several years in China, and a series of achievements have been obtained for assurance of energy supply. To allow more distributed generators and increase energy efficiency, the current energy system needs to be improved with the aim of evolving to energy Internet.

2.1. State-of-the-Art Development of Energy Internet

In 2009, the State Grid Corporation of China (SGCC) declared that they would start up the strong and smart grid plan in China and they would focus on four working areas, including strong grid, extensive interconnection, high intelligence, and open interaction. In 2010, "the 12th Five-Year Plan" launched by SGCC affirmed achievements on the upgrades of wildly interconnected power grid and transmission system, for example, pharos measurement units (PMUs), online security and stability, large-scale wind turbines, and solar photovoltaics monitoring. However, in the early 2010s, the power market in China was almost in the state of monopoly. To ensure the safety of power systems, power plants were deployed in a centralized way and the power transaction was almost operated in the planned model in which the electricity price was fixed without any adjustments neither in peak hours nor in trough hours. Limitation of the traditional communication network architecture leads to the passive consumption of power energy and low efficiency of energy utilization. However, there was no obvious change occurring in these years for this in spite of the implementation of peak-valley price in minority urban cities. Hence, there is still lots of work to do for energy Internet.

With the further development of the market economy, a series of sweeping reforms are coming in China, which will result in the further openness of energy market, and will allow more distributed energy generators to access power grids. In order to build energy Internet in China, the government encourages distributed power generation and liberalized electricity transaction, which is regarded as the milestone of the energy Internet development in China.

2.2. Requirements of Communication Network

According to the current situation of energy system, Figure 1 illustrates the future vision and system framework of energy Internet in China.

Users are the terminal nodes of energy Internet. Microgrids are small self-management areas in local distribution grids, which can contribute to the utilization of renewable energy resources and improve the energy efficiency by reducing transmission loss. And the bulk power system is mainly composed of power generation systems, Ultrahigh Voltage backbone grids, responsible for the long distance power transmission to relieve the unbalance between power consumption and resource location in different regions, power distribution networks, end-users, and so forth. To guarantee the safety and stability of power grid, energy flows and information flows will be deeply integrated with each other under the support of ICT.

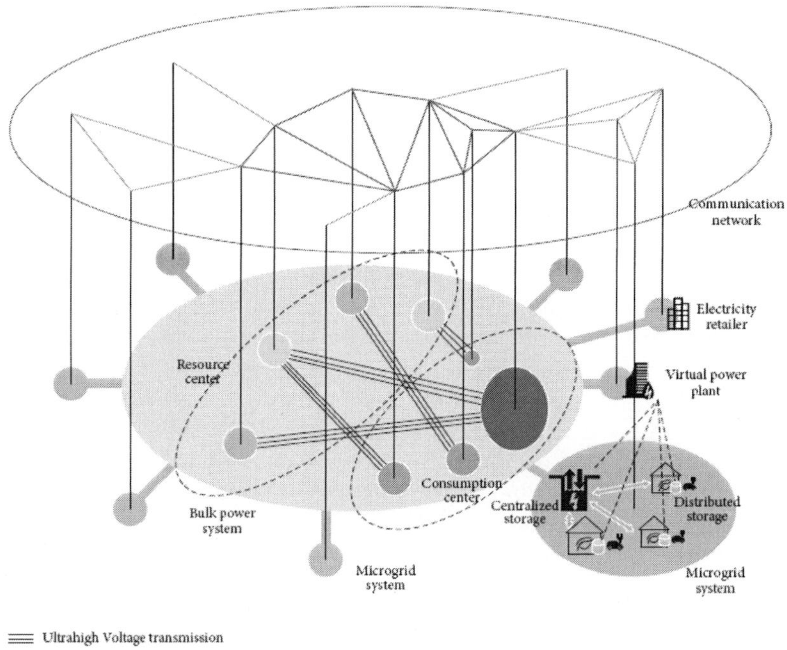

Figure 1: Framework and vision of energy Internet in China.

Though ICT has been already involved in traditional power grid to strengthen the intelligence of the power system, the communication capabilities in traditional power grid were very weak, especially in China. Compared with traditional power grid, energy Internet is characterized by the access of massive distributed DGs, highly intelligent control, highly effective energy utilization, flexible energy trading online, and series of novel business scenarios. As DGs have features like small capacity, high quantity, and fluctuant and uneven distribution, the reliable low-latency managements of fluctuant generators and dynamic consumption of DGs by communication networks are indispensable. Meanwhile, in the distributed and customer-based energy Internet, increasing information of energy production, energy transaction, and control also requires advanced and interconnected communication network. Therefore, to implement open and liberalized energy market and accept various kinds of DGs, open, flexible, and reliable communication network framework is required.

2.3. Related Work of Communication Network Framework

Massive DGs will generate large amounts of metering, monitoring, and control data, which brings specific requirements of communication networks. IP-based networks have been considered as the infrastructure of communication networks of energy Internet [6]. However, most current researches on energy Internet have just focused on the single issues in energy Internet, such as the SOFIA (Service-Oriented Information Centric Networking), which just focuses on service-oriented application information transmission [7], and ICN (Information Centric Networking), which just emphasizes machine-to-machine data delivery [12]. The grid communication system is divided into several parts in [13], including energy management system, distribution management system, and WAMS (Wide Area Measurement System), and network issues corresponding to these different parts are usually discussed separately. Hence, rare work investigates the communication network framework with a global view so as to design an open, flexible, and reliable communication network. Furthermore, the existing work of communication network framework does not comply with the specific features of power grid in China. Therefore, it is necessary to design a kind of communication network framework to meet the requirements of energy Internet and to support the construction and development of energy Internet in China.

Fortunately, in recent years, Software Defined Networking (SDN) has attracted much attention. It proposes a flexible, effective, and reliable network framework that abstracts the control plan from the packet forwarding hardware (data plane) to an external software controller [14, 15]. Therefore, SDN is perceived to have tremendous potential for utilization in the communication network of the energy Internet.

3. SDN-ENABLED HIERARCHICAL COMMUNICATION NETWORK FRAMEWORK

As is shown in Figure 2, energy Internet is expected to involve a large number of distributed renewable energy generators and improve the efficiency of energy utilization with the combination of self-consumption of power in small scope and power transmission in long distance.

As the basic cell of energy Internet, microgrid is a stable and independent microsystem responsible for small scope power consumption. Type I users could directly obtain power energy from Type II users in the same microgrid, if there is any redundant energy produced or stored by them.

This small scope self-consumption model can not only improve the utilization efficiency of renewable energy, but also decrease the power transmission loss and cost. When this energy transaction occurs, massive state information, such as load state, generation state, and storage state of users, should be collected in real-time by the microgrid energy controller to strictly guarantee the real-time balance of power supply and demand. Hence, highly frequent interaction of information between communication terminals is typical of microgrid level. Meanwhile, the adjustment of energy supply-demand among adjacent microgrids will take place when it is beyond the self-balance abilities of only one microgrid. When this cross-domain transaction occurs, amounts of information among different microgrids will be generated.

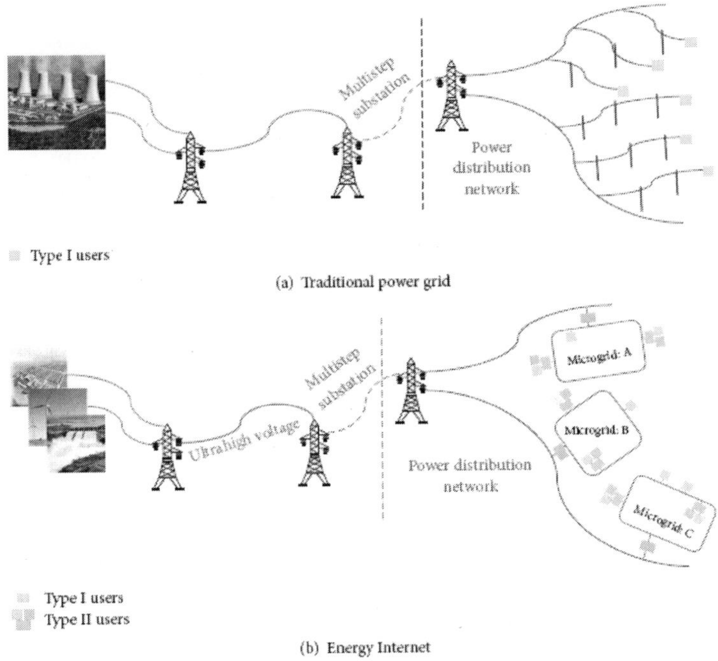

Figure 2: Differences between traditional power grid and energy Internet. Type I users (traditional users) represent those that just equal common loads, while Type II users (distributed energy users) denote those that possess abilities of power generation and storage besides consumption).

In addition, long distance transmission by UHV (Ultrahigh Voltage) would also be needed in order to realize large scope balance of energy supply and demand, such as the West-East Electricity Transmission Project in China, which is significant for the optimization of energy allocation among different regions. In this case, it is important to insure the reliable transmission of scheduling information, control information, and monitoring information as well as service operation and management in wide area.

In order to enhance the efficiency of communication system, communication genre and information frequency should be concerned specially. Therefore, we propose an SDN-enabled hierarchical framework of communication network, which can be implemented by the following two parts.

3.1. Microgrid Cluster Level Communication Network Framework

As is shown in Figure 3, several adjacent microgrids can constitute a local microgrid cluster. In each microgrid, there are several switches managed by a centralized local domain controller. The local domain Forwarding Information Base (FIB), containing all routing information inside the microgrid, can be established by the local domain controller. By forwarding this FIB message in local domain, the major communication requirements caused by small scope energy self-consumption can be met, which occupies the majority of energy and communication businesses in microgrid. Moreover, one or more switches in each microgrid are selected as edge switches to connect with those in other domains or the aggregation switch controlled by a centralized cluster controller. This cluster controller also manages those local domain controllers within its domain. Thus communication among different microgrids can be realized under the control of cluster controllers. In this cluster level framework, it has been adequately considered that the more frequent message interaction within local domains always occurs compared with that among multidomains, which is a typical feature of energy Internet communication and is usually caused by the energy self-consumption within local domains. This framework can tremendously contribute to the improvement of communication efficiency.

3.2. Global Grid Level Communication Network Framework

As is shown in Figure 4, the global control domain can be constructed by the large-scale interconnection of cluster controllers, which take charge of the aggregation switches and local domain controllers within their domain. The consistent global view of the whole network can be established by the cooperation of these distributed global controllers, or called cluster controllers. Based on this, the wide area measurement and scheduling can be achieved.

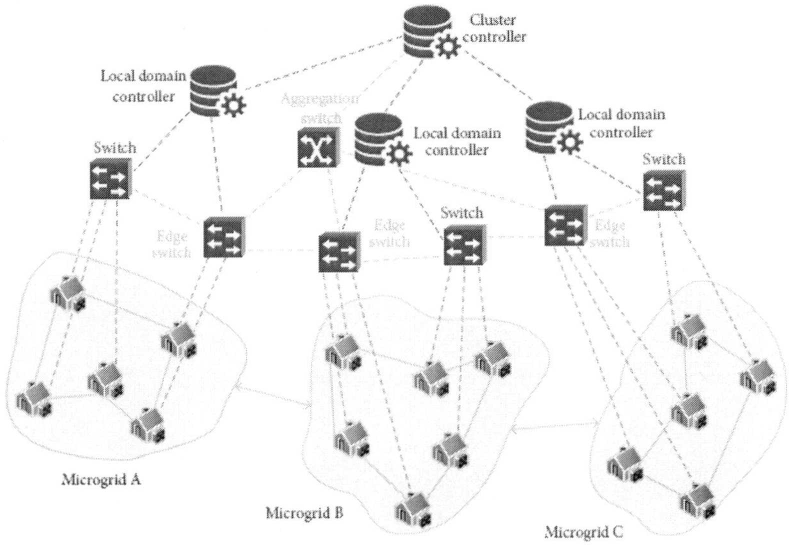

Figure 3: SDN-enabled microgrid cluster level communication network framework.

In brief, this hierarchical communication network framework, from local domain to global domain, is in accordance with the hierarchical energy network framework, from local energy self-consumption to wide area energy scheduling. Different level controllers are responsible for different network functions and this hierarchical framework would make communication networks of energy Internet more reliable.

3.3. Characteristics of Proposed Framework

As is shown in Figure 5, SDN-enabled communication network framework can be divided into four tiers, that is, data plane, control plane, orchestration tier, and application tier. Different tiers are responsible for different functions of the network. By decoupling data plane and control plane on the basis of SDN, three characteristics of the aforementioned SDN-enabled network framework can be summarized as follows.

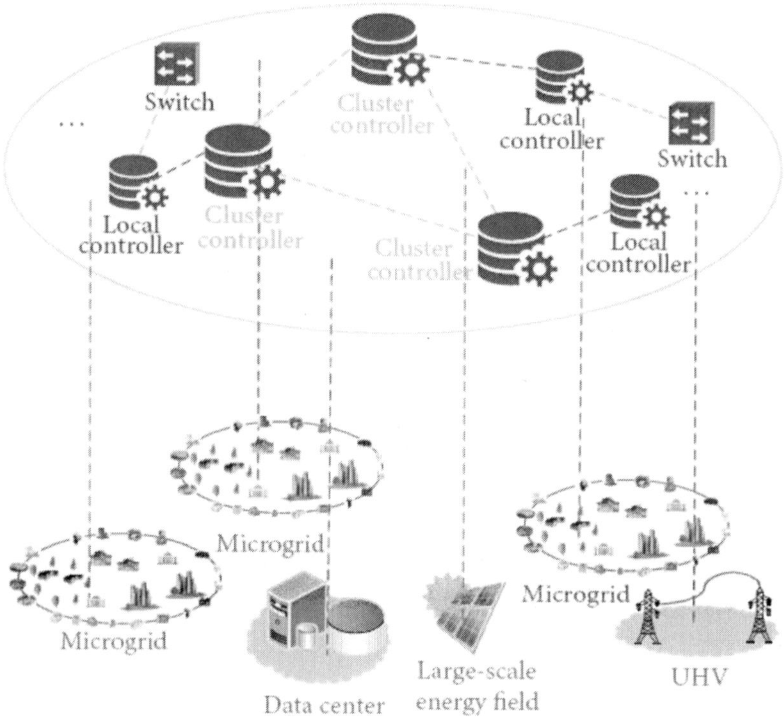

Figure 4: SDN-enabled global grid level communication network framework.

Flexibility. SDN allows network administrators to configure network functions flexibly by software. This is done by decoupling control plane from the data plane. Hence, through the north interface of SDN controller, flexible coordination of energy management and communication network management could be achieved. In addition, since the controller has a global view of the whole network topology, it can find the optimal forwarding path and control traffic flow according to different strategies, such as low-latency driven or security driven ones.

Efficiency. Owning to the highly frequent information interaction always occurring inside microgrid, most of message forwarding tasks can be accomplished according to the flow table distributed by the local domain controller. Only if it fails to provide necessary routing information will the message be delivered to the cluster controller. Compared with other SDN-enabled communication network frameworks, such as the flat controller model in [16], the proposed hierarchical framework can reduce communication delay and lessen the burden of cluster controllers effectively.

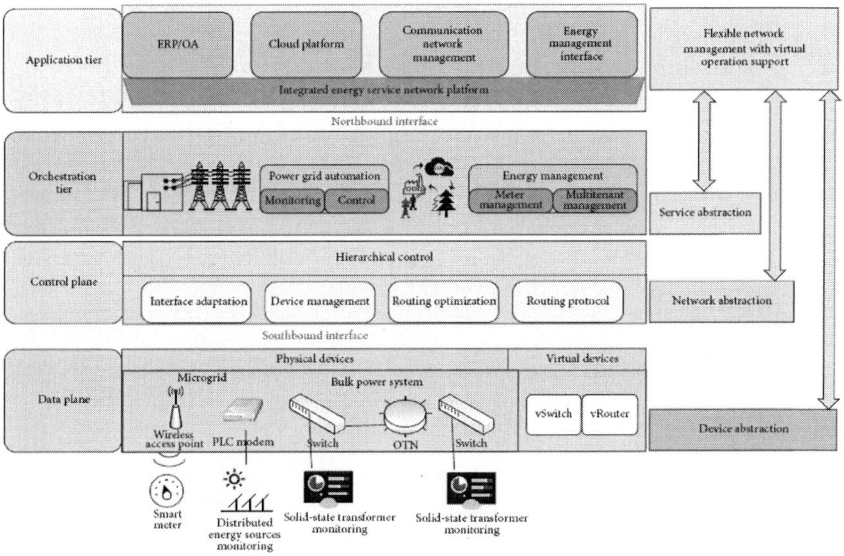

Figure 5: SDN-enabled communication network framework in energy Internet.

Reliability. Global control domain consisted of a series of distributed cluster controllers which can survive from the danger of single point failure. In addition, benefiting from the global view, when one or more communication links break down, infrastructure sharing from other links will take place under the control of the controller to achieve fast recovery, by which the reliability of communication network can be exactly strengthened.

4. APPLICATION CASES OF SDN-ENABLED COMMUNICATION NETWORK IN ENERGY INTERNET

With the influence of the "Internet," energy Internet is also expected to be qualified for more complex and flexible businesses, which cannot be realized without the support of prominent communication network. Two most typical cases will be shown as follows, which can also provide credible evidence that SDN-enabled communication network is required in energy Internet.

4.1. Virtual Power Plants (VPPs)

At present, power industry is undergoing a period of marketization at home and abroad. For instance, Chinese government has enacted the correlated policies to promote the marketization of power distribution businesses. It can break the monopoly of SGCC and CSG (China Southern Power Grid) in power transmission and distribution, which will create opportunities for the springing up of new power operators.

However, those newborn operators have no enough abilities or no permission to build their own power grid infrastructure. Under this background, the VPP will become an effective approach to relieving their insufficiency of infrastructure.

The south protocol and north protocol can enable more flexible and dynamic configures of network resources. By the north interfaces of SDN-enabled framework, VPPs can logically abstract and integrate distributed utility resources in different microgrids, such as DGs, storage devices, and controllable loads, in order to realize the self-governed management and optimization towards local resources [17] without affecting each other. It can enable different virtual operators to share the same infrastructure but implement their own operations and businesses independently.

4.2. Energy E-Commerce

The primary prospection of energy Internet is to realize energy sharing, which means loads can get supplies from those near DGs with rich power [13]. For instance, when there is a pair of users having made agreement on energy trading via a third-party platform, the seller will send its power to the third-party platform in terms of the preceding agreement. Then the buyer can obtain the same amount of electricity from the third-party platform as depicted in Figure 6.

This third-party platform driven energy e-commerce is regarded as another prospective scenario under the background of the marketization of power industry. Compared with traditional network, the programmability and openness of SDN can make it easier to achieve the management of network resources and the deployment of new businesses.

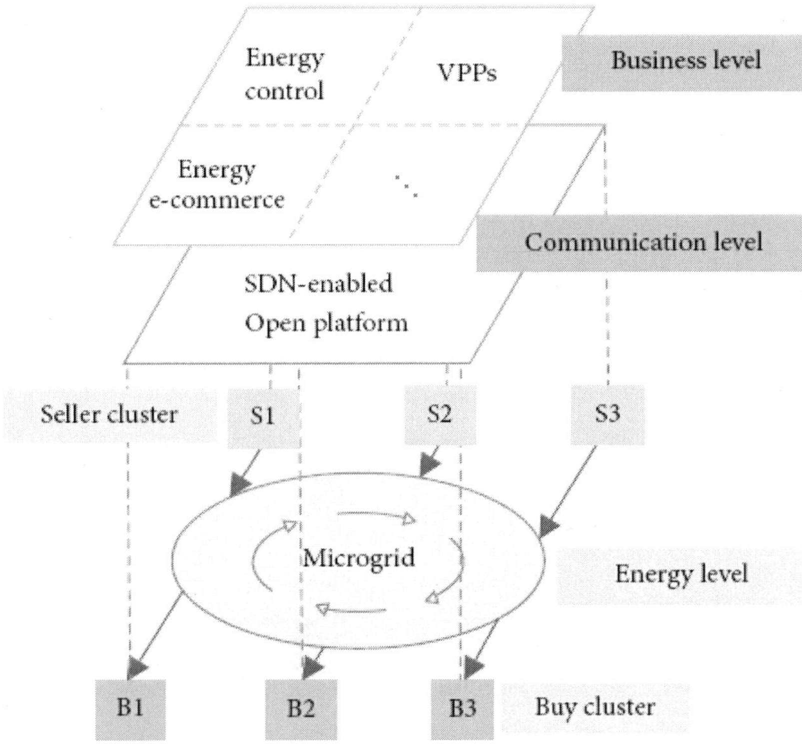

Figure 6: Multiple and flexible businesses based on SDN.

In order to illustrate how this SDN-enabled hierarchical architecture can successfully support these open businesses more clearly, we will give a case of intradomain or interdomain energy trading and then briefly analyze the deployment of flow rules and the orchestration of hierarchical controllers in this subsection. As is shown, Figure 7(a) displays the complete network architecture, while Figure 7(b) displays the logical links of data plane in global topology maintained by cluster controllers.

And we note that in order to make the diagram more legible there are some unimportant links that have been omitted, such as links between the local controller and the common switch, as the deployment of flow rules and the orchestration of hierarchical controllers in SDN are not our main concern. Here, we will just give a simple analysis.

Actually, there are some related excellent studies that have already been done, such as [18–22].

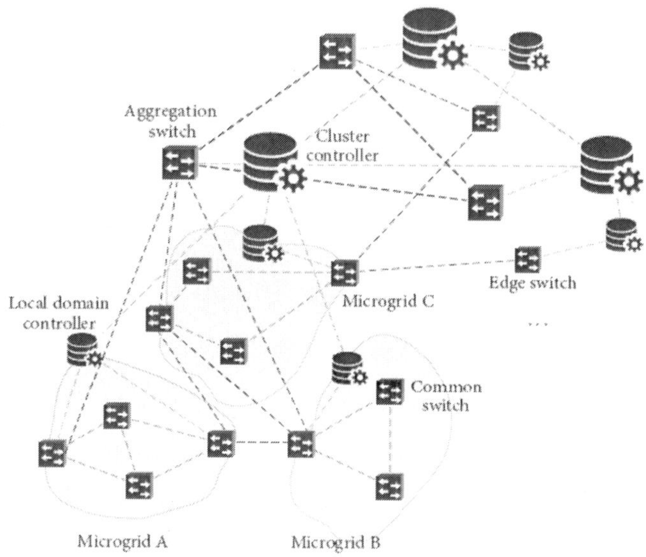

(a) An example of complete network

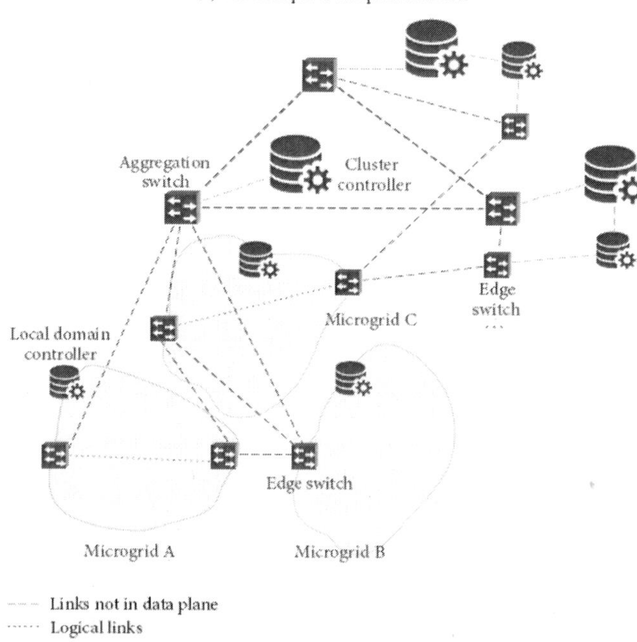

(b) Global view of data plane maintained by cluster controllers

Figure 7: A case of SDN-enabled hierarchical architecture in energy e-commerce.

Firstly, as for the local topology, the local controller can periodically construct a LLDP (Link Layer Discovery Protocol) packet for each switch port. If there is any new link between two different switch ports found, a packet-in message will be triggered. Then the local controller receives this message and infers that there is a link existing between the two involved switches and makes a record. In this process, edge switches and interdomain links can also be found. In addition, local controller can take advantage of Dijkstra-based routing algorithms, or other algorithms, to calculate shortest paths [23] and generate the local FIB. As for global topology, to reduce the difficulties of calculating global paths, the size of global topology is required to be limited. Thus instead of providing all details of the local topology in each local domain, the global view only contains edge switches, aggregation switches, interdomain links, and logical intradomain links, as is shown in Figure 7(b). Up to now, there are several multidomain routing algorithms in SDN that have been well researched, including the calculation of logical intradomain routes, such as [24, 25]. Given the limited space, we will not give more details about these. We note that each local controller just maintains the detailed routing information within its local scope and cannot obtain the views of other microgrids, while all cluster controllers have consistent global logic views. And all what switches should do is to forward messages to the next hop switch or the default switch according to the flow table distributed by controllers. If there is no rule matched, it will ask local controller for route messages.

Secondly, in the real process of message forwarding, when frequent intramicrogrid energy trading occurs, which is the most common event in energy e-commerce, massive local information exchange requirements will be produced at the same time. And all switches are OpenFlow switches and can forward messages according to the flow table sent by the local controller with high speed. If there is a new flow arriving, the source switch will send a packet-in message to the local controller to require a new flow entry. In this process, rare interdomain information will be produced and nearly no access requests to cluster controllers will occur, while when energy trading among several adjacent microgrids in the same microgrid cluster occurs, large amounts of interdomain information exchange requirements will be generated. Once the source local controller infers that the message is an interdomain one and no local rules matched, it will send requests to the cluster controller. And the cluster controller then determines a global path and sends a reply to each local controller whose domain is passed through by the determined path. Each reply contains the information of each domain's ingress and egress switches or ports. Next, local controller receives the route reply and expands this logical link to its corresponding physical path and installs rules along the involved switches within its scope. Furthermore, when large scope energy transmission occurs, such as interprovince power transmissions based on UHV, which just have 13 lines in China up to now, more than one cluster controller and corresponding aggregation switches will be involved. Because all cluster controllers have consistent global views, the global path can be calculated by the nearest cluster controller instead of asking routing information from all cluster controllers whose domain is passed through. In this process, aggregation switches controlled by cluster controllers directly will take part in the message forwarding among these far-distance microgrids to reduce end-to-end delay. Once there is an aggregation switch coming, the cluster controller will be asked to deploy table rules in corresponding aggregation switched, besides local controllers. By the above deployment of flow rules and orchestration of hierarchical controllers, SDN-enabled hierarchical architecture can adapt to energy Internet perfectly.

In summary, the openness and flexibility of SDN will make it behave better than traditional IP-based network in these complex business scenarios. The hierarchical framework brings higher efficiency and preferable global performance. These are the original motivations for our research on SDN-enabled communication network in energy Internet.

5. PERFORMANCE ANALYSIS OF SDN-ENABLED COMMUNICATION NETWORK FRAMEWORK

According to the above analysis, obviously SDN-enabled network will play prominent roles in energy Internet on account of its openness and flexibility. Meanwhile it is necessary to do sufficient investigations on the performance of SDN-enabled network, including availability (low-latency) and reliability.

5.1. Availability

The performance of communication network can be influenced by several factors of bandwidth, latency, channel quality, and so forth. Compared to the Internet, latency issues of communication network play more important roles in the protection and control of power system, especially for the crucial nodes, such as substations, energy control centers, and other vital devices. As is shown in Table 1, IEEE has classified the information types of power systems into several categories. To ensure the security of power systems, private networks, such as TDM + SDH, traditionally transmit higher priority businesses. Although latency issues are not the inherent characteristics of IP-based network, there is the tendency to be all-IP for the communication network in energy Internet owing to its characteristics of businesses, flexibility, and inexpensive cost [26]. Fortunately, SDN-enabled communication network framework could reduce the latency of network to make it competent for power systems. Table 2 depicts the latency of an SDN-enabled network with 1 GB/s bandwidth and 200 km long links in the case of transmitting 1250-byte data [11]. From the comparison of Tables 1 and 2, it is obvious to find that SDN-enabled networks could meet the latency requirements for either internal substation or external substation of power systems with reasonable strategies.

Table 1: Communication latency requirements for electric substation automation [10].

Information types	Internal substation	External substation
Protecting information	4 ms	8–12 ms
Monitoring and control information	16 ms	1 s
Operations and maintenance information	1 s	10 s
Text strings	2 s	10 s
Processed data files	10 s	30 s
Program files	1 min	10 min
Image files	10 s	1 min
Audio and video data streams	1 s	1 s

Table 2: Network latency in SDN-enabled communication network [11].

Operation type	Propagation latency/us	Processing latency/us	Queuing latency/us	Sending latency/us	Minimum total latency/ms
The simple transmission with single flow table	1000	10	$[0, \infty)$	10	1.02
The complex transmission with multiclass flow table	1000	500	$[0, \infty)$	10	1.51

There are two reasons contributing to the reduction of queue and cache latency. Firstly, compared with traditional IP-based networks, SDN-enabled networks greatly improve the speed of flow forwarding on account of the separation of control plane and data plane, which could considerably reduce processing latency. Secondly, with the global view, it is easier for the controller to deploy optimal strategies for congestion control and load balancing, which could greatly reduce the unpredictable latency produced by traffic burst and hence improve the stability and controllability of network latency. All these could be utilized to reduce the latency of communication network.

However, when forwarding new packets in an SDN-enabled network, the interactions between switches and controllers would produce extra latency. Especially when massive mice flows occur, frequent requesting to controllers will increase the round-trip time. Fortunately, the hierarchical framework proposed in this paper can greatly ease the burdens of global controllers. Recent work [18] shows that the hierarchical controller mode could lead to more than 90% events being processed locally, which makes the workload of global controllers go down to nearly 1/300 of that in normal OpenFlow networks, and the round-trip time is reduced.

In addition, there are plenty of strategies investigated to reduce the latency of SDN-enabled networks further, such as CheetahFlow [27], DIFANE [28], DevoFlow [29], and FlowShadow [30]. Mice flows account for a large portion of the total number of flows usually corresponding to the most important information in power grid, such as protection and control information. CheetahFlow is a forecasting scheme which can install flow entries to the switches proactively on the basis of historical communication records to reduce setup latency. This scheme is expert in reducing extra latency in SDN via forwarding most of the flows in terms of the advanced rules in data plane without asking for the decision of the controllers. When a mess of mice flows occur, the controller would be frequently invoked and the network performance would be apparently impaired. It applies SVM (Support Vector Machine) to identify frequent communication pairs with high accuracy. Then the forwarding rules with the shortest paths between frequent pairs will be installed in advance, which is of great significance in power systems due to the existence of numerous frequent and significant pairs, such as energy controllers and transformers.

5.2. Reliability

Reliability is another challenge of IP-based networks, which is important for power systems. Fortunately, with the development of SDN, various flow optimization and congestion control technologies have been proposed and many simulations of latency for SDN have also been done [31]. As depicted above, the distributed global controllers are conductive to avoid single point failures, and SDN-enabled fast recovery from failures also makes great contribution in avoiding congestion and packet loss.

In general, the recovery process in communication network could be divided into two steps: the failure detection and network recovery. Firstly, credible failure detection is the basis of the whole recovery process. Multiple efficient protocols and schemes on failure detection have been established, such as BFD (Bidirectional Forwarding Detection) [32] and OpenFlow Fast Failover Group Table [33]. The BFD protocol is successfully used in providing fast and low-cost failure detection for higher-plane control protocols, with a speed of millisecond level. The OpenFlow Fast Failover Group Table, supported in OpenFlow switches and independent of the controllers, could be configured to monitor the state of ports and interfaces, as well as switch forwarding actions accordingly.

Secondly, network recovery is usually complex and time-consuming in both traditional IP-based network and SDN-enabled networks. Plenty of work, contributing to the reduction of recovery latency, has been done up to now. Meanwhile multiple SDN-enabled fast recovery schemes have shown great potential. For instance, when failures are detected, the recovery process proposed in [33] could be divided into two steps: the switch-initiated recovery based on preconfigured backup path pairs to guarantee end-to-end connectivity and the controller-initiated recovery based on new optimal paths calculated by controllers. This fast failover scheme realizes the fastest recovery time of 3.3 ms through combining preconfigured backup paths and fast link failure detection in SDN, which shows an enormous improvement compared to present average recovery time varying from 28.2 to 48 ms.

6. TESTBED AND EXPERIMENTAL RESULTS

The performance of flexibility brought by SDN is obvious; thus we verify the latency and reliability in this section. In our proposed hierarchical communication network framework, the global grid level communication network is composed of several microgrid cluster level communication networks. As the microgrid is the basic unit of energy Internet, in this section, we consider a single microgrid scenario where information terminals of energy devices communicate with each other through three OpenFlow switches managed by one controller. If the latency and reliability of the communication network are ensured, the performance of communication network in energy Internet could be ensured evidently. Therefore, a testbed based on communication network of microgrid is built and experimental results are presented.

6.1. Testbed Implementation

A typical microgrid is implemented, which contains AC and DC loads, renewable energy resources, and energy storage devices. Meanwhile, based on the physical energy infrastructure, a SDN-enabled communication network which consists of a SDN domain controller, several OpenFlow switches, and a large number of information terminals is also established as shown in Figure 8. In this testbed, SDN controller Floodlight, which could provide a Web GUI for network operator, is implemented on a server which has physical links with switches. The information terminals of energy devices communicate with each other by sending ICMP packets. Three x86 PC modules installed with 64-bit Ubuntu 12.04.3, 3.8.0-25-generic Linux Kernel and OpenvSwitch2.3.0 are used as SDN switches. Each switch is equipped with 2-core 1.8 GHz Intel Celeron 1037U CPU, 2 G RAM, and 6 Intel PCI-E 1000 M network interface cards. To easily configure network parameters, all devices are set in the same network segment 192.168.1.x. When switches and information terminals get connected with controller, the state of network will be displayed on Web GUI.

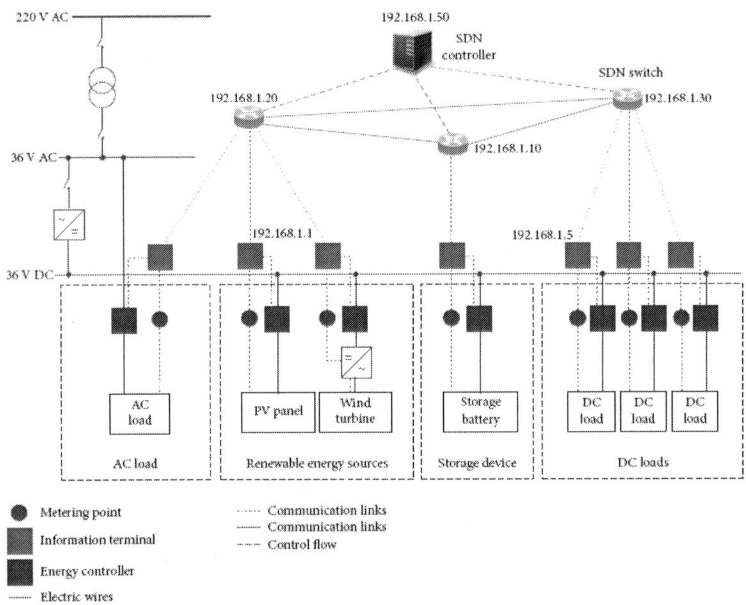

Figure 8: Implementation of testbed for communication network of microgrid.

6.2. Experimental Results

(1) Latency. First of all, the mode of OpenvSwitch is set to standalone, which means, without a controller, the switch could forward packets in a traditional way. Thus, as illustrated in Figure 9(a), the average RTT

between two information terminals is measured and calculated, respectively, in proposed SDN-enabled framework and traditional communication network framework. If the SDN controller is shut down, the proposed SDN-enabled network framework will turn into traditional network framework. With the proposed framework, it is obvious that packets always have a lower latency less than 1 ms except for the first one. The reason is that the switch does not know how to forward packets by optimal routing path for the first time, until the controller discovers the links among switches and sends flow tables to the switches along the routing path, which introduces extra latency in this discovery and delivery process. Our results also coincide with the measurements in [27, 29]. Meanwhile, the latency of packets with the traditional network framework is a little bit higher than that with the proposed network framework. It is because each switch acts as a regular MAC-learning switch when the controller cannot be contacted. In addition, compared with traditional network framework, the delay jitter of SDN-enabled network framework is lower.

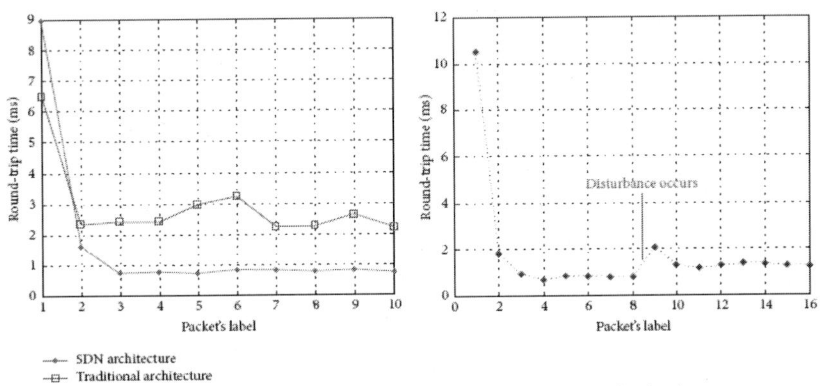

Figure 9: Round-trip time of SDN-enabled network.

(2) Reliability. Reliability of communication networks plays a significant role in ensuring the stability of energy Internet. The SDN-enabled network has an inherent advantage in enhancing communication network reliability as infrastructure sharing could be easily implemented by the SDN controller. When disturbance occurs in a communication link, the packets transmitted via this path will be forwarded by switches according to the flow table delivered from the controller. As depicted in Figure 9(b), when the link between switch 2 (with IP address 192.168.1.20) and switch 3

(with IP address 192.168.1.30) is disturbed, the communication link will recover fast and the RTT increases slightly with packets forwarded by switch 1 (with IP address 192.168.1.10). Such fast recovery mechanism is significant for the reliability of communication network in energy Internet, especially for the transmission of energy control and monitor information.

7. CONCLUSION AND FUTURE WORK

In this paper, we have summarized the state-of-the-art development for energy Internet in China and analyzed the requirements such as flexibility, latency, and reliability for communication networks in energy Internet. Then related work of communication network frameworks in energy Internet is discussed. Furthermore, a novel SDN-enabled hierarchical communication network framework for energy Internet is proposed. At last, performances such as latency and reliability of this novel communication network framework are verified by theoretical analyses and experiments. Actually, this proposed network framework could be applied in not only the power grid of China, but also other countries with hierarchical grid.

In our future work, specific methods and strategies related to security issues in this SDN-based framework will be investigated to support the development of energy Internet. Besides the latency and reliability analyzed above, security is also significant for communication networks in energy Internet. With the vast DG's access, the authentication and data protection for users and equipment become more vital and complex than before. Meanwhile, the security problems in SDN have already attracted widespread attention. SDN-enabled security schemes characterized by openness and intercommunity could make more advantageous performances compared with traditional physical isolation schemes. The centralization of control plane makes it possible to guarantee the global consistent security. The controller can also provide more fine-grained security control via configuring global security approaches from the network view. Hence, the SDN-enabled security schemes would be an effective approach for data protection in energy Internet.

CONFLICTS OF INTEREST

The authors declare that there are no conflicts of interest regarding the publication of this paper.

REFERENCES

1. N. Golmie, A. Scaglione, L. Lampe, and E. Yeh, "Guest editorial - Smart grid communications," IEEE Journal on Selected Areas in Communications, vol. 30, no. 6, pp. 1025-1026, 2012.
2. Q. Huang and J. Baliga, "FREEDM System: Role of power electronics and power semiconductors in developing an energy internet," in Proceedings of the 21st International Symposium on Power Semiconductor Devices and IC's, pp. 9–12, IEEE, Barcelona, Spain, June 2009.
3. Smart Grid System Report, United States Department of Energy, Washington DC, August 2014.
4. Federation of German Industries (BDI), Internet of Energy: ICT for Energy Markets of the Future, vol. 29, Berlin, Germany, December 2008.
5. J. Boyd, "An internet-inspired electricity grid," IEEE Spectrum, vol. 50, no. 1, pp. 12–14, 2013.
6. Z. Liu, Global Energy Internet, China Electric Power Press, Beijing, China, February 2015.
7. K. Katsaros, W. Chai, N. Wang, G. Pavlou, H. Bontius, and M. Paolone, "Information-centric networking for machine-to-machine data delivery: A case study in smart grid applications," IEEE Network, vol. 28, no. 3, pp. 58–64, 2014.
8. A. Macana, N. Quijano, and E. Mojica-Nava, "A survey on cyber physical energy systems and their applications on smart grids," in Proceedings of the 2011 IEEE PES Conference on Innovative Smart Grid Technologies Latin America, ISGT LA 2011, col, October 2011.
9. N. Bui, A. P. Castellani, P. Casari, and M. Zorzi, "The internet of energy: a web-enabled smart grid system," IEEE Network, vol. 26, no. 4, pp. 39–45, 2012. 2004.
10. Y. Lyu, "Chuanhe Huang, Yonghong Jia, , Simulation of switchs processing delay in software defined network," Journal of Computer Network and Applications, vol. 34, no. 9, pp. 2472–2475, 2014.
11. Q. Wu, Z. Li, J. Zhou et al., "SOFIA: Toward service-oriented information centric networking," IEEE Network, vol. 28, no. 3, pp. 12–18, 2014.
12. J.-W. Cao, Y.-X. Wan, and G.-Y. Tu, "Information system architecture for smart grids," Chinese Journal of Computers, vol. 36, no. 1, pp. 143–167, 2013.
13. Z. Jianchao, S. Boon-Chong, L. Tek-Tjing, and F. Chuan Heng, "Opportunities for software-defined networking in smart grid," in Proceedings of the 9th International Conference on Information, Communications and Signal Processing, ICICS 2013, twn, December 2013.
14. J. Rubio-Loyola, A. Galis, A. Astorga et al., "Scalable service deployment on software-defined networks," IEEE Communications Magazine, vol. 49, no. 12, pp. 84–93, 2011.
15. W. Xia, Y. Wen, C. H. Foh, D. Niyato, and H. Xie, "A survey on software-defined networking," IEEE Communications Surveys & Tutorials, vol. 17, no. 1, pp. 27–51, 2015.
16. Z. Wei, S. Yu, G. Sun, Y. Sun, Y. Yuan, and D. Wang, "The Concept and Development of Virtual Power Plants," Automation of Electric Power Systems, vol. 37, no. 13, pp. 1–3, 2013.
17. S. Hassas Yeganeh and Y. Ganjali, "Kandoo: a framework for efficient and scalable offloading of control applications," in Proceedings of the Proceeding of the 1st ACM International Workshop on Hot Topics in Software Defined Networks (HotSDN '12), pp. 19–24, New York, NY, USA, August 2012.
18. R. Vilalta, A. Mayoral, J. Baranda et al., "Hierarchical SDN orchestration of wireless and optical networks with E2E provisioning and recovery for future 5G networks," in Proceedings of the Optical Fiber Communications Conference and Exhibition, OFC, pp. 1–3, IEEE, USA, March 2016.
19. J. S. Choi and X. Li, "Hierarchical distributed topology discovery protocol for multi-domain SDN networks," IEEE Communications Letters, vol. 21, no. 4, pp. 773–776, 2017.
20. J.-J. Huang, Y.-Y. Chen, C. Chen, and Y. H. Chu, "Weighted routing in hierarchical multi-domain SDN controllers," in Proceedings of the 17th Asia-Pacific Network Operations and Management Symposium, APNOMS 2015, pp. 356–359, kor, August 2015.

21. Y. Liu, A. Hecker, R. Guerzoni, Z. Despotovic, and S. Beker, "On optimal hierarchical SDN," in Proceedings of the IEEE International Conference on Communications, ICC 2015, pp. 5374–5379, gbr, June 2015.
22. Li, The Design of Realization of Routing Algorithm in SDN, Beijing University of Posts and Telecommunications, Beijing, China, 2016.
A. Tootoonchian and Y. Ganjali, "HyperFlow: A distributed control plane for OpenFlow," in Proceedings of the Internet Network Management Conference, Research on Enterprise Networking, April 2010.
23. T. Koponen, M. Casado, N. Gude et al., "Onix: a distributed control platform for large-scale production networks," in Proceedings of the Operating Systems Design and Implementation, pp. 351–364, The ACM, Vancouver, BC, Canada, 2010.
24. W. Wang, Y. Xu, and M. Khanna, "A survey on the communication architectures in smart grid," Computer Networks, vol. 55, no. 15, pp. 3604–3629, 2011.
25. Z. Su, T. Wang, Y. Xia, and M. Hamdi, "CheetahFlow: Towards low latency software-defined network," in Proceedings of the 2014 1st IEEE International Conference on Communications, ICC 2014, pp. 3076–3081, aus, June 2014.
26. M. Yu, J. Rexford, M. J. Freedman, and J. Wang, "Scalable flow-based networking with DIFANE," in Proceedings of the 7th International Conference on Autonomic Computing, SIGCOMM 2010, pp. 351–362, ind, September 2010.
A. R. Curtis, J. C. Mogul, J. Tourrilhes, P. Yalagandula, P. Sharma, and S. Banerjee, "DevoFlow: Scaling flow management for high-performance networks," in Proceedings of the ACM SIGCOMM, pp. 254–265, New York, NY, USA, August 2011.
27. Y. Wang, D. Tai, T. Zhang et al., "Flowshadow: A fast path for uninterrupted packet processing in SDN switches," in Proceedings of the 11th ACM/IEEE Symposium on Architectures for Networking and Communications Systems, ANCS 2015, pp. 205-206, usa, May 2015.
28. P. T. Congdon, P. Mohapatra, M. Farrens, and V. Akella, "Simultaneously reducing latency and power consumption in openflow switches," IEEE/ACM Transactions on Networking, vol. 22, no. 3, pp. 1007–1020, 2014.
29. Katz and D. Ward, "Bidirectional Forwarding Detection (BFD)," (Proposed Standard) RFC5880, Internet Engineering Task Force, 2010.
30. N. L. M. Van Adrichem, B. J. Van Asten, and F. A. Kuipers, "Fast recovery in software-defined networks," in Proceedings of the 3rd European Workshop on Software-Defined Networks, EWSDN 2014, pp. 61–66, hun, September 2014.

CHAPTER 13

Cyberspace as a new arena for terroristic propaganda: an updated examination

Elizabeth Minei 1 and Jonathan Matusitz2

1. University of OklahomaNormanUSA

2. Seminole State CollegeUniversity of Central Florida, Partnership Center (#UP 3009)SanfordUSA

ABSTRACT

This paper analyzes the role of propaganda use in cyberterrorism. The main premise is that cyberterrorists display various semiotic gestures (e.g., the use of images and Internet videos) to communicate their intents to the public at large. In doing so, they communicate themes—these themes range from hate to anger. Cyberterrorism, then, is a form of theater or spectacle in which terrorists exploit cyberspace to trigger feelings of panic and overreaction in the target population. In many cases, this form of propaganda is the primary means of communication for various cyberterrorist groups to convey their intents. Internet sites also produce numerous opportunities for in-group communication and publicity.

1. INTRODUCTION

In this paper, the role of propaganda use in cyberterrorism is being analyzed. The main premise is that cyberterrorists display various propagandist gestures (e.g., through the use of images and Internet videos) to communicate their intents to the public at large. In doing so, they communicate themes—these themes range from hate to anger. Cyberterrorism, then, is a form of theater or spectacle in which terrorists exploit cyberspace to trigger feelings of panic and overreaction in the target population. In many cases, this form of propaganda is the primary means of communication for various cyberterrorist groups to convey their intents. Internet sites also produce numerous opportunities for in-group communication and publicity. This analysis fills a gap in research on both propaganda and cyberterrorism in that the vast majority of studies on terrorism propaganda, so far, have focused on traditional terrorism, but very little on cyberterrorism (Steuter and Wills 2009).

In this analysis, the first section offers general perspectives on cyberterrorism. As such, the authors describe cyberterrorism, its origins, and the various forms and techniques used by cyber attackers. Also provided in this section is a short explanation of the function of semiotics in cyberterrorism. What comes subsequently is the heart of the present analysis: an examination of propaganda use in cyberterrorism. It begins with historical perspectives of propaganda use; then, it delves into specific cases of propagandist gestures with respect to cyberterrorist acts. For instance, following the London bombings in 2005, "The Martyrdom Will of Mohammad Sidique Khan" became a viral video launched by a Muslim cyberterrorist group. Another example is that of Irhabi007, an attacker playing cat-and-mouse games with authorities through his websites. The next-to-last section of this analysis examines a case study of cyberterrorist propaganda—specifically, a propagandist act of the World Fantabulous Defacers (WFD)—by using semiotics and explains how the cyberterrorist act works both as a symbol and as terrorism. This analysis ends with a discussion section that also offers suggestions for future research.

1.1 General perspectives on cyberterrorism

This section describes cyberterrorism, the origin of the word and the various forms and techniques used by cyber attackers. It also provides a short explanation of the function of semiotics in cyberterrorism.

1.1.1 Cyberterrorism: definition

In order to understand the full scope of how destructive and powerful cyberterrorism can be, it is important to gain a basic understanding of the actual word. The word "cyberterrorism" comes from the portmanteau of "cyberspace" (i.e., the makeup of data, algorithms, and computer networks) and "terrorism" (i.e., premeditated, politically motivated violence committed against innocent persons or noncombatants)

(Conway 2002; Deutsch 1997). Cyberterrorism, in and of itself, is a method of attack designed to damage, tamper with, or destroy critical points of national infrastructure by controlling and manipulating computer networks (Denning 1999, 2000; Libicki 2009; Sloan 2006). The prefix "cyber" suggests that this type of terrorism occurs throughout cyberspace and is, in turn, accessible through computers (Conway 2002). The basic premise of traditional terrorism is the threat, or the actual use of violence against people or property, with the intention of inflicting enough harm to garner attention, create fear, and influence decision-making (Sloan 1981). A different concept than conventional crime, terrorism has roots in strong ideological motives, often with a goal of imposing principles and beliefs by illegal and violent means (Axelrod and Nicoletti 2009).

Though most instances of cyberterrorism occur through Internet use, it is important to recognize that the lesser utilized mechanisms of the telephone also play a role in conducting denial-of-service attacks (i.e., D.O.S. attacks), which render computer networks inaccessible, inoperable, or ineffectual, thus easing the transmission and distribution of propaganda by the attacker (Howard 2009). One such example of a D.O.S. attack would be a victim who is injured attempting to get help by dialing 911, only to be met with continuous dropped phone calls or just a dead line (Brown 2006). In causing attacks, a cyberterrorist has access to any given nation vulnerable to attacks of a grand scale. What this means is that irreparable damage can be caused due to a nation's heavy reliance on critical infrastructure that is rooted in computer networks (Lewis 2002). Using a universal weapon as seemingly harmless as the computer, cyberterrorists have at their fingertips a medium that allows them to cause great damage with minor consequence (Gorge 2007). Files can be stolen and corrupted, computer viruses can be spread, and these are all due to the easy access provided by the Internet. In some cases, a multiplied threat exists when the attacker is a former employee, familiar with the computer network, and wishing to cause harm (Misra 2003). The destruction of websites, knowingly crashing selected networks, causing denial of service in crisis situations, spreading malicious computer viruses, causing physical destruction and tampering with financial interactions, all while inducing panic and causing psychological harm to targets, are all utilized methods commonly known as information warfare (Paul 2008).

This form of attack holds greater appeal than that of the conventional methods used in the past for many reasons. For example, the costs of such an attack greatly diminish when, all things considered, the equipment needed for such an attack does not go beyond that of a computer and an online connection rather than the traditional weapons of guns or bombs used in terror situations of the past (Weimann 2005). Previous examples of traditional terrorist attacks (carried out in real time) required massive amounts of organized locations in which attackers utilized software such as robotic networks that globally hijack any number of targets and render them helpless (Aaviksoo 2008). It is precisely this lack of physical presence in regard to a target that provides a foundation for the rationale behind why cyberterrorism is a preferred method.

A high level of anonymity comes with a lack of borders, barriers, and authority that leaves an attacker virtually without consequence to target anyone or anything across the globe (Weimann 2005). This notion reflects the idea that crimes committed via computers are of a global nature in which unleashing worms and viruses that steal information are not limited on a small scale, but can occur between entire countries and nations when attackers are given free rein to commit crimes internationally, against individuals, corporations, and governments (Cassell 2006). Western infrastructures have been a primary target; so have highly populated areas, which will remain primary venues that become susceptible to attacks (Gunaratna 2005). Combined with the notion that cyberterrorism is both inexpensive and anonymous, as well as remote, an attacker is not forced into physically demanding high-risk situations; nor do they have to be as crafty to outwit security systems (Weimann 2005).

The rationale for the occurrence of cyberterrorism has included that of political motivation (Baudrillard 2002). When emblematic western infrastructures such as banks, hotels, and utilities are considered, the sheer volume of targets becomes endless, causing the focus for an attacker to switch to a strategic nature, where the motivation for an attack is fueled by the amount of damage that can be done (Gunaratna 2005). An appealing factor in the equation of cyberterrorism is that the attacks are conducted from a location removed from the target (Weimann 2005). An attacker can handpick a target based on vulnerability in various areas of government, health, commerce, and utilities (Brown 2006). Examples that fall under the assertion of causing damage from a remote location could be that of an attacker opening a dam and releasing flood waters, causing a nuclear power plant meltdown, or causing an oil pipeline to burst (Brownlie 1963). Because these utilities are run on complex computer systems, there is a vulnerability that is easy for an attacker to penetrate and exploit (Weimann 2005). For this reason, the shift from traditional methods of attack to the more modern form of cyberterrorism is appealing because physical demands are diminished, the risk of death decreases, and the amount of time contributed by an attacker has less of a psychological effect. This, in turn, eases the burden for terror organizations to maintain the number of members dedicated to the cause (Weimann 2005).

Lastly, and most importantly, there is a media motivational aspect for attackers (Weimann 2005). As a concrete example of the motivation derived from media attention, in cases such as the I LOVE YOU virus, a virus that caused an estimated $10 billion in damages on 350,000 computers in over 20 different countries (Deal, Gage and Schueneman 2001), the media coverage garnered from that incident was larger in volume than could be expected had the incident occurred in one place (Subramanya and Lakshminarasimhan 2001). When each incident is covered with such depth by the media, an inflated sense of importance and meaning is attributed to each attack.

1.1.2 Cyberterrorism: a semiotic perspective

Cyberterrorist acts can be carried out through the Internet, a public communication channel. Cyberterrorism is publicized and propagated via new media communication. Consequently, it is fundamentally through semiotics and the exploitation of new media that cyberterrorists find success in achieving their chief goals. Semiotics is the study of signs (Berger 1989; Chandler 2002; Luskin 1996; Nöth 1995; Sebeok 1994). A sign is something that stands for something else or that can be created to represent something else (Deely 1990; Peirce 1934). The Internet is a sign system; it is an astronomical assemblage of codes and images thanks to which users can construct meanings and symbols. According to semioticians, humans do not face a "simple" objective reality. Rather, what humans see are signs and symbols within a communication framework, whereby the communication of messages is deemed quintessential to the creation of meaning (Fiske 1982). From this vantage point, meaning is not absolute; nor is it static. Meaning is an active process subject to constant transformation (Benford 1998).

Now that there is a foundation for understanding exactly what cyberterrorism is and the scope—both concrete and symbolic—it encompasses, a focus on the communicative aspect is warranted. It is not enough to know that these attacks are occurring. One must seek to uncover not only the method of communication, but also the meaning behind the communication. One note to mention when attempting to analyze the "intent" of another is the very concept of "intent." When talking about motives, one must keep in mind that such a concept is intangible and as such will be immeasurable. As scholars who are not exactly certain of the exact motive behind the actions of an individual, we must examine overall behavior to tease out patterns and analyze the symbolic meaning behind those actions. In doing so, an understanding of propaganda is needed to place symbolic meaning in context.

1.2 Uses of propaganda: general perspectives

Throughout the vast history of war, there have been many documented cases in which propaganda has been used as a catalyst for empowering terror organizations and providing them motivation for large-scale operations or attacks. By definition, propaganda is a mode of communication aiming at swaying the attitude of people toward some cause (Bernays and Miller 2004). For example, propaganda ignited motivation during wartime to increase membership in the armed forces (Lasswell 1971). It was also used as a means of trickery (Krippendorff and Bock 2008), as a way to or to gain a tactical advantage against the enemy (George 1959) or, most importantly, as a way to dehumanize the enemy by creating a realm of "the other" (Keen 1991). Verton (2003) explains that al-Qaeda cells now operate with the assistance of large databases containing details of potential targets in the US. They use the Internet to collect intelligence on those targets, especially critical economic nodes, and modern software enables them to study structural weaknesses in facilities as well as predict the cascading failure effect of attacking certain systems (p. 109).

This Internet-based approach is considered postmodern, where the premise is that communication is directionless and leadership is not needed, nor does it exist (Matusitz 2008a, b). The Internet serves as the perfect medium for the trajectory of the modern terrorist: the cyberterrorist. While the tool (the Internet) has been indentified, previous research by Conway (2002) and Weimann (2006) shows that primary means of communication, intentional or otherwise, between cyberterrorist and their targets happen through a variety of employed propaganda. Jowell and O'Donnell (2006) state that "propaganda is the deliberate, systematic attempt to shape perceptions, manipulate cognitions, and direct behavior to achieve a response that furthers the desired intent of the propagandist" (p. 7).

The portrayal of the "other" (i.e., enemy) through propaganda is a method in which negative messages become continuously perpetuated. As such, the formation of in-groups occurs, which allows for beliefs and expectations to form and laws to emerge that dictate how the enemy is portrayed. Once these perceptions of an enemy form, they add motivation behind an attack (Keen 1991). When there is talk about "the other," entire cultures become faceless, nameless, feeling-less entities that are the target of violence, and hate (Keen 1991). The language used in World War II propaganda consisted of "us" versus "them" mentality messages with terms such as "Commie bear," "Nazi Swine," and "Dog of Capitalism" (Keen 1991, p. 86), all of which dehumanize a given target. Because the use of propaganda is so powerful, it is important to understand how these various types of propaganda are effective, exactly what types are available for use and what is the driving force behind that power.

In regards to the question of power, Keen (1991) suggests that propagandist messages involve certain influential indicators that influence the subconscious psyche of a culture. To begin, it is essential to recognize the media as a strong and prominent outlet for terrorists to communicate propaganda (Cowen 2006). Another prominent medium in which propaganda is used as a means of communication is through the Internet (Hoffman 2003). A traditional method of terrorist communication previously employed was the use of video as a quick and effective method of relaying terrorist messages. In addition to the main focus of the use of video being a cheap and easy means of distributing propaganda for their cause, a more aggressive and destructive utilization of propaganda using the computer and Internet is through virus spreading (Weimann 2006). In the first half of 2005, documented worldwide cyber attacks from viruses reached a recorded 237, a 50 % increase from the same time period, 1 year earlier (Hoopes 2005).

Propaganda that follows the traditional model instructs an attacker to spend time effectively gathering intelligence on specific targets as a way to ensure that the maximum amount of damage that could possibly occur actually comes to fruition in each incident (Mathieu 2007). Certain tactics that are put into place start with extensive target analysis, intelligence gathering, and a network of command and control are considered necessities when attacking a target. All of these are designed to utilize many different directions to assault a target (Desouza and Hensgen 2003). The merging of traditional methods of attack with modern ones can be reflected in the way cyberterrorists pinpoint targets through the use of computers and by way of propaganda, recruitment, collection of data and information gathering, and member-to-member communication—through forums and videos via the Internet (Weimann 2006). An even more in-depth scope of these computer-based activities includes message posting, launching campaigns of a psychological nature, gathering information on potential targets, allowing for the synchronization of agendas and actions, allotting funds to specific areas, and using videos to conduct virtual terror training (Tzfati and Weimann 2002).

Continuing on with the understanding of the role of the media in current terrorist operations, it has been recognized that the media can manipulate and form desired images in respect to the minds of the public (Laqueur 2006). The example of the I LOVE YOU virus was a prime opportunity for media coverage on a massive scale. Such immense media coverage empowers terrorist organizations and provides motivation for continued attacks. Publicity and media are considered a necessity in the world of cyberterrorism, outlining two of the primary themes in the motivation of the attackers. Jenkins (1975) proposes that

propaganda terrorist attacks are often carefully choreographed to attract the attention of the electronic media and the international press. Taking and holding hostages increases the drama. The hostages themselves often mean nothing to the terrorists. Terrorism is aimed at the people watching, not at the actual victims. Terrorism is a theater (p. 4).

With the suggestion of the motives of terrorism rooted in theatrics, it is akin to suggesting that to be recognized in a highly visible and memorable way is the purpose for the attack, qualities that are often attributed to media coverage (Cowen 2006). What is meant by terrorism "as theater" or Debord's (2005) terrorism "as spectacle" is not an exclusive activity reserved only for a selected group, rather a particular and precise display intended for an audience from one end of the spectrum to the other; much like a sporting event or a performance (Cowen 2006). These "theatrical" qualities—lack of regulation, easy access, vast range of audiences, and rapid information transfer—have allowed the goals of terrorists to be achieved, an increasingly attractive option when terror via the Internet allows for easy causing of damage with decreased fear of getting caught (Rogers 2003). Terrorist messages such as these are clearly heard worldwide due to well-developed and well-dispersed media contacts (Kim et al. 2002).

Similarly, Internet sites produce numerous opportunities for in-group communication and publicity, documenting a trend that encapsulates cause for organizations (Arquilla and Ronfeldt 2001a, b; Arquilla, Ronfeldt and Zanini 1999). The US State Department generated a list of terrorist organizations that confirmed that at least half of the known listed organizations have websites that are used for the solicitation of money and membership as well as a way for coded messages to make its way among group members (Gordon and Ford 2002). Internet provides the luxury of nonphysical contact with another member of the group where new recruits can become affiliated and commit to carrying out terrorist attacks, never actually leaving the comfort of home. In short, the use of propaganda has become the standard norm among terror groups (Harmon 2001).

Terrorist organizations require backing from supporters in the areas of both recruiting for membership and funding in order to continue to operate. Another use for propaganda is to discredit enemies (in the form of creating "the other") all while placing the organizations in a positive light. Traditional propaganda techniques such as leaflets and publications in newspapers have now been replaced by the use of websites for financial backing and membership recruiting (Wright 1991). These leaflets and newspapers are truly an artifact of the past with the United

States Department of State reported as early as 1999, that over one-third of the known Foreign Terrorist Organization (FTOs) had their own website (McGirk 1999).

1.3 Uses of propaganda: examples of cyberterrorist groups

Popular radical groups of international significance such as Hezbollah, the Lebanese-based Shi'ite Islamic group (Conway 2002), operate Internet sites and use this outlet for various purposes such as posting articles or agendas of upcoming events, or to publish recently filmed videos, which can be accessed by anybody in the global cyber community (Deutsch 1996). Cyberterrorist organizations also feature disappearing and reappearing message boards and websites (Weimann 2006). One attacker, playing cat-and-mouse games with authorities through his websites, known as Irhabi007, emerged over the Internet as a leader of an online terrorist organization. His signature included online videos with instructions for home-made car bombs, and he also led forums criticizing American foreign policy, only to take them down and repost or list them under a different domain name (Fulghum 2005).

In November of 2005, as a tribute to a suicide bomber involved in the attacks on London, a full-length propaganda video entitled "The Martyrdom Will of Mohammad Sidique Khan" was posted by another terrorist group known as Sahaab—an arm of al-Qaeda—launched on the now-unresponsive website, www.as-sahaab.com. The video bore unassailable similarities to Irhabi007's fundamental Islamist message board that had recently disappeared prior to the attack (Kohlmann 2006). Copycat websites playing the same cat-and-mouse games began to spring up after Irhabi007's capture in 2005, with messages such as the following: "The enemies of Allah will continuously [try to close down] our website ... We ask you to register for our mailing list so that you continue to receive the latest news of the Islamic Army in Iraq." This post urged followers to continue their membership with the organization, despite seemingly inoperable websites (Kohlmann 2006).

Ultimately causing violent methods of destruction, Internet messages communicated between those cyberterrorist groups display consistent themes ranging from hate to anger (Talbot 2005). Attackers need a starting place. In order to inflict the most damage possible, an attacker needs to research various potential for damage in the process of building a target profile (Mathieu 2007). In order to utilize the Internet to its fullest extent, cyberterrorists can access a multitude of international areas and databases that contain sensitive information, such as libraries. Starting with access to legally obtained information, through legitimate search engines such as Google, attackers can gather information in the form of maps, satellite images, uploaded pictures and videos, and other texts available in seemingly harmless and innocent ways available in a public domain (Paul 2008). Browsing the Internet to gain information allows attackers to start building profiles against targets using simple resources that are also very much legal. Once the information-gathering process on a target has been completed and is recorded, an attacker can then use the Internet as a channel for carrying out the attack. The Internet, by way of computers, is the main tool available for assailants to coordinate and communicate on the method of attack (Paul 2008).

Encryption programs can be implemented to cover any harmful wrongdoing that could potentially be exposed throughout the course of the operation and, as this is being done, a system of hidden messages can be put into place (Paul 2008). Many of these messages range content-wise going so far to include instructions, step-by-step illustrated renderings of how an attack should be carried out, and detailed communicated plans enclosed in a secure network that requires a designated password to access. US Military computers have shown evidence of being a popular and frequent target by attackers. In 1998, cyberterrorists cracked into computers used by the Pentagon, using these methods of attack, and downloaded technical materials sensitive in nature (Lenzner and Vardi 2007). After a federal investigation, the source of the attacks proved to be a Moscow-based series of dial-up connections. The investigation, dubbed Moonlight Maze, was ineffective in catching the attackers.

The success of the terrorist group is directly correlated with keeping membership levels at a maximum, and as such, multiple methods of recruiting new members are a major focal point in the propaganda-based messages that are employed (Liu 2000). In past efforts to increase membership among groups, traditional methods of recruitment, such as published written work, audio–video tapes, CDs, and even local prayer leaders, have been employed as a means of promoting the cause (Paul 2008). The Internet, an updated and modern element of global terrorism, is emerging with websites and electronic forums that are used to spread ideological messages and provide hyperlinks between current operatives in cyberspace in addition to sharing graphic images depicting previous successes as a call to action for potential new members (Cronin 2006). In some instances, donations from sponsors or patrons are requested for those who wish to be supportive without being directly involved (Cronin 2006). The content of the websites offer a lesson on the history of the organization, and the cause the organization supports with the intent of enticing new members to join (Paul 2008). These websites also provide a venue for cyberterrorists to plan attacks by using a variety of methods that could not be achieved through other means.

The use of video provides another powerful arena utilized by terrorists. Video has been a vital part in the process of propaganda that is cheap and globally accessible (Weimann 2006). Films depicting anything from the morale-boosting success of radical fighters to the more macabre and disconcerting videos of executions, ambushes, and roadside bombings have emerged at a steady and continuous pace, being systematically distributed across the world (Kohlmann 2006). Terrorist group Zarqawi's media chief, Abu Mayasara, displays the power of online videos when he posted, in a forum, an online insurgent video of high-ranking members of Zarqawi's organization beheading American businessman Nicholas Berg (Glasser and Coll 2005). Mere weeks after that video was posted, additional copycat beheading videos trying to achieve the same gruesome effect as Zarqawi's conquest and dozens of new unidentified Arabic-language message boards appeared rapidly on radical Islamist websites across the Internet (Kohlmann 2006).

The main difference in film distribution, to compare past methods to present day, is that in previous years, the videos, produced and distributed in traceable brick-and-mortar establishments, allowed for easy identification and easy prosecution of offenders, whereas present-day operations are postmodern and join Internet access with software designed for video editing and virtually untraceable upload capabilities (Kohlmann 2006).

In addition to easy access and virtual inability to be traced back to any one criminal, an appeal for the use of propaganda lies heavily in the ability to induce fear on a grand scale, affecting a multitude of people. Participants who were exposed to clips of terrorism and threats to national security developed higher anxiety than those who were not exposed to such clips, according to one study (Slone 2000). Perfidy or betrayal is an applicable outcome to the use of videos that rely on deceitful methods because of a reliance on outcomes that are psychologically damaging, allowing for a tactical advantage to be achieved (Dinstein 2004). Damaging and deceitful perfidy could be explained in a more detailed manner in regard to video, when the false construction or the blatant alteration of images or recordings occurs specifically to make a false claim against a party (Army Field Manual 1956). By extension, videos communicate a message to members of an organization and are used for purposes of displaying examples of previous successful attacks on a grand scale.

Another example of the deceitful nature in the form of damaging messages communicated through video comes to light when a multitude of videos are altered to express meaning that had not been originally intended (Slone 2000). Documented cases have exhibited modified and forged footage, such as falsely spliced voice recordings that depict an enemy head of state issuing orders for war crimes, or digitally altered state uniforms that have been changed to resemble enemy attire (Shulman 1999). Tactics such as these create consequences that are short term and steeped in deceit of a political nature. The consequences that occur long term—that of increased fatalities, extended periods of war, and schisms in the restoration of peace—destroy any foundation of peace that have been gained previously (Army Field Manual 1956). Additionally, propaganda allows for the perpetuation of "the other," continuing the mindset of damaging nationalistic pride which "is the language of blood: a call to arms which can end in the horrors of ethnic cleansing" (Billig 1995, p. 48).

To date, evidence suggests that through means of technology—video, internet, and media coverage—messages through propaganda are worthy of mention because of the implications they carry from a communicative perspective. It has been suggested that restricted media coverage of terrorist attacks would in turn decrease the amount of terrorist attacks that occur afterward because a primary communicative intent—media coverage and recognition—was not being met (Cowen 2006). If this is the case, an interesting perspective to look for in the data would be the ties that connect the media, propaganda, and the communicative messages that are being conveyed.

1.4 Combining semiotics and propaganda in a case study of cyberterrorism

This section provides a semiotic analysis of a case study of cyberterrorist propaganda and gives an explanation as to how the cyberterrorist act works both as a symbol and as terrorism. The case study focuses on a propagandist act committed by the World Fantabulous Defacers (WFD). This organization is a Middle-Eastern alliance of 12 cyberterrorist groups strongly opposed to the Indian presence in Kashmir and the occupation of Palestine by Israel. They have been reported in the news for wreaking havoc on websites (Aparna, Bolli and Bock 2008). In 2002, WFD hacked into the official website of Israeli Prime Minister Ariel Sharon and defaced it, causing thousands of dollars in damage. As a title, they wrote, "The Face of the World's Biggest Murderer" (Verton 2003). They also inserted a dreadful picture of an injured Palestinian child and propagandist statements such as "Long Live Hizballah! Long Live Palestine! Long Live Chechnya, Kashmir, Kosovo, and Bosnia!" (Bunt 2003). At the bottom of the website, they incorporated a message with the signature of the group (Verton 2003).

The WFD's hacking into Sharon's official website illustrates the misdeed of a cyberterrorist group that had the capability to do far more damage and potentially create a national crisis in Israel (Verton 2003). Put simply, their misdeed constitutes a semiotic act encapsulated in messages and a horrific photo. By gaining such visibility, terrorists are now able to proliferate terror in cyberspace and evoke fear. While militant Palestinians blow up Israeli buildings, they can also use the Internet to cause harm to their enemies. This very attack was carried out by Palestinians sympathetic to their particular cause. Fear was generated and destruction was caused out of a political intent. The very act of defacing the Israeli Prime Minister's official website may have caused thousands of dollars in damage, but, according to Bunt (1999, 2003), another objective of WFD was to diffuse Islamic supremacy.

It is fundamentally through semiotics and the exploitation of new media that the World Fantabulous Defacers found success in spreading propaganda. Semiotics is a tool to decode signs, their meanings and associations, and their evolution. The evolution, in this case study, is translated in a shift from traditional propaganda to e-propaganda (Karagiannis and Wagner 2007). Mandaville (2001) identifies a significant relationship between the Internet and Islamism. He points to the digitalization of Islamic terrorism. The Internet, it seems, has become an inseparable tool of Islamism. On the bright side, semiotics can also be an efficient tool for scholars and experts to detect and defeat cyber threats (Desouza and Hensgen 2005).

2. RESULTS AND FUTURE DIRECTIONS

What this analysis has demonstrated is that cyberterrorists exploit diverse semiotic gestures, through the use of images and Internet videos, to communicate their intents to the public at large. In doing so, cyberterrorists communicate themes that range from hate to anger. From this vantage point, cyberterrorism is a form of theater or spectacle in which terrorists benefit from the endless opportunities that cyberspace offers to generate feelings of panic and overreaction in the target population. Cyberterrorism is a semiotic act; be it a message, a symbol, or an image on a website. Our computer-based universe is wrapped up with images, signs, and symbols. Truly, there is a powerful semiotic dimension to cyberterrorism.

So, through propagandist gestures and the use of various symbolic systems, cyberterrorists are capable of communicating their intents. The intent is to utilize any output necessary to play upon the fears to the public and by association, enhancing the power cyberterrorists wield. More specifically, this output is represented in coverage by the media generating increased attention and heightening the theatrical element behind each attack. Our society is wrapped up with images, signs, and symbols. Given this, there is a powerful semiotic dimension to cyberterrorism. Without a doubt, it can involve sending images of fear. We saw it with the cyberterrorist act committed by the World Fantabulous Defacers (WFD) in 2002. It is essentially by means of semiotics and the utilization of new media that WFD managed to successfully spread their propagandist messages. In like fashion, the full-length propaganda video entitled "The Martyrdom Will of Mohammad Sidique Khan" was posted by another terrorist group known as Sahaab—an arm of al-Qaeda—launched on the now-unresponsive website, www.as-sahaab.com. The creators of the video had one goal in mind: to instill feelings of panic in viewers, through powerful images (Kohlmann 2006).

Also demonstrated is a carefully crafted network of Internet savvy members of cyberterrorist organizations who communicate power and status through online video clips, websites, and through methods of destruction ranging from the malicious (denial of service) to the irreparably devastating (death). The motives of cyberterrorists are the same as those of conventional terrorists: to send images of fear. In the same way that terrorism is, first and foremost, a process of communication between terrorists and target audiences (Tuman 2003), a key objective of cyberterrorists is as old as the one by conventional terrorists: to send a powerful signal whose meaning is intended to frighten and to coerce.

The interesting notion, as mentioned before with the cat-and-mouse nature of Islamist cyberterrorist Irhabi007 (Kohlmann 2006), is that these terrorist websites are frequently put up and taken down so they can cause their damage and still be maintained for another day. The general scope for the use of websites is so vast that they provide a forum, or a safe haven for any level of content that a cyberterrorist feels is necessary to air to keep motivation for the cause intact, for reasons of member recruitment or to raise funds from supporters. While the primary goal of terrorism is a process of communication between terrorists and target audiences (Tuman 2003), cyberterrorism also seeks to send a powerful signal meant to frighten and coerce the target. This analysis detailed the various motivations behind small- and large-scale targets and the emotional aspects of fear for safety and lack of faith in the government that accrues from being targeted.

For future research, it might prove interesting to continue investigating the relationship between cyberterrorism and new media (i.e., Internet and other information technologies). Without the existence of these, cyberterrorism is doomed to failure. In fact, scholars should examine the two following questions: How different would cyberterrorism be without semiotics? And what would cyberterrorism be without Internet-facilitated propaganda? The use of communication technologies by cyberterrorists is an essential requirement for the success of their propagandist and semiotic gestures. In order to cause massive overreaction from the public, cyberterrorists rely on those new media to agitate the target population by exploiting images that, once produced, can be exploited again later and be re-used to new effect.

As we can see, cyberterrorism represents a mighty tool of communication, persuasion, and propaganda. Since billions of human beings are becoming increasingly interconnected through computers and the Internet, cyberspace creates both benefits and disadvantages for human communities. The danger of cyberterrorism is real; though it has been underestimated by many, it can add a great deal to our anxieties.

REFERENCES

1. Aaviksoo J (2008) Cyber-terrorism. Vital Speeches Day 74(1):28–32
2. Aparna R, Bolli M, Bock M (2008) Practice of war: production, reproduction and communication of armed violence. Berghahn Books, New York
3. Army Field Manual (1956) Department of the Army. Washington, DC
4. Arquilla J, Ronfeldt D (2001a) Networks and netwars: the future of terror, crime, and militancy. RAND, Santa Monica
5. Arquilla J, Ronfeldt DR (2001b) Networks, netwars, and the fight for the future. First Monday 6(10):1–25
6. Arquilla J, Ronfeldt D, Zanini M (1999) Networks, netwar and information-age terrorism. In: Lesser IO, Hoffman B, Arquilla J, Ronfeldt DF, Zanini M, Jenkins BM (eds) Countering the new terrorism. RAND, Santa Monica, pp 39–88
7. Axelrod EM, Nicoletti J (2009) Violence goes to the Internet: avoiding the snare of the net. Charles C. Thomas Publisher, Springfield, IL
8. Baudrillard J (2002) The spirit of terrorism and the requiem for the Twin Towers. Verso, New York
9. Benford G (1998) A scientist's notebook. Fantasy Sci Fict 95:117–128
10. Berger A (1989) Signs in contemporary culture. Sheffield, Salem, WI
11. Bernays E, Miller MC (2004) Propaganda. Ig Publishing, Brooklyn, NY
12. Billig M (1995) Banal nationalism. Sage, Thousand Oaks, CA
13. Brown D (2006) A proposal for an international convention to regulate the use of information systems in armed conflict. Harvard Int Law J 47(1):179–221
14. Brownlie I (1963) International law and the use of force by states. Clarendon Press, Oxford
15. Bunt G (1999) Virtually Islamic. University of Wales Press, Cardiff
16. Bunt G (2003) Islam in the digital age. Pluto Press, London
17. Cassell BL (2006) Criminal network: to catch crooks in cyberspace. Wall St J—Eastern Edition, p A1
18. Chandler D (2002) Semiotics: the basics. Routledge, New York
19. Conway M (2002) What is cyberterrorism? Curr Hist 2:436–440
20. Cowen T (2006) Terrorism as theater: analysis and policy implications. Public Choice 128(1):233–244
21. Cronin AK (2006) How al-Qaida ends: the decline and demise of terrorist groups. Int Secur 31(1):7–48
22. Deal C, Gage A, Schueneman R (2001) Viral contagia in cyberspace. Milit Rev 81(2):1–17

23. Deely J (1990) Basics of semiotics. Tartu University Press, Tartu
24. Denning DE (1999) Cyberterrorism. Testimony before the Special Oversight Panel on Terrorism Committee on Armed Services U.S. House of Representatives. Georgetown Town University, Washington, DC
25. Denning DE (2000) Hacktivism: an emerging threat to diplomacy. Foreign Serv J 1(1):10–17
26. Desouza KC, Hensgen T (2003) Technological forecasting and social change. Sci Direct 70(4):385–396
27. Desouza KC, Hensgen T (2005) Managing information in complex organizations: semiotics and signals, complexity and chaos. M. E. Sharpe, Armonk, NY
28. Deutsch JM (1996) Statement before the US Senate Governmental Affairs Committee. Permanent Subcommittee on Investigations, Washington, DC
29. Deutsch JM (1997) Terrorism. Foreign Policy 108:10–22
30. Dinstein Y (2004) The conduct of hostilities under the law of international armed conflict. Cambridge University Press, Cambridge
31. Fiske J (1982) Introduction to communication studies. Methuen, New York
32. Fulghum DA (2005) Aviation. Week Space Technol 163(16):1
33. George AL (1959) Propaganda analysis: a study of inferences made from Nazi propaganda in World War II. Row, Peterson & Co., Evanston, IL
34. Glasser SB, Coll S (2005) The web as weapon. Washington Post, p A10
35. Gordon S, Ford R (2002) Cyberterrorism? Comput Secur 21(7):636–647
36. Gorge M (2007) Cyberterrorism: hype or reality? Comput Fraud Secur 2:9–12
37. Gunaratna R (2005) The prospect of global terrorism. Society 42(6):31–35
38. Harmon CC (2001) Terrorism today. Frank Cass Publishers, London
39. Hoffman B (2003) Al Qaeda, trends in terrorism, and future potentialities: an assessment. Stud Confl Terrorism 26:427–440
40. Hoopes N (2005) New focus on cyber-terrorism. Christ Sci Monitor 97(184):1
41. Howard R (2009) Cyber fraud: tactics, techniques and procedures. Auerbach, New York
42. Jenkins B (1975) International terrorism. Crescent Publication, Los Angeles
43. Jowell G, O'Donnell V (2006) Propaganda and persuasion. Sage, Thousand Oaks, CA
44. Karagiannis N, Wagner P (2007) Varieties of world making: beyond globalization. Liverpool University Press, Liverpool
45. Keen S (1991) Faces of the enemy: reflections of the hostile imagination. Harper Collins, London
46. Kim S, Scheufele DA, Shanahan JE (2002) Agenda-setting, priming, framing and second-levels in local politics. Journal Mass Commun Q 79(1):7–25
47. Kohlmann EF (2006) The real online terrorist threat. Foreign Affairs 85(5):115–124
48. Krippendorff K, Bock MA (2008) The content an analysis reader. Sage, Thousand Oaks, CA
49. Laqueur W (2006) No end to war: terrorism in the twenty-first century. Continuum, New York
50. Lasswell HD (1971) Propaganda technique in world war. MIT Press, Cambridge, MA
51. Lenzner R, Vardi N (2007) The next threat. Forbes 174(5):15–21
52. Lewis J (2002) Assessing the risks of cyberterrorism, cyber war, and other cyber threats. Center for Strategic and International Studies (CSIS), Washington, DC
53. Libicki MC (2009) Cyberdeterrence and cyberwar. RAND, Santa Monica
54. Liu K (2000) Semiotics in information systems engineering. Cambridge University Press, Cambridge
55. Luskin BJ (1996) Toward an understanding of media psychology. T H E J 23:82–85
56. Mandaville P (2001) Transnational Muslim politics: reimagining the ummah. Routledge, London
57. Mathieu G (2007) Cyberterrorism: hype or reality? Comput Fraud Secur 2:9–12
58. Matusitz J (2008a) Cyberterrorism: postmodern state of chaos. Inf Secur J Glob Perspect 17(4):179–187
59. Matusitz J (2008b) Postmodernism and networks of cyberterrorists. J Digit Forensic Pract 2(1):17–26
60. McGirk T (1999) Wired for warfare. Time Int 7:A11

61. Misra S (2003) High-tech terror. Am City Cty 118(6):1
62. Nöth W (1995) Handbook of semiotics. Indiana University Press, Bloomington, IN
63. Paul C (2008) Information operations: doctrine and practice. Praeger, Westport CT
64. Peirce CS (1934) Collected papers: volume V. Pragmatism and pragmaticism. Harvard University Press, Cambridge, MA
65. Rogers M (2003) The psychology of cyber-terrorism. In: Silke A (ed) Terrorist, victims, and society: psychological perspectives on terrorism and its consequence. John Wiley, London, pp 72–92
66. Sebeok TA (1994) Signs: an introduction to semiotics. University of Toronto Press, Toronto
67. Shulman MR (1999) Discrimination in the laws of information warfare. Columbia J Transnational Law 37:939–967
68. Sloan S (1981) A study in political violence: the Indonesian experience. University of Oklahoma Press, Norman, OK
69. Sloan S (2006) Terrorism: the present threat in context. Berg Publishers, Oxford
70. Slone M (2000) Response to media coverage of terrorism. J Conflict Resolut 44(4):508–522
71. Steuter E, Wills D (2009) At war with metaphor: media, propaganda, and racism in the war on terror. Lexington Books, Landham, MD
72. Subramanya SR, Lakshminarasimhan N (2001) Computer viruses. IEEE Potentials 20(4):16–19
73. Talbot D (2005) Terror's server. Technology Review 1:46–52
74. Tuman JS (2003) Communicating terror: the rhetorical dimensions of terrorism. Sage, Thousand Oaks, CA
75. Tzfati Y, Weimann G (2002) www.terrorism.com: Terror on the Internet. Stud Confl Terrorism 25(5):317–332
76. Verton D (2003) Black ice: the invisible threat of cyber-terrorism. McGraw-Hill, New York
77. Weimann G (2005) Cyberterrorism: the sum of all fears? Stud Confl Terrorism 48(2):129–149
78. Weimann G (2006) Terror on the internet: the new arena, the new challenges. USIP Press Books, Washington, DC
79. Wright J (1991) Terrorist propaganda: the red army faction and the provisional IRA. St. Martin's Press, New York

CHAPTER 14

Designing a Softwarized Network Deployed on a Fleet of Drones for Rural Zone Monitoring

Corrado Rametta and Giovanni Schembra *

Department of Electrical, Electronics and Informatics Engineering—University of Catania, Catania 95125, Italy

ABSTRACT

In the last decade, the differences in the information communication technology (ICT) infrastructures between urban and rural areas have registered a tremendous increase. ICT infrastructures could strongly help rural communities where many operations are time consuming, labor-intensive and expensive due to limited access and large distances to cover. One of the most attractive solutions, which is widely recognized as promising for filling this gap, is the use of drone fleets. In this context, this paper proposes a video monitoring platform as a service (VMPaaS) for wide rural areas not covered by Internet access. The platform is realized with a Software-Defined Network (SDN)/Network Functions Virtualization (NFV)-based flying ad-hoc network (FANET), whose target is providing a flexible and dynamic connectivity backbone, and a set of drones equipped with high-resolution cameras, each transmitting a video stream of a portion of the considered area. After describing the architecture of the proposed platform, service chains to realize the video delivery service are described, and an analytical model is defined to evaluate the computational load of the platform nodes in such a way so as to allow the network orchestrator to decide the backbone drones where running the virtual functions, and the relative resources to be allocated. Numerical analysis is carried out in a case study.

Keywords: digital divide; fleet of drones; video monitoring; software-defined networks (SDNs); network functions virtualization (NFV); quality of service (QoS); analytical models; performance evaluation

1. INTRODUCTION

With the rapid development of digital information technology, digital convergence (i.e., integration of a variety of all types of information such as data, voice and video through convergence terminals and services) is expected to lead people to a smart society in which anyone can use personalized services anywhere and anytime [1]. Unfortunately, the reality is that there is an ever-increasing difference between information communication technology (ICT) infrastructures when comparing urban and rural areas. This is the so-called digital divide, which is mainly due to the business situation where broadcasting and communication operators are reluctant to invest in rural ICT infrastructure, which seems much less profitable [2].

However, ICT infrastructures could strongly help rural communities and cooperatives where many operations, such as inspection and maintenance, are time consuming, labor-intensive and expensive due to limited access and large distances to cover. For these reasons, new programs are reported in a number of recent studies, and solutions are required in projects relating to rural ICTs for bridging information and service gaps between rural and urban communities (see [3,4]).

One of the most attractive solutions, which is widely recognized as promising for filling this gap, is the use of aircrafts without a human pilot aboard, commonly known as unmanned aerial vehicles (UAVs) or drones. Originally produced mostly in military applications, recently they are beginning to be used outside that domain [5,6,7], in large part because they can execute the "dull, dirty, and dangerous" tasks over extended time periods [8]. According to a recent study [9], civil UAV drones are now vastly outnumbering military ones, with a market only in the United States that could reach USD$560 million at the end of 2017. Thanks to their versatility, flexibility, easy installation and relatively small operating expenses, they are applied to many scenarios as commercial, scientific, recreational, and agricultural ones. Common applications include search and destroy operations, border surveillance, wind estimation, disaster relief, remote sensing, traffic monitoring and precision agriculture [10,11].

In the first period, these various application opportunities have encouraged researchers and developers to focus more on improving the flight efficiency of a single drone. However, in many real-world situations there is a need to develop a drone system that is able to last much longer than the endurance of an individual UAV [12,13,14,15]. A solution is to use a fleet of small-scale drones combined with methods and algorithms that leverage collaboration between multiple (possibly miniature) drones. This is the case, for example, of the idea in [16], where the authors proposed a technique of autonomous battery change/recharge stations, which are equivalent to refueling stations. Additional advantages over the use of a single drone are in terms of covered area, load balancing, mission scalability, time efficiency, and fault tolerance.

A number of applications have been proposed for fleets of drones such as managing disaster situations [17,18], retrieving information from sensors deployed in areas that are not easy for humans to access, or even transmitting live audio/video from sports events involving fast-moving people, such as bicycle races or skiing competitions.

Of course, employing a fleet of drones as a team requires strong connectivity among drones, as discussed in [19,20,21], where a multi-drone communication platform is defined to support applications that require coordination of multiple drones, and in [22], where the concept of a flying ad-hoc network (FANET) is introduced as a highly mobile wireless mesh network [23,24,25].

Three elements that can support this trend in the immediate future are cloud computing and the two recent networking paradigms, software-defined networks (SDNs) and networks functions virtualization (NFV). Cloud computing is a new Internet-based computing paradigm that provides shared computer processing resources and data to any device on demand, so enabling ubiquitous, on-demand access to a pool of configurable resources (e.g., computer networks, servers, storage, applications and services) which can be rapidly provisioned and released with minimal management effort. SDNs and NFV, on the other hand, are two paradigms for network softwarization, the first aimed at decoupling the control plane from the data plane [26,27], and the second enabling the network infrastructure to be virtualized as building block classes and functions managed by a centralized orchestration entity called management and orchestration (MANO) [28,29,30,31,32]. Deployment of SDN has been extensive in fixed infrastructure-based networks, especially in networks within data centers. More recently, both academia and the industry are manifesting increasing interest in application of

SDN in dynamic mobile wireless environments [33,34,35,36,37,38]. More specifically, SDN results very suitable for UAV networks where nodes are non-permanent, connectivity is intermittent and channels may be impaired. In this context, SDN is able to easily change flow paths dynamically after topology modifications due for example to link intermittence, or node failures because of battery drainage.

Up to now, at the best of our knowledge, works using both softwarized and non-softwarized networks of drones in an agriculture scenario are limited to sensor applications, where the network is able to gather data from sensors (e.g., soil humidity [39], gases or smoke from fires, air quality in different layers of the atmosphere [40], etc.) in order to react with some action like, for example, efficiently spraying pesticides and fertilizers on crops [41].

Application of a joint SDN/NFV paradigm has led some researchers to overcome the limitation of drone systems developed for specific applications. Authors in [42,43] introduced for the first time the idea of integrating UAVs with the cloud, and then in [44,45] proposed leveraging on the SDN and NFV to realize a cloud platform for developing drone applications for accessing UAVs through a third party. Drone connectivity scenarios have already been considered in recent 3GPP Release 14 documents [46], but are limited to consideration of the remote control of drones. A step ahead is done in [47], which considers the utilization of drones equipped with base stations (BS) to realize a multi-tier drone-cell network to complement the terrestrial HetNets, and propose a management framework based on the SDN/NFV paradigm.

However, one of the main challenges in deploying cloud and fog computing paradigms on fleet of drones is battery duration, since computing hardware is powered by the same energy source of the drone engine: an excessive computing power required by the fog-computing node installed on a drone would compromise its flight duration.

With all this in mind, this paper proposes a video monitoring platform as a service (VMPaaS) for wide rural areas not covered by Internet access. The platform is realized with a FANET, whose target is providing connectivity backbone, and a set of drones equipped with high-resolution cameras, each transmitting a video stream of a portion of the considered area. This platform, thanks to its flexibility due to the application of the cloud/fog and the SDN/NFV paradigms, allows, on the one hand, third-party users to contribute to the whole service by installing new cameras on the area or launching new video-transmitter drones that automatically connect to the platform, and on the other hand, users to connect to the platform and, through their terminal, choose one or more cameras to receive video flows of interest.

The main contributions of this paper are:

(1) definition of the platform architecture, which is realized as a "video monitoring as a service" (VMaaS), constituted by a backbone mesh network providing connectivity and computation services to video transmitters, whose selection can be dynamically decided by users according to the portions of rural areas they want to monitor. Specific architectures of both backbone mesh nodes and platform orchestrator are also provided;

(2) definition of the service chains to realize the video delivery service; specifically, the paper describes the service chains of both Acquirer and the Edge Streamer nodes;

(3) definition of an analytical model to evaluate the computational load of the platform nodes, in such a way so as to allow the network orchestrator to decide the backbone drones where running the virtual functions.

(4) application of the proposed model to a case study, in order to analyze the impact of each element of the service chains to the overall computational cost.

The paper is structured as follows. Section 2 provides an architectural and implementation description of the platform. Section 3introduces the service chains defined to realize the platform service. Section 4 models the computational load of the platform nodes. Section 5 considers a case study and provides a numerical analysis aimed at showing how the model can be used to design and manage the platform. Finally, Section 6 draws some conclusions and describe possible future work.

2. VIDEO MONITORING PLATFORM DESCRIPTION

The scenario we refer to in this paper is shown in Figure 1. It is a rural area where a fleet of drones realizes a video monitoring service for all the people that work there, or have any interest in monitoring it. It is constituted by a wireless mesh network that behaves as a backbone to allow easy and dynamic connections of video transmitter and video receiver devices. As illustrated in the sequel, the proposed platform is designed as a "video monitoring as a service" (VMaaS), which is managed by a video monitoring platform provider. It is not deployed for a specific user, but has the objective of capturing videos of a wide rural area, providing a service that can be used by any customer that has the interest of monitoring one or more portions of it.

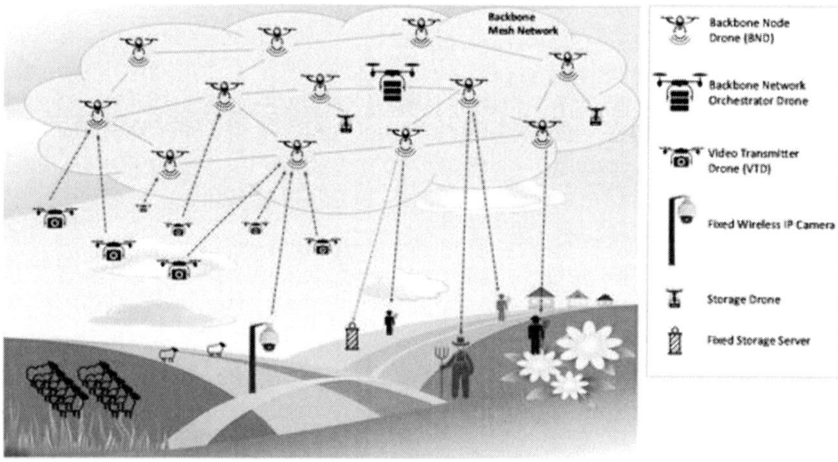

Figure 1. Reference scenario.

The main elements of the video monitoring platform are described in Section 2.1, while Section 2.2 presents its architecture. Finally, Section 2.3 will describe the platform orchestrator, with its management role at both network and application layers.

2.1. Platform Elements

As shown in Figure 1, the video monitoring platform is constituted by a backbone mesh network and a number of video transmitter devices.

The backbone mesh network, whose nodes are the backbone node drones (BND), is a flying ad-hoc network (FANET), an ad-hoc network that is a particular class of Mobile Ad-hoc NETworks (MANET), also classifiable as a subset of Vehicular Ad-hoc NETworks (VANET) [34]. Generally, FANETs nodes may be highly mobile, so causing connectivity problems and frequent topology changes. However, for the scenario we are considering in this paper, where the only target is to cover a given rural area, we can assume that they follow a global path plan, that is, all the BNDs slowly move on a predetermined path with a regular mobility model. Moreover, by timely designing of network node density, it is possible to guaranteeing connectivity even in case of failures of some nodes. Therefore, their number, protocols and techniques they apply to setup and maintain connectivity, and the relative routing and battery recharging policies are out of the scope of this paper, and can be considered as a matter of future work. Interested readers can refer to the wide literature regarding FANETs [23,24,25] and data communications in unmanned aerial vehicles (UAV) [16,48].

The architecture of the backbone mesh network nodes is presented in Figure 2. Their target is not only providing connectivity at the network level, but also running the virtual service elements constituting the platform at the application level, that is, the acquirers and the edge streamers comprising the video broadcasting infrastructure described in Section 2.2. For this purpose, they are equipped with one or more computing units hosting an NFV infrastructure (NFVI) point of presence (POP). A general-purpose x86 hardware, like for example Intel Nuke MiniPC or even RaspberryPi, can be used to deploy a virtualization environment that allows running virtual machines (VM). Each VM is used to host a specific virtual network or application function (VNF and VAF, respectively), according to the NFV paradigm. VM Dom0 is always running to host the operating system. A virtual SDN-compliant software switch (e.g., an OpenvSwitch [49]) is also installed and run on each backbone node drone to connect local VMs to each other, to the ones running on the neighboring backbone network node drones, and to some transmitter and receiver devices, all under the centralized control of a remote SDN Controller. A WiFi network interface equipped with an omnidirectional antenna allows physical communications in the wireless mesh network.

In our prototype, we used CentOS release 6.4 as host operating system (OS), directly installed on the bare metal, whereas we have chosen Xen Hypervisor [50] as a VM hypervisor. It behaves as a middleware software, enabling both virtual system management and hardware resource sharing with the aim of executing multiple computer operating systems on the same hardware concurrently. Xen Hypervisor is a free and open-source software developed by the University of Cambridge Computer Laboratory, available for x86-64, IA-32 and ARM architectures, and supporting a form of virtualization known as para-virtualization. Thanks to the para-virtualization paradigm, it is possible to obtain a faster execution of the VMs as compared with the traditional approaches. More in detail, Xen Hypervisor allows virtual machines to share with each other the x86-64 hardware directly, without the need to specify the resources to be allocated for the virtualized hardware preventively. Thanks to this peculiarity, the host OS only acts as a console to operate with the virtualization manager, enabling commands as create, destroy and migrate.

Video transmission is realized with video transmitter drones and fixed wireless IP cameras, all sending video of portions of the considered rural area. Video transmitter drones are drones equipped with high-resolution cameras that dynamically connect to the closest BND to access the video monitoring platform. Fixed wireless IP cameras are video cameras installed on the ground, for example on poles, and likewise video transmitter drones, access the platform through the closest BND.

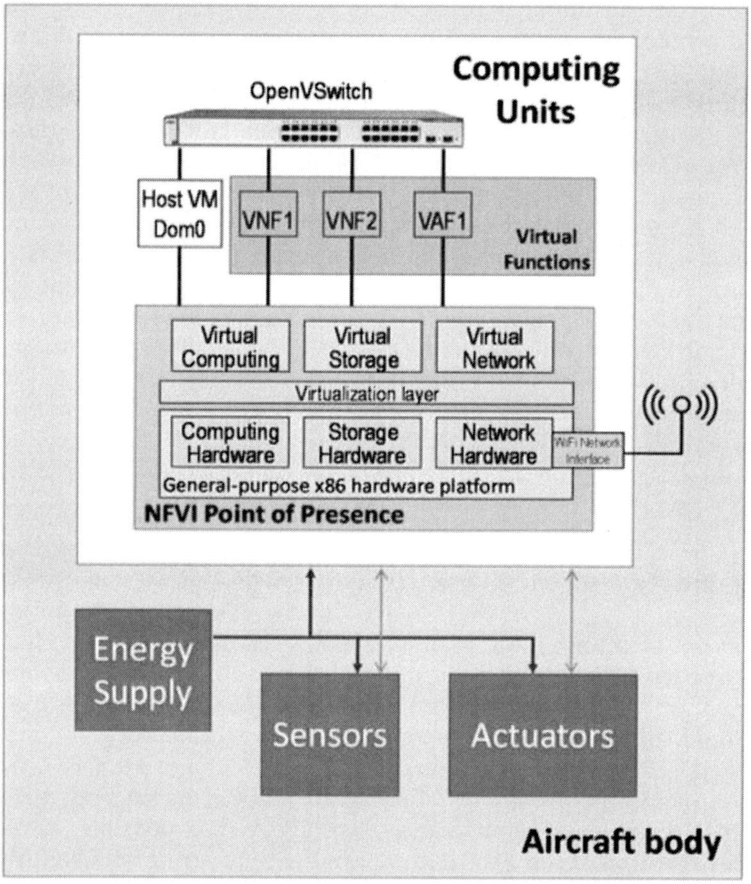

Figure 2. Backbone Mesh Network Node Architecture. VNF: virtual network function; VM: virtual machines; NFVI: network functions virtualization infrastructure; VAF: virtual application function.

Receivers of the video monitoring service provided by the above platform are people that, for some reason, need to monitor one or more portions of the rural area. To this purpose, they have a receiver device, which can be either a smartphone, a tablet or a personal computer with a client application installed. From this client application, a user is able to select the rural area portions he is interested to, by choosing them from a map of the area. Moreover, it can be decided to watch a live video stream of the selected areas, recoding it thanks to the storage service provided by the platform, or play out some video stream video stream recorded in the past.

Thanks to the SDN paradigm used by the backbone mesh network, each video flow generated by a video transmitter and entering the backbone network is automatically re-routed to the devices of all the users interested in it. In addition, thanks to the NFV facilities of the backbone, each flow can be elaborated to receive some network and application functions implemented as pieces of software in some drone node of the network, as for example information encryption or event-analysis for alarm triggering setup by the clients.

Let us note that the application of the joint SDN/NFV paradigm allows service continuity even in the case that video transmitters and users change their access point to the backbone network, due for example to movements of users, video transmitter drones and backbone node drones.

2.2. Video Monitoring Platform Architecture

The video monitoring platform architecture is sketched in Figure 3. It is logically constituted by a Video Broadcasting Infrastructure leveraging on the connectivity service provided by the backbone mesh network described so far. Based on the number of users connected to the platform, and the access points related to their current geographical positions, the video monitoring platform provider sets up and dynamically manages the number of nodes and resources involved in the service. This is done through a softwarized approach based on SDN and NFV.

More specifically, a video delivery tree (VDT) is created for the multipoint video stream generated by each video transmitter. This is a tree structure made up of virtual instances of network and application functions running on the backbone drone nodes, which is responsible for receiving a video stream from a video transmitter and delivering it to the interested end users of the service.

The platform may expose additional functionalities to the end users, such as transcoding of a high-quality video stream to a lower-quality video format in order to fit both end-user and network requirements. If transcoding of the same flow is requested by more than one client, this task is assigned to some of the platform nodes according to the position of the requesting clients. To this purpose, a video delivery forest is realized for each multipoint video stream generated by a video transmitter. A video delivery forest is constituted by one VDT for each quality video format requested by clients for the same flow.

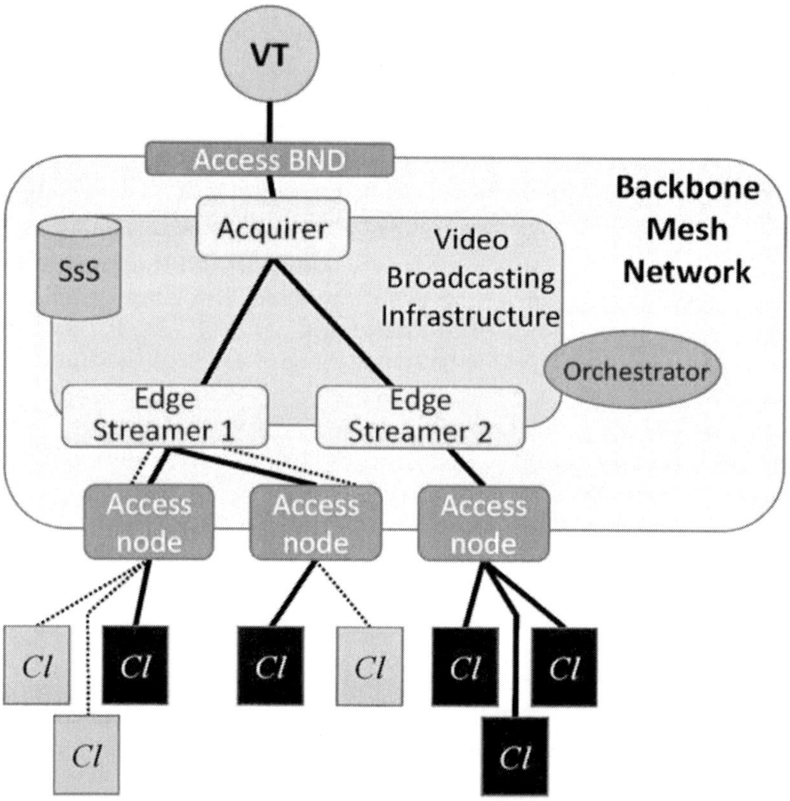

Figure 3. Video monitoring platform architecture. VT: video transmitter.

In the platform architecture sketched in Figure 3, we can see a video delivery forest constituted by two VDTs. In the figure, we can observe a video transmitter (VT) that accesses the backbone mesh network through a backbone node drone (BND) that works as network access point, in order to transmit a given video stream to some interested clients (Cl). In this example, clients access the backbone mesh network through three different access BNDs. Clients shown in the figure belong to two sets, the former requiring the content at the original quality (black clients), and the latter at a lower quality that is achieved by transcoding (grey clients).

Each video delivery forest is constituted by one acquirer and one or more edge streamers. The *acquirer* is the ingress node of video transmitters to the video broadcasting infrastructure, and represents the root of their VDTs. Its main tasks are recognizing media streams, notifying the orchestrator about the upcoming transmissions, and receiving transmission instructions from the orchestrator in terms of a list of IP addresses of the backbone node drones running the edge streamers where the media streams have to be forwarded. For each flow, the acquirer is run on a VM dynamically instantiated by the orchestrator on an SDN/NFV drone node of the backbone mesh network, in order to be as closer as possible to the relative video transmitter.

The *edge streamers* are the leaves of the VDTs, and serve the platform clients. Likewise, the acquirers receive instructions from the orchestrator regarding the IP addresses of the clients that have requested to receive the specific flow of each VDT. If only one transcoding quality has been requested, and requesting clients are mobile users accessing the platform through the same network access node, the transcoding function is installed only on the edge streamer running on that node. Instead, if the same transcoding quality is requested by clients assigned to different edge streamers, the relative transcoding function can be installed on either those edge streamers or the acquirer.

Finally, another key element in the proposed platform is the *storage sub-system* (*SsS*). Its task is to store video flows. Thanks to it, the platform has the facility of allowing clients to record stream, in such a way that it will be available in the future in off-line mode. More specifically, the acquirer splits video streams, which have to be stored, in sub-streams that can be saved on different drones of the backbone mesh network, named *storage drones*. In order to increase the storage capacity of the SsS, a set of fixed storage servers are installed on the ground to store old flows that will likely not be requested frequently. In our prototype, the acquirers use Forward Error Correction (FEC) to encode video streams to introduce some redundancy, in such a way that, even if some drones used for storing sub-streams of the same main stream are temporarily not available when a Client request to watch a flow, this flow can be rebuilt. For each flow to be stored, the choice of the number of involved storage drones and fixed storage servers is in charge of the orchestrator.

2.3. Platform Orchestration

A platform element that plays a very important role is the backbone network orchestrator drone, in the following indicated as *orchestrator*. It is a dedicated drone communicating with all the platform components through the backbone network. Its goal is to coordinate the behavior of all the elements of the NFV infrastructure (NFVI) [51], that is, the SDN switches and the virtual machines (VMs) used on the network nodes to run both the network functions and the elements of the video broadcasting infrastructure, i.e., the acquirers and the edge streamers.

More specifically, tasks of the orchestrator are allocating, migrating and terminating VMs, controlling traffic paths, managing and orchestrating service chains according to the run-time evolution of the network traffic, the requirements of the video monitoring platform provider and the service-level agreements (SLAs) with the customers.

The orchestrator architecture, following the management and orchestration (MANO) document [28], is shown in Figure 4. Its main elements are:

(a) Platform Front-end: it is the manager of this specific service of video monitoring, and works as the access interface of the orchestrator for the users of this service. The Front-end is an http server aiming at handling the RESTful requests from clients. Application data are stored in a relational database containing the following information:

- Users with their profile and subscription agreements
- For each video transmitter, its geographical position and its access permissions
- For each user, the set of portions of rural to be monitored, the list recorded contents with the location of the stored sub-streams to compose it, and other additional information like the triggering alarms.

When clients access the service through their web-based devices or their dedicated mobile Apps, they directly communicate with the platform front-end, which uses his database, in order to synchronize the information with the local user's devices. Then, for each action requested by the users, the front-end receives a request and forwards it to the NFV orchestrator residing in the management and orchestration (MANO) segment to be processed and implemented on the video broadcasting infrastructure. More in depth, as a first action, the front-end verifies the user identity. If the entering user is a client, the front-end sends it the list of the available transmitting elements and their current localization on the monitored area. The client can furthermore choose to access his own archive of previously registered contents.

On the other hand, when new transmitting elements are attached to the backbone network, or some transmitter drone changes its current location, the platform front-end notifies this to the NFV orchestrator to reconfigure the mesh backbone network and the video broadcasting infrastructure.

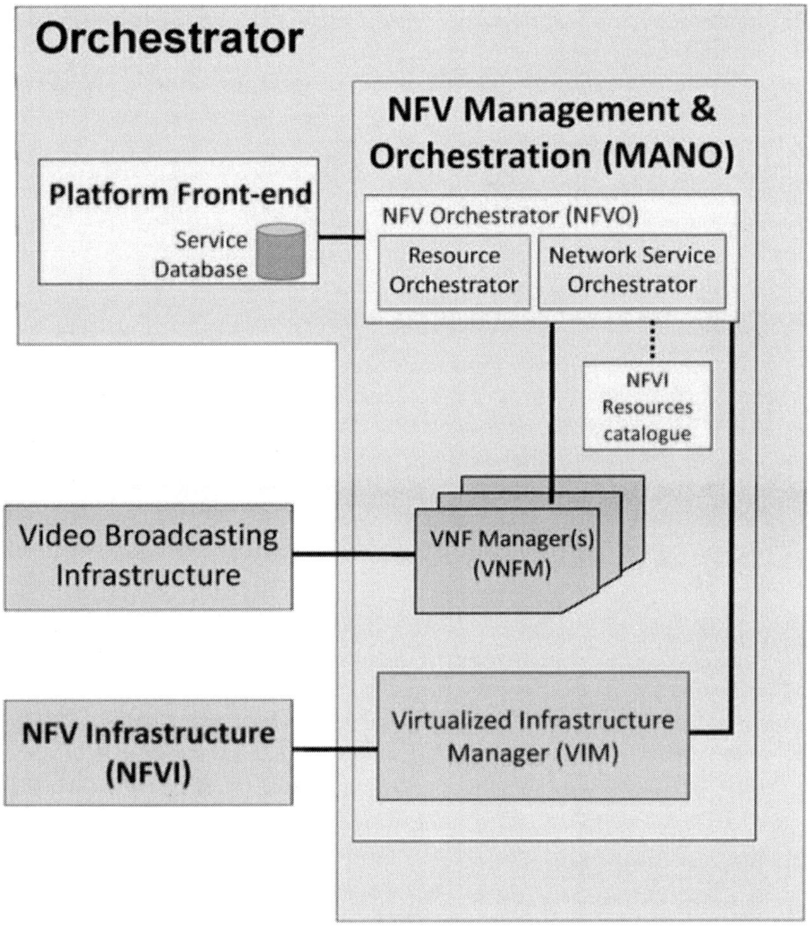

Figure 4. Orchestrator architecture. NFV: network functions virtualization.

(b) Virtualized infrastructure manager (VIM): it is the core application of a softwarized network, acting as a sort of operating system for the network; it sends rules to the hardware and software nodes of the NFV infrastructure about port forwarding, and chooses optimal paths for application data delivery; in addition, it decides the amount of resources, in terms of bandwidth, computing and memory, that each node has reserved to support each elementary service;

(c) VNF manager: it has the capability for managing the lifecycle of virtual machines running both network (e.g., deep packet inspectors, load balancers) and application functions (i.e., all the functions related to streaming, forwarding and storage). Its choices are based on the rules and information coming from the NFVO element, and is in charge of creating, migrating and destroying VMs, communicating with the hypervisors running on the network nodes;

(d) NFV orchestrator (NFVO): it gathers information about the network (topology, number of connected clients, required contents, availability of backbone node drones, etc.) and, according to specific algorithms and policies, decides how to manage resources of the network devices. More specifically, it has the following main functions:

- It is responsible for the implementation of the requests coming from the platform front-end; this is done by configuring and managing the VDTs. More specifically, the NFVO is invoked every time the front-end: (a) receives a connection request from either a client or a video transmitter; (b) a client requests a new connection to a video transmitter; in this case a path has to be created from the video transmitter to it; (c) a video transmitter starts the transmission of a new flow;
- It monitors the network status, the usage of wireless links in the mesh network, the RAM/CPU usage of each computation node and each virtual machine running networking or application functions, with the targets of deciding allocation of physical and virtual resources that will be assigned to specific requests, and selecting the most efficient end-to-end paths between video transmitters and receivers.

The policies implemented by the NFVO can refer to a wide range of aspects, like energy consumption, end-to-end delay between source and destination of data flows, number of hops of the path, overall number of virtual machines active at the same time, quality of service (QoS) and quality of experience (QoE), Service Level Agreement (SLA) with the customers, etc. The implemented policies may aim at achieving consolidation, by minimizing the number of drones involved in the forwarding procedure of the media streams from the transmitters to the destination clients. The computational load model described in Section 4 is one of the key elements to design these policies.

3. SERVICE CHAINS TO REALIZE THE VIDEO BROADCASTING INFRASTRUCTURE ELEMENTS

In the proposed platform, each video transmitter is the source of one multipoint video stream that can be transcoded to different qualities and/or stored according to the requests coming from the clients. Consequently, as already said so far, the platform topology can be considered as a forest, that is, a set of trees that have the edge streamer nodes as leaves. More specifically, since each flow can be transcoded at different encoding qualities in different backbone node drones (BNDs), it follows that each flow is transmitted through a forest that is constituted by as many VDTs (transcoded VDTs) as the number of encoding qualities requested for it. The roots of these subtrees are the platform nodes where the transcoders are located. So, given an original flow *f*, the flow derived by it with a quality *q*will be identified as [f,q], and the transcoded VDT carrying [f,q] will be indicated as T[f,q]. Management policies of the VDTs are in charge of the NFVO block residing in the orchestrator. This is a challenging and very broad topic widely discussed in past and current literature [52,53]. Although the whole management problem is out of the scope of this paper, the computational load model described in the following section is a fundamental piece of it.

Let us now describe the service chains running in the BNDs to implement both the acquirers, that manage traffic coming from video transmitters towards the platform, and the edge streamers, that manage traffic coming from the platform towards the clients.

The service chain related to the Acquirer is shown in Figure 5a. Traffic coming from VTs enters a load balancer (LB) block, which subdivides it to the computation units that are currently active in the BND. The number of active computation units and the video flows that have to be managed by each computation unit are decided by the orchestrator that applies consolidation policies in order to concentrate the load on the smallest number of computation units for energy-saving purposes.

When a video flow enters a computation unit, it is first analyzed by a deep packet inspector (DPI) block that forwards it to an acquirer (A) block, which is the root of the relative VDT. Then, if the flow has to be transcoded, it enters the transcoding section, which is constituted by a transcoder (TC) block for each required quality level. If more than one TC is needed for the same flow, the flow is first replicated by a point-to-multipoint (PM) block. Finally, the video flow, either original or transcoded, enters another PM block to create as many copies of the flow as the number of edge streamers that are present on the considered VDT. If some clients have requested to store a flow, a copy of it is created by another PM block and sent to the storage (ST) block. This last block saves only one copy of each video flow if at least one recording request has arrived to the system, and even if more than one recording requests have been received by the orchestrator for the same flow. In order to limit the unavailability probability of the drone where the flow is saved, the ST makes a FEC encoding [54], splitting the flow in M different parts such that, if any F of them, with $F \leq M$, are available, the flow can be rebuilt. The flow parts are then sent to M different storage drones or fixed storage servers to be saved. The numbers M and F, and the IP addresses of the M different storage elements are provided to the ST block by the orchestrator.

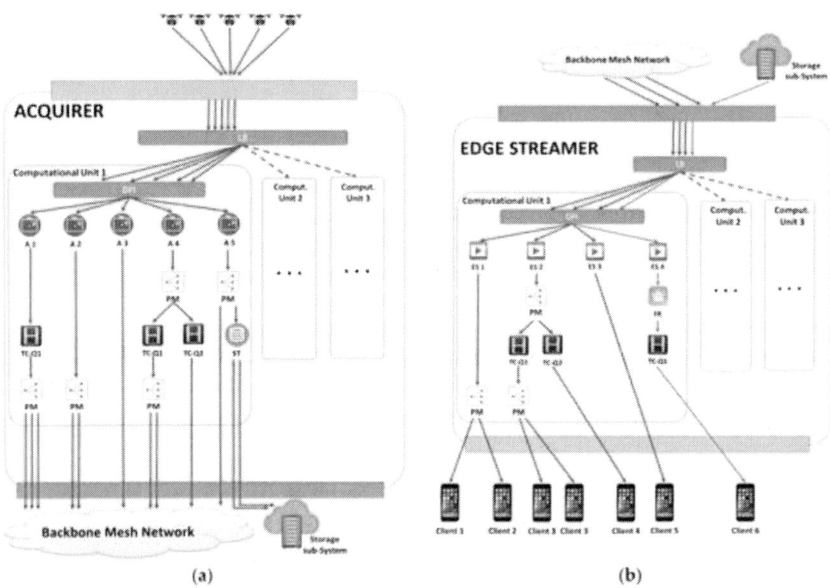

Figure 5. Platform service chains. (**a**) acquirer service chain; (**b**) edge streamer service chain.

The service chain of the edge streamer nodes is represented in Figure 5b. In these nodes, flows arrive from acquirers through the backbone mesh network, specifically by the acquirers that have some children in the considered edge streamer node. Focusing on a specific flow, which can be either with the original quality or a quality q obtained for transcoding, it is first managed by a LB block and a DPI block with the same functionalities explained so far when we referred to Figure 5a. Then, the flow arrives to the edge streamer (ES) block, which is the block that is in charge of the communications with all the clients assigned to it. Finally, as in the acquirer nodes, the video flow enters the transcoding section if transcoding is required in this node, and then in the point-to-multipoint section to be replicated to all the clients that have to receive it. Moreover, if some client requires watching a stored video flow, its ES requests the component sub-flows to F storage drones decided by the orchestrator, in order to reassemble it, and passes the received parts to the flow rebuilder (FR) block, which creates again the flow with the original quality, applying an inverse FEC. Then the flow traverses a transcoding section if transcoding is needed, and finally is delivered to the requesting client.

4. COMPUTATIONAL MODEL OF THE BACKBONE NODE DRONES

In this section, considering the service chains described above, we model the computational load of the backbone node drones hosting the platform elements. Let us note that each drone can be, at the same time, the ingress node for some VTs and the egress node for some clients. For this reason, limiting our attention to the traffic related to the considered platform, in the generic backbone drone $\wp$the total network traffic is the sum of the traffic entering from the VTs (for the acquirer role of $\wp$) and the traffic entering from the other backbone drones, to be forwarded to the clients (for the edge streamer role of $\wp$).

The overall computational load of the generic drone $\wp$ is:

$$\Omega^{(ALL)} = \Omega^{(ACn)} + \Omega^{(ESn)} \tag{1}$$

where $\Omega^{(ACn)}$ and $\Omega^{(ESn)}$ are the computational loads related to the acquirer and the edge streamer roles, respectively. They can be calculated as the sum of the contributions due to each element of the service chains shown in Figure 5:

$$\Omega^{(ACn)} = \Omega_{LB}^{(ACn)} + \Omega_{DPI}^{(ACn)} + \Omega_{A}^{(ACn)} + \Omega_{PM}^{(ACn)} + \Omega_{TC}^{(ACn)} + \Omega_{ST}^{(ACn)} \tag{2}$$

$$\Omega^{(ESn)} = \Omega_{LB}^{(ESn)} + \Omega_{DPI}^{(ESn)} + \Omega_{ES}^{(ESn)} + \Omega_{PM}^{(ESn)} + \Omega_{FR}^{(ESn)} + \Omega_{TC}^{(ESn)} \tag{3}$$

where each element, representing the computational load of all the blocks depicted in Figure 5, will be defined in Section 4.1 and Section 4.2.

The components of the acquirer computational load will be derived in Section 4.1, while the ones related to the edge streamer will be derived in Section 4.2.

Following the literature [55], we model the load of a VM hosting a virtual function with a linear model constituted by a base part needed to maintain the VM active, and a part proportional to the managed traffic. Therefore, in the following, for the generic VM *v*hosting the generic virtual function *V*, we will indicate the base computational load needed to run *v* as φv, and the computational load per unit of flow related to the virtual function *V* as ξV.

4.1. Acquirers

Let us consider the service chain related to the acquirer running in the generic drone ℘. Let NF be the number of VTs attached to ℘. Referring to Figure 5a, the whole acquirer computational load is the sum of the loads related to all the blocks highlighted in that figure, as expressed in (2).

According to the linear model of the computational load, the computational load of the load balancer is:

$$\Omega_{LB}^{(ACn)} = \varphi_{LB} + \xi_{LB} \sum_{f=1}^{N_F} \lambda_f \tag{4}$$

where λf is the bit rate of the flow *f*.

The computational load for the deep packet inspectors can be calculated taking into account that we have one DPI for each computation unit that is active in the drone ℘, and the whole traffic coming from the VTs is distributed to the DPI blocks of the active computation units. Therefore, the overall computational load due to the DPI blocks is:

$$\Omega_{DPI}^{(ACn)} = N_S \cdot \varphi_{DPI} + \xi_{DPI} \sum_{f=1}^{N_F} \lambda_f \tag{5}$$

where NS is the number of computation units in the considered drone ℘.

In order to calculate the computational load due to the acquirer blocks, notice that we have an instance of the acquirer block for each entering flow, and therefore:

$$\Omega_A^{(ACn)} = N_F \cdot \varphi_A + \xi_A \sum_{f=1}^{N_F} \lambda_f \qquad (6)$$

Let us now derive the computational load due to the point-to-multipoint (PM) blocks. For this purpose, let us note that we have two sets of PM blocks. The first set is constituted by PM blocks that replicate flows to be sent to the transcoders if they have to be transcoded. More in depth, we have one PM block for each flow *f* that has to be transcoded in the considered drone $\wp$, event represented by the indicator function I(CQ)$\wp$(f) defined as follows:

$$I_{\wp}^{(CQ)}(f) = \begin{cases} 1 & \text{if the flow } f \text{ has to be transcoded in the drone } \wp \\ 0 & \text{otherwise} \end{cases} \qquad (7)$$

The generic PM block of this set, the one that manages the generic flow *f*, is loaded by a bit rate λf, and has a computational load per unit of flow, ξPM, that depends on the number of replicas it has to do, that is equal to the number N(CQ)$\wp$(f) of transcodings that the drone $\wp$ has to do on the flow *f*, plus one if it has been requested the storage of the flow. In order to represent this last event, let us define the following indicator function:

$$I^{(SsS)}(f) = \begin{cases} 1 & \text{if some user has requested to store the flow } f \\ 0 & \text{otherwise} \end{cases} \qquad (8)$$

The second set is constituted by the PM blocks that create replicas of the flows for the edge streamers in the related VDTs. To this purpose, for the generic flow f that has to be forwarded by the drone $\wp$ to some edge streamers at an output quality qOUT, we indicate its bit rate as γqOUT, and define the indicator function $I_{>1}^{(ESn)}\left(T_{[f,q_{OUT}]}\right)$ as follows:

$$I_{>1}^{(ESn)}\left(T_{[f,q_{OUT}]}\right) = \begin{cases} 1 & \text{if the number of ES nodes on the tree } T_{[f,q_{OUT}]} \text{ is} > 1 \\ 0 & \text{otherwise} \end{cases} \qquad (9)$$

Each of these last PM blocks has to manage a flow bit rate γqOUT and has a computational load per unit of flow, ξPM, that depends on the number of replicas it has to do, that is equal to the number $N_{f,q_{OUT}}^{(ESn)}$ of edge streamers nodes on the related VDT T[f,qOUT]. Therefore, we have:

$$\Omega_{PM}^{(ACn)} = \sum_{f=1}^{N_F} \left\{ \left[I_{\wp}^{(CQ)}(f) \text{ or } I^{(SsS)}(f) \right] \cdot \varphi_{PM} + \xi_{PM} \left(N_{\wp}^{(CQ)}(f) + I^{(SsS)}(f) \right) \cdot \lambda_f + \right. \\ \left. + \sum_{q_{OUT}=0}^{Q_L} I_{>1}^{(ESn)} \left(T_{[f,q_{OUT}]} \right) \cdot \left[\varphi_{PM} + \xi_{PM} \left(N_{f,q_{OUT}}^{(ESn)} \right) \cdot \gamma_{q_{OUT}} \right] \right\} \tag{10}$$

where QL is the number of possible quality levels, and qOUT=0 indicates the original quality, that is, γ0=λf.

The computational load due to the transcoder (TC) blocks can be derived taking into account that we have one TC block for each flow that has to be transcoded, and for each requested encoding quality, that is:

$$\Omega_{TC}^{(ACn)} = \sum_{f=1}^{N_F} \sum_{q_{OUT}=1}^{Q_L} I_{\wp}^{(CsQ)}(f, q_{OUT}) \cdot \left[\varphi_{TC} + \xi_{TC}(q_{OUT}) \cdot \lambda_f \right] \tag{11}$$

where we have considered that the parameter ξTC(qOUT) depends on the out transcoding quality, as noted experimentally. The function I(CsQ)℘(f,qOUT) in (11) is an indicator function of transcoding at the specific quality level qOUT, defined as follows:

$$I_{\wp}^{(CsQ)}(f, q_{OUT}) = \begin{cases} 1 & \text{if the drone } \wp \text{ has to transcode the flow } f \text{ at quality } q_{OUT} \\ 0 & \text{otherwise} \end{cases} \tag{12}$$

Finally, the computational load due to the storage (ST) blocks depends on the bit rate of the flows to be stored, and therefore we have:

$$\Omega_{ST}^{(ACn)} = \varphi_{ST} + \xi_{ST} \sum_{f=1}^{N_F} I^{(SsS)}(f) \cdot \lambda_f \tag{13}$$

4.2. Edge Streamers

According to (3), let us derive the computational load due to the edge streamer chain, as represented in Figure 5b.

In order to evaluate the computational load of the load balancer, let us observe that this block is loaded by a traffic bit rate given by the sum of two terms, the first related to the live streaming flows coming from the acquirers, and the second related to the stored flows requested by the clients connected to the considered edge streamer.

The first term is the aggregated bit rate of all the live streaming flows directed to the clients accessing the platform through the edge streamer running in the considered drone $\wp$. In order to calculate it, for a generic live streaming flow fL encoded at a quality level qOUT, let us define the indicator function I(VDT)$\wp$(fL,qOUT) of the fact that the considered edge streamer in the drone $\wp$ is on the VDT T[fL,qOUT], that is, some clients connected to the platform through the drone $\wp$ have requested to receive the flow fL at quality qOUT. Thus, this function is defined as follows:

$$I_{\wp}^{(VDT)}(f_L, q_{OUT}) = \begin{cases} 1 & \text{if the drone } \wp \text{ belongs to the VDT } T_{[f_L, q_{OUT}]} \\ 0 & \text{otherwise} \end{cases} \quad (14)$$

On the other hand, the second term can be calculated as the sum of the bit rates of the stored flows requested by clients connected to the platform through the drone $\wp$. To this purpose, for a generic stored flow fS, let us define the following indicator function:

$$I_{\wp}^{(St)}(f_S) = \begin{cases} 1 & \text{if some Client connected to the drone } \wp \text{ has requested the stored flow } f_S \\ 0 & \text{otherwise} \end{cases} \quad (15)$$

The total input bit rate of the ES node in the drone $\wp$ is:

$$\lambda_{IN}^{(ESn)} = \sum_{f_L=1}^{N_F} \sum_{q_{OUT}=0}^{Q_L} I_{\wp}^{(VDT)}(f_L, q_{OUT}) \cdot \gamma_{q_{OUT}} + \sum_{f_S \in \aleph^{(S)}} \lambda_{f_S} I_{\wp}^{(St)}(f_S) \quad (16)$$

where ℵ(S) is the set of stored flows, and λfS the bit rate of the stored flow fS. Now, we can calculate the computational load of the load balancer block as follows:

$$\Omega_{LB}^{(ESn)} = \varphi_{LB} + \xi_{LB} \lambda_{IN}^{(ESn)} \quad (17)$$

The computational load of the DPI block can be calculated as in (5), taking into account that in this case the input bit rate is λ(ESn)IN. Therefore, we have:

$$\Omega_{DPI}^{(ESn)} = N_S \cdot \varphi_{DPI} + \xi_{DPI} \lambda_{IN}^{(ESn)} \quad (18)$$

In order to calculate the computational load of the edge streamer (ES) blocks, we note that we have one ES for each live streaming flow crossing the drone $\wp$, and an additional ES for each client that has requested to watch a stored video stream. Therefore, we have:

$$\Omega_{ES}^{(ESn)} = \sum_{f_L=1}^{N_F} \sum_{q_{IN}=0}^{Q_L} I_{\wp}^{(VDT)}(f_L, q_{IN}) \cdot \left[\varphi_{ES} + \xi_{ES}\gamma_{q_{IN}}\right] + \sum_{f_S \in \aleph^{(S)}} I_{\wp}^{(St)}(f_S) \cdot \left[\varphi_{ES} + \xi_{ES}\lambda_{f_S}\right] \tag{19}$$

Let us now derive the computational load for the point-to-multipoint (PM) blocks in the edge streamer of the drone $\wp$. It is the sum of two terms: the first one considers the PMs used to send the video flows to the transcoding blocks and, for a given flow [fL,qIN], it is present if this flow has to be transcoded to at least two quality levels; the second term accounts for the point-to-multipoint transmission of each flow to more than one client. Therefore, if we indicate the number of clients connected to the VDT T[fL,qOUT] through the edge streamer in the drone $\wp$ as N(Cl,$\wp$)[fL,qOUT], and define the following indicator function:

$$I_{>1}^{(Cl,\wp)}\left(T_{[f_L,q_{OUT}]}\right) = \begin{cases} 1 & \text{if the number of Clients connected through the ES } \wp \\ & \text{on the tree } T_{[f_L,q_{OUT}]} \text{ is greater than 1} \\ 0 & \text{otherwise} \end{cases} \tag{20}$$

we have:

$$\Omega_{PM}^{(ESn)} = \sum_{f_L=1}^{N_F} \sum_{q_{IN}=0}^{Q_L} I_{\wp}^{(VDT)}(f_L, q_{IN}) \cdot \left\{ I_{\wp}^{(CQ)}([f_L, q_{IN}]) \cdot \left[\varphi_{PM} + \xi_{PM}\left(N_{\wp}^{(CQ)}([f_L, q_{IN}])\right)\gamma_{q_{IN}}\right] + \right.$$
$$\left. + \sum_{q_{OUT}=1}^{Q_L} I_{>1}^{(Cl,\wp)}\left(T_{[f_L,q_{OUT}]}\right) \cdot \left[\varphi_{PM} + \xi_{PM}\left(N_{[f_L,q_{OUT}]}^{(Cl,\wp)}\right)\gamma_{q_{OUT}}\right] \right\} \tag{21}$$

The computational load of the flow rebuilder (FR) block can be easily derived considering that the edge streamer node $\wp$ has one FR for each stored flow requested by clients connected to this node. Therefore, we have:

$$\Omega_{FR}^{(ESn)} = \sum_{f_S \in \aleph^{(S)}} I_{\wp}^{(St)}(f_S) \cdot \left(\varphi_{FR} + \xi_{FR}\lambda_{f_S}\right) \tag{22}$$

Finally, the computational load of the transcoder (TC) blocks can be derived considering all the flows that should be transcoded in the edge streamer, that is, both the live streaming flows and the stored flows. Therefore, if we indicate the generic live streaming flow as [fL,qIN], and the generic stored flow as fS, we have:

$$\Omega_{TC}^{(ES\vartheta)} = \sum_{f_L=1}^{N_F} \sum_{q_{IN}=1}^{Q_L} \sum_{q_{OUT}=1}^{q_{IN}} I_{\wp}^{(C\vartheta Q)}([f_L, q_{OUT}]) \cdot [\varphi_{TC} + \xi_{TC}(q_{OUT}) \cdot \gamma_{q_{IN}}] + \sum_{f_S \in \aleph^{(S)}} \sum_{q_{OUT}=1}^{q_{IN}} I_{\wp}^{(S\vartheta)}(f_S) \cdot \left[\varphi_{TC} + \xi_{TC}(q_{OUT}) \cdot \lambda_{f_S}\right] \tag{23}$$

5. NUMERICAL RESULTS

In this section, we consider a case study constituted by a fleet of forty drones covering a wide rural area, and working as nodes of the backbone mesh network, all equipped by an SDN/NFV infrastructure to host virtual functions for the video monitoring service. As said in Section 2.1, protocols and techniques applied to setup and maintain connectivity are out of the scope of this paper, and therefore we are limited to assuming that the FANET supporting the backbone mesh network guarantees connectivity with the required throughput between each pair of adjacent nodes.

Each backbone node drone carries a package of five Intel NUC Mini PC with processor INTEL i5-3330 @ 3.00 GHz, 64 bits. The monitoring network is constituted by 50 fixed wireless IP cameras installed in strategic points on the territory, and powered with solar energy, and a number of video transmitter drones flying on the same area to integrate video covering of the considered rural zone; this last number has been varied in our numerical analysis in the interval between 0 and 150, in order to have a total number of video transmitters ranging between 50 and 200. Some additional nodes complete the network, one working as backbone network orchestrator drone, four as storage drones, and two installed on the ground to work as fixed storage servers.

We have realized two different analyses. In the first analysis, we have varied the number of video transmitters as indicated so far, i.e., in the range [50, 200], while, in the second analysis, we considered a constant number of video transmitters, set to 200, and we varied the number of acquirer nodes active in the network. In our study we assumed that one-third of the video transmitters encode video at 400 kbit/s, one-third at 500 kbit/s and one-third at 600 kbit/s. The number of video receivers for each video transmitter has been randomly chosen in the set [1,5]. Moreover, 10% of video flows are requested to be recorded.

Video receivers can set the destination quality with QL=6 different levels, the lowest corresponding to a bit rate of 50 kbit/s, and the others with an increment of 50 kbit/s, so ranging between 50 kbit/s and 300 kbit/s. We assumed that 30% of the clients are able to receive video at the maximum quality, while the remaining ones require a quality levels randomly chosen among the six available ones.

In the first analysis, we have considered the presence of 5 acquirers and 10 edge streamers, whose position in the backbone network is decided by the network orchestrator to minimize their average distance from the video transmitters and the video receivers, respectively. Obtained results are averaged on 200 simulation runs, each characterized by a different position of the video transmitter drones, chosen in a random way. Parameters characterizing the computational load of each virtual function have been derived experimentally by running them on virtual machines created with 1 core, a RAM of 1024 MB, and a storage space of 5 GB, and using an Ubuntu operating system with Java and gcc. Each virtual machine in idle state uses 0.1% of the processor. The measured parameters are listed in Table 1.

Table 1. Load parameters of the virtual functions, measured experimentally.

Virtual Functions	ϕ		ξ	
Load Balancer	0.40%		0.0012%	
Deep Packet Inspector	0.90%		0.0011%	
Acquirer	0.12%		0.0013%	
Edge Streamer	0.20%		0.0015%	
Point-to-Multipoint	0.12%		0.0013%	
Transcoder (Q1–Q6)	0.11%	Q1	Q2	Q3
		0.0050%	0.0064%	0.0078%
		Q4	Q5	Q6
		0.0092%	0.0106%	0.0120%
Transcoder (low quality)	0.11%		0.005%	
Storage	0.12%		0.03%	
Flow Rebuilder	0.12%		0.08%	

In order to evaluate the contribution of each virtual function to the overall computational load, in Figure 6 we show their computational loads averaged over all the drones hosting them. As expected, they increase in both the acquirers (see Figure 6a) and the edge streamers (see Figure 6b) with the number of video transmitters. Moreover, we can observe that the PM block is the most CPU-hungry in the acquirers, while it occupies the least portion of CPU in the edge streamers. The first reason is due to the high number of edge streamers, each requiring a copy of each flow, copies that have to be created in the acquirers. The second reason is related to the presence of the transcoding function, which is mostly put on the acquirers because, for the majority of the flows, there are clients requesting the same quality level and attached to different edge streamers; in this case, the transcoders are put on the root of the tree, that is, on the acquirer.

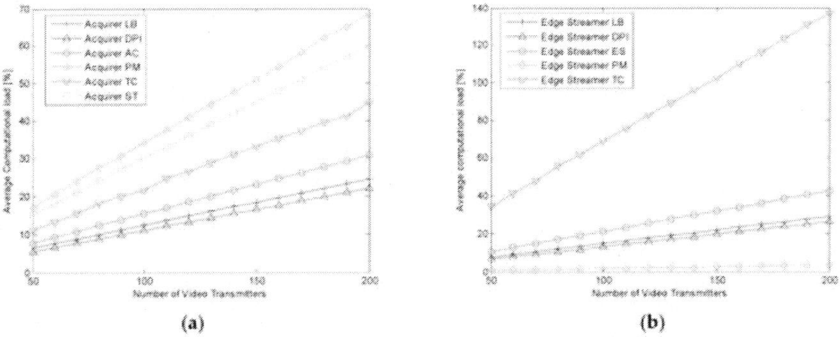

Figure 6. Average computational load. (**a**) acquirer blocks; (**b**) edge streamer blocks. LB: load balancer; DPI: deep packet inspector; ES: edge streamer; PM: point-to-multipoint; TC: Transcoder.

The model proposed in the paper can be used by the orchestrator to evaluate, and then optimize, the number of computation units to activate on each drone. For this reason, we have presented in Figure 7 the mean value of the number of active computation units needed in each drone.

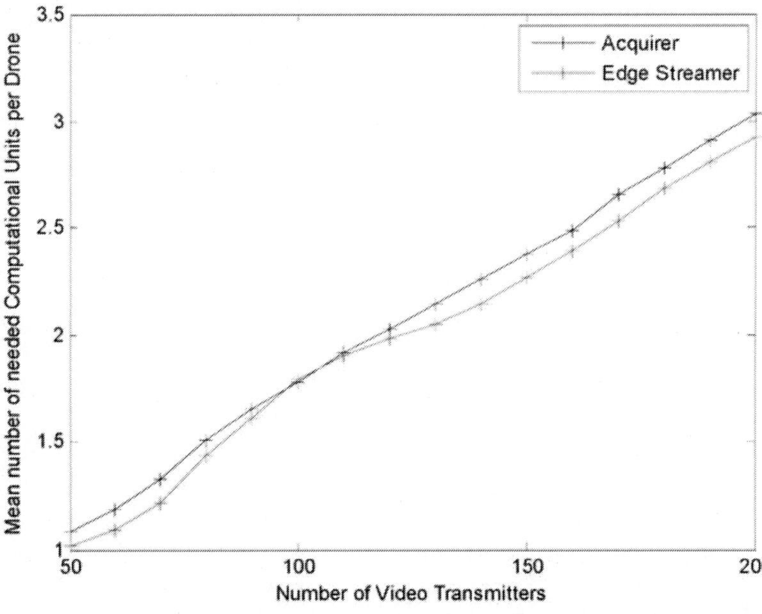

Figure 7. Computation units needed per drone.

In order to show the total information that is available to the orchestrator for its decisions, we have analyzed a specific situation where the rural area is covered by 200 video transmitters, i.e., 50 fixed cameras and 150 video transmitter drones, connected to the backbone mesh network with a fixed topology. Figure 8 shows the detailed computational load in the acquirers and in the edge streamers, while Figure 9 summarizes the number of needed computation units in each acquirer and in each edge streamer to support the load, taking into account that each computation units can support at most a load of 100%. Using this information, the orchestrator can decide to switch off some backbone drones, or switch on some of them to migrate on it some virtual function in order to decrease the load of other drones that need to save some energy to extend their flight life.

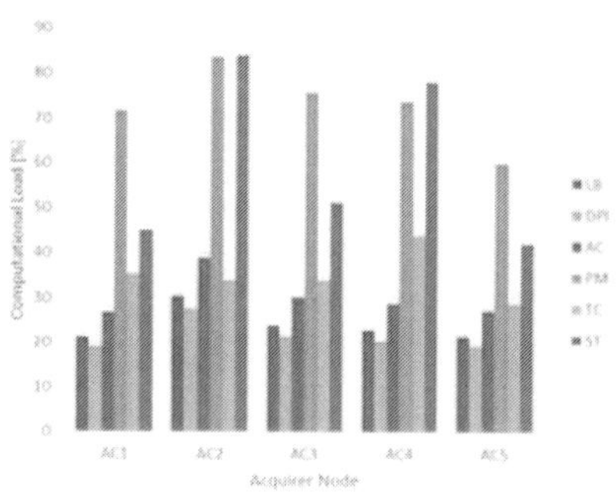

(a)

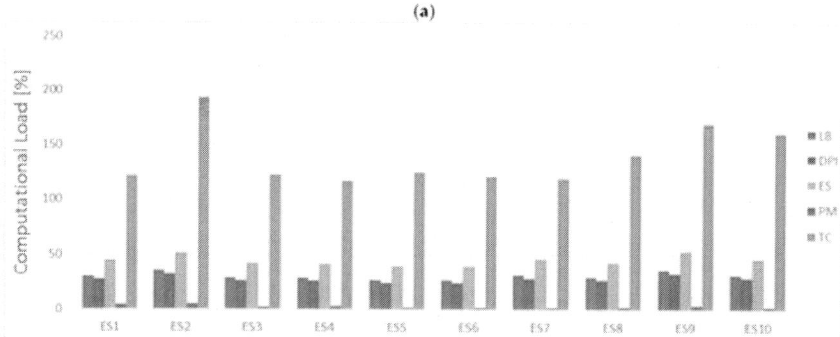

(b)

Figure 8. Per-block computational load. (**a**) computational load of each block in each acquirer; (**b**) computational load of each block in each edge streamer. TC: transcoder.

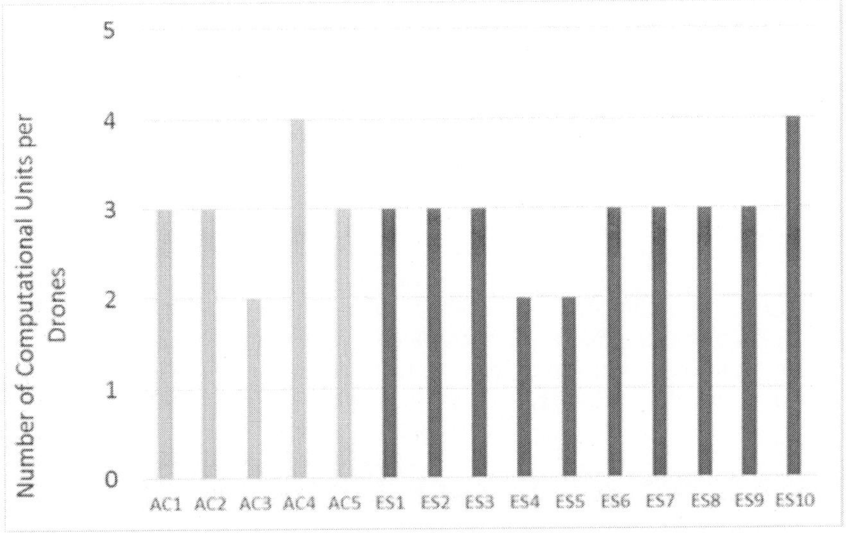

Figure 9. Number of needed computational units per drone.

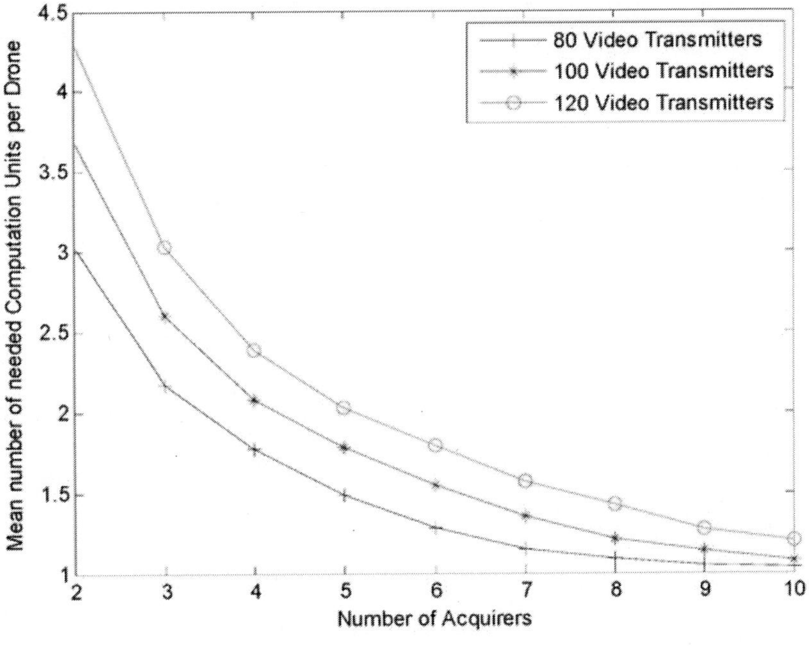

Figure 10. Mean number of needed computational units per drone versus the number of acquirers.

Finally, to this purpose Figure 10 presents the mean number of active computation units needed in a single backbone drone by varying the number of acquirer nodes in the network, and for different numbers of video transmitters.

6. CONCLUSIONS

With the final goal of filling the gap of ICT technologies between rural and urban areas, this paper proposes a video monitoring platform for wide rural areas not covered by Internet access. In order to be flexible and dynamically adaptive, the platform is designed as a FANET of drones leveraging on the recent SDN/NFV paradigm. This constitutes the backbone of the platform, where a variable number of video transmitter drones and fixed video transmitters can be connected automatically to provide clients with video flows of some requested portions of the monitored rural area.

First, the paper introduces the platform architecture and the service chains to realize the video delivery service. Then, an analytical model is defined to evaluate the computational load of the platform nodes, and it is applied to a case study for numerical analysis.

As a future work, we plan to apply the proposed model to define some orchestration and resource allocation policies that the platform orchestrator can apply to manage the entire platform, also in presence of variability in terms of number of drones in the wireless mesh network, their mutual position, and the access to the backbone of the video transmitter drones.

ACKNOWLEDGMENTS

This work has been partially supported by the INPUT (In-Network Programmability for next-generation personal cloUd service supporT) project funded by the European Commission under the Horizon 2020 Programme (Call H2020-ICT-2014-1, Grant no. 644672).

AUTHOR CONTRIBUTIONS

Corrado Rametta has mainly contributed to the definition of the video monitoring platform and has developed the software to derive numerical results. Giovanni Schembra has conceived the scenario and defined the service chains and the analytical model. Both the Authors have designed the experiments and contributed to write the paper.

CONFLICTS OF INTEREST

The authors declare no conflict of interest.

REFERENCES

1. Byanyuma, M.; Kalolo, S.; Mrutu, S.I.; Nyakyi, C.; Sam, A. Affordable broadband connectivity for rural areas. In Proceedings of the 2013 Pan African International Conference on Information Science, Computing and Telecommunications (PACT), Lusaka, Zambia, 13–17 July, 2013; pp. 62–65.
2. Kim, H.; Lee, E. Expanding ICT infrastructure for rural areas in Korea. In Proceedings of the 2013 15th International Conference on Advanced Communications Technology (ICACT), PyeongChang, South Kore, 27–30 January 2013; pp. 312–316.
3. National Information Society Agency of Korea. Report on Pilot Projects for Rural BcN Stimulation; South Korea, 2011.
4. National Information Society Agency of Korea. Broadband Convergence Network annual Report 2011; South Korea, 2011.
5. Argrow, B.; Lawrence, D.; Rasmussen, E. UAV systems for sensor dispersal, telemetry, and visualization in hazardous environments. In Proceedings of the 43rd Aerospace Sciences Meeting and Exhibit, Reno, NV, USA, 10–13 January 2005.
6. Messous, M.A.; Senouci, S.M.; Sedjelmaci, H. Network connectivity and area coverage for UAV fleet mobility model with energy constraint. In Proceedings of the IEEE Wireless Communications and Networking Conference, Doha, Qatar, 3–6 April 2016; pp. 1–6.
7. Coronado, P.; Stetina, F.; Jacob, D. New technologies to support NASA's mission to planet earth satellite remote sensing product validation: The use of an unmanned autopiloted vehicle (UAV) as a platform to conduct remote sensing. In Proceedings of the SPIE Robotic and Semi-Robotic Ground Vehicle Technology, Orlando, FL, USA, 13 April 1998; Volume 3366, pp. 38–49.
8. Eyes of the Army: U.S. Army Unmanned Aircraft Systems Roadmap 2010–2035. U.S. Army UAS Center of Excellence. Available online: http://www.fas.org/irp/ program/ collect/ uas-army.pdf (accessed on 20 March 2017).
9. Wagner, B. Civilian market for unmanned aircraft struggles to take flight. National Defense Magazine. October 2007. Available online: http://www.national defense magazine.org/archive/2007/October/Pages/CivilianMarket2488.aspx (accessed on 20 March 2017).
10. Vescoukis, V.; Doulamis, N.; Karagiorgou, S. A service oriented architecture for decision support systems in environmental crisis management. Future Gener. Comput. Syst. 2012, 28, 593–604.
11. Allen, G.; Goodale, T.; Radke, T.; Russell, M.; Seidel, E.; Davis, K.; Dolkas, K.N.; Doulamis, N.D.; Kielmann, T.; Merzky, A.; et al. Enabling applications on the grid: A gridlab overview. Int. J. High Perform. Comput. Appl. 2003, 17, 449–466.
12. Nigam, N.; Kroo, I. Persistent surveillance using multiple unmanned air vehicles. In Proceedings of the IEEE Aerospace Conference, Big Sky, MT, USA, 1–8 March 2008; pp. 1–14.

13. Tozer, T.; Grace, D. High-altitude platforms for wireless communications. Electron. Commun. Eng. J. 2001, 13, 127–137.
14. Ryan, A.; Hedrick, J. A mode-switching path planner for UAV-assisted search and rescue. In Proceedings of the 44th IEEE Conference on Decision and Control, Seville, Spain, 12–15 December 2005; pp. 1471–1476.
15. Weiss, L.G. Autonomous robots in the fog of war. IEEE Spectr. 2011, 48, 30.
16. Ure, N.K.; Chowdhary, G.; Toksoz, T.; How, J.P.; Vavrina, M.A.; Vian, J. An Automated Battery Management System to Enable Persistent Missions with Multiple Aerial Vehicles. IEEE/ASME Trans. Mechatron. 2015, 20, 275–286.
17. Giulietti, F.; Pollini, L.; Innocenti, M. Autonomous formation flight. IEEE Control Syst. 2000, 20, 34–44.
18. Schumacher, C.J.; Kumar, R. Adaptive control of uavs in close-coupled formation flight. In Proceedings of the American Control Conference, Chicago, IL, USA, 28–30 June 2000; pp. 849–853.
19. Lee, J.; Kim, K.; Yoo, S.; Chung, A.Y.; Lee, J.Y.; Park, S.J.; Kim, H. Constructing a reliable and fast recoverable network for drones. In Proceedings of the 2016 IEEE International Conference on Communications (ICC), Kuala Lumpur, Malaysia, 23–27 May 2016; pp. 1–6.
20. Chung, A.Y.; Jung, J.; Kim, K.; Lee, H.K.; Lee, J.; Lee, S.K.; Yoo, S.; Kim, H. Poster: Swarming drones can connect you to the network. In Proceedings of the 13th Annual International Conference on Mobile Systems, Applications, and Services, ACM, Florence, Italy, 19–22 May 2015; p. 477.
21. Yoo, S.; Kim, K.; Jung, J.; Chung, A.Y.; Lee, J.; Lee, S.K.; Lee, H.K.; Kim, H. Poster: A multi-drone platform for empowering drones' teamwork. In Proceedings of the 21st Annual International Conference on Mobile Computing and Networking, ACM, Paris, France, 7–11 September 2015; pp. 275–277.
22. Zafar, W.; Khan, B.M. Flying Ad-Hoc Networks: Technological and Social Implications. IEEE Technol. Soc. Mag. 2016, 35, 67–74.
23. Santi, P. Topology Control in Wireless Ad Hoc and Sensor Networks; Wiley: Hoboken, NJ, USA, 2005.
24. Lombardo, A.; Licandro, F.; Schembra, G. Multipath Routing and Rate-Controlled Video Encoding in Wireless Video Surveillance Networks. Multimed. Syst. 2008, 14, 155–165.
25. Chandler, P.R.; Pachter, M.; Rasmussen, S. Uav cooperative control. In Proceedings of the 2001 American Control Conference, Arlington, VA, USA, 25–27 June 2001; pp. 50–55.
26. Nunes, B.; Mendonca, M.; Nguyen, X.-N.; Obraczka, K.; Turletti, T. A Survey of Software-Defined Networking: Past, Present, and Future of Programmable Networks. IEEE Commun. Surv. Tutor. 2014, 16, 1617–1634.
27. Lombardo, A.; Manzalini, A.; Riccobene, V.; Schembra, G. An Analytical Tool for Performance Evaluation of Software Defined Networking Services. In Proceedings of the IEEE SDNMO 2014, Krakow, Poland, 9 May 2014.
28. ETSI NFV Group Specification. Network Function Virtualization (NFV) Management and Orchestration, -December 2014. Available online: http://www.etsi.org/ deliver/ etsi_gs/NFV-MAN/001_099/001/01.01.01_60/gs_NFV-MAN001v010101p.pdf(accessed on 20 March 2017).
29. Jain, R.; Paul, S. Network Virtualization and Software Defined Networking for Cloud Computing: A Survey. IEEE Commun. Mag. 2013, 51, 24–31.
30. D'Amico, V.; Lombardo, A.; Melita, M.; Rametta, C.; Schembra, G. An SDN/NFV Telco Operator Platform for Video Broadcasting. IEEE Commun. Mag. 2016, 54, 122–128.
31. Faraci, G.; Lombardo, A.; Schembra, G. A Processor-Sharing Scheduling Strategy for NFV Nodes. J. Electr. Comput. Eng.2016, 2016, 1.
32. Faraci, G.; Schembra, G. An Analytical Model to Design and Manage a Green SDN/NFV CPE Node. IEEE Trans. Netw. Serv. Manag. 2015, 12, 435–450.
33. Betzler, A.; Quer, F.; Camps-Mur, D.; Demirkol, I.; Garcia-Villegas, E. On the benefits of wireless SDN in networks of constrained edge devices. In 2016 European Conference on Networks and Communications (EuCNC), Athens, Greece, June 27–30 2016; pp. 37–41.
34. Gupta, L.; Jain, R.; Vaszkun, G. Survey of Important Issues in UAV Communication Networks. IEEE Commun. Surv. Tutor.2016, 18, 1123–1152.

35. Mendonca, M.; Astuto, B.N.; Obraczka, K.; Turletti, T. Software defined networking for heterogeneous networks. IEEE MMTC E-Lett. 2013, 8, 36–39.
36. Costanzo, S.; Galluccio, L.; Morabito, G.; Palazzo, S. Software defined wireless networks: Unbridling SDNs. In Proceedings of the European Workshop on Software Defined Networking (EWSDN'12), Darmstadt, Germany, 25–28 October 2012; pp. 1–6.
37. Lombardo, A.; Panarello, C.; Schembra, G. A Model-Assisted Cross-Layer Design of an Energy-Efficient Mobile Video Cloud. IEEE Trans. Multimed. 2014, 16, 2307–2322.
38. Incarbone, G.; Schembra, G. A Business Model for Multimedia Streaming in Mobile Clouds. IEEE Trans. Netw. Serv. Manag.2014, 11, 376–389.
39. Sara, M.; Jawhar, I.; Nader, M. A Softwarization Architecture for UAVs and WSNs as Part of the Cloud Environment. In Proceedings of the IEEE International Conference on Cloud Engineering Workshop (IC2EW), Berlin, Germany, 4–8 April 2016; pp. 13–18.
40. Varela, G.; Caamamo, P.; Orjales, F.; Deibe, A.; López-Peña, F.; Duro, R.J. Swarm Intelligence Based Approach for Real Time UAV Team Coordination in Search Operations. In Proceedings of the 2011 Third World Congress on Nature and Biologically Inspired Computing (NaBIC), Salamanca, Spain, 19–21 October 2011; pp. 365–370.
41. Costa, F.G.; Ueyama, J.; Braun, T.; Pessin, G.; Osório, F.S.; Vargas, P.A. The use of unmanned aerial vehicles and wireless sensor network in agricultural applications. In Proceedings of the 2012 IEEE International Geoscience and Remote Sensing Symposium (IGARSS), 2012; pp. 5045–5048.
42. Mahmoud, S.; Mohamed, N. Collaborative UAVs Cloud. In Proceedings of the 2014 International Conference on Unmanned Aircraft Systems (ICUAS), Orlando, FL, USA, 27–30 May 2014; pp. 365–373.
43. Mahmoud, S.; Mohamed, N.; Al-Jaroodi, J. Integrating UAVs into the Cloud Using the Concept of the Web of Things. J. Robot.2015, 2015, 10.
44. Mahmoud, S.; Mohamed, N. Broker Architecture for Collaborative UAVs Cloud Computing. In Proceedings of the 2015 International Conference on Collaboration Technologies and Systems (CTS 2015), Atlanta, GA, USA, 1–5 June 2015.
45. Mahmoud, S.; Mohamed, N. Toward a Cloud Platform for UAV Resources and Services. In Proceedings of the IEEE 4th Symposium on Network Cloud Computing and Applications, Munich, Germany, 11–12 June 2015.
46. 3GPP. Feasibility study on new services and markeets technology enablers for critical communications. Technical Report Number 22.862. June 2016. Available online: https://portal.3gpp.org/desktopmodules/Specifications/SpecificationDetails.aspx?specificationId=3014 (accessed on 20 March 2017).
47. Bor-Yaliniz, I.; Yanikomeroglu, H. The New Frontier in RAN Heterogeneity: Multi-Tier Drone-Cells. IEEE Commun. Mag.2016, 54, 48–55.
48. Matolak, D.W. Unmanned aerial vehicles: Communications challenges and future aerial networking. In Proceedings of the 2015 International Conference on Computing, Networking and Communications (ICNC), Garden Grove, CA, USA, 16–19 February 2015; pp. 567–572.
49. Open vSwitch. Available online: http://openvswitch.org/ (accessed on 20 March 2017).
50. The Xen Project. Available online: https://www.xenproject.org/ (accessed on 20 March 2017).
51. ETSI GS NFV—INF 001, v1.1.1, Network Functions Virtualization (NFV): Infrastructure Overview. 01-2015. Available online:http://www.etsi.org/deliver/etsi_gs/NFV-INF/001_099/ 001/01.01.01_60/gs_nfv-inf001v010101p.pdf (accessed on 20 March 2017).
52. Marcondes, C.; Santos, T.; Godoy, A.; Viel, C.; Teixeira, C. CastFlow: Clean-slate multicast approach using in-advance path processing in programmable networks. In Proceedings of the IEEE Symposium on Computers and Communications (ISCC) 2012, Cappadocia, Turkey, 1–4 July 2012.
53. Kotani, D.; Suzuki, K.; Shimonishi, H. A design and implementation of OpenFlow controller handling IP multicast with fast tree switching. In Proceedings of the IEEE/IPSJ International Symposium on Applications and the Internet (SAINT) 2012, Izmir, Turkey, 16–20 July 2012.

54. Luyi, S.; Jinyi, F.; Xiaohua, Y. Forward Error Correction. In Proceedings of the 2012 Fourth International Conference on Computational and Information Sciences, Chongqing, China, 17–19 August 2012; pp. 37–40.
55. Enokido, T.; Aikebaier, A.; Takizawa, M. An extended simple power consumption model for selecting a server to perform computation type processes in digital ecosystems. IEEE Trans. Ind. Inform. 2014, 10, 1627–1636.

INDEX